# GETTING STARTED

## Welcome

Congratulations, you have just gained access to the highes
Solutions Architect Associate Certification Exam. Over 20.0
average of 4.5/5 stars and find that these Practice Questions are the closest to the real AWS exam. With
this Ultimate Exam Prep you too have the chance to pass the exam with flying colors!

While we can't update the title of this book, all 390 Practice Questions have been fully updated to cover
the latest SAA-C02 version of the exam. The SAA-C02 exam covers a broad set of AWS services and the
aim of providing these Practice Tests is to prepare you thoroughly for the real exam so that you get to
pass first time with confidence.

There are 6 practice exams with 65 questions each, and each set of practice exams includes questions
from all domains of the latest SAA-C02 exam. All 390 practice questions were designed to reflect the
difficulty of the real AWS exam. With these Practice Tests, you'll know when you are ready to pass your
AWS Solutions Architect exam first time! We recommend re-taking these practice tests until you
consistently score 80% or higher - that's when you're ready to sit the exam and achieve a great score!

If you want easy to pass questions, then these Practice Tests are not for you! Our students love these high-
quality practice tests because they simulate the actual certification exam and help them understand the
AWS concepts. Students who have recently passed the AWS exam confirm that our AWS practice questions
closely match the exam pattern and difficulty.

I hope you get great value from this resource and feel confident that you'll ace your AWS Certified Solutions
Architect Associate exam through diligent study of these questions.

Wishing you all the best with your AWS Certification exam.

*Neal Davis*

Neal Davis

**AWS Solution Architect & Founder of Digital Cloud Training**

# How to best use this resource

We have organized the practice questions into 6 sets and each set is repeated once <u>without</u> answers and explanations and once <u>with</u> answers and explanations. This allows you to choose from two methods of preparation.

## 1. Exam simulation

To simulate the exam experience, use the "PRACTICE QUESTIONS ONLY" sets. Grab a pen and paper to record your answers for all 65 questions. After completing each set, check your answers using the "PRACTICE QUESTIONS, ANSWERS & EXPLANATIONS" section.

To calculate your total score, sum up the number of correct answers and multiply them by 1.54 (weighting out of 100%) to get your percentage score out of 100%. For example, if you got 50 questions right, the calculation would be 50 x 1.54 = 77%. The pass mark of the official AWS exam is 72%.

## 2. Training mode

To use the practice questions as a learning tool, use the "PRACTICE QUESTIONS, ANSWERS & EXPLANATIONS" sets to view the answers, read the explanations and look up the reference links as you move through the questions.

# Key Training Advice

**AIM FOR A MINIMUM SCORE OF 80%**: Although the actual AWS exam has a pass mark of 72%, we recommend that you repeatedly retake our AWS practice exams until you consistently score 80% or higher. We encourage you to put in the work and study the explanations in detail! Once you achieve the recommended score in the practice tests - you are ready to sit the exam and achieve a great score!

**CONFORM WITH EXAM BLUEPRINT**: Using our AWS Certified Solutions Architect Associate practice exams helps you gain experience with the test question format and how the questions in the real AWS exam are structured. With our practice tests, you will be adequately prepared for the real AWS exam.

**DEEPEN YOUR KNOWLEDGE**: Please note that though we match the AWS exam pattern, our AWS practice exams are NOT brain dumps. Please don't expect to pass the real AWS certification exam by simply memorizing answers. Instead, we encourage you to use our AWS Solutions Architect practice tests to deepen your knowledge. This is your best chance to successfully pass your exam no matter what questions you are presented with in your real exam.

# Your Pathway to Success

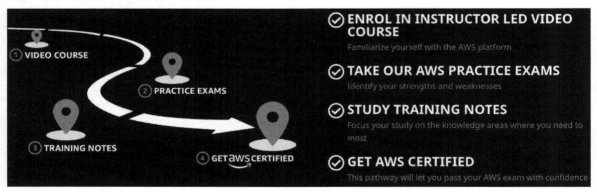

**Instructor-led Video Course**

If you are new to AWS, we'd suggest first enrolling in the online instructor-led AWS Certified Solutions Architect Associate Video Course from Digital Cloud Training to familiarize yourself with the AWS platform before assessing your exam readiness with these practice exams.

**Online practice exam simulator**

If you are looking for more practice questions online, use the online exam simulator on the Digital Cloud Training website. With over 500 practice questions, you get to evaluate your progress and identify your strengths and weaknesses. Simply the best way to assess your exam readiness! We offer multiple learning modes and a pool of over 500 questions that are regularly updated.

**Training Notes**

As a final step, use the Training Notes for the AWS Certified Solutions Architect from Digital Cloud to get a more detailed understanding of the AWS services and focus your study on the knowledge areas where you need to most. Deep dive into the SAA-C02 exam objectives with 300 pages of detailed facts, tables and diagrams to shortcut your time to success.

# Limited Time Bonus Offer

As a special bonus, we are now offering **FREE Access to the Exam Simulator** on the Digital Cloud Training website. The exam simulator randomly selects 65 questions from our pool of over 500 unique questions - mimicking the real AWS exam environment. The practice exam has the same format, style, time limit, and passing score as the real AWS exam.

Navigate to the BONUS OFFER section at end of this book for instructions on how to claim your bonus.

# Contact, Support & Sharing

We want you to get great value from these training resources. If for any reason you are not 100% satisfied, please message us at feedback@digitalcloud.training. We promise to address all questions and concerns, typically within 24hrs. We really want you to have a 5-star learning experience!

For technical support, contact us at:
support@digitalcloud.training.

If you enjoy reading reviews, please consider paying it forward. Reviews really matter - they guide students and help us continuously improve our courses. We celebrate every honest review and truly appreciate it. We'd be thrilled if you could leave a rating at amazon.com/ryp.

The AWS platform is evolving quickly, and the exam tracks these changes with a typical lag of around 6 months. We are therefore reliant on student feedback to keep track of what is appearing in the exam. Our private Facebook group is a great place to ask questions and share knowledge and exam tips with the AWS community. Join the discussion and share your exam feedback to our Facebook group:

https://www.facebook.com/groups/awscertificationqa

# TABLE OF CONTENTS

# SET 1: PRACTICE QUESTIONS ONLY

*Or go directly to Set 1: Practice Questions, Answers & Explanations*

## 1. Question

A company has deployed Amazon RedShift for performing analytics on user data. When using Amazon RedShift, which of the following statements are correct in relation to availability and durability? (choose 2)

1. RedShift always keeps three copies of your data
2. Single-node clusters support data replication
3. RedShift provides continuous/incremental backups
4. Manual backups are automatically deleted when you delete a cluster
5. RedShift always keeps five copies of your data

## 2. Question

You are a Solutions Architect at Digital Cloud Training. A client from a large multinational corporation is working on a deployment of a significant amount of resources into AWS. The client would like to be able to deploy resources across multiple AWS accounts and regions using a single toolset and template. You have been asked to suggest a toolset that can provide this functionality?

1. Use a CloudFormation template that creates a stack and specify the logical IDs of each account and region
2. Use a CloudFormation StackSet and specify the target accounts and regions in which the stacks will be created
3. Use a third-party product such as Terraform that has support for multiple AWS accounts and regions
4. This cannot be done, use separate CloudFormation templates per AWS account and region

## 3. Question

A new Big Data application you are developing will use hundreds of EC2 instances to write data to a shared file system. The file system must be stored redundantly across multiple AZs within a region and allow the EC2 instances to concurrently access the file system. The required throughput is multiple GB per second.

From the options presented which storage solution can deliver these requirements?

1. Amazon EBS using multiple volumes in a RAID 0 configuration
2. Amazon EFS
3. Amazon S3
4. Amazon Storage Gateway

## 4. Question

An application running on an external website is attempting to initiate a request to your company's website on AWS using API calls. A problem has been reported in which the requests are failing with an error that includes the following text:

"**Cross-Origin Request Blocked: The Same Origin Policy disallows reading the remote resource**"

**You have been asked to resolve the problem, what is the most likely solution?**

1. Enable CORS on the APIs resources using the selected methods under the API Gateway
2. The ACL on the API needs to be updated
3. The IAM policy does not allow access to the API
4. The request is not secured with SSL/TLS

## 5. Question

**You need to configure an application to retain information about each user session and have decided to implement a layer within the application architecture to store this information.**

**Which of the options below could be used? (choose 2)**

1. A workflow service such as Amazon Simple Workflow Service (SWF)
2. Sticky sessions on an Elastic Load Balancer (ELB)
3. A block storage service such as Elastic Block Store (EBS)
4. A relational data store such as Amazon RDS
5. A key/value store such as ElastiCache Redis

## 6. Question

**The data scientists in your company are looking for a service that can process and analyze real-time, streaming data. They would like to use standard SQL queries to query the streaming data.**

**Which combination of AWS services would deliver these requirements?**

1. Kinesis Data Streams and Kinesis Data Analytics
2. Kinesis Data Streams and Kinesis Firehose
3. ElastiCache and EMR
4. DynamoDB and EMR

## 7. Question

**Which of the following approaches provides the lowest cost for Amazon elastic block store snapshots while giving you the ability to fully restore data?**

1. Maintain a single snapshot; the latest snapshot is both incremental and complete
2. Maintain the most current snapshot; archive the original to Amazon Glacier
3. Maintain two snapshots: the original snapshot and the latest incremental snapshot
4. Maintain the original snapshot; subsequent snapshots will overwrite one another

## 8. Question

**You are undertaking a project to make some audio and video files that your company uses for onboarding new staff members available via a mobile application. You are looking for a cost-effective way to convert the files from their current formats into formats that are compatible with smartphones and tablets. The files are currently stored in an S3 bucket.**

**What AWS service can help with converting the files?**

1. Rekognition

2. Elastic Transcoder
3. Data Pipeline
4. Amazon Personalize

## 9. Question

You are a Solutions Architect at Digital Cloud Training. A large multi-national client has requested a design for a multi-region, multi-master database. The client has requested that the database be designed for fast, massively scaled applications for a global user base. The database should be a fully managed service including the replication.

Which AWS service can deliver these requirements?

1. S3 with Cross Region Replication
2. RDS with Multi-AZ
3. DynamoDB with Global Tables and Cross Region Replication
4. EC2 instances with EBS replication

## 10. Question

A customer has asked you to recommend the best solution for a highly available database. The database is a relational OLTP type of database and the customer does not want to manage the operating system the database runs on. Failover between AZs must be automatic.

Which of the below options would you suggest to the customer?

1. Use RDS in a Multi-AZ configuration
2. Use DynamoDB
3. Use RedShift in a Multi-AZ configuration
4. Install a relational database on EC2 instances in multiple AZs and create a cluster

## 11. Question

An application you manage uses Auto Scaling and a fleet of EC2 instances. You recently noticed that Auto Scaling is scaling the number of instances up and down multiple times in the same hour. You need to implement a remediation to reduce the amount of scaling events. The remediation must be cost-effective and preserve elasticity. What design changes would you implement? (choose 2)

1. Modify the Auto Scaling group termination policy to terminate the newest instance first
2. Modify the Auto Scaling group cool-down timers
3. Modify the CloudWatch alarm period that triggers your Auto Scaling scale down policy
4. Modify the Auto Scaling policy to use scheduled scaling actions
5. Modify the Auto Scaling group termination policy to terminate the oldest instance first

## 12. Question

One of your EC2 instances runs an application process that saves user data to an attached EBS volume. The EBS volume was attached to the EC2 instance after it was launched and is unencrypted. You would like to encrypt the data that is stored on the volume as it is considered sensitive however you cannot shutdown the instance due to other application processes that are running.

What is the best method of applying encryption to the sensitive data without any downtime?

1. Create an encrypted snapshot of the current EBS volume. Restore the snapshot to the EBS volume
2. Create and mount a new encrypted EBS volume. Move the data to the new volume and then delete the old volume
3. Unmount the volume and enable server-side encryption. Re-mount the EBS volume
4. Leverage the AWS Encryption CLI to encrypt the data on the volume

## 13. Question

You are planning to launch a RedShift cluster for processing and analyzing a large amount of data. The RedShift cluster will be deployed into a VPC with multiple subnets. Which construct is used when provisioning the cluster to allow you to specify a set of subnets in the VPC that the cluster will be deployed into?

1. Subnet Group
2. Availability Zone (AZ)
3. DB Subnet Group
4. Cluster Subnet Group

## 14. Question

A Solutions Architect is responsible for a web application that runs on EC2 instances that sit behind an Application Load Balancer (ALB). Auto Scaling is used to launch instances across 3 Availability Zones. The web application serves large image files and these are stored on an Amazon EFS file system. Users have experienced delays in retrieving the files and the Architect has been asked to improve the user experience.

What should the Architect do to improve user experience?

1. Cache static content using CloudFront
2. Reduce the file size of the images
3. Move the digital assets to EBS
4. Use Spot instances

## 15. Question

A Solutions Architect is deploying an Auto Scaling Group (ASG) and needs to determine what CloudWatch monitoring option to use. Which of the statements below would assist the Architect in making his decision? (choose 2)

1. Basic monitoring is enabled by default if the ASG is created from the CLI
2. Detailed monitoring is chargeable and must always be manually enabled
3. Detailed monitoring is free and can be manually enabled
4. Detailed monitoring is enabled by default if the ASG is created from the CLI
5. Basic monitoring is enabled by default if the ASG is created from the console

## 16. Question

A Linux instance running in your VPC requires some configuration changes to be implemented locally and you need to run some commands. Which of the following can be used to securely connect to the instance?

1. SSL/TLS certificate

2. Public key
3. Key Pairs
4. EC2 password

## 17. Question

**Your company would like to restrict the ability of most users to change their own passwords whilst continuing to allow a select group of users within specific user groups.**

**What is the best way to achieve this? (choose 2)**

1. Under the IAM Password Policy deselect the option to allow users to change their own passwords
2. Create an IAM Policy that grants users the ability to change their own password and attach it to the groups that contain the users
3. Create an IAM Policy that grants users the ability to change their own password and attach it to the individual user accounts
4. Create an IAM Role that grants users the ability to change their own password and attach it to the groups that contain the users
5. Disable the ability for all users to change their own passwords using the AWS Security Token Service

## 18. Question

**A colleague from your company's IT Security team has notified you of an Internet-based threat that affects a certain port and protocol combination. You have conducted an audit of your VPC and found that this port and protocol combination is allowed on an Inbound Rule with a source of 0.0.0.0/0. You have verified that this rule only exists for maintenance purposes and need to make an urgent change to block the access.**

**What is the fastest way to block access from the Internet to the specific ports and protocols?**

1. You don't need to do anything; this rule will only allow access to VPC based resources
2. Update the security group by removing the rule
3. Delete the security group
4. Add a deny rule to the security group with a higher priority

## 19. Question

**You are an entrepreneur building a small company with some resources running on AWS. As you have limited funding, you're extremely cost conscious. Which AWS service can send you alerts via email or SNS topic when you are forecast to exceed your funding capacity so you can take action?**

1. Cost & Usage reports
2. AWS Billing Dashboard
3. AWS Budgets
4. Cost Explorer

## 20. Question

**Your company is starting to use AWS to host new web-based applications. A new two-tier application will be deployed that provides customers with access to data records. It is important that the application is highly responsive and retrieval times are optimized. You're looking for a persistent data**

store that can provide the required performance. From the list below what AWS service would you recommend for this requirement?

1. Kinesis Data Streams
2. ElastiCache with the Memcached engine
3. ElastiCache with the Redis engine
4. RDS in a multi-AZ configuration

## 21. Question

A Solutions Architect is developing an encryption solution. The solution requires that data keys are encrypted using envelope protection before they are written to disk.

Which solution option can assist with this requirement?

1. AWS Certificate Manager
2. AWS KMS API
3. IAM Access Key
4. API Gateway with STS

## 22. Question

A solutions Architect is designing a new workload where an AWS Lambda function will access an Amazon DynamoDB table.

What is the MOST secure means of granting the Lambda function access to the DynamoDB table?

1. Create an identity and access management (IAM) role with the necessary permissions to access the DynamoDB table, and assign the role to the Lambda function
2. Create a DynamoDB username and password and give them to the Developer to use in the Lambda function
3. Create an identity and access management (IAM) user and create access and secret keys for the user. Give the user the necessary permissions to access the DynamoDB table. Have the Developer use these keys to access the resources
4. Create an identity and access management (IAM) role allowing access from AWS Lambda and assign the role to the DynamoDB table

## 23. Question

An e-commerce application is hosted in AWS. The last time a new product was launched, the application experienced a performance issue due to an enormous spike in traffic. Management decided that capacity must be doubled this week after the product is launched.

What is the MOST efficient way for management to ensure that capacity requirements are met?

1. Add Amazon EC2 Spot instances
2. Add a Step Scaling policy
3. Add a Simple Scaling policy
4. Add a Scheduled Scaling action

## 24. Question

A colleague has asked you some questions about how AWS charge for DynamoDB. He is interested in knowing what type of workload DynamoDB is best suited for in relation to cost and how AWS charges for DynamoDB? (choose 2)

1. DynamoDB is more cost effective for read heavy workloads
2. DynamoDB is more cost effective for write heavy workloads
3. Priced based on provisioned throughput (read/write) regardless of whether you use it or not
4. You provision for expected throughput but are only charged for what you use
5. DynamoDB scales vertically by adding additional nodes

## 25. Question

A user is testing a new service that receives location updates from 5,000 rental cars every hour. Which service will collect data and automatically scale to accommodate production workload?

1. Amazon API Gateway
2. Amazon EBS
3. Amazon Kinesis Firehose
4. Amazon EC2

## 26. Question

A research company is developing a data lake solution in Amazon S3 to analyze huge datasets. The solution makes infrequent SQL queries only. In addition, the company wants to minimize infrastructure costs.

Which AWS service should be used to meet these requirements?

1. Amazon Redshift Spectrum
2. Amazon Aurora
3. Amazon Athena
4. Amazon RDS for MySQL

## 27. Question

An application runs on two EC2 instances in private subnets split between two AZs. The application needs to connect to a CRM SaaS application running on the Internet. The vendor of the SaaS application restricts authentication to a whitelist of source IP addresses and only 2 IP addresses can be configured per customer.

What is the most appropriate and cost-effective solution to enable authentication to the SaaS application?

1. Configure redundant Internet Gateways and update the routing tables for each subnet
2. Configure a NAT Gateway for each AZ with an Elastic IP address •
3. Use multiple Internet-facing Application Load Balancers with Elastic IP addresses
4. Use a Network Load Balancer and configure a static IP for each AZ

## 28. Question

A recent security audit uncovered some poor deployment and configuration practices within your VPC. You need to ensure that applications are deployed in secure configurations.

How can this be achieved in the most operationally efficient manner?

1.  Remove the ability for staff to deploy applications
2.  Use AWS Inspector to apply secure configurations
3.  Manually check all application configurations before deployment
4.  Use CloudFormation with securely configured templates

## 29. Question

The application development team in your company has a new requirement for the deployment of a container solution. You plan to use the AWS Elastic Container Service (ECS). The solution should include load balancing of incoming requests across the ECS containers and allow the containers to use dynamic host port mapping so that multiple tasks from the same service can run on the same container host.

Which AWS load balancing configuration will support this?

1.  You cannot run multiple copies of a task on the same instance, because the ports would conflict
2.  Use a Network Load Balancer (NLB) and host-based routing
3.  Use a Classic Load Balancer (CLB) and create a static mapping of the ports
4.  Use an Application Load Balancer (ALB) and map the ECS service to the ALB

## 30. Question

To improve security in your AWS account you have decided to enable multi-factor authentication (MFA). You can authenticate using an MFA device in which two ways? (choose 2)

1.  Using biometrics
2.  Locally to EC2 instances
3.  Through the AWS Management Console
4.  Using the AWS API
5.  Using a key pair

## 31. Question

The company you work for has a presence across multiple AWS regions. As part of disaster recovery planning you are formulating a solution to provide a regional DR capability for an application running on a fleet of Amazon EC2 instances that are provisioned by an Auto Scaling Group (ASG). The applications are stateless and read and write data to an S3 bucket. You would like to utilize the current AMI used by the ASG as it has some customizations made to it.

What are the steps you might take to enable a regional DR capability for this application? (choose 2)

1.  Enable cross region replication on the S3 bucket and specify a destination bucket in the DR region
2.  Modify the launch configuration for the ASG in the DR region and specify the AMI
3.  Copy the AMI to the DR region and create a new launch configuration for the ASG that uses the AMI
4.  Enable multi-AZ for the S3 bucket to enable synchronous replication to the DR region
5.  Modify the permissions of the AMI so it can be used across multiple regions

## 32. Question

A Solutions Architect needs to improve performance for a web application running on EC2 instances launched by an Auto Scaling group. The instances run behind an ELB Application Load Balancer. During heavy use periods the ASG doubles in size and analysis has shown that static content stored on the EC2 instances is being requested by users in a specific geographic location.

How can the Solutions Architect reduce the need to scale and improve the application performance?

1. Re-deploy the application in a new VPC that is closer to the users making the requests
2. Create an Amazon CloudFront distribution for the site and redirect user traffic to the distribution
3. Store the contents on Amazon EFS instead of the EC2 root volume
4. Implement Amazon Redshift to create a repository of the content closer to the users

## 33. Question

You are a Solutions Architect at Digital Cloud Training. One of your clients has requested that you design a solution for distributing load across a number of EC2 instances across multiple AZs within a region. Customers will connect to several different applications running on the client's servers through their browser using multiple domain names and SSL certificates. The certificates are stored in AWS Certificate Manager (ACM).

What is the optimal architecture to ensure high availability, cost effectiveness, and performance?

1. Launch a single ALB, configure host-based routing for the domain names and bind an SSL certificate to each routing rule
2. Launch a single ALB and bind multiple SSL certificates to the same secure listener. Clients will use the Server Name Indication (SNI) extension
3. Launch a single ALB and bind multiple SSL certificates to multiple secure listeners
4. Launch multiple ALBs and bind separate SSL certificates to each ELB

## 34. Question

The website for a new application received around 50,000 requests each second and the company wants to use multiple applications to analyze the navigation patterns of the users on their website so they can personalize the user experience.

What can a Solutions Architect use to collect page clicks for the website and process them sequentially for each user?

1. Amazon SQS standard queue
2. AWS CloudTrail trail
3. Amazon Kinesis Streams
4. Amazon SQS FIFO queue

## 35. Question

A retail organization is deploying a new application that will read and write data to a database. The company wants to deploy the application in three different AWS Regions in an active-active configuration. The databases need to replicate to keep information in sync.

Which solution best meets these requirements?

1. Amazon DynamoDB with global tables
2. Amazon Athena with Amazon S3 cross-region replication

3. AWS Database Migration Service with change data capture
4. Amazon Aurora Global Database

## 36. Question

You are building an application that will collect information about user behavior. The application will rapidly ingest large amounts of dynamic data and requires very low latency. The database must be scalable without incurring downtime. Which database would you recommend for this scenario?

1. RedShift
2. DynamoDB
3. RDS with MySQL
4. RDS with Microsoft SQL

## 37. Question

You have been asked to implement a solution for capturing, transforming and loading streaming data into an Amazon RedShift cluster. The solution will capture data from Amazon Kinesis Data Streams. Which AWS services would you utilize in this scenario? (choose 2)

1. Kinesis Data Firehose for capturing the data and loading it into RedShift
2. Kinesis Video Streams for capturing the data and loading it into RedShift
3. Lambda for transforming the data
4. EMR for transforming the data
5. AWS Data Pipeline for transforming the data

## 38. Question

A company is deploying a big data and analytics workload. The analytics will be run from a fleet of thousands of EC2 instances across multiple AZs. Data needs to be stored on a shared storage layer that can be mounted and accessed concurrently by all EC2 instances. Latency is not a concern however extremely high throughput is required.

What storage layer would be most suitable for this requirement?

1. Amazon EFS in Max I/O mode
2. Amazon EFS in General Purpose mode
3. Amazon EBS PIOPS
4. Amazon S3

## 39. Question

Your company is reviewing their information security processes. One of the items that came out of a recent audit is that there is insufficient data recorded about requests made to a few S3 buckets. The security team requires an audit trail for operations on the S3 buckets that includes the requester, bucket name, request time, request action, and response status.

Which action would you take to enable this logging?

1. Create a CloudWatch metric that monitors the S3 bucket operations and triggers an alarm
2. Enable server access logging for the S3 buckets to save access logs to a specified destination bucket
3. Create a CloudTrail trail that audits S3 bucket operations
4. Enable S3 event notifications for the specific actions and setup an SNS notification

## 40. Question

A Solutions Architect is designing a new architecture that will use an Amazon EC2 Auto Scaling group.

Which of the following factors determine the health check grace period? (choose 2)

1. How long the bootstrap script takes to run
2. How long it takes for the Auto Scaling group to detect a failure
3. How much of the application code is embedded in the AMI
4. How many Amazon CloudWatch alarms are configured for status checks
5. How frequently the Auto Scaling group scales up or down

## 41. Question

A call center application consists of a three-tier application using Auto Scaling groups to automatically scale resources as needed. Users report that every morning at 9:00am the system becomes very slow for about 15 minutes. A Solutions Architect determines that a large percentage of the call center staff starts work at 9:00am, so Auto Scaling does not have enough time to scale to meet demand.

How can the Architect fix the problem?

1. Permanently keep a steady state of instance that is needed at 9:00am to guarantee available resources, but use Spot Instances
2. Use Reserved Instances to ensure the system has reserved the right amount of capacity for the scaling events
3. Create an Auto Scaling scheduled action to scale out the necessary resources at 8:30am each morning
4. Change the Auto Scaling group's scale out event to scale based on network utilization

## 42. Question

Your company keeps unstructured data on a filesystem. You need to provide access to employees via EC2 instances in your VPC. Which storage solution should you choose?

1. Amazon EBS
2. Amazon Snowball
3. Amazon EFS
4. Amazon S3

## 43. Question

You are a Solutions Architect at a media company and you need to build an application stack that can receive customer comments from sporting events. The application is expected to receive significant load that could scale to millions of messages within a short space of time following high-profile matches. As you are unsure of the load required for the database layer what is the most cost-effective way to ensure that the messages are not dropped?

1. Use RDS Auto Scaling for the database layer which will automatically scale as required
2. Create an SQS queue and modify the application to write to the SQS queue. Launch another application instance the polls the queue and writes messages to the database
3. Use DynamoDB and provision enough write capacity to handle the highest expected load
4. Write the data to an S3 bucket, configure RDS to poll the bucket for new messages

## 44. Question

A company needs to store data for 5 years. The company will need to have immediate and highly available access to the data at any point in time but will not require frequent access.

Which lifecycle action should be taken to meet the requirements while reducing costs?

1. Transition objects from Amazon S3 Standard to the GLACIER storage class
2. Transition objects from Amazon S3 Standard to Amazon S3 One Zone-Infrequent Access (S3 One Zone-IA)
3. Transition objects to expire after 5 years
4. Transition objects from Amazon S3 Standard to Amazon S3 Standard-Infrequent Access (S3 Standard-IA)

## 45. Question

A Solutions Architect is designing an application that will run on Amazon ECS behind an Application Load Balancer (ALB). For security reasons, the Amazon EC2 host instances for the ECS cluster are in a private subnet.

What should be done to ensure that the incoming traffic to the host instances is from the ALB only?

1. Update the EC2 cluster security group to allow incoming access from the IP address of the ALB only
2. Modify the security group used by the EC2 cluster to allow incoming traffic from the security group used by the ALB only
3. Create network ACL rules for the private subnet to allow incoming traffic on ports 32768 through 61000 from the IP address of the ALB only
4. Enable AWS WAF on the ALB and enable the ECS rule

## 46. Question

A Solutions Architect is designing a highly-scalable system to track records. Records must remain available for immediate download for three months, and then the records must be deleted.

What's the most appropriate decision for this use case?

1. Store the files on Amazon EFS, and create a lifecycle policy to remove the files after three months
2. Store the files on Amazon S3, and create a lifecycle policy to remove the files after three months
3. Store the files on Amazon EBS, and create a lifecycle policy to remove the files after three months
4. Store the files on Amazon Glacier, and create a lifecycle policy to remove the files after three months

## 47. Question

A Solutions Architect needs to allow another AWS account programmatic access to upload objects to his bucket. The Solutions Architect needs to ensure that he retains full control of the objects uploaded to the bucket. How can this be done?

1. The Architect will need to instruct the user in the other AWS account to grant him access when uploading objects
2. The Architect will need to take ownership of objects after they have been uploaded
3. The Architect can use a resource-based bucket policy that grants cross-account access and include a conditional statement that only allows uploads if full control access is granted to the Architect

4. The Architect can use a resource-based ACL with an IAM policy that grants cross-account access and include a conditional statement that only allows uploads if full control access is granted to the Architect

## 48. Question

You are creating a design for a web-based application that will be based on a web front-end using EC2 instances and a database back-end. This application is a low priority and you do not want to incur costs in general day to day management. Which AWS database service can you use that will require the least operational overhead?

1. DynamoDB
2. EMR
3. RedShift
4. RDS

## 49. Question

A company's Amazon RDS MySQL DB instance may be rebooted for maintenance and to apply patches. This database is critical and potential user disruption must be minimized.

What should the Solution Architect do in this scenario?

1. Set up an Amazon RDS MySQL cluster
2. Create an RDS MySQL Read Replica
3. Set the Amazon RDS MySQL to Multi-AZ
4. Create an Amazon EC2 instance MySQL cluster

## 50. Question

You would like to share some documents with public users accessing an S3 bucket over the Internet. What are two valid methods of granting public read permissions so you can share the documents? (choose 2)

1. Grant public read access to the objects when uploading
2. Grant public read on all objects using the S3 bucket ACL
3. Share the documents using CloudFront and a static website
4. Use the AWS Policy Generator to create a bucket policy for your Amazon S3 bucket granting read access to public anonymous users
5. Share the documents using a bastion host in a public subnet

## 51. Question

You have created a private Amazon CloudFront distribution that serves files from an Amazon S3 bucket and is accessed using signed URLs. You need to ensure that users cannot bypass the controls provided by Amazon CloudFront and access content directly.

How can this be achieved? (choose 2)

1. Create an origin access identity and associate it with your distribution
2. Modify the Edge Location to restrict direct access to Amazon S3 buckets
3. Modify the permissions on the origin access identity to restrict read access to the Amazon S3 bucket

4. Create a new signed URL that requires users to access the Amazon S3 bucket through Amazon CloudFront
5. Modify the permissions on the Amazon S3 bucket so that only the origin access identity has read and download permissions

## 52. Question

Your company shares some HR videos stored in an Amazon S3 bucket via CloudFront. You need to restrict access to the private content so users coming from specific IP addresses can access the videos and ensure direct access via the Amazon S3 bucket is not possible.

How can this be achieved?

1. Configure CloudFront to require users to access the files using a signed URL, and configure the S3 bucket as a website endpoint
2. Configure CloudFront to require users to access the files using signed cookies, and move the files to an encrypted EBS volume
3. Configure CloudFront to require users to access the files using signed cookies, create an origin access identity (OAI) and instruct users to login with the OAI
4. Configure CloudFront to require users to access the files using a signed URL, create an origin access identity (OAI) and restrict access to the files in the Amazon S3 bucket to the OAI

## 53. Question

There is a temporary need to share some video files that are stored in a private S3 bucket. The consumers do not have AWS accounts and you need to ensure that only authorized consumers can access the files. What is the best way to enable this access?

1. Enable public read access for the S3 bucket
2. Use CloudFront to distribute the files using authorization hash tags
3. Generate a pre-signed URL and distribute it to the consumers
4. Configure an allow rule in the Security Group for the IP addresses of the consumers

## 54. Question

You would like to provide some on-demand and live streaming video to your customers. The plan is to provide the users with both the media player and the media files from the AWS cloud. One of the features you need is for the content of the media files to begin playing while the file is still being downloaded.

What AWS services can deliver these requirements? (choose 2)

1. Store the media files in an S3 bucket
2. Use CloudFront with a Web and RTMP distribution
3. Store the media files on an EBS volume
4. Use CloudFront with an RTMP distribution
5. Store the media files on an EC2 instance

## 55. Question

The company you work for is currently transitioning their infrastructure and applications into the AWS cloud. You are planning to deploy an Elastic Load Balancer (ELB) that distributes traffic for a web application running on EC2 instances. You still have some application servers running on-premise and you would like to distribute application traffic across both your AWS and on-premises resources.

**How can this be achieved?**

1. Provision a Direct Connect connection between your on-premises location and AWS and create a target group on an ALB to use IP based targets for both your EC2 instances and on-premises servers
2. Provision a Direct Connect connection between your on-premises location and AWS and create a target group on an ALB to use Instance ID based targets for both your EC2 instances and on-premises servers
3. Provision an IPSec VPN connection between your on-premises location and AWS and create a CLB that uses cross-zone load balancing to distributed traffic across EC2 instances and on-premises servers
4. This cannot be done, ELBs are an AWS service and can only distributed traffic within the AWS cloud

## 56. Question

A Solutions Architect is developing a mobile web app that will provide access to health-related data. The web apps will be tested on Android and iOS devices. The Architect needs to run tests on multiple devices simultaneously and to be able to reproduce issues, and record logs and performance data to ensure quality before release.

**What AWS service can be used for these requirements?**

1. AWS Cognito
2. AWS Device Farm
3. AWS Workspaces
4. Amazon Appstream 2.0

## 57. Question

There is a new requirement to implement in-memory caching for a Financial Services application due to increasing read-heavy load. The data must be stored persistently. Automatic failover across AZs is also required.

**Which two items from the list below are required to deliver these requirements? (choose 2)**

1. ElastiCache with the Memcached engine
2. Multi-AZ with Cluster mode and Automatic Failover enabled
3. ElastiCache with the Redis engine
4. Multiple nodes placed in different AZs
5. Read replica with failover mode enabled

## 58. Question

An application you are designing receives and processes files. The files are typically around 4GB in size and the application extracts metadata from the files which typically takes a few seconds for each file. The pattern of updates is highly dynamic with times of little activity and then multiple uploads within a short period of time.

**What architecture will address this workload the most cost efficiently?**

1. Upload files into an S3 bucket, and use the Amazon S3 event notification to invoke a Lambda function to extract the metadata

2. Store the file in an EBS volume which can then be accessed by another EC2 instance for processing
3. Place the files in an SQS queue, and use a fleet of EC2 instances to extract the metadata
4. Use a Kinesis data stream to store the file, and use Lambda for processing

## 59. Question

A Solutions Architect needs to transform data that is being uploaded into S3. The uploads happen sporadically and the transformation should be triggered by an event. The transformed data should then be loaded into a target data store.

**What services would be used to deliver this solution in the MOST cost-effective manner? (choose 2)**

1. Use AWS Glue to extract, transform and load the data into the target data store
2. Configure CloudFormation to provision a Kinesis data stream to transform the data and load it into S3
3. Configure S3 event notifications to trigger a Lambda function when data is uploaded and use the Lambda function to trigger the ETL job
4. Configure CloudFormation to provision AWS Data Pipeline to transform the data
5. Configure a CloudWatch alarm to send a notification to CloudFormation when data is uploaded

## 60. Question

A company has divested a single business unit and needs to move the AWS account owned by the business unit to another AWS Organization. How can this be achieved?

1. Migrate the account using the AWS Organizations console
2. Create a new account in the destination AWS Organization and migrate resources
3. Create a new account in the destination AWS Organization and share the original resources using AWS Resource Access Manager
4. Migrate the account using AWS CloudFormation

## 61. Question

A new application is to be published in multiple regions around the world. The Architect needs to ensure only 2 IP addresses need to be whitelisted. The solution should intelligently route traffic for lowest latency and provide fast regional failover.

**How can this be achieved?**

1. Launch EC2 instances into multiple regions behind an ALB and use Amazon CloudFront with a pair of static IP addresses
2. Launch EC2 instances into multiple regions behind an NLB and use AWS Global Accelerator
3. Launch EC2 instances into multiple regions behind an ALB and use a Route 53 failover routing policy
4. Launch EC2 instances into multiple regions behind an NLB with a static IP address

## 62. Question

An e-commerce web application needs a highly scalable key-value database. Which AWS database service should be used?

1. Amazon DynamoDB
2. Amazon ElastiCache

3. Amazon RedShift
4. Amazon RDS

## 63. Question

An Architect needs to find a way to automatically and repeatably create many member accounts within an AWS Organization. The accounts also need to be moved into an OU and have VPCs and subnets created.

**What is the best way to achieve this?**

1. Use the AWS Management Console
2. Use CloudFormation with scripts
3. Use the AWS Organizations API
4. Use the AWS CLI

## 64. Question

A company has acquired another business and needs to migrate their 50TB of data into AWS within 1 month. They also require a secure, reliable and private connection to the AWS cloud.

**How are these requirements best accomplished?**

1. Provision an AWS Direct Connect connection and migrate the data over the link
2. Launch a Virtual Private Gateway (VPG) and migrate the data over the AWS VPN
3. Migrate data using AWS Snowball. Provision an AWS VPN initially and order a Direct Connect link
4. Provision an AWS VPN CloudHub connection and migrate the data over redundant links

## 65. Question

An organization in the health industry needs to create an application that will transmit protected health data to thousands of service consumers in different AWS accounts. The application servers run on EC2 instances in private VPC subnets. The routing for the application must be fault tolerant.

**What should be done to meet these requirements?**

1. Create a proxy server in the service provider VPC to route requests from service consumers to the application servers
2. Create an internal Application Load Balancer in the service provider VPC and put application servers behind it
3. Create a virtual private gateway connection between each pair of service provider VPCs and service consumer VPCs
4. Create a VPC endpoint service and grant permissions to specific service consumers to create a connection

# SET 1: PRACTICE QUESTIONS, ANSWERS & EXPLANATIONS

## 1. Question

A company has deployed Amazon RedShift for performing analytics on user data. When using Amazon RedShift, which of the following statements are correct in relation to availability and durability? (choose 2)

1. RedShift always keeps three copies of your data
2. Single-node clusters support data replication
3. RedShift provides continuous/incremental backups
4. Manual backups are automatically deleted when you delete a cluster
5. RedShift always keeps five copies of your data

**Answer: 1,3**

**Explanation:**

- RedShift always keeps three copies of your data and provides continuous/incremental backups
- Corrections:
- Single-node clusters do not support data replication
- Manual backups are not automatically deleted when you delete a cluster

**References:**

https://digitalcloud.training/certification-training/aws-solutions-architect-associate/database/amazon-redshift/

## 2. Question

You are a Solutions Architect at Digital Cloud Training. A client from a large multinational corporation is working on a deployment of a significant amount of resources into AWS. The client would like to be able to deploy resources across multiple AWS accounts and regions using a single toolset and template. You have been asked to suggest a toolset that can provide this functionality?

1. Use a CloudFormation template that creates a stack and specify the logical IDs of each account and region
2. Use a CloudFormation StackSet and specify the target accounts and regions in which the stacks will be created
3. Use a third-party product such as Terraform that has support for multiple AWS accounts and regions
4. This cannot be done, use separate CloudFormation templates per AWS account and region

**Answer: 2**

**Explanation:**

- AWS CloudFormation StackSets extends the functionality of stacks by enabling you to create, update, or delete stacks across multiple accounts and regions with a single operation
- Using an administrator account, you define and manage an AWS CloudFormation template, and use the template as the basis for provisioning stacks into selected target accounts across specified regions. An administrator account is the AWS account in which you create stack sets

- A stack set is managed by signing in to the AWS administrator account in which it was created. A target account is the account into which you create, update, or delete one or more stacks in your stack set
- Before you can use a stack set to create stacks in a target account, you must set up a trust relationship between the administrator and target accounts
- A regular CloudFormation template cannot be used across regions and accounts. You would need to create copies of the template and then manage updates
- You do not need to use a third-party product such as Terraform as this functionality can be delivered through native AWS technology

**References:**

https://digitalcloud.training/certification-training/aws-solutions-architect-associate/management-tools/aws-cloudformation/

https://docs.aws.amazon.com/AWSCloudFormation/latest/UserGuide/stacksets-concepts.html

## 3. Question

A new Big Data application you are developing will use hundreds of EC2 instances to write data to a shared file system. The file system must be stored redundantly across multiple AZs within a region and allow the EC2 instances to concurrently access the file system. The required throughput is multiple GB per second.

From the options presented which storage solution can deliver these requirements?

1. Amazon EBS using multiple volumes in a RAID 0 configuration
2. Amazon EFS
3. Amazon S3
4. Amazon Storage Gateway

**Answer: 2**

**Explanation:**

- Amazon EFS is the best solution as it is the only solution that is a file-level storage solution (not block/object-based), stores data redundantly across multiple AZs within a region and you can concurrently connect up to thousands of EC2 instances to a single filesystem
- Amazon EBS volumes cannot be accessed by concurrently by multiple instances
- Amazon S3 is an object store, not a file system
- Amazon Storage Gateway is a range of products used for on-premises storage management and can be configured to cache data locally, backup data to the cloud and also provides a virtual tape backup solution

**References:**

https://digitalcloud.training/certification-training/aws-solutions-architect-associate/storage/amazon-efs/

## 4. Question

An application running on an external website is attempting to initiate a request to your company's website on AWS using API calls. A problem has been reported in which the requests are failing with an error that includes the following text:

**"Cross-Origin Request Blocked: The Same Origin Policy disallows reading the remote resource"**

**You have been asked to resolve the problem, what is the most likely solution?**

1. Enable CORS on the APIs resources using the selected methods under the API Gateway
2. The ACL on the API needs to be updated
3. The IAM policy does not allow access to the API
4. The request is not secured with SSL/TLS

**Answer: 1**

**Explanation:**

- Can enable Cross Origin Resource Sharing (CORS) for multiple domain use with Javascript/AJAX:
    - Can be used to enable requests from domains other the APIs domain
    - Allows the sharing of resources between different domains
    - The method (GET, PUT, POST etc.) for which you will enable CORS must be available in the API Gateway API before you enable CORS
    - If CORS is not enabled and an API resource received requests from another domain the request will be blocked
    - Enable CORS on the APIs resources using the selected methods under the API Gateway
- IAM policies are not used to control CORS and there is no ACL on the API to update
- This error would display whether using SSL/TLS or not

**References:**

https://digitalcloud.training/certification-training/aws-solutions-architect-associate/networking-and-content-delivery/amazon-api-gateway/

## 5. Question

**You need to configure an application to retain information about each user session and have decided to implement a layer within the application architecture to store this information.**

**Which of the options below could be used? (choose 2)**

1. A workflow service such as Amazon Simple Workflow Service (SWF)
2. Sticky sessions on an Elastic Load Balancer (ELB)
3. A block storage service such as Elastic Block Store (EBS)
4. A relational data store such as Amazon RDS
5. A key/value store such as ElastiCache Redis

**Answer: 2,5**

**Explanation:**

- In order to address scalability and to provide a shared data storage for sessions that can be accessible from any individual web server, you can abstract the HTTP sessions from the web servers themselves. A common solution to for this is to leverage an In-Memory Key/Value store such as Redis and Memcached.
- Sticky sessions, also known as session affinity, allow you to route a site user to the particular web server that is managing that individual user's session. The session's validity can be determined by a number of methods, including a client-side cookie or via configurable duration parameters that

can be set at the load balancer which routes requests to the web servers. You can configure sticky sessions on Amazon ELBs.
- Relational databases are not typically used for storing session state data due to their rigid schema that tightly controls the format in which data can be stored.
- Workflow services such as SWF are used for carrying out a series of tasks in a coordinated task flow. They are not suitable for storing session state data.
- In this instance the question states that a caching layer is being implemented and EBS volumes would not be suitable for creating an independent caching layer as they must be attached to EC2 instances.

**References:**

https://aws.amazon.com/caching/session-management/


## 6. Question

The data scientists in your company are looking for a service that can process and analyze real-time, streaming data. They would like to use standard SQL queries to query the streaming data.

**Which combination of AWS services would deliver these requirements?**

1. Kinesis Data Streams and Kinesis Data Analytics
2. Kinesis Data Streams and Kinesis Firehose
3. ElastiCache and EMR
4. DynamoDB and EMR


**Answer: 1**

**Explanation:**

- Kinesis Data Streams enables you to build custom applications that process or analyze streaming data for specialized needs
- Amazon Kinesis Data Analytics is the easiest way to process and analyze real-time, streaming data. Kinesis Data Analytics can use standard SQL queries to process Kinesis data streams and can ingest data from Kinesis Streams and Kinesis Firehose but Firehose cannot be used for running SQL queries
- DynamoDB is a NoSQL database that can be used for storing data from a stream but cannot be used to process or analyze the data or to query it with SQL queries. Elastic Map Reduce (EMR) is a hosted Hadoop framework and is not used for analytics on streaming data

**References:**

https://digitalcloud.training/certification-training/aws-solutions-architect-associate/analytics/amazon-kinesis/


## 7. Question

Which of the following approaches provides the lowest cost for Amazon elastic block store snapshots while giving you the ability to fully restore data?

1. Maintain a single snapshot; the latest snapshot is both incremental and complete
2. Maintain the most current snapshot; archive the original to Amazon Glacier
3. Maintain two snapshots: the original snapshot and the latest incremental snapshot
4. Maintain the original snapshot; subsequent snapshots will overwrite one another

**Answer: 1**

**Explanation:**

- You can backup data on an EBS volume by periodically taking snapshots of the volume. The scenario is that you need to reduce storage costs by maintaining as few EBS snapshots as possible whilst ensuring you can restore all data when required.
- If you take periodic snapshots of a volume, the snapshots are incremental which means only the blocks on the device that have changed after your last snapshot are saved in the new snapshot. Even though snapshots are saved incrementally, the snapshot deletion process is designed such that you need to retain only the most recent snapshot in order to restore the volume
- You cannot just keep the original snapshot as it will not be incremental and complete
- You do not need to keep the original and latest snapshot as the latest snapshot is all that is needed
- There is no need to archive the original snapshot to Amazon Glacier. EBS copies your data across multiple servers in an AZ for durability

**References:**

https://digitalcloud.training/certification-training/aws-solutions-architect-associate/compute/amazon-ebs/

# 8. Question

You are undertaking a project to make some audio and video files that your company uses for onboarding new staff members available via a mobile application. You are looking for a cost-effective way to convert the files from their current formats into formats that are compatible with smartphones and tablets. The files are currently stored in an S3 bucket.

**What AWS service can help with converting the files?**

1. Rekognition
2. Elastic Transcoder
3. Data Pipeline
4. Amazon Personalize

**Answer: 2**

**Explanation:**

- Amazon Elastic Transcoder is a highly scalable, easy to use and cost-effective way for developers and businesses to convert (or "transcode") video and audio files from their source format into versions that will playback on devices like smartphones, tablets and PCs
- Amazon Personalize is a machine learning service that makes it easy for developers to create individualized recommendations for customers using their applications
- Data Pipeline helps you move, integrate, and process data across AWS compute and storage resources, as well as your on-premises resources
- Rekognition is a deep learning-based visual analysis service

**References:**

https://digitalcloud.training/certification-training/aws-solutions-architect-associate/media-services/amazon-elastic-transcoder/

## 9. Question

You are a Solutions Architect at Digital Cloud Training. A large multi-national client has requested a design for a multi-region, multi-master database. The client has requested that the database be designed for fast, massively scaled applications for a global user base. The database should be a fully managed service including the replication.

Which AWS service can deliver these requirements?

1. S3 with Cross Region Replication
2. RDS with Multi-AZ
3. DynamoDB with Global Tables and Cross Region Replication
4. EC2 instances with EBS replication

Answer: 3

Explanation:

- Cross-region replication allows you to replicate across regions:
  - Amazon DynamoDB global tables provides a fully managed solution for deploying a multi-region, multi-master database
  - When you create a global table, you specify the AWS regions where you want the table to be available
  - DynamoDB performs all of the necessary tasks to create identical tables in these regions, and propagate ongoing data changes to all of them
- RDS with Multi-AZ is not multi-master (only one DB can be written to at a time), and does not span regions
- S3 is an object store not a multi-master database
- There is no such thing as EBS replication. You could build your own database stack on EC2 with DB-level replication but that is not what is presented in the answer

References:

https://digitalcloud.training/certification-training/aws-solutions-architect-associate/database/amazon-dynamodb/

## 10. Question

A customer has asked you to recommend the best solution for a highly available database. The database is a relational OLTP type of database and the customer does not want to manage the operating system the database runs on. Failover between AZs must be automatic.

Which of the below options would you suggest to the customer?

1. Use RDS in a Multi-AZ configuration
2. Use DynamoDB
3. Use RedShift in a Multi-AZ configuration
4. Install a relational database on EC2 instances in multiple AZs and create a cluster

Answer: 1

Explanation:

- Amazon Relational Database Service (Amazon RDS) is a managed service that makes it easy to set up, operate, and scale a relational database in the cloud. With RDS you can configure Multi-AZ which creates a replica in another AZ and synchronously replicates to it (DR only)
- RedShift is used for analytics OLAP not OLTP
- If you install a DB on an EC2 instance you will need to manage to OS yourself and the customer wants it to be managed for them
- DynamoDB is a managed database of the NoSQL type. NoSQL DBs are not relational DBs

**References:**

https://digitalcloud.training/certification-training/aws-solutions-architect-associate/compute/aws-auto-scaling/

## 11. Question

**An application you manage uses Auto Scaling and a fleet of EC2 instances. You recently noticed that Auto Scaling is scaling the number of instances up and down multiple times in the same hour. You need to implement a remediation to reduce the amount of scaling events. The remediation must be cost-effective and preserve elasticity. What design changes would you implement? (choose 2)**

1. Modify the Auto Scaling group termination policy to terminate the newest instance first
2. Modify the Auto Scaling group cool-down timers
3. Modify the CloudWatch alarm period that triggers your Auto Scaling scale down policy
4. Modify the Auto Scaling policy to use scheduled scaling actions
5. Modify the Auto Scaling group termination policy to terminate the oldest instance first

**Answer: 2,3**

**Explanation:**

- The cooldown period is a configurable setting for your Auto Scaling group that helps to ensure that it doesn't launch or terminate additional instances before the previous scaling activity takes effect so this would help. After the Auto Scaling group dynamically scales using a simple scaling policy, it waits for the cooldown period to complete before resuming scaling activities
- The CloudWatch Alarm Evaluation Period is the number of the most recent data points to evaluate when determining alarm state. This would help as you can increase the number of datapoints required to trigger an alarm
- The order in which Auto Scaling terminates instances is not the issue here, the problem is that the workload is dynamic and Auto Scaling is constantly reacting to change, and launching or terminating instances
- Using scheduled scaling actions may not be cost-effective and also affects elasticity as it is less dynamic

**References:**

https://docs.aws.amazon.com/AmazonCloudWatch/latest/monitoring/AlarmThatSendsEmail.html#alarm-evaluation

https://digitalcloud.training/certification-training/aws-solutions-architect-associate/compute/aws-auto-scaling/

## 12. Question

One of your EC2 instances runs an application process that saves user data to an attached EBS volume. The EBS volume was attached to the EC2 instance after it was launched and is unencrypted. You would like to encrypt the data that is stored on the volume as it is considered sensitive however you cannot shutdown the instance due to other application processes that are running.

**What is the best method of applying encryption to the sensitive data without any downtime?**

1. Create an encrypted snapshot of the current EBS volume. Restore the snapshot to the EBS volume
2. Create and mount a new encrypted EBS volume. Move the data to the new volume and then delete the old volume
3. Unmount the volume and enable server-side encryption. Re-mount the EBS volume
4. Leverage the AWS Encryption CLI to encrypt the data on the volume

**Answer: 2**

**Explanation:**

- You cannot restore a snapshot of a root volume without downtime
- There is no direct way to change the encryption state of a volume
- Either create an encrypted volume and copy data to it or take a snapshot, encrypt it, and create a new encrypted volume from the snapshot

**References:**

https://digitalcloud.training/certification-training/aws-solutions-architect-associate/compute/amazon-ebs/

## 13. Question

You are planning to launch a RedShift cluster for processing and analyzing a large amount of data. The RedShift cluster will be deployed into a VPC with multiple subnets. Which construct is used when provisioning the cluster to allow you to specify a set of subnets in the VPC that the cluster will be deployed into?

1. Subnet Group
2. Availability Zone (AZ)
3. DB Subnet Group
4. Cluster Subnet Group

**Answer: 4**

**Explanation:**

- You create a cluster subnet group if you are provisioning your cluster in your virtual private cloud (VPC)
- A cluster subnet group allows you to specify a set of subnets in your VPC
- When provisioning a cluster, you provide the subnet group and Amazon Redshift creates the cluster on one of the subnets in the group
- A DB Subnet Group is used by RDS
- A Subnet Group is used by ElastiCache
- Availability Zones are part of the AWS global infrastructure, subnets reside within AZs but in RedShift you provision the cluster into Cluster Subnet Groups

**References:**

https://digitalcloud.training/certification-training/aws-solutions-architect-associate/database/amazon-redshift/

https://docs.aws.amazon.com/redshift/latest/mgmt/working-with-cluster-subnet-groups.html

## 14. Question

A Solutions Architect is responsible for a web application that runs on EC2 instances that sit behind an Application Load Balancer (ALB). Auto Scaling is used to launch instances across 3 Availability Zones. The web application serves large image files and these are stored on an Amazon EFS file system. Users have experienced delays in retrieving the files and the Architect has been asked to improve the user experience.

**What should the Architect do to improve user experience?**

1. Cache static content using CloudFront
2. Reduce the file size of the images
3. Move the digital assets to EBS
4. Use Spot instances

**Answer: 1**

**Explanation:**

- CloudFront is ideal for caching static content such as the files in this scenario and would increase performance
- Moving the files to EBS would not make accessing the files easier or improve performance
- Reducing the file size of the images may result in better retrieval times, however CloudFront would still be the preferable option
- Using Spot EC2 instances may reduce EC2 costs but it won't improve user experience

**References:**

https://digitalcloud.training/certification-training/aws-solutions-architect-associate/networking-and-content-delivery/amazon-cloudfront/

## 15. Question

A Solutions Architect is deploying an Auto Scaling Group (ASG) and needs to determine what CloudWatch monitoring option to use. Which of the statements below would assist the Architect in making his decision? (choose 2)

1. Basic monitoring is enabled by default if the ASG is created from the CLI
2. Detailed monitoring is chargeable and must always be manually enabled
3. Detailed monitoring is free and can be manually enabled
4. Detailed monitoring is enabled by default if the ASG is created from the CLI
5. Basic monitoring is enabled by default if the ASG is created from the console

**Answer: 4,5**

**Explanation:**

- Basic monitoring sends EC2 metrics to CloudWatch about ASG instances every 5 minutes
- Detailed can be enabled and sends metrics every 1 minute (it is always chargeable)
- When the launch configuration is created from the CLI detailed monitoring of EC2 instances is enabled by default
- When you enable Auto Scaling group metrics, Auto Scaling sends sampled data to CloudWatch every minute

**References:**

https://digitalcloud.training/certification-training/aws-solutions-architect-associate/compute/aws-auto-scaling/

## 16. Question

A Linux instance running in your VPC requires some configuration changes to be implemented locally and you need to run some commands. Which of the following can be used to securely connect to the instance?

1. SSL/TLS certificate
2. Public key
3. Key Pairs
4. EC2 password

**Answer: 3**

**Explanation:**

- A key pair consists of a public key that AWS stores, and a private key file that you store
- For Windows AMIs, the private key file is required to obtain the password used to log into your instance
- For Linux AMIs, the private key file allows you to securely SSH into your instance
- The "EC2 password" might refer to the operating system password. By default, you cannot login this way to Linux and must use a key pair. However, this can be enabled by setting a password and updating the /etc/ssh/sshd_config file
- You cannot login to an EC2 instance using certificates/public keys

**References:**

https://digitalcloud.training/certification-training/aws-solutions-architect-associate/compute/amazon-ec2/

## 17. Question

Your company would like to restrict the ability of most users to change their own passwords whilst continuing to allow a select group of users within specific user groups.

**What is the best way to achieve this? (choose 2)**

1. Under the IAM Password Policy deselect the option to allow users to change their own passwords
2. Create an IAM Policy that grants users the ability to change their own password and attach it to the groups that contain the users
3. Create an IAM Policy that grants users the ability to change their own password and attach it to the individual user accounts

4. Create an IAM Role that grants users the ability to change their own password and attach it to the groups that contain the users
5. Disable the ability for all users to change their own passwords using the AWS Security Token Service

**Answer: 1,2**

**Explanation:**

- A password policy can be defined for enforcing password length, complexity etc. (applies to all users)
- You can allow or disallow the ability to change passwords using an IAM policy and you should attach this to the group that contains the users, not to the individual users themselves
- You cannot use an IAM role to perform this function
- The AWS STS is not used for controlling password policies

**References:**

https://digitalcloud.training/certification-training/aws-solutions-architect-associate/security-identity-compliance/aws-iam/

## 18. Question

A colleague from your company's IT Security team has notified you of an Internet-based threat that affects a certain port and protocol combination. You have conducted an audit of your VPC and found that this port and protocol combination is allowed on an Inbound Rule with a source of 0.0.0.0/0. You have verified that this rule only exists for maintenance purposes and need to make an urgent change to block the access.

What is the fastest way to block access from the Internet to the specific ports and protocols?

1. You don't need to do anything; this rule will only allow access to VPC based resources
2. Update the security group by removing the rule
3. Delete the security group
4. Add a deny rule to the security group with a higher priority

**Answer: 2**

**Explanation:**

- Security group membership can be changed whilst instances are running
- Any changes to security groups will take effect immediately
- You can only assign permit rules in a security group, you cannot assign deny rules
- If you delete the security you will remove all rules and potentially cause other problems
- You do need to make the update, as it's the VPC based resources you're concerned about

**References:**

https://digitalcloud.training/certification-training/aws-solutions-architect-associate/networking-and-content-delivery/amazon-vpc/

## 19. Question

You are an entrepreneur building a small company with some resources running on AWS. As you have limited funding, you're extremely cost conscious. Which AWS service can send you alerts via email or SNS topic when you are forecast to exceed your funding capacity so you can take action?

1. Cost & Usage reports
2. AWS Billing Dashboard
3. AWS Budgets
4. Cost Explorer

**Answer: 3**

**Explanation:**

- AWS Budgets gives you the ability to set custom budgets that alert you when your costs or usage exceed (or are forecasted to exceed) your budgeted amount. Budget alerts can be sent via email and/or Amazon Simple Notification Service (SNS) topic
- The AWS Cost Explorer is a free tool that allows you to view charts of your costs
- The AWS Billing Dashboard can send alerts when you're bill reaches certain thresholds but you must use AWS Budgets to created custom budgets that notify you when you are forecast to exceed a budget
- The AWS Cost and Usage report tracks your AWS usage and provides estimated charges associated with your AWS account but does not send alerts

**References:**

https://aws.amazon.com/aws-cost-management/aws-budgets/

## 20. Question

Your company is starting to use AWS to host new web-based applications. A new two-tier application will be deployed that provides customers with access to data records. It is important that the application is highly responsive and retrieval times are optimized. You're looking for a persistent data store that can provide the required performance. From the list below what AWS service would you recommend for this requirement?

1. Kinesis Data Streams
2. ElastiCache with the Memcached engine
3. ElastiCache with the Redis engine
4. RDS in a multi-AZ configuration

**Answer: 3**

**Explanation:**

ElastiCache is a web service that makes it easy to deploy and run Memcached or Redis protocol-compliant server nodes in the cloud. The in-memory caching provided by ElastiCache can be used to significantly improve latency and throughput for many read-heavy application workloads or compute-intensive workloads

There are two different database engines with different characteristics as per below:

**Memcached**

- Not persistent
- Cannot be used as a data store
- Supports large nodes with multiple cores or threads
- Scales out and in, by adding and removing nodes

**Redis**

- Data is persistent
- Can be used as a datastore
- Not multi-threaded
- Scales by adding shards, not nodes

Kinesis Data Streams is used for processing streams of data, it is not a persistent data store

RDS is not the optimum solution due to the requirement to optimize retrieval times which is a better fit for an in-memory data store such as ElastiCache

**References:**

https://digitalcloud.training/certification-training/aws-solutions-architect-associate/database/amazon-elasticache/

## 21. Question

**A Solutions Architect is developing an encryption solution. The solution requires that data keys are encrypted using envelope protection before they are written to disk.**

**Which solution option can assist with this requirement?**

1. AWS Certificate Manager
2. AWS KMS API
3. IAM Access Key
4. API Gateway with STS

**Answer: 2**

**Explanation:**

- The AWS KMS API can be used for encrypting data keys (envelope encryption)
- AWS Certificate Manager is a service that lets you easily provision, manage, and deploy public and private Secure Sockets Layer/Transport Layer Security (SSL/TLS) certificates for use with AWS services and your internal connected resources
- The AWS Security Token Service (STS) is a web service that enables you to request temporary, limited-privilege credentials for AWS Identity and Access Management (IAM) users or for users that you authenticate (federated users)
- IAM access keys are used for signing programmatic requests you make to AWS

**References:**

https://docs.aws.amazon.com/kms/latest/APIReference/Welcome.html

## 22. Question

A solutions Architect is designing a new workload where an AWS Lambda function will access an Amazon DynamoDB table.

What is the MOST secure means of granting the Lambda function access to the DynamoDB table?

1. Create an identity and access management (IAM) role with the necessary permissions to access the DynamoDB table, and assign the role to the Lambda function
2. Create a DynamoDB username and password and give them to the Developer to use in the Lambda function
3. Create an identity and access management (IAM) user and create access and secret keys for the user. Give the user the necessary permissions to access the DynamoDB table. Have the Developer use these keys to access the resources
4. Create an identity and access management (IAM) role allowing access from AWS Lambda and assign the role to the DynamoDB table

**Answer: 1**

**Explanation:**

- The most secure method is to use an IAM role so you don't need to embed any credentials in code and can tightly control the services that your Lambda function can access. You need to assign the role to the Lambda function, NOT to the DynamoDB table
- You should not provide a username and password to the Developer to use with the function. This is insecure – always avoid using credentials in code!
- You should not use an access key and secret ID to access DynamoDB. Again, this means embedding credentials in code which should be avoided.

**References:**

https://aws.amazon.com/blogs/security/how-to-create-an-aws-iam-policy-to-grant-aws-lambda-access-to-an-amazon-dynamodb-table/

## 23. Question

An e-commerce application is hosted in AWS. The last time a new product was launched, the application experienced a performance issue due to an enormous spike in traffic. Management decided that capacity must be doubled this week after the product is launched.

What is the MOST efficient way for management to ensure that capacity requirements are met?

1. Add Amazon EC2 Spot instances
2. Add a Step Scaling policy
3. Add a Simple Scaling policy
4. Add a Scheduled Scaling action

**Answer: 4**

**Explanation:**

- Scheduled scaling: Scaling based on a schedule allows you to set your own scaling schedule for predictable load changes. To configure your Auto Scaling group to scale based on a schedule, you create a scheduled action. This is ideal for situations where you know when and for how long you are going to need the additional capacity

- Step scaling: step scaling policies increase or decrease the current capacity of your Auto Scaling group based on a set of scaling adjustments, known as step adjustments. The adjustments vary based on the size of the alarm breach. This is more suitable to situations where the load unpredictable
- Simple scaling: AWS recommend using step over simple scaling in most cases. With simple scaling, after a scaling activity is started, the policy must wait for the scaling activity or health check replacement to complete and the cooldown period to expire before responding to additional alarms (in contrast to step scaling). Again, this is more suitable to unpredictable workloads
- EC2 Spot Instances: adding spot instances may decrease EC2 costs but you still need to ensure they are available. The main requirement of the question is that the performance issues are resolved rather than the cost being minimized

**References:**

https://docs.aws.amazon.com/autoscaling/ec2/userguide/as-scale-based-on-demand.html

https://digitalcloud.training/certification-training/aws-solutions-architect-associate/compute/aws-auto-scaling/

## 24. Question

**A colleague has asked you some questions about how AWS charge for DynamoDB. He is interested in knowing what type of workload DynamoDB is best suited for in relation to cost and how AWS charges for DynamoDB? (choose 2)**

1. DynamoDB is more cost effective for read heavy workloads
2. DynamoDB is more cost effective for write heavy workloads
3. Priced based on provisioned throughput (read/write) regardless of whether you use it or not
4. You provision for expected throughput but are only charged for what you use
5. DynamoDB scales vertically by adding additional nodes

**Answer: 1,3**

**Explanation:**

- DynamoDB is more cost effective for read heavy workloads. This is due to the read capacity units (RCU) being half the price of the write capacity units (WCU).
- With DynamoDB you are charged based on the provisioned throughput you assign (RCUs/WCUs) regardless of whether you use it or not. With the DynamoDB Auto Scaling feature you can now have DynamoDB dynamically adjust provisioned throughput capacity on your behalf, in response to actual traffic patterns. However, this is not provided as an answer option.
- DynamoDB scales horizontally and the mechanism by which this happens is transparent to consumers. It does not scale vertically by adding nodes.

**References:**

https://digitalcloud.training/certification-training/aws-solutions-architect-associate/database/amazon-dynamodb/

https://docs.aws.amazon.com/amazondynamodb/latest/developerguide/AutoScaling.html

## 25. Question

A user is testing a new service that receives location updates from 5,000 rental cars every hour. Which service will collect data and automatically scale to accommodate production workload?

1. Amazon API Gateway
2. Amazon EBS
3. Amazon Kinesis Firehose
4. Amazon EC2

**Answer: 3**

**Explanation:**

- What we need here is a service that can ~~streaming~~ collect streaming data. The only option available is Kinesis Firehose which captures, transforms, and loads streaming data into "destinations" such as S3, RedShift, Elasticsearch and Splunk
- Amazon EC2 is not suitable for collecting streaming data
- EBS is a block-storage service in which you attach volumes to EC2 instances, this does not assist with collecting streaming data (see previous point)
- Amazon API Gateway is used for hosting and managing APIs not for receiving streaming data

**References:**

https://digitalcloud.training/certification-training/aws-solutions-architect-associate/analytics/amazon-kinesis/

## 26. Question

A research company is developing a data lake solution in Amazon S3 to analyze huge datasets. The solution makes infrequent SQL queries only. In addition, the company wants to minimize infrastructure costs.

Which AWS service should be used to meet these requirements?

1. Amazon Redshift Spectrum
2. Amazon Aurora
3. Amazon Athena
4. Amazon RDS for MySQL

**Answer: 3**

**Explanation:**

- Amazon Athena is an interactive query service that makes it easy to analyze data in Amazon S3 using standard SQL. Athena is serverless, so there is no infrastructure to manage, and you pay only for the queries that you run – this satisfies the requirement to minimize infrastructure costs for infrequent queries.
- Amazon RedShift Spectrum is a feature of Amazon Redshift that enables you to run queries against exabytes of unstructured data in Amazon S3, with no loading or ETL required. However, RedShift nodes run on EC2 instances, so for infrequent queries this will not minimize infrastructure costs.
- Amazon RDS and Aurora are not suitable solutions for analyzing datasets on S3 – these are both relational databases typically used for transactional (not analytical) workloads.

**References:**

https://digitalcloud.training/certification-training/aws-solutions-architect-associate/analytics/amazon-athena/

https://docs.aws.amazon.com/athena/latest/ug/what-is.html

## 27. Question

An application runs on two EC2 instances in private subnets split between two AZs. The application needs to connect to a CRM SaaS application running on the Internet. The vendor of the SaaS application restricts authentication to a whitelist of source IP addresses and only 2 IP addresses can be configured per customer.

What is the most appropriate and cost-effective solution to enable authentication to the SaaS application?

1. Configure redundant Internet Gateways and update the routing tables for each subnet
2. Configure a NAT Gateway for each AZ with an Elastic IP address
3. Use multiple Internet-facing Application Load Balancers with Elastic IP addresses
4. Use a Network Load Balancer and configure a static IP for each AZ

**Answer: 2**

**Explanation:**

- In this scenario you need to connect the EC2 instances to the SaaS application with a source address of one of two whitelisted public IP addresses to ensure authentication works.
- A NAT Gateway is created in a specific AZ and can have a single Elastic IP address associated with it. NAT Gateways are deployed in public subnets and the route tables of the private subnets where the EC2 instances reside are configured to forward Internet-bound traffic to the NAT Gateway. You do pay for using a NAT Gateway based on hourly usage and data processing, however this is still a cost-effective solution
- A Network Load Balancer can be configured with a single static IP address (the other types of ELB cannot) for each AZ. However, using a NLB is not an appropriate solution as the connections are being made outbound from the EC2 instances to the SaaS app and ELBs are used for distributing inbound connection requests to EC2 instances (only return traffic goes back through the ELB)
- An ALB does not support static IP addresses and is not suitable for a proxy function
- AWS Route 53 is a DNS service and is not used as an outbound proxy server so is not suitable for this scenario

**References:**

https://digitalcloud.training/certification-training/aws-solutions-architect-associate/compute/elastic-load-balancing/

## 28. Question

A recent security audit uncovered some poor deployment and configuration practices within your VPC. You need to ensure that applications are deployed in secure configurations.

How can this be achieved in the most operationally efficient manner?

1. Remove the ability for staff to deploy applications
2. Use AWS Inspector to apply secure configurations

3. Manually check all application configurations before deployment
4. Use CloudFormation with securely configured templates

**Answer: 4**

**Explanation:**

- CloudFormation helps users to deploy resources in a consistent and orderly way. By ensuring the CloudFormation templates are created and administered with the right security configurations for your resources, you can then repeatedly deploy resources with secure settings and reduce the risk of human error
- Removing the ability of staff to deploy resources does not help you to deploy applications securely as it does not solve the problem of how to do this in an operationally efficient manner
- Manual checking of all application configurations before deployment is not operationally efficient
- Amazon Inspector is an automated security assessment service that helps improve the security and compliance of applications deployed on AWS. It is not used to secure the actual deployment of resources, only to assess the deployed state of the resources

**References:**

https://digitalcloud.training/certification-training/aws-solutions-architect-associate/management-tools/aws-cloudformation/


## 29. Question

The application development team in your company has a new requirement for the deployment of a container solution. You plan to use the AWS Elastic Container Service (ECS). The solution should include load balancing of incoming requests across the ECS containers and allow the containers to use dynamic host port mapping so that multiple tasks from the same service can run on the same container host.

**Which AWS load balancing configuration will support this?**

1. You cannot run multiple copies of a task on the same instance, because the ports would conflict
2. Use a Network Load Balancer (NLB) and host-based routing
3. Use a Classic Load Balancer (CLB) and create a static mapping of the ports
4. Use an Application Load Balancer (ALB) and map the ECS service to the ALB

**Answer: 4**

**Explanation:**

- It is possible to associate a service on Amazon ECS to an Application Load Balancer (ALB) for the Elastic Load Balancing (ELB) service
- An Application Load Balancer allows dynamic port mapping. You can have multiple tasks from a single service on the same container instance.
- The Classic Load Balancer requires that you statically map port numbers on a container instance. You cannot run multiple copies of a task on the same instance, because the ports would conflict
- An NLB does not support host-based routing (ALB only), and this would not help anyway

**References:**

https://digitalcloud.training/certification-training/aws-solutions-architect-associate/compute/amazon-ecs/

https://digitalcloud.training/certification-training/aws-solutions-architect-associate/compute/elastic-load-balancing/

## 30. Question

**To improve security in your AWS account you have decided to enable multi-factor authentication (MFA). You can authenticate using an MFA device in which two ways? (choose 2)**

1. Using biometrics
2. Locally to EC2 instances
3. Through the AWS Management Console
4. Using the AWS API
5. Using a key pair

**Answer: 3,4**

**Explanation:**

You can authenticate using an MFA device in the following ways:

- Through the AWS Management Console – the user is prompted for a user name, password and authentication code
- Using the AWS API – restrictions are added to IAM policies and developers can request temporary security credentials and pass MFA parameters in their AWS STS API requests
- Using the AWS CLI by obtaining temporary security credentials from STS (aws sts get-session-token)

**References:**

https://digitalcloud.training/certification-training/aws-solutions-architect-associate/security-identity-compliance/aws-iam/

## 31. Question

**The company you work for has a presence across multiple AWS regions. As part of disaster recovery planning you are formulating a solution to provide a regional DR capability for an application running on a fleet of Amazon EC2 instances that are provisioned by an Auto Scaling Group (ASG). The applications are stateless and read and write data to an S3 bucket. You would like to utilize the current AMI used by the ASG as it has some customizations made to it.**

**What are the steps you might take to enable a regional DR capability for this application? (choose 2)**

1. Enable cross region replication on the S3 bucket and specify a destination bucket in the DR region
2. Modify the launch configuration for the ASG in the DR region and specify the AMI
3. Copy the AMI to the DR region and create a new launch configuration for the ASG that uses the AMI
4. Enable multi-AZ for the S3 bucket to enable synchronous replication to the DR region
5. Modify the permissions of the AMI so it can be used across multiple regions

**Answer: 1,3**

**Explanation:**

- There are two parts to this solution. First you need to copy the S3 data to each region (as the instances are stateless), then you need to be able to deploy instances from an ASG using the same AMI in each regions.
  - CRR is an Amazon S3 feature that automatically replicates data across AWS Regions. With CRR, every object uploaded to an S3 bucket is automatically replicated to a destination bucket in a different AWS Region that you choose, this enables you to copy the existing data across to each region
  - AMIs of both Amazon EBS-backed AMIs and instance store-backed AMIs can be copied between regions. You can then use the copied AMI to create a new launch configuration (remember that you cannot modify an ASG launch configuration, you must create a new launch configuration)
- There's no such thing as Multi-AZ for an S3 bucket (it's an RDS concept)
- Changing permissions on an AMI doesn't make it usable from another region, the AMI needs to be present within each region to be used

References:

https://digitalcloud.training/certification-training/aws-solutions-architect-associate/storage/amazon-s3/

https://digitalcloud.training/certification-training/aws-solutions-architect-associate/compute/amazon-ebs/

## 32. Question

A Solutions Architect needs to improve performance for a web application running on EC2 instances launched by an Auto Scaling group. The instances run behind an ELB Application Load Balancer. During heavy use periods the ASG doubles in size and analysis has shown that static content stored on the EC2 instances is being requested by users in a specific geographic location.

How can the Solutions Architect reduce the need to scale and improve the application performance?

1. Re-deploy the application in a new VPC that is closer to the users making the requests
2. Create an Amazon CloudFront distribution for the site and redirect user traffic to the distribution
3. Store the contents on Amazon EFS instead of the EC2 root volume
4. Implement Amazon Redshift to create a repository of the content closer to the users

Answer: 2

Explanation:

- This is a good use case for CloudFront. CloudFront is a content delivery network (CDN) that caches content closer to users. You can cache the static content on CloudFront using the EC2 instances as origins for the content. This will improve performance (as the content is closer to the users) and reduce the need for the ASG to scale (as you don't need the processing power of the EC2 instances to serve the static content).
- Re-deploying the application in a VPC closer to the users may reduce latency (and therefore improve performance), but it doesn't solve the problem of reducing the need for the ASG to scale.
- Using EFS instead of the EC2 root volume does not solve either problem.
- RedShift cannot be used to create content repositories to get content closer to users, it's a data warehouse used for analytics.

References:

https://digitalcloud.training/certification-training/aws-solutions-architect-associate/networking-and-content-delivery/amazon-cloudfront/

https://aws.amazon.com/caching/cdn/

## 33. Question

You are a Solutions Architect at Digital Cloud Training. One of your clients has requested that you design a solution for distributing load across a number of EC2 instances across multiple AZs within a region. Customers will connect to several different applications running on the client's servers through their browser using multiple domain names and SSL certificates. The certificates are stored in AWS Certificate Manager (ACM).

What is the optimal architecture to ensure high availability, cost effectiveness, and performance?

1. Launch a single ALB, configure host-based routing for the domain names and bind an SSL certificate to each routing rule
2. Launch a single ALB and bind multiple SSL certificates to the same secure listener. Clients will use the Server Name Indication (SNI) extension
3. Launch a single ALB and bind multiple SSL certificates to multiple secure listeners
4. Launch multiple ALBs and bind separate SSL certificates to each ELB

**Answer: 2**

**Explanation:**

- You can use a single ALB and bind multiple SSL certificates to the same listener
- With Server Name Indication (SNI) a client indicates the hostname to connect to. SNI supports multiple secure websites using a single secure listener
- You cannot have the same port in multiple listeners so adding multiple listeners would not work. Also, when using standard HTTP/HTTPS the port will always be 80/443 so you must be able to receive traffic on the same ports for multiple applications and still be able to forward to the correct instances. This is where host-based routing comes in
- With host-based routing you can route client requests based on the Host field (domain name) of the HTTP header allowing you to route to multiple domains from the same load balancer (and share the same listener)
- You do not need multiple ALBs and it would not be cost-effective

**References:**

https://digitalcloud.training/certification-training/aws-solutions-architect-associate/compute/elastic-load-balancing/

## 34. Question

The website for a new application received around 50,000 requests each second and the company wants to use multiple applications to analyze the navigation patterns of the users on their website so they can personalize the user experience.

What can a Solutions Architect use to collect page clicks for the website and process them sequentially for each user?

1. Amazon SQS standard queue
2. AWS CloudTrail trail

3. Amazon Kinesis Streams
4. Amazon SQS FIFO queue

**Answer: 3**

**Explanation:**

- This is a good use case for Amazon Kinesis streams as it is able to scale to the required load, allow multiple applications to access the records and process them sequentially
- Amazon Kinesis Data Streams enables real-time processing of streaming big data. It provides ordering of records, as well as the ability to read and/or replay records in the same order to multiple Amazon Kinesis Applications
- Amazon Kinesis streams allows up to 1 MiB of data per second or 1,000 records per second for writes per shard. There is no limit on the number of shards so you can easily scale Kinesis Streams to accept 50,000 per second
- The Amazon Kinesis Client Library (KCL) delivers all records for a given partition key to the same record processor, making it easier to build multiple applications reading from the same Amazon Kinesis data stream
- Standard SQS queues do not ensure that messages are processed sequentially and FIFO SQS queues do not scale to the required number of transactions a second
- CloudTrail is used for auditing and is not useful here

**References:**

https://docs.aws.amazon.com/streams/latest/dev/service-sizes-and-limits.html

https://aws.amazon.com/kinesis/data-streams/faqs/

https://digitalcloud.training/certification-training/aws-solutions-architect-associate/analytics/amazon-kinesis/

## 35. Question

A retail organization is deploying a new application that will read and write data to a database. The company wants to deploy the application in three different AWS Regions in an active-active configuration. The databases need to replicate to keep information in sync.

**Which solution best meets these requirements?**

1. Amazon DynamoDB with global tables
2. Amazon Athena with Amazon S3 cross-region replication
3. AWS Database Migration Service with change data capture
4. Amazon Aurora Global Database

**Answer: 1**

**Explanation:**

- Amazon DynamoDB global tables provide a fully managed solution for deploying a multi-region, multi-master database. This is the only solution presented that provides an active-active configuration where reads and writes can take place in multiple regions with full bi-directional synchronization.
- Amazon Athena with S3 cross-region replication is not suitable. This is not a solution that provides a transactional database solution (Athena is used for analytics), or active-active synchronization.

- Amazon Aurora Global Database provides read access to a database in multiple regions — it does not provide active-active configuration with bi-directional synchronization (though you can failover to your read-only DBs and promote them to writable).

**References:**

https://digitalcloud.training/certification-training/aws-solutions-architect-associate/database/amazon-dynamodb/

https://aws.amazon.com/blogs/database/how-to-use-amazon-dynamodb-global-tables-to-power-multiregion-architectures/

## 36. Question

**You are building an application that will collect information about user behavior. The application will rapidly ingest large amounts of dynamic data and requires very low latency. The database must be scalable without incurring downtime. Which database would you recommend for this scenario?**

1. RedShift
2. DynamoDB
3. RDS with MySQL
4. RDS with Microsoft SQL

**Answer: 2**

**Explanation:**

- Amazon Dynamo DB is a fully managed NoSQL database service that provides fast and predictable performance with seamless scalability
- Push button scaling means that you can scale the DB at any time without incurring downtime
- DynamoDB provides low read and write latency
- RDS uses EC2 instances so you have to change your instance type/size in order to scale compute vertically
- RedShift uses EC2 instances as well, so you need to choose your instance type/size for scaling compute vertically, but you can also scale horizontally by adding more nodes to the cluster
- Rapid ingestion of dynamic data is not an ideal use case for RDS or RedShift

**References:**

https://digitalcloud.training/certification-training/aws-solutions-architect-associate/database/amazon-dynamodb/

## 37. Question

**You have been asked to implement a solution for capturing, transforming and loading streaming data into an Amazon RedShift cluster. The solution will capture data from Amazon Kinesis Data Streams. Which AWS services would you utilize in this scenario? (choose 2)**

1. Kinesis Data Firehose for capturing the data and loading it into RedShift
2. Kinesis Video Streams for capturing the data and loading it into RedShift
3. Lambda for transforming the data
4. EMR for transforming the data
5. AWS Data Pipeline for transforming the data

**Answer: 1,3**

**Explanation:**

- For this solution Kinesis Data Firehose can be used as it can use Kinesis Data Streams as a source and can capture, transform, and load streaming data into a RedShift cluster. Kinesis Data Firehose can invoke a Lambda function to transform data before delivering it to destinations
- Kinesis Video Streams makes it easy to securely stream video from connected devices to AWS for analytics, machine learning (ML), and other processing, this solution does not involve video streams
- AWS Data Pipeline is used for processing and moving data between compute and storage services. It does not work with streaming data as Kinesis does
- Elastic Map Reduce (EMR) is used for processing and analyzing data using the Hadoop framework. It is not used for transforming streaming data

**References:**

https://digitalcloud.training/certification-training/aws-solutions-architect-associate/analytics/amazon-kinesis/

## 38. Question

A company is deploying a big data and analytics workload. The analytics will be run from a fleet of thousands of EC2 instances across multiple AZs. Data needs to be stored on a shared storage layer that can be mounted and accessed concurrently by all EC2 instances. Latency is not a concern however extremely high throughput is required.

What storage layer would be most suitable for this requirement?

1. Amazon EFS in Max I/O mode
2. Amazon EFS in General Purpose mode
3. Amazon EBS PIOPS
4. Amazon S3

**Answer: 1**

**Explanation:**

- Amazon EFS file systems in the Max I/O mode can scale to higher levels of aggregate throughput and operations per second with a tradeoff of slightly higher latencies for file operations
- Amazon S3 is not a storage layer that can be mounted and accessed concurrently
- Amazon EBS volumes cannot be shared between instances

**References:**

https://digitalcloud.training/certification-training/aws-solutions-architect-associate/storage/amazon-efs/

https://docs.aws.amazon.com/efs/latest/ug/performance.html

## 39. Question

Your company is reviewing their information security processes. One of the items that came out of a recent audit is that there is insufficient data recorded about requests made to a few S3 buckets. The security team requires an audit trail for operations on the S3 buckets that includes the requester, bucket name, request time, request action, and response status.

**Which action would you take to enable this logging?**

1. Create a CloudWatch metric that monitors the S3 bucket operations and triggers an alarm
2. Enable server access logging for the S3 buckets to save access logs to a specified destination bucket
3. Create a CloudTrail trail that audits S3 bucket operations
4. Enable S3 event notifications for the specific actions and setup an SNS notification

**Answer: 2**

**Explanation:**

- Server access logging provides detailed records for the requests that are made to a bucket. To track requests for access to your bucket, you can enable server access logging. Each access log record provides details about a single access request, such as the requester, bucket name, request time, request action, response status, and an error code, if relevant
- For capturing IAM/user identity information in logs you would need to configure AWS CloudTrail Data Events (however this does not audit the bucket operations required in the question)
- Amazon S3 event notifications can be sent in response to actions in Amazon S3 like PUTs, POSTs, COPYs, or DELETEs.S3 event notifications records the request action but not the other requirements of the security team
- CloudWatch metrics do not include the bucket operations specified in the question

**References:**

https://digitalcloud.training/certification-training/aws-solutions-architect-associate/storage/amazon-s3/

https://docs.aws.amazon.com/AmazonS3/latest/dev/ServerLogs.html

## 40. Question

A Solutions Architect is designing a new architecture that will use an Amazon EC2 Auto Scaling group.

**Which of the following factors determine the health check grace period? (choose 2)**

1. How long the bootstrap script takes to run
2. How long it takes for the Auto Scaling group to detect a failure
3. How much of the application code is embedded in the AMI
4. How many Amazon CloudWatch alarms are configured for status checks
5. How frequently the Auto Scaling group scales up or down

**Answer: 1,3**

**Explanation:**

- Amazon EC2 Auto Scaling waits until the health check grace period ends before checking the health status of the instance. The length of the health check grace period needs to consider the warm-up time for your instances. This includes the time to start the application. Application code in the AMI as well as bootstrap scripts could delay application start-up, so you'd want to consider these factors when determining the health check grace period.
- How many times the Auto Scaling group scales up or down is not relevant to the health check grace period, every instance will need to go through this when launched and you need to ensure the instances start before the period ends.

- It's not relevant how many CloudWatch alarms are configured for status checks as status checks are not acted on until the health check grace period ends.
- Detecting a failure is related to how quickly Auto Scaling can react and terminate and replace an instance, it's not relevant to the health check grace period.

**References:**

https://docs.aws.amazon.com/autoscaling/ec2/userguide/healthcheck.html

https://digitalcloud.training/certification-training/aws-solutions-architect-associate/compute/aws-auto-scaling/

## 41. Question

A call center application consists of a three-tier application using Auto Scaling groups to automatically scale resources as needed. Users report that every morning at 9:00am the system becomes very slow for about 15 minutes. A Solutions Architect determines that a large percentage of the call center staff starts work at 9:00am, so Auto Scaling does not have enough time to scale to meet demand.

**How can the Architect fix the problem?**

1. Permanently keep a steady state of instance that is needed at 9:00am to guarantee available resources, but use Spot Instances
2. Use Reserved Instances to ensure the system has reserved the right amount of capacity for the scaling events
3. Create an Auto Scaling scheduled action to scale out the necessary resources at 8:30am each morning
4. Change the Auto Scaling group's scale out event to scale based on network utilization

**Answer: 3**

**Explanation:**

- Scheduled scaling: Scaling based on a schedule allows you to set your own scaling schedule for predictable load changes. To configure your Auto Scaling group to scale based on a schedule, you create a scheduled action. This is ideal for situations where you know when and for how long you are going to need the additional capacity
- Changing the scale-out events to scale based on network utilization may not assist here. We're not certain the network utilization will increase sufficiently to trigger an Auto Scaling scale out action as the load may be more CPU/memory or number of connections. The main problem however is that we need to ensure the EC2 instances are provisioned ahead of demand not in response to demand (which would incur a delay whilst the EC2 instances "warm up")
- Using reserved instances ensures capacity is available within an AZ, however the issue here is not that the AZ does not have capacity for more instances, it is that the instances are not being launched by Auto Scaling ahead of the peak demand
- Keeping a steady state of Spot instances is not a good solution. Spot instances may be cheaper, but this is not guaranteed and keeping them online 24hrs a day is wasteful and could prove more expensive

**References:**

https://digitalcloud.training/certification-training/aws-solutions-architect-associate/compute/aws-auto-scaling/

https://docs.aws.amazon.com/autoscaling/ec2/userguide/schedule_time.html

## 42. Question

Your company keeps unstructured data on a filesystem. You need to provide access to employees via EC2 instances in your VPC. Which storage solution should you choose?

1. Amazon EBS
2. Amazon Snowball
3. Amazon EFS
4. Amazon S3

**Answer: 3**

**Explanation:**

- EFS is the only storage system presented that provides a file system. EFS is accessed by mounting filesystems using the NFS v4.1 protocol from your EC2 instances. You can concurrently connect up to thousands of instances to a single EFS filesystem
- Amazon S3 is an object-based storage system that is accessed over a REST API
- Amazon EBS is a block-based storage system that provides volumes that are mounted to EC2 instances but cannot be shared between EC2 instances
- Amazon Snowball is a device used for migrating very large amounts of data into or out of AWS

**References:**

https://digitalcloud.training/certification-training/aws-solutions-architect-associate/storage/amazon-efs/

## 43. Question

You are a Solutions Architect at a media company and you need to build an application stack that can receive customer comments from sporting events. The application is expected to receive significant load that could scale to millions of messages within a short space of time following high-profile matches. As you are unsure of the load required for the database layer what is the most cost-effective way to ensure that the messages are not dropped?

1. Use RDS Auto Scaling for the database layer which will automatically scale as required
2. Create an SQS queue and modify the application to write to the SQS queue. Launch another application instance the polls the queue and writes messages to the database
3. Use DynamoDB and provision enough write capacity to handle the highest expected load
4. Write the data to an S3 bucket, configure RDS to poll the bucket for new messages

**Answer: 2**

**Explanation:**

- Amazon Simple Queue Service (Amazon SQS) is a web service that gives you access to message queues that store messages waiting to be processed. SQS offers a reliable, highly-scalable, hosted queue for storing messages in transit between computers and is used for distributed/decoupled applications.
- This is a great use case for SQS as the messages you don't have to over-provision the database layer or worry about messages being dropped
- RDS Auto Scaling does not exist. With RDS you have to select the underlying EC2 instance type to use and pay for that regardless of the actual load on the DB. Note that a new feature released in June 2019 does allow Auto Scaling for the RDS storage, but not the compute layer.

With DynamoDB there are now 2 pricing options:

- Provisioned capacity has been around forever and is one of the incorrect answers to this question. With provisioned capacity you have to specify the number of read/write capacity units to provision and pay for these regardless of the load on the database.
- With the the new On-demand capacity mode DynamoDB is charged based on the data reads and writes your application performs on your tables. You do not need to specify how much read and write throughput you expect your application to perform because DynamoDB instantly accommodates your workloads as they ramp up or down. it might be a good solution to this question but is not an available option.

**References:**

https://digitalcloud.training/certification-training/aws-solutions-architect-associate/application-integration/amazon-sqs/

## 44. Question

A company needs to store data for 5 years. The company will need to have immediate and highly available access to the data at any point in time but will not require frequent access.

Which lifecycle action should be taken to meet the requirements while reducing costs?

1. Transition objects from Amazon S3 Standard to the GLACIER storage class
2. Transition objects from Amazon S3 Standard to Amazon S3 One Zone-Infrequent Access (S3 One Zone-IA)
3. Transition objects to expire after 5 years
4. Transition objects from Amazon S3 Standard to Amazon S3 Standard-Infrequent Access (S3 Standard-IA)

**Answer: 4**

**Explanation:**

- This is a good use case for S3 Standard-IA which provides immediate access and 99.9% availability.
- Expiring the objects after 5 years is going to delete them at the end of the 5-year period, but you still need to work out the best storage solution to use before then, and this answer does not provide a solution.
- The S3 One Zone-IA tier provides immediate access, but the availability is lower at 99.5% so this is not the best option.
- The Glacier storage class does not provide immediate access. You can retrieve within hours or minutes, but you do need to submit a job to retrieve the data.

**References:**

https://aws.amazon.com/s3/storage-classes/

https://digitalcloud.training/certification-training/aws-solutions-architect-associate/storage/amazon-s3/

## 45. Question

A Solutions Architect is designing an application that will run on Amazon ECS behind an Application Load Balancer (ALB). For security reasons, the Amazon EC2 host instances for the ECS cluster are in a private subnet.

What should be done to ensure that the incoming traffic to the host instances is from the ALB only?

1. Update the EC2 cluster security group to allow incoming access from the IP address of the ALB only
2. Modify the security group used by the EC2 cluster to allow incoming traffic from the security group used by the ALB only
3. Create network ACL rules for the private subnet to allow incoming traffic on ports 32768 through 61000 from the IP address of the ALB only
4. Enable AWS WAF on the ALB and enable the ECS rule

**Answer: 2**

**Explanation:**

- The best way to accomplish this requirement is to restrict incoming traffic to the Security Group used by the ALB. This will ensure that only the ALB (and its nodes) will be able to connect to the EC2 instances in the ECS cluster.
- You should not use the IP address of the ALB in the Security Group rules as an ALB has multiple nodes in each AZ in which it has subnets defined. Always use security groups whenever you can.
- Network ACLs work at the subnet level. It is preferable to use Security Groups which work at the instance level. Also, you should not use the IP of the ALB as it will have multiple nodes / IPs and it would be cumbersome to setup and administer.
- Enabling a WAF is useful when you need to protect against malicious code. However, this is not a requirement for this solution, you just need to restrict incoming traffic to the ALB.

**References:**

https://digitalcloud.training/certification-training/aws-solutions-architect-associate/compute/elastic-load-balancing/

## 46. Question

**A Solutions Architect is designing a highly-scalable system to track records. Records must remain available for immediate download for three months, and then the records must be deleted.**

**What's the most appropriate decision for this use case?**

1. Store the files on Amazon EFS, and create a lifecycle policy to remove the files after three months
2. Store the files on Amazon S3, and create a lifecycle policy to remove the files after three months
3. Store the files on Amazon EBS, and create a lifecycle policy to remove the files after three months
4. Store the files on Amazon Glacier, and create a lifecycle policy to remove the files after three months

**Answer: 2**

**Explanation:**

- With S3 you can create a lifecycle action using the "expiration action element" which expires objects (deletes them) at the specified time
- S3 lifecycle actions apply to any storage class, including Glacier, however Glacier would not allow immediate download
- There is no lifecycle policy available for deleting files on EBS and EFS
- NOTE: The new Amazon Data Lifecycle Manager (DLM) feature automates the creation, retention, and deletion of EBS snapshots but not the individual files within an EBS volume. This is a new feature that may not yet feature on the exam

**References:**

https://digitalcloud.training/certification-training/aws-solutions-architect-associate/storage/amazon-s3/

## 47. Question

A Solutions Architect needs to allow another AWS account programmatic access to upload objects to his bucket. The Solutions Architect needs to ensure that he retains full control of the objects uploaded to the bucket. How can this be done?

1. The Architect will need to instruct the user in the other AWS account to grant him access when uploading objects
2. The Architect will need to take ownership of objects after they have been uploaded
3. The Architect can use a resource-based bucket policy that grants cross-account access and include a conditional statement that only allows uploads if full control access is granted to the Architect
4. The Architect can use a resource-based ACL with an IAM policy that grants cross-account access and include a conditional statement that only allows uploads if full control access is granted to the Architect

**Answer: 3**

**Explanation:**

- You can use a resource-based bucket policy to allow another AWS account to upload objects to your bucket and use a conditional statement to ensure that full control permissions are granted to a specific account identified by an ID (e.g. email address)
- You cannot use a resource-based ACL with IAM policy as this configuration does not support conditional statements
- Taking ownership of objects is not a concept that is valid in Amazon S3 and asking the user in the other AWS account to grant access when uploading is not a good method as technical controls to enforce this behavior are preferred

**References:**

https://docs.aws.amazon.com/AmazonS3/latest/dev/example-bucket-policies.html

https://aws.amazon.com/premiumsupport/knowledge-center/cross-account-access-s3/

https://digitalcloud.training/certification-training/aws-solutions-architect-associate/storage/amazon-s3/

## 48. Question

You are creating a design for a web-based application that will be based on a web front-end using EC2 instances and a database back-end. This application is a low priority and you do not want to incur costs in general day to day management. Which AWS database service can you use that will require the least operational overhead?

1. DynamoDB
2. EMR
3. RedShift
4. RDS

**Answer: 1**

**Explanation:**

- Out of the options in the list, DynamoDB requires the least operational overhead as there are no backups, maintenance periods, software updates etc. to deal with
- RDS, RedShift and EMR all require some operational overhead to deal with backups, software updates and maintenance periods

**References:**

https://digitalcloud.training/certification-training/aws-solutions-architect-associate/database/amazon-dynamodb/

## 49. Question

A company's Amazon RDS MySQL DB instance may be rebooted for maintenance and to apply patches. This database is critical and potential user disruption must be minimized.

**What should the Solution Architect do in this scenario?**

1. Set up an Amazon RDS MySQL cluster
2. Create an RDS MySQL Read Replica
3. Set the Amazon RDS MySQL to Multi-AZ
4. Create an Amazon EC2 instance MySQL cluster

**Answer: 3**

**Explanation:**

- With RDS in multi-AZ configuration system upgrades like OS patching, DB Instance scaling and system upgrades, are applied first on the standby, before failing over and modifying the other DB Instance. This means the database is always available with minimal disruption.
- You cannot create a "RDS MySQL cluster" with Amazon RDS. If you want to create a MySQL cluster you need to install on EC2 (which is another option presented). If you install in EC2 you must manage the whole process of patching and failover yourself as it's not a managed solution.
- Amazon RDS MySQL Read Replicas can serve reads but not writes so there would be a disruption if the application is writing to the DB while the system updates are taking place.

**References:**

https://digitalcloud.training/certification-training/aws-solutions-architect-associate/database/amazon-rds/

https://docs.aws.amazon.com/AmazonRDS/latest/UserGuide/USER_UpgradeDBInstance.Maintenance.html

## 50. Question

You would like to share some documents with public users accessing an S3 bucket over the Internet. What are two valid methods of granting public read permissions so you can share the documents? (choose 2)

1. Grant public read access to the objects when uploading
2. Grant public read on all objects using the S3 bucket ACL
3. Share the documents using CloudFront and a static website

4. Use the AWS Policy Generator to create a bucket policy for your Amazon S3 bucket granting read access to public anonymous users
5. Share the documents using a bastion host in a public subnet

**Answer: 1,4**

**Explanation:**

- Access policies define access to resources and can be associated with resources (buckets and objects) and users
- You can use the AWS Policy Generator to create a bucket policy for your Amazon S3 bucket. Bucket policies can be used to grant permissions to objects
- You can define permissions on objects when uploading and at any time afterwards using the AWS Management Console.
- You cannot use a bucket ACL to grant permissions to objects within the bucket. You must explicitly assign the permissions to each object through an ACL attached as a subresource to that object
- Using an EC2 instance as a bastion host to share the documents is not a feasible or scalable solution
- You can configure an S3 bucket as a static website and use CloudFront as a front-end however this is not necessary just to share the documents and imposes some constraints on the solution

**References:**

https://digitalcloud.training/certification-training/aws-solutions-architect-associate/storage/amazon-s3/

## 51. Question

You have created a private Amazon CloudFront distribution that serves files from an Amazon S3 bucket and is accessed using signed URLs. You need to ensure that users cannot bypass the controls provided by Amazon CloudFront and access content directly.

How can this be achieved? (choose 2)

1. Create an origin access identity and associate it with your distribution
2. Modify the Edge Location to restrict direct access to Amazon S3 buckets
3. Modify the permissions on the origin access identity to restrict read access to the Amazon S3 bucket
4. Create a new signed URL that requires users to access the Amazon S3 bucket through Amazon CloudFront
5. Modify the permissions on the Amazon S3 bucket so that only the origin access identity has read and download permissions

**Answer: 1,5**

**Explanation:**

- If you're using an Amazon S3 bucket as the origin for a CloudFront distribution, you can either allow everyone to have access to the files there, or you can restrict access. If you limit access by using CloudFront signed URLs or signed cookies you also won't want people to be able to view files by simply using the direct URL for the file. Instead, you want them to only access the files by using the CloudFront URL, so your protections work. This can be achieved by creating an OAI and associating it with your distribution and then modifying the permissions on the S3 bucket to only allow the OAI to access the files
- You do not modify permissions on the OAI – you do this on the S3 bucket

- If users are accessing the S3 files directly, a new signed URL is not going to stop them
- You cannot modify edge locations to restrict access to S3 buckets

**References:**

https://docs.aws.amazon.com/AmazonCloudFront/latest/DeveloperGuide/private-content-restricting-access-to-s3.html

## 52. Question

**Your company shares some HR videos stored in an Amazon S3 bucket via CloudFront. You need to restrict access to the private content so users coming from specific IP addresses can access the videos and ensure direct access via the Amazon S3 bucket is not possible.**

**How can this be achieved?**

1. Configure CloudFront to require users to access the files using a signed URL, and configure the S3 bucket as a website endpoint
2. Configure CloudFront to require users to access the files using signed cookies, and move the files to an encrypted EBS volume
3. Configure CloudFront to require users to access the files using signed cookies, create an origin access identity (OAI) and instruct users to login with the OAI
4. Configure CloudFront to require users to access the files using a signed URL, create an origin access identity (OAI) and restrict access to the files in the Amazon S3 bucket to the OAI

**Answer: 4**

**Explanation:**

- A signed URL includes additional information, for example, an expiration date and time, that gives you more control over access to your content. You can also specify the IP address or range of IP addresses of the users who can access your content
- If you use CloudFront signed URLs (or signed cookies) to limit access to files in your Amazon S3 bucket, you may also want to prevent users from directly accessing your S3 files by using Amazon S3 URLs. To achieve this, you can create an origin access identity (OAI), which is a special CloudFront user, and associate the OAI with your distribution. You can then change the permissions either on your Amazon S3 bucket or on the files in your bucket so that only the origin access identity has read permission (or read and download permission)
- Users cannot login with an OAI
- You cannot use CloudFront and an OAI when you're S3 bucket is configured as a website endpoint
- You cannot use CloudFront to pull data directly from an EBS volume

**References:**

https://docs.aws.amazon.com/AmazonCloudFront/latest/DeveloperGuide/private-content-restricting-access-to-s3.html

https://digitalcloud.training/certification-training/aws-solutions-architect-associate/storage/amazon-s3/

## 53. Question

**There is a temporary need to share some video files that are stored in a private S3 bucket. The consumers do not have AWS accounts and you need to ensure that only authorized consumers can access the files. What is the best way to enable this access?**

1. Enable public read access for the S3 bucket
2. Use CloudFront to distribute the files using authorization hash tags
3. Generate a pre-signed URL and distribute it to the consumers
4. Configure an allow rule in the Security Group for the IP addresses of the consumers

**Answer: 3**

**Explanation:**

- S3 pre-signed URLs can be used to provide temporary access to a specific object to those who do not have AWS credentials. This is the best option
- Enabling public read access does not restrict the content to authorized consumers
- You cannot use CloudFront as hash tags are not a CloudFront authentication mechanism
- Security Groups do not apply to S3 buckets

**References:**

https://digitalcloud.training/certification-training/aws-solutions-architect-associate/storage/amazon-s3/

## 54. Question

You would like to provide some on-demand and live streaming video to your customers. The plan is to provide the users with both the media player and the media files from the AWS cloud. One of the features you need is for the content of the media files to begin playing while the file is still being downloaded.

**What AWS services can deliver these requirements? (choose 2)**

1. Store the media files in an S3 bucket
2. Use CloudFront with a Web and RTMP distribution
3. Store the media files on an EBS volume
4. Use CloudFront with an RTMP distribution
5. Store the media files on an EC2 instance

**Answer: 1,2**

**Explanation:**

- For serving both the media player and media files you need two types of distributions:
  - A web distribution for the media player
  - An RTMP distribution for the media files
- RTMP:
  - Distribute streaming media files using Adobe Flash Media Server's RTMP protocol
  - Allows an end user to begin playing a media file before the file has finished downloading from a CloudFront edge location
  - Files must be stored in an S3 bucket (not an EBS volume or EC2 instance)

**References:**

https://digitalcloud.training/certification-training/aws-solutions-architect-associate/networking-and-content-delivery/amazon-cloudfront/

## 55. Question

The company you work for is currently transitioning their infrastructure and applications into the AWS cloud. You are planning to deploy an Elastic Load Balancer (ELB) that distributes traffic for a web application running on EC2 instances. You still have some application servers running on-premise and you would like to distribute application traffic across both your AWS and on-premises resources.

How can this be achieved?

1. Provision a Direct Connect connection between your on-premises location and AWS and create a target group on an ALB to use IP based targets for both your EC2 instances and on-premises servers
2. Provision a Direct Connect connection between your on-premises location and AWS and create a target group on an ALB to use Instance ID based targets for both your EC2 instances and on-premises servers
3. Provision an IPSec VPN connection between your on-premises location and AWS and create a CLB that uses cross-zone load balancing to distributed traffic across EC2 instances and on-premises servers
4. This cannot be done, ELBs are an AWS service and can only distributed traffic within the AWS cloud

Answer: 1

Explanation:

- The ALB (and NLB) supports IP addresses as targets
- Using IP addresses as targets allows load balancing any application hosted in AWS or on-premises using IP addresses of the application back-ends as targets
- You must have a VPN or Direct Connect connection to enable this configuration to work
- You cannot use instance ID based targets for on-premises servers and you cannot mix instance ID and IP address target types in a single target group
- The CLB does not support IP addresses as targets

References:

https://digitalcloud.training/certification-training/aws-solutions-architect-associate/compute/elastic-load-balancing/

https://aws.amazon.com/blogs/aws/new-application-load-balancing-via-ip-address-to-aws-on-premises-resources/

## 56. Question

A Solutions Architect is developing a mobile web app that will provide access to health-related data. The web apps will be tested on Android and iOS devices. The Architect needs to run tests on multiple devices simultaneously and to be able to reproduce issues, and record logs and performance data to ensure quality before release.

What AWS service can be used for these requirements?

1. AWS Cognito
2. AWS Device Farm
3. AWS Workspaces
4. Amazon Appstream 2.0

Answer: 2

**Explanation:**

- AWS Device Farm is an app testing service that lets you test and interact with your Android, iOS, and web apps on many devices at once, or reproduce issues on a device in real time
- Amazon Cognito lets you add user sign-up, sign-in, and access control to your web and mobile apps quickly and easily. It is not used for testing
- Amazon WorkSpaces is a managed, secure cloud desktop service
- Amazon AppStream 2.0 is a fully managed application streaming service

**References:**

https://aws.amazon.com/device-farm/

## 57. Question

There is a new requirement to implement in-memory caching for a Financial Services application due to increasing read-heavy load. The data must be stored persistently. Automatic failover across AZs is also required.

Which two items from the list below are required to deliver these requirements? (choose 2)

1. ElastiCache with the Memcached engine
2. Multi-AZ with Cluster mode and Automatic Failover enabled
3. ElastiCache with the Redis engine
4. Multiple nodes placed in different AZs
5. Read replica with failover mode enabled

**Answer: 2,3**

**Explanation:**

- Redis engine stores data persistently
- Memcached engine does not store data persistently
- Redis engine supports Multi-AZ using read replicas in another AZ in the same region
- You can have a fully automated, fault tolerant ElastiCache-Redis implementation by enabling both cluster mode and multi-AZ failover
- Memcached engine does not support Multi-AZ failover or replication

**References:**

https://digitalcloud.training/certification-training/aws-solutions-architect-associate/database/amazon-elasticache/

## 58. Question

An application you are designing receives and processes files. The files are typically around 4GB in size and the application extracts metadata from the files which typically takes a few seconds for each file. The pattern of updates is highly dynamic with times of little activity and then multiple uploads within a short period of time.

What architecture will address this workload the most cost efficiently?

1. Upload files into an S3 bucket, and use the Amazon S3 event notification to invoke a Lambda function to extract the metadata
2. Store the file in an EBS volume which can then be accessed by another EC2 instance for processing

3. Place the files in an SQS queue, and use a fleet of EC2 instances to extract the metadata
4. Use a Kinesis data stream to store the file, and use Lambda for processing

**Answer: 1**

**Explanation:**

- Storing the file in an S3 bucket is the most cost-efficient solution, and using S3 event notifications to invoke a Lambda function works well for this unpredictable workload
- Kinesis data streams runs on EC2 instances and you must therefore provision some capacity even when the application is not receiving files. This is not as cost-efficient as storing them in an S3 bucket prior to using Lambda for the processing
- SQS queues have a maximum message size of 256KB. You can use the extended client library for Java to use pointers to a payload on S3 but the maximum payload size is 2GB
- Storing the file in an EBS volume and using EC2 instances for processing is not cost efficient

**References:**

https://digitalcloud.training/certification-training/aws-solutions-architect-associate/storage/amazon-s3/

https://docs.aws.amazon.com/AmazonS3/latest/dev/NotificationHowTo.html

## 59. Question

A Solutions Architect needs to transform data that is being uploaded into S3. The uploads happen sporadically and the transformation should be triggered by an event. The transformed data should then be loaded into a target data store.

What services would be used to deliver this solution in the MOST cost-effective manner? (choose 2)

1. Use AWS Glue to extract, transform and load the data into the target data store
2. Configure CloudFormation to provision a Kinesis data stream to transform the data and load it into S3
3. Configure S3 event notifications to trigger a Lambda function when data is uploaded and use the Lambda function to trigger the ETL job
4. Configure CloudFormation to provision AWS Data Pipeline to transform the data
5. Configure a CloudWatch alarm to send a notification to CloudFormation when data is uploaded

**Answer: 1,3**

**Explanation:**

- S3 event notifications triggering a Lambda function is completely serverless and cost-effective
- AWS Glue can trigger ETL jobs that will transform that data and load it into a data store such as S3
- Kinesis Data Streams is used for processing data, rather than extracting and transforming it. The Kinesis consumers are EC2 instances which are not as cost-effective as serverless solutions
- AWS Data Pipeline can be used to automate the movement and transformation of data, it relies on other services to actually transform the data

**References:**

https://docs.aws.amazon.com/AmazonS3/latest/dev/NotificationHowTo.html

https://aws.amazon.com/glue/

## 60. Question

A company has divested a single business unit and needs to move the AWS account owned by the business unit to another AWS Organization. How can this be achieved?

1. Migrate the account using the AWS Organizations console
2. Create a new account in the destination AWS Organization and migrate resources
3. Create a new account in the destination AWS Organization and share the original resources using AWS Resource Access Manager
4. Migrate the account using AWS CloudFormation

**Answer: 1**

**Explanation:**

- Accounts can be migrated between organizations. To do this you must have root or IAM access to both the member and master accounts. Resources will remain under the control of the migrated account.
- You do not need to use AWS CloudFormation. You can use the Organizations API or AWS CLI for when there are many accounts to migrate and therefore you could use CloudFormation for any additional automation but it is not necessary for this scenario.
- You do not need to create a new account in the destination AWS Organization as you can just migrate the existing account.

**References:**

https://digitalcloud.training/certification-training/aws-solutions-architect-associate/management-tools/aws-organizations/

https://aws.amazon.com/premiumsupport/knowledge-center/organizations-move-accounts/

## 61. Question

A new application is to be published in multiple regions around the world. The Architect needs to ensure only 2 IP addresses need to be whitelisted. The solution should intelligently route traffic for lowest latency and provide fast regional failover.

How can this be achieved?

1. Launch EC2 instances into multiple regions behind an ALB and use Amazon CloudFront with a pair of static IP addresses
2. Launch EC2 instances into multiple regions behind an NLB and use AWS Global Accelerator
3. Launch EC2 instances into multiple regions behind an ALB and use a Route 53 failover routing policy
4. Launch EC2 instances into multiple regions behind an NLB with a static IP address

**Answer: 2**

**Explanation:**

- AWS Global Accelerator uses the vast, congestion-free AWS global network to route TCP and UDP traffic to a healthy application endpoint in the closest AWS Region to the user. This means it will intelligently route traffic to the closest point of presence (reducing latency). Seamless failover is ensured as AWS Global Accelerator uses anycast IP address which means the IP does not change when failing over between regions so there are no issues with client caches having incorrect entries that need to expire. This is the only solution that provides deterministic failover.

- An NLB with a static IP is a workable solution as you could configure a primary and secondary address in applications. However, this solution does not intelligently route traffic for lowest latency.
- A Route 53 failover routing policy uses a primary and standby configuration. Therefore, it sends all traffic to the primary until it fails a health check at which time it sends traffic to the secondary. This solution does not intelligently route traffic for lowest latency.
- Amazon CloudFront cannot be configured with "a pair of static IP addresses".

**References:**

https://digitalcloud.training/certification-training/aws-solutions-architect-associate/networking-and-content-delivery/aws-global-accelerator/

https://aws.amazon.com/global-accelerator/

https://aws.amazon.com/global-accelerator/faqs/

https://docs.aws.amazon.com/global-accelerator/latest/dg/what-is-global-accelerator.html


## 62. Question

**An e-commerce web application needs a highly scalable key-value database. Which AWS database service should be used?**

1. Amazon DynamoDB
2. Amazon ElastiCache
3. Amazon RedShift
4. Amazon RDS


**Answer: 1**

**Explanation:**

- A key-value database is a type of nonrelational (NoSQL) database that uses a simple key-value method to store data. A key-value database stores data as a collection of key-value pairs in which a key serves as a unique identifier. Amazon DynamoDB is a fully managed NoSQL database service that provides fast and predictable performance with seamless scalability – this is the best database for these requirements.
- Amazon RDS is a relational (SQL) type of database, not a key-value / nonrelational database.
- Amazon RedShift is a data warehouse service used for online analytics processing (OLAP) workloads.
- Amazon ElastiCache is an in-memory caching database. This is not a nonrelational key-value database.

**References:**

https://aws.amazon.com/nosql/key-value/

https://digitalcloud.training/certification-training/aws-solutions-architect-associate/database/amazon-dynamodb/

## 63. Question

An Architect needs to find a way to automatically and repeatably create many member accounts within an AWS Organization. The accounts also need to be moved into an OU and have VPCs and subnets created.

### What is the best way to achieve this?

1. Use the AWS Management Console
2. Use CloudFormation with scripts
3. Use the AWS Organizations API
4. Use the AWS CLI

Answer: 2

Explanation:

- The best solution is to use a combination of scripts and AWS CloudFormation. You will also leverage the AWS Organizations API. This solution can provide all of the requirements.
- You can create member accounts with the AWS Organizations API. However, you cannot use that API to configure the account and create VPCs and subnets.
- Using the AWS Management Console is not a method of automatically creating the resources.
- You can do all tasks using the AWS CLI but it is better to automate the process using AWS CloudFormation.

References:

https://digitalcloud.training/certification-training/aws-solutions-architect-associate/management-tools/aws-organizations/

https://aws.amazon.com/blogs/security/how-to-use-aws-organizations-to-automate-end-to-end-account-creation/

## 64. Question

A company has acquired another business and needs to migrate their 50TB of data into AWS within 1 month. They also require a secure, reliable and private connection to the AWS cloud.

### How are these requirements best accomplished?

1. Provision an AWS Direct Connect connection and migrate the data over the link
2. Launch a Virtual Private Gateway (VPG) and migrate the data over the AWS VPN
3. Migrate data using AWS Snowball. Provision an AWS VPN initially and order a Direct Connect link
4. Provision an AWS VPN CloudHub connection and migrate the data over redundant links

Answer: 3

Explanation:

- AWS Direct Connect provides a secure, reliable and private connection. However, lead times are often longer than 1 month so it cannot be used to migrate data within the timeframes. Therefore, it is better to use AWS Snowball to move the data and order a Direct Connect connection to satisfy the other requirement later on. In the meantime, the organization can use an AWS VPN for secure, private access to their VPC.

- A VPG is the AWS-side of an AWS VPN. A VPN does not provide a private connection and is not reliable as you can never guarantee the latency over the Internet.
- AWS VPN CloudHub is a service for connecting multiple sites into your VPC over VPN connections. It is not used for aggregating links and the limitations of Internet bandwidth from the company where the data is stored will still be an issue. It also uses the public Internet so is not a private or reliable connection.

**References:**

https://digitalcloud.training/certification-training/aws-solutions-architect-associate/networking-and-content-delivery/aws-direct-connect/

https://digitalcloud.training/certification-training/aws-solutions-architect-associate/migration/aws-snowball/

https://aws.amazon.com/snowball/

https://aws.amazon.com/directconnect/


## 65. Question

**An organization in the health industry needs to create an application that will transmit protected health data to thousands of service consumers in different AWS accounts. The application servers run on EC2 instances in private VPC subnets. The routing for the application must be fault tolerant.**

**What should be done to meet these requirements?**

1. Create a proxy server in the service provider VPC to route requests from service consumers to the application servers
2. Create an internal Application Load Balancer in the service provider VPC and put application servers behind it
3. Create a virtual private gateway connection between each pair of service provider VPCs and service consumer VPCs
4. Create a VPC endpoint service and grant permissions to specific service consumers to create a connection

**Answer: 4**

**Explanation:**

- What you need to do here is offer the service through a service provider offering. This is a great use case for a VPC endpoint service using AWS PrivateLink (referred to as an endpoint service). Other AWS principals can then create a connection from their VPC to your endpoint service using an interface VPC endpoint. You are acting as the service provider and offering the service to service consumers. This configuration uses a Network Load Balancer and can be fault tolerant by configuring multiple subnets in which the EC2 instances are running.
- Creating a virtual private gateway connection between each pair of service provider VPCs and service consumer VPCs would be extremely cumbersome and is not the best option.
- Creating an internal ALB would not work as you need consumers from outside your VPC to be able to connect.
- Using a proxy service is possible but would not scale as well and would present a single point of failure unless there is some load balancing to multiple proxies (not mentioned).

**References:**

https://docs.aws.amazon.com/vpc/latest/userguide/endpoint-service.html

https://digitalcloud.training/certification-training/aws-solutions-architect-associate/networking-and-content-delivery/amazon-vpc/

# SET 2: PRACTICE QUESTIONS ONLY

*Or go directly to Set 2: Practice Questions, Answers & Explanations*

## 1. Question

An EC2 instance that you manage has an IAM role attached to it that provides it with access to Amazon S3 for saving log data to a bucket. A change in the application architecture means that you now need to provide the additional ability for the application to securely make API requests to Amazon API Gateway.

**Which two methods could you use to resolve this challenge? (choose 2)**

1. You cannot modify the IAM role assigned to an EC2 instance after it has been launched. You'll need to recreate the EC2 instance and assign a new IAM role
2. Create an IAM role with a policy granting permissions to Amazon API Gateway and add it to the EC2 instance as an additional IAM role
3. Create a new IAM role with multiple IAM policies attached that grants access to Amazon S3 and Amazon API Gateway, and replace the existing IAM role that is attached to the EC2 instance
4. Delegate access to the EC2 instance from the API Gateway management console
5. Add an IAM policy to the existing IAM role that the EC2 instance is using granting permissions to access Amazon API Gateway

## 2. Question

An AWS workload in a VPC is running a legacy database on an Amazon EC2 instance. Data is stored on a 2000GB Amazon EBS (gp2) volume. At peak load times, logs show excessive wait time.

**What should be implemented to improve database performance using persistent storage?**

1. Change the EC2 instance type to one with EC2 instance store volumes
2. Migrate the data on the EBS volume to provisioned IOPS SSD (io1)
3. Migrate the data on the Amazon EBS volume to an SSD-backed volume
4. Change the EC2 instance type to one with burstable performance

## 3. Question

A DynamoDB database you manage is randomly experiencing heavy read requests that are causing latency. What is the simplest way to alleviate the performance issues?

1. Create DynamoDB read replicas
2. Create an ElastiCache cluster in front of DynamoDB
3. Enable DynamoDB DAX
4. Enable EC2 Auto Scaling for DynamoDB

## 4. Question

A company's Amazon EC2 instances were terminated or stopped, resulting in a loss of important data that was stored on attached EC2 instance stores. They want to avoid this happening in the future and need a solution that can scale as data volumes increase with the LEAST amount of management and configuration.

**Which storage is most appropriate?**

1. Amazon EBS
2. Amazon EFS
3. Amazon S3
4. Amazon RDS

## 5. Question

A bank is writing new software that is heavily dependent upon the database transactions for write consistency. The application will also occasionally generate reports on data in the database and will do joins across multiple tables. The database must automatically scale as the amount of data grows.

**Which AWS service should be used to run the database?**

1. Amazon RedShift
2. Amazon DynamoDB
3. Amazon Aurora
4. Amazon S3

## 6. Question

A Solutions Architect is designing a web application that runs on Amazon EC2 instances behind an Elastic Load Balancer. All data in transit must be encrypted.

**Which solution options meet the encryption requirement? (choose 2)**

1. Use an Application Load Balancer (ALB) in passthrough mode, then terminate SSL on EC2 instances
2. Use an Application Load Balancer (ALB) with a TCP listener, then terminate SSL on EC2 instances
3. Use a Network Load Balancer (NLB) with a TCP listener, then terminate SSL on EC2 instances
4. Use an Application Load Balancer (ALB) with an HTTPS listener, then install SSL certificates on the ALB and EC2 instances
5. Use a Network Load Balancer (NLB) with an HTTPS listener, then install SSL certificates on the NLB and EC2 instances

## 7. Question

A VPC has a fleet of EC2 instances running in a private subnet that need to connect to Internet-based hosts using the IPv6 protocol. What needs to be configured to enable this connectivity?

1. AWS Direct Connect
2. An Egress-Only Internet Gateway
3. VPN CloudHub
4. A NAT Gateway

## 8. Question

The Perfect Forward Secrecy (PFS) security feature uses a derived session key to provide additional safeguards against the eavesdropping of encrypted data. Which two AWS services support PFS? (choose 2)

1. EC2
2. EBS

3. CloudFront
4. Auto Scaling
5. Elastic Load Balancing

## 9. Question

A client needs to implement a shared directory system. Requirements are that it should provide a hierarchical structure, support strong data consistency, and be accessible from multiple accounts, regions and on-premises servers using their AWS Direct Connect link.

**Which storage service would you recommend to the client?**

1. Amazon S3
2. Amazon EBS
3. Amazon Storage Gateway
4. Amazon EFS

## 10. Question

You are deploying a two-tier web application within your VPC. The application consists of multiple EC2 instances and an Internet-facing Elastic Load Balancer (ELB). The application will be used by a small number of users with fixed public IP addresses and you need to control access so only these users can access the application.

**What would be the BEST methods of applying these controls? (choose 2)**

1. Configure the EC2 instance's Security Group to allow traffic from only the specific IP sources
2. Configure the local firewall on each EC2 instance to only allow traffic from the specific IP sources
3. Configure the ELB Security Group to allow traffic from only the specific IP sources
4. Configure the ELB to send the X-Forwarded-For header and configure the EC2 instances to filter traffic based on the source IP information in the header
5. Configure certificates on the clients and use client certificate authentication on the ELB

## 11. Question

The operations team in your company are looking for a method to automatically respond to failed status check alarms that are being received from an EC2 instance. The system in question is experiencing intermittent problems with its operating system software.

**Which two steps will help you to automate the resolution of the operating system software issues? (choose 2)**

1. Configure an EC2 action that recovers the instance
2. Create a CloudWatch alarm that monitors the "StatusCheckFailed_Instance" metric
3. Configure an EC2 action that terminates the instance
4. Configure an EC2 action that reboots the instance
5. Create a CloudWatch alarm that monitors the "StatusCheckFailed_System" metric

## 12. Question

An application is hosted on the U.S west coast. Users there have no problems, but users on the east coast are experiencing performance issues. The users have reported slow response times with the search bar autocomplete and display of account listings.

**How can you improve the performance for users on the east coast?**

1. Setup cross-region replication and use Route 53 geolocation routing
2. Create an ElastiCache database in the U.S east region
3. Create a DynamoDB Read Replica in the U.S east region
4. Host the static content in an Amazon S3 bucket and distribute it using CloudFront

## 13. Question

An application that you will be deploying in your VPC requires 14 EC2 instances that must be placed on distinct underlying hardware to reduce the impact of the failure of a hardware node. The instances will use varying instance types. What configuration will cater to these requirements taking cost-effectiveness into account?

1. Use a Cluster Placement Group within a single AZ
2. Use a Spread Placement Group across two AZs
3. Use dedicated hosts and deploy each instance on a dedicated host
4. You cannot control which nodes your instances are placed on

## 14. Question

A Solutions Architect requires a highly available database that can deliver an extremely low RPO. Which of the following configurations uses synchronous replication?

1. RDS Read Replica across AWS regions
2. DynamoDB Read Replica
3. RDS DB instance using a Multi-AZ configuration
4. EBS volume synchronization

## 15. Question

A large media site has multiple applications running on Amazon ECS. A Solutions Architect needs to use content metadata to route traffic to specific services.

**What is the MOST efficient method to fulfil this requirement?**

1. Use an AWS Classic Load Balancer with a host-based routing rule to route traffic to the correct service
2. Use the AWS CLI to update an Amazon Route 53 hosted zone to route traffic as services get updated
3. Use an AWS Application Load Balancer with a path-based routing rule to route traffic to the correct service
4. Use Amazon CloudFront to manage and route traffic to the correct service

## 16. Question

Developers regularly create and update CloudFormation stacks using API calls. For security reasons you need to ensure that users are restricted to a specified template. How can this be achieved?

1. Store the template on Amazon S3 and use a bucket policy to restrict access
2. Create an IAM policy with a Condition: TemplateURL parameter
3. Create an IAM policy with a Condition: StackPolicyURL parameter
4. Create an IAM policy with a Condition: ResourceTypes parameter

## 17. Question

During an application load testing exercise, the Amazon RDS database was seen to cause a performance bottleneck.

Which steps can be taken to improve the database performance? (choose 2)

1. Change the RDS database instance to multiple Availability Zones
2. Scale up to a larger RDS instance type
3. Redirect read queries to RDS read replicas
4. Use RDS in a separate AWS Region
5. Scale out using an Auto Scaling group for RDS

## 18. Question

You are looking for a method to distribute onboarding videos to your company's numerous remote workers around the world. The training videos are located in an S3 bucket that is not publicly accessible. Which of the options below would allow you to share the videos?

1. Use ElastiCache and attach the S3 bucket as a cache origin
2. Use CloudFront and use a custom origin pointing to an EC2 instance
3. Use a Route 53 Alias record the points to the S3 bucket
4. Use CloudFront and set the S3 bucket as an origin

## 19. Question

The development team in your company has created a new application that you plan to deploy on AWS which runs multiple components in Docker containers. You would prefer to use AWS managed infrastructure for running the containers as you do not want to manage EC2 instances.

Which of the below solution options would deliver these requirements? (choose 2)

1. Put your container images in the Elastic Container Registry (ECR)
2. Put your container images in a private repository
3. Use the Elastic Container Service (ECS) with the EC2 Launch Type
4. Use CloudFront to deploy Docker on EC2
5. Use the Elastic Container Service (ECS) with the Fargate Launch Type

## 20. Question

A Solutions Architect must design a storage solution for incoming billing reports in CSV format. The data will be analyzed infrequently and discarded after 30 days.

Which combination of services will be MOST cost-effective in meeting these requirements?

1. Use AWS Data Pipeline to import the logs into a DynamoDB table
2. Import the logs into an RDS MySQL instance
3. Import the logs to an Amazon Redshift cluster
4. Write the files to an S3 bucket and use Amazon Athena to query the data

## 21. Question

You are a Solutions Architect for a systems integrator. Your client is growing their presence in the AWS cloud and has applications and services running in a VPC across multiple availability zones within a region. The client has a requirement to build an operational dashboard within their on-premise data center within the next few months. The dashboard will show near real time statistics and therefore must be connected over a low latency, high performance network.

**What would be the best solution for this requirement?**

1. Use redundant VPN connections to two VGW routers in the region, this should give you access to the infrastructure in all AZs
2. Order multiple AWS Direct Connect connections that will be connected to multiple AZs
3. Order a single AWS Direct Connect connection to connect to the client's VPC. This will provide access to all AZs within the region
4. You cannot connect to multiple AZs from a single location

## 22. Question

A company hosts a popular web application that connects to an Amazon RDS MySQL DB instance running in a private VPC subnet that was created with default ACL settings. The web servers must be accessible only to customers on an SSL connection. The database should only be accessible to web servers in a public subnet.

**Which solution meets these requirements without impacting other running applications? (choose 2)**

1. Create a network ACL on the DB subnet, allow MySQL port 3306 inbound for web servers, and deny all outbound traffic
2. Create a DB server security group that allows the HTTPS port 443 inbound and specify the source as a web server security group
3. Create a DB server security group that allows MySQL port 3306 inbound and specify the source as a web server security group
4. Create a web server security group that allows HTTPS port 443 inbound traffic from Anywhere (0.0.0.0/0) and apply it to the web servers
5. Create a network ACL on the web server's subnet, allow HTTPS port 443 inbound, and specify the source as 0.0.0.0/0

## 23. Question

A developer is creating a solution for a real-time bidding application for a large retail company that allows users to bid on items of end-of-season clothing. The application is expected to be extremely popular and the back-end DynamoDB database may not perform as required.

**How can the Solutions Architect enable in-memory read performance with microsecond response times for the DynamoDB database?**

1. Increase the provisioned throughput
2. Configure Amazon DAX
3. Enable read replicas
4. Configure DynamoDB Auto Scaling

## 24. Question

A Solutions Architect must select the most appropriate database service for two use cases. A team of data scientists perform complex queries on a data warehouse that take several hours to complete. Another team of scientists need to run fast, repeat queries and update dashboards for customer support staff.

**Which solution delivers these requirements MOST cost-effectively?**

1. RedShift for the analytics use case and RDS for the customer support dashboard
2. RedShift for both use cases
3. RDS for both use cases
4. RedShift for the analytics use case and ElastiCache in front of RedShift for the customer support dashboard

## 25. Question

A Solutions Architect is designing a shared service for hosting containers from several customers on Amazon ECS. These containers will use several AWS services. A container from one customer must not be able to access data from another customer.

**Which solution should the Architect use to meet the requirements?**

1. IAM Instance Profile for EC2 instances
2. IAM roles for tasks
3. Network ACL
4. IAM roles for EC2 instances

## 26. Question

A Solutions Architect needs to deploy an HTTP/HTTPS service on Amazon EC2 instances that will be placed behind an Elastic Load Balancer. The ELB must support WebSockets.

**How can the Architect meet these requirements?**

1. Launch a Layer-4 Load Balancer
2. Launch a Network Load Balancer (NLB)
3. Launch an Application Load Balancer (ALB)
4. Launch a Classic Load Balancer (CLB)

## 27. Question

You would like to create a highly available web application that serves static content using multiple On-Demand EC2 instances.

**Which of the following will help you to achieve this? (choose 2)**

1. Direct Connect
2. DynamoDB and ElastiCache
3. Elastic Load Balancer and Auto Scaling
4. Amazon S3 and CloudFront
5. Multiple Availability Zones

## 28. Question

The security team in your company is defining new policies for enabling security analysis, resource change tracking, and compliance auditing. They would like to gain visibility into user activity by recording API calls made within the company's AWS account. The information that is logged must be encrypted. This requirement applies to all AWS regions in which your company has services running.

**How will you implement this request? (choose 2)**

1. Create a CloudTrail trail and apply it to all regions
2. Create a CloudTrail trail in each region in which you have services
3. Enable encryption with a single KMS key
4. Enable encryption with multiple KMS keys
5. Use CloudWatch to monitor API calls

## 29. Question

A client plans to migrate an on-premise multi-tier application to AWS. The application is integrated with industry-standard message brokers. The client wants to migrate from the existing message broker without rewriting application code. Which service should be used?

1. Amazon Step Functions
2. Amazon MQ
3. Amazon SQS
4. Amazon SNS

## 30. Question

A Solutions Architect is designing a front-end that accepts incoming requests for back-end business logic applications. The Architect is planning to use Amazon API Gateway, which statements are correct in relation to the service? (choose 2)

1. API Gateway is a web service that gives businesses and web application developers an easy and cost-effective way to distribute content with low latency and high data transfer speeds
2. API Gateway is a collection of resources and methods that are integrated with back-end HTTP endpoints, Lambda functions or other AWS services
3. Throttling can be configured at multiple levels including Global and Service Call
4. API Gateway uses the AWS Application Auto Scaling service to dynamically adjust provisioned throughput capacity on your behalf, in response to actual traffic patterns
5. API Gateway is a network service that provides an alternative to using the Internet to connect customers' on-premise sites to AWS

## 31. Question

You have deployed a highly available web application across two AZs. The application uses an Auto Scaling Group (ASG) and an Application Load Balancer (ALB) to distribute connections between the EC2 instances that make up the web front-end. The load has increased and the ASG has launched new instances in both AZs, however you noticed that the ALB is only distributing traffic to the EC2 instances in one AZ.

From the options below, what is the most likely cause of the issue?

1. The ALB does not have a public subnet defined in both AZs
2. The ASG has not registered the new instances with the ALB
3. The EC2 instances in one AZ are not passing their health checks
4. Cross-zone load balancing is not enabled on the ALB

## 32. Question

A Solutions Architect has created a VPC design that meets the security requirements of their organization. Any new applications that are deployed must use this VPC design.

**How can project teams deploy, manage, and delete VPCs that meet this design with the LEAST administrative effort?**

1. Use AWS Elastic Beanstalk to deploy both the VPC and the application
2. Clone the existing authorized VPC for each new project
3. Run a script that uses the AWS Command Line interface to deploy the VPC
4. Deploy an AWS CloudFormation template that defines components of the VPC

## 33. Question

A new mobile application that your company is deploying will be hosted on AWS. The users of the application will use mobile devices to upload small amounts of data on a frequent basis. It is expected that the number of users connecting each day could be over 1 million. The data that is uploaded must be stored in a durable and persistent data store. The data store must also be highly available and easily scalable.

**Which AWS service would you use?**

1. Redshift
2. Kinesis
3. RDS
4. DynamoDB

## 34. Question

You have created a file system using Amazon Elastic File System (EFS) which will hold home directories for users. What else needs to be done to enable users to save files to the EFS file system?

1. Create a separate EFS file system for each user and grant read-write-execute permissions on the root directory to the respective user. Then mount the file system to the users' home directory
2. Instruct the users to create a subdirectory on the file system and mount the subdirectory to their home directory
3. Modify permissions on the root directory to grant read-write-execute permissions to the users. Then create a subdirectory and mount it to the users' home directory
4. Create a subdirectory for each user and grant read-write-execute permissions to the users. Then mount the subdirectory to the users' home directory

## 35. Question

You would like to host a static website for digitalcloud.training on AWS. You will be using Route 53 to direct traffic to the website. Which of the below steps would help you achieve your objectives? (choose 2)

1. Create an "SRV" record that points to the S3 bucket
2. Use any existing S3 bucket that has public read access enabled
3. Create an "Alias" record that points to the S3 bucket
4. Create a "CNAME" record that points to the S3 bucket
5. Create an S3 bucket named digitalcloud.training

## 36. Question

Your organization is deploying a multi-language website on the AWS Cloud. The website uses CloudFront as the front-end and the language is specified in the HTTP request:

- http://d12345678aabbcc0.cloudfront.net/main.html?language=en
- http://d12345678aabbcc0.cloudfront.net/main.html?language=sp
- http://d12345678aabbcc0.cloudfront.net/main.html?language=fr

You need to configure CloudFront to deliver the cached content. What method can be used?

1. Query string parameters
2. Signed Cookies
3. Origin Access Identity
4. Signed URLs

## 37. Question

Your company runs a two-tier application on the AWS cloud that is composed of a web front-end and an RDS database. The web front-end uses multiple EC2 instances in multiple Availability Zones (AZ) in an Auto Scaling group behind an Elastic Load Balancer. Your manager is concerned about a single point of failure in the RDS database layer.

What would be the most effective approach to minimizing the risk of an AZ failure causing an outage to your database layer?

1. Take a snapshot of the database
2. Increase the DB instance size
3. Enable Multi-AZ for the RDS DB instance
4. Create a Read Replica of the RDS DB instance in another AZ

## 38. Question

A client is in the design phase of developing an application that will process orders for their online ticketing system. The application will use a number of front-end EC2 instances that pick-up orders and place them in a queue for processing by another set of back-end EC2 instances. The client will have multiple options for customers to choose the level of service they want to pay for.

The client has asked how he can design the application to process the orders in a prioritized way based on the level of service the customer has chosen?

1. Create multiple SQS queues, configure exactly-once processing and set the maximum visibility timeout to 12 hours
2. Create a combination of FIFO queues and Standard queues and configure the applications to place messages into the relevant queue based on priority
3. Create multiple SQS queues, configure the front-end application to place orders onto a specific queue based on the level of service requested and configure the back-end instances to sequentially poll the queues in order of priority
4. Create a single SQS queue, configure the front-end application to place orders on the queue in order of priority and configure the back-end instances to poll the queue and pick up messages in the order they are presented

## 39. Question

A bespoke application consisting of three tiers is being deployed in a VPC. You need to create three security groups. You have configured the WebSG (web server) security group and now need to configure the AppSG (application tier) and DBSG (database tier). The application runs on port 1030 and the database runs on 3306.

**Which rules should be created according to security best practice? (choose 2)**

1. On the AppSG security group, create a custom TCP rule for TCP 1030 and configure the DBSG security group as the source
2. On the DBSG security group, create a custom TCP rule for TCP 3306 and configure the WebSG security group as the source
3. On the WebSG security group, create a custom TCP rule for TCP 1030 and configure the AppSG security group as the source
4. On the AppSG security group, create a custom TCP rule for TCP 1030 and configure the WebSG security group as the source
5. On the DBSG security group, create a custom TCP rule for TCP 3306 and configure the AppSG security group as the source


## 40. Question

An organization is migrating data to the AWS cloud. An on-premises application uses Network File System shares and must access the data without code changes. The data is critical and is accessed frequently.

**Which storage solution should a Solutions Architect recommend to maximize availability and durability?**

1. AWS Storage Gateway – File Gateway
2. Amazon Simple Storage Service
3. Amazon Elastic Block Store
4. Amazon Elastic File System


## 41. Question

One of your clients has asked you for some advice on an issue they are facing regarding storage. The client uses an on-premise block-based storage array which is getting close to capacity. The client would like to maintain a configuration where reads/writes to a subset of frequently accessed data are performed on-premise whilst also alleviating the local capacity issues by migrating data into the AWS cloud.

**What would you suggest as the BEST solution to the client's current problems?**

1. Implement a Storage Gateway Virtual Tape Library, backup the data and then delete the data from the array
2. Implement a Storage Gateway Volume Gateway in cached mode
3. Use S3 copy command to copy data into the AWS cloud
4. Archive data that is not accessed regularly straight into Glacier

## 42. Question

You have launched a Spot instance on EC2 for working on an application development project. In the event of an interruption what are the possible behaviors that can be configured? (choose 2)

1. Save
2. Stop
3. Hibernate
4. Pause
5. Restart

## 43. Question

An application launched on Amazon EC2 instances needs to publish personally identifiable information (PII) about customers using Amazon SNS. The application is launched in private subnets within an Amazon VPC.

Which is the MOST secure way to allow the application to access service endpoints in the same region?

1. Use a NAT gateway
2. Use a proxy instance
3. Use AWS PrivateLink
4. Use an Internet Gateway

## 44. Question

You work as a Solutions Architect at Digital Cloud Training. You are working on a disaster recovery solution that allows you to bring up your applications in another AWS region. Some of your applications run on EC2 instances and have proprietary software configurations with embedded licenses. You need to create duplicate copies of your EC2 instances in the other region.

What would be the best way to do this? (choose 2)

1. Create new EC2 instances from the snapshots
2. Create an AMI of each EC2 instance and copy the AMIs to the other region
3. Copy the snapshots to the other region and create new EC2 instances from the snapshots
4. Create snapshots of the EBS volumes attached to the instances
5. Create new EC2 instances from the AMIs

## 45. Question

You are a Solutions Architect at Digital Cloud Training. A client of yours is using API Gateway for accepting and processing a large number of API calls to AWS Lambda. The client's business is rapidly growing and he is therefore expecting a large increase in traffic to his API Gateway and AWS Lambda services.

The client has asked for advice on ensuring the services can scale without any reduction in performance. What advice would you give to the client? (choose 2)

1. API Gateway scales manually through the assignment of provisioned throughput
2. AWS Lambda automatically scales up by using larger instance sizes for your functions
3. API Gateway scales up to the default throttling limit, with some additional burst capacity available
4. API Gateway can only scale up to the fixed throttling limits
5. AWS Lambda scales concurrently executing functions up to your default limit

## 46. Question

Your client is looking for a way to use standard templates for describing and provisioning their infrastructure resources on AWS. Which AWS service can be used in this scenario?

1. Auto Scaling
2. CloudFormation
3. Elastic Beanstalk
4. Simple Workflow Service (SWF)

## 47. Question

A company is launching a new application and expects it to be very popular. The company requires a database layer that can scale along with the application. The schema will be frequently changes and the application cannot afford any downtime for database changes.

Which AWS service allows the company to achieve these requirements?

1. Amazon RDS MySQL
2. Amazon RedShift
3. Amazon Aurora
4. Amazon DynamoDB

## 48. Question

You would like to grant additional permissions to an individual ECS application container on an ECS cluster that you have deployed. You would like to do this without granting additional permissions to the other containers that are running on the cluster.

How can you achieve this?

1. Create a separate Task Definition for the application container that uses a different Task Role
2. In the same Task Definition, specify a separate Task Role for the application container
3. You cannot implement granular permissions with ECS containers
4. Use EC2 instances instead as you can assign different IAM roles on each instance

## 49. Question

A mobile client requires data from several application-layer services to populate its user interface. What can the application team use to decouple the client interface from the underlying services behind them?

1. Application Load Balancer
2. AWS Device Farm
3. Amazon API Gateway
4. Amazon Cognito

## 50. Question

A customer has a production application running on Amazon EC2. The application frequently overwrites and deletes data, and it is essential that the application receives the most up-to-date version of the data whenever it is requested.

Which service is most appropriate for these requirements?

1. Amazon RedShift
2. Amazon S3
3. Amazon RDS
4. AWS Storage Gateway

## 51. Question

You are running a Hadoop cluster on EC2 instances in your VPC. The EC2 instances are launched by an Auto Scaling Group (ASG) and you have configured the ASG to scale out and in as demand changes. One of the instances in the group is the Hadoop Master Node and you need to ensure that it is not terminated when your ASG processes a scale in action.

What is the best way this can be achieved without interrupting services?

1. Change the DeleteOnTermination value for the EC2 instance
2. Use the Instance Protection feature to set scale in protection for the Hadoop Master Node
3. Move the Hadoop Master Node to another ASG that has the minimum and maximum instance settings set to 1
4. Enable Deletion Protection for the EC2 instance

## 52. Question

As a Solutions Architect at Digital Cloud Training you are helping a client to design a multi-tier web application architecture. The client has requested that the architecture provide low-latency connectivity between all servers and be resilient across multiple locations.

They would also like to use their existing Microsoft SQL licenses for the database tier. The client needs to maintain the ability to access the operating systems of all servers for the installation of monitoring software.

How would you recommend the database tier is deployed?

1. Amazon RDS with Microsoft SQL Server
2. Amazon RDS with Microsoft SQL Server in a Multi-AZ configuration
3. Amazon EC2 instances with Microsoft SQL Server and data replication within an AZ
4. Amazon EC2 instances with Microsoft SQL Server and data replication between two different AZs

## 53. Question

A Solutions Architect needs to design a solution that will allow Website Developers to deploy static web content without managing server infrastructure. All web content must be accessed over HTTPS with a custom domain name. The solution should be scalable as the company continues to grow.

Which of the following will provide the MOST cost-effective solution?

1. AWS Lambda function with Amazon API Gateway
2. Amazon EC2 instance with Amazon EBS
3. Amazon CloudFront with an Amazon S3 bucket origin
4. Amazon S3 with a static website

## 54. Question

An EBS-backed EC2 instance has been configured with some proprietary software that uses an embedded license. You need to move the EC2 instance to another Availability Zone (AZ) within the region. How can this be accomplished? Choose the best answer.

1. Use the AWS Management Console to select a different AZ for the existing instance
2. Create an image from the instance. Launch an instance from the AMI in the destination AZ
3. Take a snapshot of the instance. Create a new EC2 instance and perform a restore from the snapshot
4. Perform a copy operation to move the EC2 instance to the destination AZ

## 55. Question

A Solutions Architect must design a solution that encrypts data in Amazon S3. Corporate policy mandates encryption keys be generated and managed on premises. Which solution should the Architect use to meet the security requirements?

1. SSE-S3: Server-side encryption with Amazon-managed master key
2. AWS CloudHSM
3. SSE-KMS: Server-side encryption with AWS KMS managed keys
4. SSE-C: Server-side encryption with customer-provided encryption keys

## 56. Question

A data-processing application runs on an i3.large EC2 instance with a single 100 GB EBS gp2 volume. The application stores temporary data in a small database (less than 30 GB) located on the EBS root volume. The application is struggling to process the data fast enough, and a Solutions Architect has determined that the I/O speed of the temporary database is the bottleneck.

What is the MOST cost-efficient way to improve the database response times?

1. Put the temporary database on a new 50-GB EBS gp2 volume
2. Move the temporary database onto instance storage
3. Put the temporary database on a new 50-GB EBS io1 volume with a 3000 IOPS allocation
4. Enable EBS optimization on the instance and keep the temporary files on the existing volume

## 57. Question

You need to enable sign in on your mobile app using social identity providers including Amazon, Facebook and Google. How can you enable this capability?

1. Simple AD
2. Amazon Cognito
3. Access keys
4. IAM Policies

## 58. Question

A Solutions Architect is developing a new web application on AWS that needs to be able to scale to support unpredictable workloads. The Architect prefers to focus on value-add activities such as software development and product roadmap development rather than provisioning and managing instances.

**Which solution is most appropriate for this use case?**

1. Amazon API Gateway and AWS Lambda
2. Amazon API Gateway and Amazon EC2
3. Amazon CloudFront and AWS Lambda
4. Elastic Load Balancing with Auto Scaling groups and Amazon EC2

## 59. Question

An application you manage exports data from a relational database into an S3 bucket. The data analytics team wants to import this data into a RedShift cluster in a VPC in the same account. Due to the data being sensitive the security team has instructed you to ensure that the data traverses the VPC without being routed via the public Internet.

**Which combination of actions would meet this requirement? (choose 2)**

1. Create and configure an Amazon S3 VPC endpoint
2. Set up a NAT gateway in a private subnet to allow the Amazon RedShift cluster to access Amazon S3
3. Create a NAT gateway in a public subnet to allows the Amazon RedShift cluster to access Amazon S3
4. Create a cluster Security Group to allow the Amazon RedShift cluster to access Amazon S3
5. Enable Amazon RedShift Enhanced VPC routing

## 60. Question

Your company is opening a new office in the Asia Pacific region. Users in the new office will need to read data from an RDS database that is hosted in the U.S. To improve performance, you are planning to implement a Read Replica of the database in the Asia Pacific region. However, your Chief Security Officer (CSO) has explained to you that the company policy dictates that all data that leaves the U.S must be encrypted at rest. The master RDS DB is not currently encrypted.

**What options are available to you? (choose 2)**

1. You can create an encrypted Read Replica that is encrypted with a different key
2. You can create an encrypted Read Replica that is encrypted with the same key
3. You can use an ELB to provide an encrypted transport layer in front of the RDS DB
4. You can enable encryption for the master DB by creating a new DB from a snapshot with encryption enabled
5. You can enable encryption for the master DB through the management console

## 61. Question

An application receives images uploaded by customers and stores them on Amazon S3. An AWS Lambda function then processes the images to add graphical elements. The processed images need to be available for users to download for 30 days, after which time they can be deleted. Processed images can be easily recreated from original images. The Original images need to be immediately available for 30 days and be accessible within 24 hours for another 90 days.

**Which combination of Amazon S3 storage classes is most cost-effective for the original and processed images? (choose 2)**

1. Store the original images in STANDARD for 30 days, transition to DEEP_ARCHIVE for 180 days, then expire the data
2. Store the processed images in ONEZONE_IA and then expire the data after 30 days
3. Store the processed images in STANDARD and then transition to GLACIER after 30 days
4. Store the original images in STANDARD_IA for 30 days and then transition to DEEP_ARCHIVE
5. Store the original images in STANDARD for 30 days, transition to GLACIER for 180 days, then expire the data

## 62. Question

A web application is running on a fleet of Amazon EC2 instances using an Auto Scaling Group. It is desired that the CPU usage in the fleet is kept at 40%.

How should scaling be configured?

1. Use a custom CloudWatch alarm to monitor CPU usage and notify the ASG using Amazon SNS
2. Use a simple scaling policy that launches instances when the average CPU hits 40%
3. Use a step scaling policy that uses the PercentChangeInCapacity value to adjust the group size as required
4. Use a target tracking policy that keeps the average aggregate CPU utilization at 40%

## 63. Question

A shared services VPC is being setup for use by several AWS accounts. An application needs to be securely shared from the shared services VPC. The solution should not allow consumers to connect to other instances in the VPC.

How can this be setup with the least administrative effort? (choose 2)

1. Create a Network Load Balancer (NLB)
2. Setup VPC peering between each AWS VPC
3. Configure security groups to restrict access
4. Use AWS PrivateLink to expose the application as an endpoint service
5. Use AWS ClassicLink to expose the application as an endpoint service

## 64. Question

An application running on Amazon EC2 needs to regularly download large objects from Amazon S3. How can performance be optimized for high-throughput use cases?

1. Issue parallel requests and use byte-range fetches
2. Use AWS Global Accelerator
3. Use Amazon S3 Transfer acceleration
4. Use Amazon CloudFront to cache the content

## 65. Question

A new application will run across multiple Amazon ECS tasks. Front-end application logic will process data and then pass that data to a back-end ECS task to perform further processing and write the data to a datastore. The Architect would like to reduce-interdependencies so failures do no impact other components.

Which solution should the Architect use?

1. Create an Amazon Kinesis Firehose delivery stream that delivers data to an Amazon S3 bucket, configure the front-end to write data to the stream and the back-end to read data from Amazon S3
2. Create an Amazon SQS queue and configure the front-end to add messages to the queue and the back-end to poll the queue for messages
3. Create an Amazon Kinesis Firehose delivery stream and configure the front-end to add data to the stream and the back-end to read data from the stream
4. Create an Amazon SQS queue that pushes messages to the back-end. Configure the front-end to add messages to the queue

# SET 2: PRACTICE QUESTIONS, ANSWERS & EXPLANATIONS

## 1. Question

An EC2 instance that you manage has an IAM role attached to it that provides it with access to Amazon S3 for saving log data to a bucket. A change in the application architecture means that you now need to provide the additional ability for the application to securely make API requests to Amazon API Gateway.

Which two methods could you use to resolve this challenge? (choose 2)

1. You cannot modify the IAM role assigned to an EC2 instance after it has been launched. You'll need to recreate the EC2 instance and assign a new IAM role
2. Create an IAM role with a policy granting permissions to Amazon API Gateway and add it to the EC2 instance as an additional IAM role
3. Create a new IAM role with multiple IAM policies attached that grants access to Amazon S3 and Amazon API Gateway, and replace the existing IAM role that is attached to the EC2 instance
4. Delegate access to the EC2 instance from the API Gateway management console
5. Add an IAM policy to the existing IAM role that the EC2 instance is using granting permissions to access Amazon API Gateway

**Answer: 3,5**

**Explanation:**

- There are two possible solutions here. In one you create a new IAM role with multiple policies, in the other you add a new policy to the existing IAM role.
- Contrary to one of the incorrect answers, you can modify IAM roles after an instance has been launched – this was changed quite some time ago now. However, you cannot add multiple IAM roles to a single EC2 instance. If you need to attach multiple policies you must attach them to a single IAM role. There is no such thing as delegating access using the API Gateway management console

**References:**

https://digitalcloud.training/certification-training/aws-solutions-architect-associate/compute/amazon-ec2/

## 2. Question

An AWS workload in a VPC is running a legacy database on an Amazon EC2 instance. Data is stored on a 2000GB Amazon EBS (gp2) volume. At peak load times, logs show excessive wait time.

What should be implemented to improve database performance using persistent storage?

1. Change the EC2 instance type to one with EC2 instance store volumes
2. Migrate the data on the EBS volume to provisioned IOPS SSD (io1)
3. Migrate the data on the Amazon EBS volume to an SSD-backed volume
4. Change the EC2 instance type to one with burstable performance

**Answer: 2**

**Explanation:**

- The data is already on an SSD-backed volume (gp2), therefore, to improve performance the best option is to migrate the data onto a provisioned IOPS SSD (io1) volume type which will provide improved I/O performance and therefore reduce wait times
- Using an instance store volume may provide high performance but the data is not persistent so it is not suitable for a database
- Burstable performance instances provide a baseline of CPU performance with the ability to burst to a higher level when required. However, the issue in this scenario is disk wait time, not CPU performance, therefore we need to improve I/O not CPU performance

**References:**

https://digitalcloud.training/certification-training/aws-solutions-architect-associate/compute/amazon-ebs/

https://docs.aws.amazon.com/AWSEC2/latest/UserGuide/EBSVolumeTypes.html

https://docs.aws.amazon.com/AWSEC2/latest/UserGuide/burstable-performance-instances.html

## 3. Question

**A DynamoDB database you manage is randomly experiencing heavy read requests that are causing latency. What is the simplest way to alleviate the performance issues?**

1. Create DynamoDB read replicas
2. Create an ElastiCache cluster in front of DynamoDB
3. Enable DynamoDB DAX
4. Enable EC2 Auto Scaling for DynamoDB

**Answer: 3**

**Explanation:**

- DynamoDB offers consistent single-digit millisecond latency. However, DynamoDB + DAX further increases performance with response times in microseconds for millions of requests per second for read-heavy workloads
- ElastiCache in front of DynamoDB is not the best answer as DynamoDB DAX is a simpler implementation and provides the required performance improvements
- There's no such thing as DynamoDB Read Replicas (Read Replicas are an RDS concept)
- You cannot use EC2 Auto Scaling with DynamoDB. You can use Application Auto Scaling to scales DynamoDB but as the spikes in read traffic are random and Auto Scaling needs time to adjust the capacity of the DB it wouldn't be as responsive as using DynamoDB DAX

**References:**

https://aws.amazon.com/dynamodb/dax/

https://digitalcloud.training/certification-training/aws-solutions-architect-associate/database/amazon-dynamodb/

## 4. Question

**A company's Amazon EC2 instances were terminated or stopped, resulting in a loss of important data that was stored on attached EC2 instance stores. They want to avoid this happening in the future and**

need a solution that can scale as data volumes increase with the LEAST amount of management and configuration.

**Which storage is most appropriate?**

1. Amazon EBS
2. Amazon EFS
3. Amazon S3
4. Amazon RDS

**Answer: 2**

**Explanation:**

- Amazon EFS is a fully managed service that requires no changes to your existing applications and tools, providing access through a standard file system interface for seamless integration. It is built to scale on demand to petabytes without disrupting applications, growing and shrinking automatically as you add and remove files. This is an easy solution to implement and the option that requires the least management and configuration
- An instance store provides temporary block-level storage for an EC2 instance. If you terminate the instance you lose all data. The alternative is to use Elastic Block Store volumes which are also block-level storage devices but the data is persistent. However, EBS is not a fully managed solution and doesn't grow automatically as your data requirements increase – you would need to increase the volume size and then extend your filesystem
- Amazon S3 is an object storage solution and as the data is currently sitting on a block storage you would need to develop some way to use the REST API to upload/manage data on S3 – this is not the easiest solution to implement
- Amazon RDS is a relational database service, the question is not looking for a database, just a way of storing data

**References:**

https://digitalcloud.training/certification-training/aws-solutions-architect-associate/storage/amazon-efs/

https://aws.amazon.com/efs/

## 5. Question

A bank is writing new software that is heavily dependent upon the database transactions for write consistency. The application will also occasionally generate reports on data in the database and will do joins across multiple tables. The database must automatically scale as the amount of data grows.

**Which AWS service should be used to run the database?**

1. Amazon RedShift
2. Amazon DynamoDB
3. Amazon Aurora
4. Amazon S3

**Answer: 3**

**Explanation:**

- We can exclude RedShift as we're looking for a transactional DB, not a data warehouse, and we can exclude S3 as it is an object store, not a relational database

- We can then examine the three key requirements here to determine the choice of database:
- Write consistency: DynamoDB is eventually consistent for writes, whereas Aurora provides low-latency write consistency
- Joins across multiple tables: This can be provided by Aurora as it is a relational database but not by DynamoDB as it is a NoSQL database
- Automatically scaling storage: DynamoDB uses push-button scaling and can also now auto scale; Aurora storage automatically scales with the data in your cluster volume
- The best choice is therefore Aurora as it can provide write consistency, joins across tables and automatic storage scaling

**References:**

https://docs.aws.amazon.com/AmazonRDS/latest/AuroraUserGuide/Aurora.Managing.Performance.html

https://digitalcloud.training/certification-training/aws-solutions-architect-associate/database/amazon-rds/

## 6. Question

A Solutions Architect is designing a web application that runs on Amazon EC2 instances behind an Elastic Load Balancer. All data in transit must be encrypted.

**Which solution options meet the encryption requirement? (choose 2)**

1. Use an Application Load Balancer (ALB) in passthrough mode, then terminate SSL on EC2 instances
2. Use an Application Load Balancer (ALB) with a TCP listener, then terminate SSL on EC2 instances
3. Use a Network Load Balancer (NLB) with a TCP listener, then terminate SSL on EC2 instances
4. Use an Application Load Balancer (ALB) with an HTTPS listener, then install SSL certificates on the ALB and EC2 instances
5. Use a Network Load Balancer (NLB) with an HTTPS listener, then install SSL certificates on the NLB and EC2 instances

**Answer: 3,4**

**Explanation:**

- You can passthrough encrypted traffic with an NLB and terminate the SSL on the EC2 instances, so this is a valid answer.
- You can use a HTTPS listener with an ALB and install certificates on both the ALB and EC2 instances. This does not use passthrough, instead it will terminate the first SSL connection on the ALB and then re-encrypt the traffic and connect to the EC2 instances.
- You cannot use passthrough mode with an ALB and terminate SSL on the EC2 instances.
- You cannot use a TCP listener with an ALB.
- You cannot use a HTTPS listener with an NLB.

**References:**

https://digitalcloud.training/certification-training/aws-solutions-architect-associate/compute/elastic-load-balancing/

## 7. Question

A VPC has a fleet of EC2 instances running in a private subnet that need to connect to Internet-based hosts using the IPv6 protocol. What needs to be configured to enable this connectivity?

1. AWS Direct Connect
2. An Egress-Only Internet Gateway
3. VPN CloudHub
4. A NAT Gateway

**Answer: 2**

**Explanation:**

- An egress-only Internet gateway is a horizontally scaled, redundant, and highly available VPC component that allows outbound communication over IPv6 from instances in your VPC to the Internet, and prevents the Internet from initiating an IPv6 connection with your instances
- A NAT Gateway is used for enabling Internet connectivity using the IPv4 protocol only
- AWS Direct Connect is a private connection between your data center and an AWS VPC
- VPN CloudHub enables a hub-and-spoke model for communicating between multiple sites over a VPN connection

**References:**

https://docs.aws.amazon.com/vpc/latest/userguide/egress-only-internet-gateway.html

https://digitalcloud.training/certification-training/aws-solutions-architect-associate/networking-and-content-delivery/amazon-vpc/

## 8. Question

**The Perfect Forward Secrecy (PFS) security feature uses a derived session key to provide additional safeguards against the eavesdropping of encrypted data. Which two AWS services support PFS? (choose 2)**

1. EC2
2. EBS
3. CloudFront
4. Auto Scaling
5. Elastic Load Balancing

**Answer: 3,5**

**Explanation:**

- CloudFront and ELB support Perfect Forward Secrecy which creates a new private key for each SSL session
- Perfect Forward Secrecy (PFS) provides additional safeguards against the eavesdropping of encrypted data, through the use of a unique random session key
- The other services listed do not support PFS

**References:**

https://digitalcloud.training/certification-training/aws-solutions-architect-associate/networking-and-content-delivery/amazon-cloudfront/

https://digitalcloud.training/certification-training/aws-solutions-architect-associate/compute/elastic-load-balancing/

## 9. Question

A client needs to implement a shared directory system. Requirements are that it should provide a hierarchical structure, support strong data consistency, and be accessible from multiple accounts, regions and on-premises servers using their AWS Direct Connect link.

Which storage service would you recommend to the client?

1. Amazon S3
2. Amazon EBS
3. Amazon Storage Gateway
4. Amazon EFS

**Answer: 4**

**Explanation:**

- Amazon EFS provides high-performance, secure access for thousands of connections to a shared file system using a traditional file permissions model, file locking, and hierarchical directory structure via the NFSv4 protocol. It allows you to simultaneously share files between multiple Amazon EC2 instances across multiple AZs, regions, VPCs, and accounts as well as on-premises servers via AWS Direct Connect or AWS VPN. This is ideal for your business applications that need to share a common data source. For application workloads with many instances accessing the same set of files, Amazon EFS provides strong data consistency helping to ensure that any file read will reflect the last write of the file
- Amazon S3 does not support a hierarchical structure. Though you can create folders within buckets, these are actually just pointers to groups of objects. The structure is flat in Amazon S3. Also, the consistency model of Amazon S3 is read-after-write for PUTS of new objects, but only eventual consistency for overwrite PUTS and DELETES. This does not support the requirement for strong consistency
- Amazon EBS is a block-storage device that is attached to an individual instance and cannot be shared between multiple instances. EBS does not support multiple requirements in this scenario
- Amazon Storage Gateway supports multiple modes of operation but none of them provide a single shared storage location that is accessible from multiple accounts, regions and on-premise servers simultaneously

**References:**

https://aws.amazon.com/efs/features/

https://digitalcloud.training/certification-training/aws-solutions-architect-associate/storage/amazon-efs/

## 10. Question

You are deploying a two-tier web application within your VPC. The application consists of multiple EC2 instances and an Internet-facing Elastic Load Balancer (ELB). The application will be used by a small number of users with fixed public IP addresses and you need to control access so only these users can access the application.

What would be the BEST methods of applying these controls? (choose 2)

1. Configure the EC2 instance's Security Group to allow traffic from only the specific IP sources
2. Configure the local firewall on each EC2 instance to only allow traffic from the specific IP sources
3. Configure the ELB Security Group to allow traffic from only the specific IP sources

4. Configure the ELB to send the X-Forwarded-For header and configure the EC2 instances to filter traffic based on the source IP information in the header
5. Configure certificates on the clients and use client certificate authentication on the ELB

**Answer: 3,4**

**Explanation:**

- There are two practical methods of implementing these controls and these can be used in isolation or together (defence in depth). As the clients have fixed IPs you can configure a security group to control access by only permitting these addresses. The ELB security group is the correct place to implement this control. You can also configured ELB to forward the X-Forwarded-For header which means the source IP information is carried through to the EC2 instances. You are then able to configure security controls for the addresses at the EC2 instance level, for instance by using an iptables firewall
- ELB does not support client certificate authentication (API Gateway does support this)
- The EC2 instance Security Group is the wrong place to implement the allow rule

**References:**

https://digitalcloud.training/certification-training/aws-solutions-architect-associate/compute/elastic-load-balancing/

## 11. Question

The operations team in your company are looking for a method to automatically respond to failed status check alarms that are being received from an EC2 instance. The system in question is experiencing intermittent problems with its operating system software.

Which two steps will help you to automate the resolution of the operating system software issues? (choose 2)

1. Configure an EC2 action that recovers the instance
2. Create a CloudWatch alarm that monitors the "StatusCheckFailed_Instance" metric
3. Configure an EC2 action that terminates the instance
4. Configure an EC2 action that reboots the instance
5. Create a CloudWatch alarm that monitors the "StatusCheckFailed_System" metric

**Answer: 2,4**

**Explanation:**

- EC2 status checks are performed every minute and each returns a pass or a fail status. If all checks pass, the overall status of the instance is OK. If one or more checks fail, the overall status is impaired
- System status checks detect (StatusCheckFailed_System) problems with your instance that require AWS involvement to repair whereas Instance status checks (StatusCheckFailed_Instance) detect problems that require your involvement to repair
- The action to recover the instance is only supported on specific instance types and can be used only with StatusCheckFailed_System
- Configuring an action to terminate the instance would not help resolve system software issues as the instance would be terminated

**References:**

https://digitalcloud.training/certification-training/aws-solutions-architect-associate/compute/amazon-ec2/

## 12. Question

An application is hosted on the U.S west coast. Users there have no problems, but users on the east coast are experiencing performance issues. The users have reported slow response times with the search bar autocomplete and display of account listings.

How can you improve the performance for users on the east coast?

1. Setup cross-region replication and use Route 53 geolocation routing
2. Create an ElastiCache database in the U.S east region
3. Create a DynamoDB Read Replica in the U.S east region
4. Host the static content in an Amazon S3 bucket and distribute it using CloudFront

**Answer: 2**

**Explanation:**

- ElastiCache can be deployed in the U.S east region to provide high-speed access to the content. ElastiCache Redis has a good use case for autocompletion (see links below)
- This is not static content that can be hosted in an Amazon S3 bucket and distributed using CloudFront
- There's no such thing as a DynamoDB Read Replica (Read Replicas are an RDS concept)
- Cross-region replication is an Amazon S3 concept and the dynamic data that is presented by this application is unlikely to be stored in an S3 bucket

**References:**

https://aws.amazon.com/blogs/database/creating-a-simple-autocompletion-service-with-redis-part-one-of-two/

https://digitalcloud.training/certification-training/aws-solutions-architect-associate/database/amazon-elasticache/

## 13. Question

An application that you will be deploying in your VPC requires 14 EC2 instances that must be placed on distinct underlying hardware to reduce the impact of the failure of a hardware node. The instances will use varying instance types. What configuration will cater to these requirements taking cost-effectiveness into account?

1. Use a Cluster Placement Group within a single AZ
2. Use a Spread Placement Group across two AZs
3. Use dedicated hosts and deploy each instance on a dedicated host
4. You cannot control which nodes your instances are placed on

**Answer: 2**

**Explanation:**

- A spread placement group is a group of instances that are each placed on distinct underlying hardware. Spread placement groups are recommended for applications that have a small number of critical instances that should be kept separate from each other. Launching instances in a spread placement group reduces the risk of simultaneous failures that might occur when instances share the same underlying hardware
- A cluster placement group is a logical grouping of instances within a single Availability Zone. Cluster placement groups are recommended for applications that benefit from low network latency, high network throughput, or both, and if the majority of the network traffic is between the instances in the group
- Using a single instance on each dedicated host would be extremely expensive

**References:**

https://digitalcloud.training/certification-training/aws-solutions-architect-associate/compute/amazon-ec2/

https://docs.aws.amazon.com/AWSEC2/latest/UserGuide/placement-groups.html

## 14. Question

**A Solutions Architect requires a highly available database that can deliver an extremely low RPO. Which of the following configurations uses synchronous replication?**

1. RDS Read Replica across AWS regions
2. DynamoDB Read Replica
3. RDS DB instance using a Multi-AZ configuration
4. EBS volume synchronization

**Answer: 3**

**Explanation:**

- A Recovery Point Objective (RPO) relates to the amount of data loss that can be allowed, in this case a low RPO means that you need to minimize the amount of data lost so synchronous replication is required. Out of the options presented only Amazon RDS in a multi-AZ configuration uses synchronous replication
- RDS Read Replicas use asynchronous replication and are not used for DR
- DynamoDB Read Replicas do not exist
- EBS volume synchronization does not exist

**References:**

https://digitalcloud.training/certification-training/aws-solutions-architect-associate/database/amazon-rds/

## 15. Question

**A large media site has multiple applications running on Amazon ECS. A Solutions Architect needs to use content metadata to route traffic to specific services.**

**What is the MOST efficient method to fulfil this requirement?**

1. Use an AWS Classic Load Balancer with a host-based routing rule to route traffic to the correct service

2. Use the AWS CLI to update an Amazon Route 53 hosted zone to route traffic as services get updated
3. Use an AWS Application Load Balancer with a path-based routing rule to route traffic to the correct service
4. Use Amazon CloudFront to manage and route traffic to the correct service

**Answer: 3**

**Explanation:**

- The ELB Application Load Balancer can route traffic based on data included in the request including the host name portion of the URL as well as the path in the URL. Creating a rule to route traffic based on information in the path will work for this solution and ALB works well with Amazon ECS.
- The ELB Classic Load Balancer does not support any content-based routing including host or path-based.
- Using the AWS CLI to update Route 53 as to how to route traffic may work, but it is definitely not the most efficient way to solve this challenge.
- Amazon CloudFront does not have the capability to route traffic to different Amazon ECS services based on content metadata.

**References:**

https://digitalcloud.training/certification-training/aws-solutions-architect-associate/compute/elastic-load-balancing/

## 16. Question

**Developers regularly create and update CloudFormation stacks using API calls. For security reasons you need to ensure that users are restricted to a specified template. How can this be achieved?**

1. Store the template on Amazon S3 and use a bucket policy to restrict access
2. Create an IAM policy with a Condition: TemplateURL parameter
3. Create an IAM policy with a Condition: StackPolicyURL parameter
4. Create an IAM policy with a Condition: ResourceTypes parameter

**Answer: 2**

**Explanation:**

- The cloudformation:TemplateURL, lets you specify where the CloudFormation template for a stack action, such as create or update, resides and enforce that it be used
- The CloudFormation API accepts a ResourceTypes parameter. In your API call, you specify which types of resources can be created or updated. This does not control which template is used
- You can ensure that every CloudFormation stack has a stack policy associated with it upon creation with the StackPolicyURL condition. However, this parameter itself is not used to specify the template to use
- Configuring a bucket policy on the Amazon S3 bucket where you place your templates is a good idea, but it does not enforce CloudFormation create and update API requests to use the templates in the bucket.

**References:**

https://aws.amazon.com/blogs/devops/aws-cloudformation-security-best-practices/

## 17. Question

**During an application load testing exercise, the Amazon RDS database was seen to cause a performance bottleneck.**

**Which steps can be taken to improve the database performance? (choose 2)**

1. Change the RDS database instance to multiple Availability Zones
2. Scale up to a larger RDS instance type
3. Redirect read queries to RDS read replicas
4. Use RDS in a separate AWS Region
5. Scale out using an Auto Scaling group for RDS

**Answer: 2,3**

**Explanation:**

- There two main ways you can increase performance on an Amazon RDS database are 1) scale up to a larger RDS instance type with more CPU/RAM, and 2) use RDS read replicas to offload read traffic from the master database instance.
- Using multi-AZ will not increase performance, only availability. You need to deploy read replicas for offloading database queries from the master DB.
- You cannot use Auto Scaling groups for RDS instances.
- Using RDS in a separate region does not work for an application as it would be an entirely separate database service without any replication/synchronization of data.

**References:**

https://digitalcloud.training/certification-training/aws-solutions-architect-associate/database/amazon-rds/

## 18. Question

You are looking for a method to distribute onboarding videos to your company's numerous remote workers around the world. The training videos are located in an S3 bucket that is not publicly accessible. Which of the options below would allow you to share the videos?

1. Use ElastiCache and attach the S3 bucket as a cache origin
2. Use CloudFront and use a custom origin pointing to an EC2 instance
3. Use a Route 53 Alias record the points to the S3 bucket
4. Use CloudFront and set the S3 bucket as an origin

**Answer: 4**

**Explanation:**

- CloudFront uses origins which specify the origin of the files that the CDN will distribute

- Origins can be either an S3 bucket, an EC2 instance, and Elastic Load Balancer, or Route 53 – can also be external (non-AWS). When using Amazon S3 as an origin you place all of your objects within the bucket
- You cannot configure an origin with ElastiCache
- You cannot use a Route 53 Alias record to connect to an S3 bucket that is not publicly available
- You can configure a custom origin pointing to an EC2 instance but as the training videos are located in an S3 bucket this would not be helpful

**References:**

https://digitalcloud.training/certification-training/aws-solutions-architect-associate/networking-and-content-delivery/amazon-cloudfront/

## 19. Question

The development team in your company has created a new application that you plan to deploy on AWS which runs multiple components in Docker containers. You would prefer to use AWS managed infrastructure for running the containers as you do not want to manage EC2 instances.

Which of the below solution options would deliver these requirements? (choose 2)

1. Put your container images in the Elastic Container Registry (ECR)
2. Put your container images in a private repository
3. Use the Elastic Container Service (ECS) with the EC2 Launch Type
4. Use CloudFront to deploy Docker on EC2
5. Use the Elastic Container Service (ECS) with the Fargate Launch Type

**Answer: 1,5**

**Explanation:**

- If you do not want to manage EC2 instances you must use the AWS Fargate launch type which is a serverless infrastructure managed by AWS. Fargate only supports container images hosted on Elastic Container Registry (ECR) or Docker Hub
- The EC2 Launch Type allows you to run containers on EC2 instances that you manage
- Private repositories are only supported by the EC2 Launch Type
- You cannot use CloudFront (a CDN) to deploy Docker on EC2

**References:**

https://digitalcloud.training/certification-training/aws-solutions-architect-associate/compute/amazon-ecs/

## 20. Question

A Solutions Architect must design a storage solution for incoming billing reports in CSV format. The data will be analyzed infrequently and discarded after 30 days.

Which combination of services will be MOST cost-effective in meeting these requirements?

1. Use AWS Data Pipeline to import the logs into a DynamoDB table
2. Import the logs into an RDS MySQL instance
3. Import the logs to an Amazon Redshift cluster
4. Write the files to an S3 bucket and use Amazon Athena to query the data

**Answer: 4**

**Explanation:**

- Amazon S3 is great solution for storing objects such as this. You only pay for what you use and don't need to worry about scaling as it will scale as much as you need it to. Using Amazon Athena to analyze the data works well as it is a serverless service so it will be very cost-effective for use cases where the analysis is only happening infrequently. You can also configure Amazon S3 to expire the objects after 30 days.
- Importing the logs into an RDS MySQL instance is not a good solution. This is not the best storage solution for log files and its main use case as a DB is transactional rather than analytical.
- AWS Data Pipeline is used to process and move data. You can move data into DynamoDB, but this is not a good storage solution for these log files. Also, there is no analytics solution in this option.
- Importing the log files into an Amazon RedShift cluster will mean you can perform analytics on the data as this is the primary use case for RedShift (it's a data warehouse). However, this is not the most cost-effective solution as RedShift uses EC2 instances (it's not serverless) so the instances will be running all the time even though the analytics is infrequent.

**References:**

https://aws.amazon.com/athena/

https://digitalcloud.training/certification-training/aws-solutions-architect-associate/analytics/amazon-athena/

https://digitalcloud.training/certification-training/aws-solutions-architect-associate/storage/amazon-s3/

## 21. Question

You are a Solutions Architect for a systems integrator. Your client is growing their presence in the AWS cloud and has applications and services running in a VPC across multiple availability zones within a region. The client has a requirement to build an operational dashboard within their on-premise data center within the next few months. The dashboard will show near real time statistics and therefore must be connected over a low latency, high performance network.

**What would be the best solution for this requirement?**

1. Use redundant VPN connections to two VGW routers in the region, this should give you access to the infrastructure in all AZs
2. Order multiple AWS Direct Connect connections that will be connected to multiple AZs
3. Order a single AWS Direct Connect connection to connect to the client's VPC. This will provide access to all AZs within the region
4. You cannot connect to multiple AZs from a single location

**Answer: 3**

**Explanation:**

- With AWS Direct Connect you can provision a low latency, high performance private connection between the client's data center and AWS. Direct Connect connections connect you to a region and all AZs within that region. In this case the client has a single VPC so we know their resources are container within a single region and therefore a single Direct Connect connection satisfies the requirements.

- As Direct Connect connections allow you to connect to all AZs within a region you do not need to order multiple connections (but you might want to for redundancy)
- VPN connections use the public Internet and are therefore not good when you need a low latency, high performance and consistent network experience

**References:**

https://digitalcloud.training/certification-training/aws-solutions-architect-associate/networking-and-content-delivery/aws-direct-connect/

## 22. Question

A company hosts a popular web application that connects to an Amazon RDS MySQL DB instance running in a private VPC subnet that was created with default ACL settings. The web servers must be accessible only to customers on an SSL connection. The database should only be accessible to web servers in a public subnet.

Which solution meets these requirements without impacting other running applications? (choose 2)

1. Create a network ACL on the DB subnet, allow MySQL port 3306 inbound for web servers, and deny all outbound traffic
2. Create a DB server security group that allows the HTTPS port 443 inbound and specify the source as a web server security group
3. Create a DB server security group that allows MySQL port 3306 inbound and specify the source as a web server security group
4. Create a web server security group that allows HTTPS port 443 inbound traffic from Anywhere (0.0.0.0/0) and apply it to the web servers
5. Create a network ACL on the web server's subnet, allow HTTPS port 443 inbound, and specify the source as 0.0.0.0/0

**Answer: 3.4**

**Explanation:**

- A VPC automatically comes with a modifiable default network ACL. By default, it allows all inbound and outbound IPv4 traffic. Custom network ACLs deny everything inbound and outbound by default but in this case a default network ACL is being used
- Inbound connections to web servers will be coming in on port 443 from the Internet so creating a security group to allow this port from 0.0.0.0/0 and applying it to the web servers will allow this traffic
- The MySQL DB will be listening on port 3306. Therefore, the security group that is applied to the DB servers should allow 3306 inbound from the web servers security group
- The DB server is listening on 3306 so creating a rule allowing 443 inbound will not help

**References:**

https://digitalcloud.training/certification-training/aws-solutions-architect-associate/networking-and-content-delivery/amazon-vpc/

## 23. Question

A developer is creating a solution for a real-time bidding application for a large retail company that allows users to bid on items of end-of-season clothing. The application is expected to be extremely popular and the back-end DynamoDB database may not perform as required.

How can the Solutions Architect enable in-memory read performance with microsecond response times for the DynamoDB database?

1. Increase the provisioned throughput
2. Configure Amazon DAX
3. Enable read replicas
4. Configure DynamoDB Auto Scaling

**Answer: 2**

**Explanation:**

- Amazon DynamoDB Accelerator (DAX) is a fully managed, highly available, in-memory cache for DynamoDB that delivers up to a 10x performance improvement – from milliseconds to microseconds – even at millions of requests per second. You can enable DAX for a DynamoDB database with a few clicks
- Provisioned throughput is the maximum amount of capacity that an application can consume from a table or index, it doesn't improve the speed of the database or add in-memory capabilities
- DynamoDB auto scaling actively manages throughput capacity for tables and global secondary indexes so like provisioned throughput it does not provide the speed or in-memory capabilities requested
- There is no such thing as read replicas with DynamoDB

**References:**

https://aws.amazon.com/dynamodb/dax/

## 24. Question

A Solutions Architect must select the most appropriate database service for two use cases. A team of data scientists perform complex queries on a data warehouse that take several hours to complete. Another team of scientists need to run fast, repeat queries and update dashboards for customer support staff.

Which solution delivers these requirements MOST cost-effectively?

1. RedShift for the analytics use case and RDS for the customer support dashboard
2. RedShift for both use cases
3. RDS for both use cases
4. RedShift for the analytics use case and ElastiCache in front of RedShift for the customer support dashboard

**Answer: 2**

**Explanation:**

- RedShift is a columnar data warehouse DB that is ideal for running long complex queries. RedShift can also improve performance for repeat queries by caching the result and returning the cached result when queries are re-run. Dashboard, visualization, and business intelligence (BI) tools that execute repeat queries see a significant boost in performance due to result caching

- RDS may be a good fit for the fast queries (not for the complex queries) but you now have multiple DBs to manage and multiple sets of data which is not going to be cost-effective
- You could put ElastiCache in front of the RedShift DB and this would provide good performance for the fast, repeat queries. However, it is not essential and would add cost to the solution so is not the most cost-effective option available

**References:**

https://aws.amazon.com/about-aws/whats-new/2017/11/amazon-redshift-introduces-result-caching-for-sub-second-response-for-repeat-queries/

https://digitalcloud.training/certification-training/aws-solutions-architect-associate/database/amazon-redshift/


## 25. Question

**A Solutions Architect is designing a shared service for hosting containers from several customers on Amazon ECS. These containers will use several AWS services. A container from one customer must not be able to access data from another customer.**

**Which solution should the Architect use to meet the requirements?**

1. IAM Instance Profile for EC2 instances
2. IAM roles for tasks
3. Network ACL
4. IAM roles for EC2 instances


**Answer: 2**

**Explanation:**

- IAM roles for ECS tasks enabled you to secure your infrastructure by assigning an IAM role directly to the ECS task rather than to the EC2 container instance. This means you can have one task that uses a specific IAM role for access to S3 and one task that uses an IAM role to access DynamoDB
- With IAM roles for EC2 instances you assign all of the IAM policies required by tasks in the cluster to the EC2 instances that host the cluster. This does not allow the secure separation requested
- An instance profile is a container for an IAM role that you can use to pass role information to an EC2 instance when the instance starts. Again, this does not allow the secure separation requested
- Network ACLs are applied at the subnet level and would not assist here

**References:**

https://aws.amazon.com/blogs/compute/help-secure-container-enabled-applications-with-iam-roles-for-ecs-tasks/

https://digitalcloud.training/certification-training/aws-solutions-architect-associate/compute/amazon-ecs/


## 26. Question

**A Solutions Architect needs to deploy an HTTP/HTTPS service on Amazon EC2 instances that will be placed behind an Elastic Load Balancer. The ELB must support WebSockets.**

**How can the Architect meet these requirements?**

1. Launch a Layer-4 Load Balancer
2. Launch a Network Load Balancer (NLB)
3. Launch an Application Load Balancer (ALB)
4. Launch a Classic Load Balancer (CLB)

**Answer: 3**

**Explanation:**

- Both the ALB and NLB support WebSockets. However, only the ALB supports HTTP/HTTPS listeners. The NLB only supports TCP, TLS, UDP, TCP_UDP.
- The CLB does not support WebSockets.
- A "Layer-4 Load Balancer" is not suitable, we need a layer 7 load balancer for HTTP/HTTPS.

**References:**

https://digitalcloud.training/certification-training/aws-solutions-architect-associate/compute/elastic-load-balancing/

https://docs.aws.amazon.com/elasticloadbalancing/latest/application/load-balancer-listeners.html

https://docs.aws.amazon.com/elasticloadbalancing/latest/network/load-balancer-listeners.html

## 27. Question

**You would like to create a highly available web application that serves static content using multiple On-Demand EC2 instances.**

**Which of the following will help you to achieve this? (choose 2)**

1. Direct Connect
2. DynamoDB and ElastiCache
3. Elastic Load Balancer and Auto Scaling
4. Amazon S3 and CloudFront
5. Multiple Availability Zones

**Answer: 3,5**

**Explanation:**

- None of the answer options present the full solution. However, you have been asked which services will help you to achieve the desired outcome. In this case we need high availability for on-demand EC2 instances.
- A single Auto Scaling Group will enable the on-demand instances to be launched into multiple availability zones with an elastic load balancer distributing incoming connections to the available EC2 instances. This provides high availability and elasticity
- Amazon S3 and CloudFront could be used to serve static content from an S3 bucket, however the question states that the web application runs on EC2 instances
- DynamoDB and ElastiCache are both database services, not web application services, and cannot help deliver high availability for EC2 instances
- Direct Connect is used for connecting on-premise data centers into AWS using a private network connection and does not help in this situation at all.

**References:**

https://digitalcloud.training/certification-training/aws-solutions-architect-associate/networking-and-content-delivery/amazon-vpc/

https://digitalcloud.training/certification-training/aws-solutions-architect-associate/compute/elastic-load-balancing/

https://digitalcloud.training/certification-training/aws-solutions-architect-associate/compute/aws-auto-scaling/

## 28. Question

The security team in your company is defining new policies for enabling security analysis, resource change tracking, and compliance auditing. They would like to gain visibility into user activity by recording API calls made within the company's AWS account. The information that is logged must be encrypted. This requirement applies to all AWS regions in which your company has services running.

How will you implement this request? (choose 2)

1. Create a CloudTrail trail and apply it to all regions
2. Create a CloudTrail trail in each region in which you have services
3. Enable encryption with a single KMS key
4. Enable encryption with multiple KMS keys
5. Use CloudWatch to monitor API calls

**Answer: 1,3**

**Explanation:**

- CloudTrail is used for recording API calls (auditing) whereas CloudWatch is used for recording metrics (performance monitoring). The solution can be deployed with a single trail that is applied to all regions. A single KMS key can be used to encrypt log files for trails applied to all regions. CloudTrail log files are encrypted using S3 Server Side Encryption (SSE) and you can also enable encryption SSE KMS for additional security
- You do not need to create a separate trail in each region or use multiple KMS keys
- CloudWatch is not used for monitoring API calls

**References:**

https://digitalcloud.training/certification-training/aws-solutions-architect-associate/management-tools/aws-cloudtrail/

## 29. Question

A client plans to migrate an on-premise multi-tier application to AWS. The application is integrated with industry-standard message brokers. The client wants to migrate from the existing message broker without rewriting application code. Which service should be used?

1. Amazon Step Functions
2. Amazon MQ
3. Amazon SQS
4. Amazon SNS

**Answer: 2**

**Explanation:**

- Amazon MQ supports industry-standard APIs and protocols so you can migrate from your existing message broker without rewriting application code
- Amazon SQS is a message queueing service and is not compatible with industry-standard message brokers. You would need to rewrite some application code to get the application working with SQS
- Amazon SNS is a notification service, not a message broker
- Amazon Step Functions is used for coordinating multiple AWS services into serverless workflows, it is not a message broker

**References:**

https://docs.aws.amazon.com/amazon-mq/latest/developer-guide/welcome.html

https://digitalcloud.training/certification-training/aws-solutions-architect-associate/application-integration/amazon-mq/

## 30. Question

A Solutions Architect is designing a front-end that accepts incoming requests for back-end business logic applications. The Architect is planning to use Amazon API Gateway, which statements are correct in relation to the service? (choose 2)

1. API Gateway is a web service that gives businesses and web application developers an easy and cost-effective way to distribute content with low latency and high data transfer speeds
2. API Gateway is a collection of resources and methods that are integrated with back-end HTTP endpoints, Lambda functions or other AWS services
3. Throttling can be configured at multiple levels including Global and Service Call
4. API Gateway uses the AWS Application Auto Scaling service to dynamically adjust provisioned throughput capacity on your behalf, in response to actual traffic patterns
5. API Gateway is a network service that provides an alternative to using the Internet to connect customers' on-premise sites to AWS

**Answer: 2,3**

**Explanation:**

- An Amazon API Gateway is a collection of resources and methods that are integrated with back-end HTTP endpoints, Lambda function or other AWS services. API Gateway handles all of the tasks involved in accepting and processing up to hundreds of thousands of concurrent API calls. Throttling can be configured at multiple levels including Global and Service Call
- CloudFront is a web service that gives businesses and web application developers an easy and cost-effective way to distribute content with low latency and high data transfer speeds
- Direct Connect is a network service that provides an alternative to using the Internet to connect customers' on-premise sites to AWS
- DynamoDB uses the AWS Application Auto Scaling service to dynamically adjust provisioned throughput capacity on your behalf, in response to actual traffic patterns

**References:**

https://digitalcloud.training/certification-training/aws-solutions-architect-associate/networking-and-content-delivery/amazon-api-gateway/

## 31. Question

You have deployed a highly available web application across two AZs. The application uses an Auto Scaling Group (ASG) and an Application Load Balancer (ALB) to distribute connections between the EC2 instances that make up the web front-end. The load has increased and the ASG has launched new instances in both AZs, however you noticed that the ALB is only distributing traffic to the EC2 instances in one AZ.

From the options below, what is the most likely cause of the issue?

1. The ALB does not have a public subnet defined in both AZs
2. The ASG has not registered the new instances with the ALB
3. The EC2 instances in one AZ are not passing their health checks
4. Cross-zone load balancing is not enabled on the ALB

Answer: 1

Explanation:

- Cross-zone load balancing is enabled on the ALB by default. Also, if it was disabled the ALB would send traffic equally to each AZ configured regardless of the number of hosts in each AZ so some traffic would still get through
- Internet facing ELB nodes have public IPs and route traffic to the private IP addresses of the EC2 instances. You need one public subnet in each AZ where the ELB is defined
- The ASG would automatically register new instances with the ALB
- EC2 instance health checks are unlikely to be the issue here as the instances in both AZs are all being launched from the same ASG so should be identically configured
- Please refer to the AWS article linked below for detailed information on the configuration described in this scenario

References:

https://digitalcloud.training/certification-training/aws-solutions-architect-associate/compute/elastic-load-balancing/

https://aws.amazon.com/premiumsupport/knowledge-center/public-load-balancer-private-ec2/

## 32. Question

A Solutions Architect has created a VPC design that meets the security requirements of their organization. Any new applications that are deployed must use this VPC design.

How can project teams deploy, manage, and delete VPCs that meet this design with the LEAST administrative effort?

1. Use AWS Elastic Beanstalk to deploy both the VPC and the application
2. Clone the existing authorized VPC for each new project
3. Run a script that uses the AWS Command Line interface to deploy the VPC
4. Deploy an AWS CloudFormation template that defines components of the VPC

Answer: 4

Explanation:

- CloudFormation allows you to define your infrastructure through code and securely and repeatably deploy the infrastructure with minimal administrative effort. This is a perfect use case for CloudFormation.
- You can use a script to create the VPCs using the AWS CLI however this would be a lot more work to create and manage the scripts.
- You cannot clone VPCs.
- You cannot deploy the VPC through Elastic Beanstalk – you need to deploy the VPC first and then deploy your application using Beanstalk.

**References:**

https://digitalcloud.training/certification-training/aws-solutions-architect-associate/management-tools/aws-cloudformation/

https://aws.amazon.com/cloudformation/

## 33. Question

A new mobile application that your company is deploying will be hosted on AWS. The users of the application will use mobile devices to upload small amounts of data on a frequent basis. It is expected that the number of users connecting each day could be over 1 million. The data that is uploaded must be stored in a durable and persistent data store. The data store must also be highly available and easily scalable.

**Which AWS service would you use?**

1. Redshift
2. Kinesis
3. RDS
4. DynamoDB

**Answer: 4**

**Explanation:**

- Amazon DynamoDB is a fully managed NoSQL database service that provides a durable and persistent data store. You can scale DynamoDB using push button scaling which means that you can scale the DB at any time without incurring downtime. Amazon DynamoDB stores three geographically distributed replicas of each table to enable high availability and data durability
- RedShift is a data warehousing solution that is used for analytics on data, it is not used for transactional databases
- RDS is not highly available unless you use multi-AZ, which is not specified in the answer. It is also harder to scale RDS as you must change the instance size and incur downtime
- Kinesis is used for collecting, processing and analyzing streaming data. It is not used as a data store

**References:**

https://digitalcloud.training/certification-training/aws-solutions-architect-associate/database/amazon-dynamodb/

## 34. Question

You have created a file system using Amazon Elastic File System (EFS) which will hold home directories for users. What else needs to be done to enable users to save files to the EFS file system?

1. Create a separate EFS file system for each user and grant read-write-execute permissions on the root directory to the respective user. Then mount the file system to the users' home directory
2. Instruct the users to create a subdirectory on the file system and mount the subdirectory to their home directory
3. Modify permissions on the root directory to grant read-write-execute permissions to the users. Then create a subdirectory and mount it to the users' home directory
4. Create a subdirectory for each user and grant read-write-execute permissions to the users. Then mount the subdirectory to the users' home directory

**Answer: 4**

**Explanation:**

- After creating a file system, by default, only the root user (UID 0) has read-write-execute permissions. For other users to modify the file system, the root user must explicitly grant them access. One common use case is to create a "writable" subdirectory under this file system root for each user you create on the EC2 instance and mount it on the user's home directory. All files and subdirectories the user creates in their home directory are then created on the Amazon EFS file system
- You don't want to modify permission on the root directory as this will mean all users are able to access other users' files (and this is a home directory, so the contents are typically kept private)
- You don't want to create a separate EFS file system for each user, this would be a higher cost and require more management overhead
- Instructing the users to create a subdirectory on the file system themselves would not work as they will not have access to write to the directory root.

**References:**

https://docs.aws.amazon.com/efs/latest/ug/accessing-fs-nfs-permissions-per-user-subdirs.html

https://docs.aws.amazon.com/efs/latest/ug/accessing-fs-nfs-permissions.html#accessing-fs-nfs-permissions-ex-scenarios

https://digitalcloud.training/certification-training/aws-solutions-architect-associate/storage/amazon-efs/

## 35. Question

You would like to host a static website for digitalcloud.training on AWS. You will be using Route 53 to direct traffic to the website. Which of the below steps would help you achieve your objectives? (choose 2)

1. Create an "SRV" record that points to the S3 bucket
2. Use any existing S3 bucket that has public read access enabled
3. Create an "Alias" record that points to the S3 bucket
4. Create a "CNAME" record that points to the S3 bucket
5. Create an S3 bucket named digitalcloud.training

**Answer: 3,5**

**Explanation:**

- S3 can be used to host static websites and you can use a custom domain name with S3 using a Route 53 Alias record. When using a custom domain name, the bucket name must be the same as the domain name

- The Alias record is a Route 53 specific record type. Alias records are used to map resource record sets in your hosted zone to Amazon Elastic Load Balancing load balancers, Amazon CloudFront distributions, AWS Elastic Beanstalk environments, or Amazon S3 buckets that are configured as websites
- You cannot use any bucket when you want to use a custom domain name. As mentioned above you must have a bucket name that matches the domain name
- You must use an Alias record when configuring an S3 bucket as a static website – you cannot use SRV or CNAME records

**References:**

https://digitalcloud.training/certification-training/aws-solutions-architect-associate/storage/amazon-s3/

https://digitalcloud.training/certification-training/aws-solutions-architect-associate/networking-and-content-delivery/amazon-route-53/

## 36. Question

**Your organization is deploying a multi-language website on the AWS Cloud. The website uses CloudFront as the front-end and the language is specified in the HTTP request:**

- **http://d12345678aabbcc0.cloudfront.net/main.html?language=en**
- **http://d12345678aabbcc0.cloudfront.net/main.html?language=sp**
- **http://d12345678aabbcc0.cloudfront.net/main.html?language=fr**

**You need to configure CloudFront to deliver the cached content. What method can be used?**

1. Query string parameters
2. Signed Cookies
3. Origin Access Identity
4. Signed URLs

**Answer: 1**

**Explanation:**

- Query string parameters cause CloudFront to forward query strings to the origin and to cache based on the language parameter
- Signed URLs and Cookies provide additional control over access to content
- Origin access identities are used to control access to CloudFront distributions

**References:**

https://docs.aws.amazon.com/AmazonCloudFront/latest/DeveloperGuide/QueryStringParameters.html

https://digitalcloud.training/certification-training/aws-solutions-architect-associate/networking-and-content-delivery/amazon-cloudfront/

## 37. Question

**Your company runs a two-tier application on the AWS cloud that is composed of a web front-end and an RDS database. The web front-end uses multiple EC2 instances in multiple Availability Zones (AZ) in an Auto Scaling group behind an Elastic Load Balancer. Your manager is concerned about a single point of failure in the RDS database layer.**

**What would be the most effective approach to minimizing the risk of an AZ failure causing an outage to your database layer?**

1. Take a snapshot of the database
2. Increase the DB instance size
3. Enable Multi-AZ for the RDS DB instance
4. Create a Read Replica of the RDS DB instance in another AZ

**Answer: 3**

**Explanation:**

- Multi-AZ RDS creates a replica in another AZ and synchronously replicates to it. This provides a DR solution as if the AZ in which the primary DB resides fails, multi-AZ will automatically fail over to the replica instance with minimal downtime
- Read replicas are used for read heavy DBs and replication is asynchronous. Read replicas do not provide HA/DR as you cannot fail over to a read replica. They are used purely for offloading read requests from the primary DB
- Taking a snapshot of the database is useful for being able to recover from a failure so you can restore the database. However, this does not prevent an outage from happening as there will be significant downtime while you try and restore the snapshot to a new DB instance in another AZ
- Increasing the DB instance size will not provide any benefits to enabling high availability or fault tolerance, it will only serve to improve the performance of the DB

**References:**

https://digitalcloud.training/certification-training/aws-solutions-architect-associate/database/amazon-rds/

## 38. Question

A client is in the design phase of developing an application that will process orders for their online ticketing system. The application will use a number of front-end EC2 instances that pick-up orders and place them in a queue for processing by another set of back-end EC2 instances. The client will have multiple options for customers to choose the level of service they want to pay for.

The client has asked how he can design the application to process the orders in a prioritized way based on the level of service the customer has chosen?

1. Create multiple SQS queues, configure exactly-once processing and set the maximum visibility timeout to 12 hours
2. Create a combination of FIFO queues and Standard queues and configure the applications to place messages into the relevant queue based on priority
3. Create multiple SQS queues, configure the front-end application to place orders onto a specific queue based on the level of service requested and configure the back-end instances to sequentially poll the queues in order of priority
4. Create a single SQS queue, configure the front-end application to place orders on the queue in order of priority and configure the back-end instances to poll the queue and pick up messages in the order they are presented

**Answer: 3**

**Explanation:**

- The best option is to create multiple queues and configure the application to place orders onto a specific queue based on the level of service. You then configure the back-end instances to poll these queues in order or priority so they pick up the higher priority jobs first
- Creating a combination of FIFO and standard queues is incorrect as creating a mixture of queue types is not the best way to separate the messages, and there is nothing in this option that explains how the messages would be picked up in the right order
- Creating a single queue and configuring the applications to place orders on the queue in order of priority would not work as standard queues offer best-effort ordering so there's no guarantee that the messages would be picked up in the correct order
- Creating multiple SQS queues and configuring exactly-once processing (only possible with FIFO) would not ensure that the order of the messages is prioritized

**References:**

https://digitalcloud.training/certification-training/aws-solutions-architect-associate/application-integration/amazon-sqs/

## 39. Question

A bespoke application consisting of three tiers is being deployed in a VPC. You need to create three security groups. You have configured the WebSG (web server) security group and now need to configure the AppSG (application tier) and DBSG (database tier). The application runs on port 1030 and the database runs on 3306.

Which rules should be created according to security best practice? (choose 2)

1. On the AppSG security group, create a custom TCP rule for TCP 1030 and configure the DBSG security group as the source
2. On the DBSG security group, create a custom TCP rule for TCP 3306 and configure the WebSG security group as the source
3. On the WebSG security group, create a custom TCP rule for TCP 1030 and configure the AppSG security group as the source
4. On the AppSG security group, create a custom TCP rule for TCP 1030 and configure the WebSG security group as the source
5. On the DBSG security group, create a custom TCP rule for TCP 3306 and configure the AppSG security group as the source

**Answer: 4,5**

**Explanation:**

- With security groups rules are always allow rules. The best practice is to configure the source as another security group which is attached to the EC2 instances that traffic will come from. In this case you need to configure a rule that allows TCP 1030 and configure the source as the web server security group (WebSG). This allows traffic from the web servers to reach the application servers. You then need to allow communications on port 3306 (MYSQL/Aurora) from the AppSG security group to enable access to the database from the application servers

**References:**

https://docs.aws.amazon.com/vpc/latest/userguide/VPC_SecurityGroups.html

https://digitalcloud.training/certification-training/aws-solutions-architect-associate/networking-and-content-delivery/amazon-vpc/

## 40. Question

An organization is migrating data to the AWS cloud. An on-premises application uses Network File System shares and must access the data without code changes. The data is critical and is accessed frequently.

Which storage solution should a Solutions Architect recommend to maximize availability and durability?

1. AWS Storage Gateway – File Gateway
2. Amazon Simple Storage Service
3. Amazon Elastic Block Store
4. Amazon Elastic File System

**Answer: 1**

**Explanation:**

- The solution must use NFS file shares to access the migrated data without code modification. This means you can use either Amazon EFS or AWS Storage Gateway – File Gateway. Both of these can be mounted using NFS from on-premises applications. However, EFS is the wrong answer as the solution asks to maximize availability and durability. The File Gateway backs off of Amazon S3 which has much higher availability and durability than EFS which is why it is the best solution for this scenario.
- Amazon EBS is not a suitable solution as it is a block-based (not file-based like NFS) storage solution that you mount to EC2 instances in the cloud – not from on-premises applications.
- Amazon S3 does not offer an NFS interface.

**References:**

https://docs.aws.amazon.com/storagegateway/latest/userguide/CreatingAnNFSFileShare.html

https://digitalcloud.training/certification-training/aws-solutions-architect-associate/storage/amazon-efs/

## 41. Question

One of your clients has asked you for some advice on an issue they are facing regarding storage. The client uses an on-premise block-based storage array which is getting close to capacity. The client would like to maintain a configuration where reads/writes to a subset of frequently accessed data are performed on-premise whilst also alleviating the local capacity issues by migrating data into the AWS cloud.

What would you suggest as the BEST solution to the client's current problems?

1. Implement a Storage Gateway Virtual Tape Library, backup the data and then delete the data from the array
2. Implement a Storage Gateway Volume Gateway in cached mode
3. Use S3 copy command to copy data into the AWS cloud
4. Archive data that is not accessed regularly straight into Glacier

**Answer: 2**

**Explanation:**

- Backing up the data and then deleting it is not the best solution when much of the data is accessed regularly
- A Storage Gateway Volume Gateway in cached mode will store the entire dataset on S3 and a cache of the most frequently accessed data is cached on-site
- The S3 copy command doesn't help here as the data is not in S3
- You cannot archive straight into Glacier; you must store data on S3 first. Also, archiving is not the best solution to this problem

**References:**

https://digitalcloud.training/certification-training/aws-solutions-architect-associate/storage/aws-storage-gateway/

## 42. Question

**You have launched a Spot instance on EC2 for working on an application development project. In the event of an interruption what are the possible behaviors that can be configured? (choose 2)**

1. Save
2. Stop
3. Hibernate
4. Pause
5. Restart

**Answer: 2,3**

**Explanation:**

- You can specify whether Amazon EC2 should hibernate, stop, or terminate Spot Instances when they are interrupted. You can choose the interruption behavior that meets your needs. The default is to terminate Spot Instances when they are interrupted
- You cannot configure the interruption behavior to restart, save, or pause the instance

**References:**

https://digitalcloud.training/certification-training/aws-solutions-architect-associate/compute/amazon-ec2/

https://docs.aws.amazon.com/AWSEC2/latest/UserGuide/spot-interruptions.html

## 43. Question

**An application launched on Amazon EC2 instances needs to publish personally identifiable information (PII) about customers using Amazon SNS. The application is launched in private subnets within an Amazon VPC.**

**Which is the MOST secure way to allow the application to access service endpoints in the same region?**

1. Use a NAT gateway
2. Use a proxy instance
3. Use AWS PrivateLink
4. Use an Internet Gateway

**Answer: 3**

**Explanation:**

- To publish messages to Amazon SNS topics from an Amazon VPC, create an interface VPC endpoint. Then, you can publish messages to SNS topics while keeping the traffic within the network that you manage with the VPC. This is the most secure option as traffic does not need to traverse the Internet.
- Internet Gateways are used by instances in public subnets to access the Internet and this is less secure than an VPC endpoint.
- A NAT Gateway is used by instances in private subnets to access the Internet and this is less secure than an VPC endpoint.
- A proxy instance will also use the public Internet and so is less secure than a VPC endpoint.

**References:**

https://docs.aws.amazon.com/sns/latest/dg/sns-vpc-endpoint.html

https://digitalcloud.training/certification-training/aws-solutions-architect-associate/networking-and-content-delivery/amazon-vpc/

## 44. Question

**You work as a Solutions Architect at Digital Cloud Training. You are working on a disaster recovery solution that allows you to bring up your applications in another AWS region. Some of your applications run on EC2 instances and have proprietary software configurations with embedded licenses. You need to create duplicate copies of your EC2 instances in the other region.**

**What would be the best way to do this? (choose 2)**

1. Create new EC2 instances from the snapshots
2. Create an AMI of each EC2 instance and copy the AMIs to the other region
3. Copy the snapshots to the other region and create new EC2 instances from the snapshots
4. Create snapshots of the EBS volumes attached to the instances
5. Create new EC2 instances from the AMIs

**Answer: 2,5**

**Explanation:**

- In this scenario we are not looking to backup the instances but to create identical copies of them in the other region. These are often called golden images. We must assume that any data used by the instances resides in another service and will be accessible to them when they are launched in a DR situation
- You launch EC2 instances using AMIs not snapshots (you can create AMIs from snapshots). Therefore, you should create AMIs of each instance (rather than snapshots), copy the AMIs between regions and then create new EC2 instances from the AMIs
- AMIs are regional as they are backed by Amazon S3. You can only launch an AMI from the region in which it is stored. However, you can copy AMI's to other regions using the console, command line, or the API

**References:**

https://digitalcloud.training/certification-training/aws-solutions-architect-associate/compute/amazon-ec2/

## 45. Question

You are a Solutions Architect at Digital Cloud Training. A client of yours is using API Gateway for accepting and processing a large number of API calls to AWS Lambda. The client's business is rapidly growing and he is therefore expecting a large increase in traffic to his API Gateway and AWS Lambda services.

The client has asked for advice on ensuring the services can scale without any reduction in performance. What advice would you give to the client? (choose 2)

1. API Gateway scales manually through the assignment of provisioned throughput
2. AWS Lambda automatically scales up by using larger instance sizes for your functions
3. API Gateway scales up to the default throttling limit, with some additional burst capacity available
4. API Gateway can only scale up to the fixed throttling limits
5. AWS Lambda scales concurrently executing functions up to your default limit

**Answer: 3,5**

**Explanation:**

- API Gateway can scale to any level of traffic received by an API. API Gateway scales up to the default throttling limit of 10,000 requests per second and can burst past that up to 5,000 RPS. Throttling is used to protect back-end instances from traffic spikes
- Lambda uses continuous scaling – scales out not up. Lambda scales concurrently executing functions up to your default limit (1000)
- API Gateway does not use provisioned throughput – this is something that is used to provision performance in DynamoDB
- API Gateway can scale past the default throttling limits (they are not fixed; you just have to apply to have them adjusted)

**References:**

https://digitalcloud.training/certification-training/aws-solutions-architect-associate/networking-and-content-delivery/amazon-api-gateway/

https://digitalcloud.training/certification-training/aws-solutions-architect-associate/compute/aws-lambda/

## 46. Question

Your client is looking for a way to use standard templates for describing and provisioning their infrastructure resources on AWS. Which AWS service can be used in this scenario?

1. Auto Scaling
2. CloudFormation
3. Elastic Beanstalk
4. Simple Workflow Service (SWF)

**Answer: 2**

**Explanation:**

- AWS CloudFormation is a service that gives developers and businesses an easy way to create a collection of related AWS resources and provision them in an orderly and predictable fashion. AWS

CloudFormation provides a common language for you to describe and provision all the infrastructure resources in your cloud environment

- AWS Auto Scaling is used for providing elasticity to EC2 instances by launching or terminating instances based on load
- Elastic Beanstalk is a PaaS service for running managed web applications. It is not used for infrastructure deployment
- Amazon Simple Workflow Service (SWF) is a web service that makes it easy to coordinate work across distributed application components, it does not use templates for deploying infrastructure

**References:**

https://digitalcloud.training/certification-training/aws-solutions-architect-associate/management-tools/aws-cloudformation/

## 47. Question

A company is launching a new application and expects it to be very popular. The company requires a database layer that can scale along with the application. The schema will be frequently changes and the application cannot afford any downtime for database changes.

Which AWS service allows the company to achieve these requirements?

1. Amazon RDS MySQL
2. Amazon RedShift
3. Amazon Aurora
4. Amazon DynamoDB

**Answer: 4**

**Explanation:**

- DynamoDB a NoSQL DB which means you can change the schema easily. It's also the only DB in the list that you can scale without any downtime
- Amazon Aurora, RDS MySQL and RedShift all require changing instance sizes in order to scale which causes an outage. They are also all relational databases (SQL) so changing the schema is difficult

**References:**

https://digitalcloud.training/certification-training/aws-solutions-architect-associate/database/amazon-dynamodb/

## 48. Question

You would like to grant additional permissions to an individual ECS application container on an ECS cluster that you have deployed. You would like to do this without granting additional permissions to the other containers that are running on the cluster.

How can you achieve this?

1. Create a separate Task Definition for the application container that uses a different Task Role
2. In the same Task Definition, specify a separate Task Role for the application container
3. You cannot implement granular permissions with ECS containers
4. Use EC2 instances instead as you can assign different IAM roles on each instance

**Answer: 1**

**Explanation:**

- You can only apply one IAM role to a Task Definition so you must create a separate Task Definition. A Task Definition is required to run Docker containers in Amazon ECS and you can specify the IAM role (Task Role) that the task should use for permissions
- It is incorrect to say that you cannot implement granular permissions with ECS containers as IAM roles are granular and are applied through Task Definitions/Task Roles
- You can apply different IAM roles to different EC2 instances, but to grant permissions to ECS application containers you must use Task Definitions and Task Roles

**References:**

https://digitalcloud.training/certification-training/aws-solutions-architect-associate/compute/amazon-ecs/

## 49. Question

**A mobile client requires data from several application-layer services to populate its user interface. What can the application team use to decouple the client interface from the underlying services behind them?**

1. Application Load Balancer
2. AWS Device Farm
3. Amazon API Gateway
4. Amazon Cognito

**Answer: 3**

**Explanation:**

- Amazon API Gateway decouples the client application from the back-end application-layer services by providing a single endpoint for API requests
- An application load balancer distributes incoming connection requests to back-end EC2 instances. It is not used for decoupling application-layer services from mobile clients
- Amazon Cognito is used for adding sign-up, sign-in and access control to mobile apps
- AWS Device farm is an app testing service for Android, iOS and web apps

**References:**

https://digitalcloud.training/certification-training/aws-solutions-architect-associate/networking-and-content-delivery/amazon-api-gateway/

## 50. Question

**A customer has a production application running on Amazon EC2. The application frequently overwrites and deletes data, and it is essential that the application receives the most up-to-date version of the data whenever it is requested.**

**Which service is most appropriate for these requirements?**

1. Amazon RedShift
2. Amazon S3
3. Amazon RDS

4.   AWS Storage Gateway

**Answer: 3**

**Explanation:**

- This scenario asks that when retrieving data, the chosen storage solution should always return the most up-to-date data. Therefore, we must use Amazon RDS as it provides read-after-write consistency
- Amazon S3 only provides eventual consistency for overwrites and deletes
- Amazon RedShift is a data warehouse and is not used as a transactional database so this is the wrong use case for it
- AWS Storage Gateway is used for enabling hybrid cloud access to AWS storage services from on-premises

**References:**

https://digitalcloud.training/certification-training/aws-solutions-architect-associate/database/amazon-rds/

## 51. Question

You are running a Hadoop cluster on EC2 instances in your VPC. The EC2 instances are launched by an Auto Scaling Group (ASG) and you have configured the ASG to scale out and in as demand changes. One of the instances in the group is the Hadoop Master Node and you need to ensure that it is not terminated when your ASG processes a scale in action.

**What is the best way this can be achieved without interrupting services?**

1.   Change the DeleteOnTermination value for the EC2 instance
2.   Use the Instance Protection feature to set scale in protection for the Hadoop Master Node
3.   Move the Hadoop Master Node to another ASG that has the minimum and maximum instance settings set to 1
4.   Enable Deletion Protection for the EC2 instance

**Answer: 2**

**Explanation:**

- You can enable Instance Protection to protect a specific instance in an ASG from a scale in action
- Moving the Hadoop Node to another ASG would work but is impractical and would incur service interruption
- EC2 has a feature called "termination protection" not "Deletion Protection"
- The "DeleteOnTermination" value relates to EBS volumes not EC2 instances

**References:**

https://digitalcloud.training/certification-training/aws-solutions-architect-associate/compute/aws-auto-scaling/

https://aws.amazon.com/blogs/aws/new-instance-protection-for-auto-scaling/

## 52. Question

As a Solutions Architect at Digital Cloud Training you are helping a client to design a multi-tier web application architecture. The client has requested that the architecture provide low-latency connectivity between all servers and be resilient across multiple locations.

They would also like to use their existing Microsoft SQL licenses for the database tier. The client needs to maintain the ability to access the operating systems of all servers for the installation of monitoring software.

How would you recommend the database tier is deployed?

1. Amazon RDS with Microsoft SQL Server
2. Amazon RDS with Microsoft SQL Server in a Multi-AZ configuration
3. Amazon EC2 instances with Microsoft SQL Server and data replication within an AZ
4. Amazon EC2 instances with Microsoft SQL Server and data replication between two different AZs

Answer: 4

Explanation:

- As the client needs to access the operating system of the database servers, we need to use EC2 instances not RDS (which does not allow operating system access). We can implement EC2 instances with Microsoft SQL in two different AZs which provides the requested location redundancy and AZs are connected by low-latency, high throughput and redundant networking
- Implementing the solution in a single AZ would not provide the resiliency requested
- RDS is a fully managed service and you do not have access to the underlying EC2 instance (no root access)

References:

https://digitalcloud.training/certification-training/aws-solutions-architect-associate/networking-and-content-delivery/amazon-vpc/

https://digitalcloud.training/certification-training/aws-solutions-architect-associate/compute/amazon-ec2/

https://digitalcloud.training/certification-training/aws-solutions-architect-associate/database/amazon-rds/

## 53. Question

A Solutions Architect needs to design a solution that will allow Website Developers to deploy static web content without managing server infrastructure. All web content must be accessed over HTTPS with a custom domain name. The solution should be scalable as the company continues to grow.

Which of the following will provide the MOST cost-effective solution?

1. AWS Lambda function with Amazon API Gateway
2. Amazon EC2 instance with Amazon EBS
3. Amazon CloudFront with an Amazon S3 bucket origin
4. Amazon S3 with a static website

Answer: 3

Explanation:

- You can create an Amazon CloudFront distribution that uses an S3 bucket as the origin. This will allow you to serve the static content using the HTTPS protocol.
- You can create a static website using Amazon S3 with a custom domain name. However, you cannot connect to an Amazon S3 static website using HTTPS (only HTTP) so this solution does not work.
- Amazon EC2 with EBS is not a suitable solution as you would need to manage the server infrastructure (which the question states is not desired).
- AWS Lambda and API Gateway are both serverless services however this combination does not provide a solution for serving static content over HTTPS.

**References:**

https://digitalcloud.training/certification-training/aws-solutions-architect-associate/networking-and-content-delivery/amazon-cloudfront/

https://docs.aws.amazon.com/AmazonS3/latest/dev/WebsiteHosting.html

## 54. Question

An EBS-backed EC2 instance has been configured with some proprietary software that uses an embedded license. You need to move the EC2 instance to another Availability Zone (AZ) within the region. How can this be accomplished? Choose the best answer.

1. Use the AWS Management Console to select a different AZ for the existing instance
2. Create an image from the instance. Launch an instance from the AMI in the destination AZ
3. Take a snapshot of the instance. Create a new EC2 instance and perform a restore from the snapshot
4. Perform a copy operation to move the EC2 instance to the destination AZ

**Answer: 2**

**Explanation:**

- The easiest and recommended option is to create an AMI (image) from the instance and launch an instance from the AMI in the other AZ. AMIs are backed by snapshots which in turn are backed by S3 so the data is available from any AZ within the region
- You can take a snapshot, launch an instance in the destination AZ. Stop the instance, detach its root volume, create a volume from the snapshot you took and attach it to the instance. However, this is not the best option
- There's no way to move an EC2 instance from the management console
- You cannot perform a copy operation to move the instance

**References:**

https://digitalcloud.training/certification-training/aws-solutions-architect-associate/compute/amazon-ec2/

https://aws.amazon.com/premiumsupport/knowledge-center/move-ec2-instance/

## 55. Question

A Solutions Architect must design a solution that encrypts data in Amazon S3. Corporate policy mandates encryption keys be generated and managed on premises. Which solution should the Architect use to meet the security requirements?

1. SSE-S3: Server-side encryption with Amazon-managed master key
2. AWS CloudHSM
3. SSE-KMS: Server-side encryption with AWS KMS managed keys
4. SSE-C: Server-side encryption with customer-provided encryption keys

**Answer: 4**

**Explanation:**

- With SSE-C you keep the encryption keys on premises. Data is encrypted and decrypted in AWS (server-side) but you manage the keys outside of AWS. This is the correct answer.
- With SSE-S3, Amazon manage the keys for you, so this is incorrect.
- With SSE-KMS the keys are managed in the Amazon Key Management Service, so this is incorrect.
- With AWS CloudHSM your keys are held in AWS in a hardware security module. Again, the keys are not on-premises they are in AWS, so this is incorrect.

**References:**

https://digitalcloud.training/certification-training/aws-solutions-architect-associate/storage/amazon-s3/

## 56. Question

A data-processing application runs on an i3.large EC2 instance with a single 100 GB EBS gp2 volume. The application stores temporary data in a small database (less than 30 GB) located on the EBS root volume. The application is struggling to process the data fast enough, and a Solutions Architect has determined that the I/O speed of the temporary database is the bottleneck.

**What is the MOST cost-efficient way to improve the database response times?**

1. Put the temporary database on a new 50-GB EBS gp2 volume
2. Move the temporary database onto instance storage
3. Put the temporary database on a new 50-GB EBS io1 volume with a 3000 IOPS allocation
4. Enable EBS optimization on the instance and keep the temporary files on the existing volume

**Answer: 2**

**Explanation:**

- EC2 Instance Stores are high-speed ephemeral storage that is physically attached to the EC2 instance. The i3.large instance type comes with a single 475GB NVMe SSD instance store so it would be a good way to lower cost and improve performance by using the attached instance store. As the files are temporary, it can be assumed that ephemeral storage (which means the data is lost when the instance is stopped) is sufficient.
- Enabling EBS optimization will not lower cost. Also, EBS Optimization is a network traffic optimization, it does not change the I/O speed of the volume.
- Moving the DB to a new 50-GB EBS gp2 volume will not result in a performance improvement as you get IOPS allocated per GB so a smaller volume will have lower performance.
- Moving the DB to a new 50-GB EBS io1 volume with a 3000 IOPS allocation will improve performance but is more expensive so will not be the most cost-efficient solution.

**References:**

https://docs.aws.amazon.com/AWSEC2/latest/UserGuide/InstanceStorage.html

## 57. Question

You need to enable sign in on your mobile app using social identity providers including Amazon, Facebook and Google. How can you enable this capability?

1. Simple AD
2. Amazon Cognito
3. Access keys
4. IAM Policies

**Answer: 2**

**Explanation:**

- Amazon Cognito lets you easily add user sign-up and authentication to your mobile and web apps. Amazon Cognito also enables you to authenticate users through an external identity provider and provides temporary security credentials to access your app's backend resources in AWS or any service behind Amazon API Gateway
- Access keys (and secret IDs) are associated with AWS accounts in IAM and are used to sign programmatic requests that you make to AWS if you use AWS CLI commands (using the SDKs) or using AWS API operations
- IAM Policies is not a correct answer. A policy is an entity that, when attached to an identity or resource, defines their permissions. It is not used for providing authentication services through social identity providers
- Simple AD is a standalone managed directory that is powered by a Samba 4 Active Directory Compatible Server. It is not used for providing authentication services through social identity providers

**References:**

https://aws.amazon.com/cognito/faqs/

## 58. Question

A Solutions Architect is developing a new web application on AWS that needs to be able to scale to support unpredictable workloads. The Architect prefers to focus on value-add activities such as software development and product roadmap development rather than provisioning and managing instances.

Which solution is most appropriate for this use case?

1. Amazon API Gateway and AWS Lambda
2. Amazon API Gateway and Amazon EC2
3. Amazon CloudFront and AWS Lambda
4. Elastic Load Balancing with Auto Scaling groups and Amazon EC2

**Answer: 1**

**Explanation:**

- The Architect requires a solution that removes the need to manage instances. Therefore, it must be a serverless service which rules out EC2. The two remaining options use AWS Lambda at the back-end for processing. Though CloudFront can trigger Lambda functions it is more suited to customizing content delivered from an origin. Therefore, API Gateway with AWS Lambda is the most workable solution presented
- This solution will likely require other services such as S3 for content and a database service. Refer to the link below for an example scenario that use API Gateway and AWS Lambda with other services to create a serverless web application

**References:**

https://aws.amazon.com/getting-started/projects/build-serverless-web-app-lambda-apigateway-s3-dynamodb-cognito/


## 59. Question

An application you manage exports data from a relational database into an S3 bucket. The data analytics team wants to import this data into a RedShift cluster in a VPC in the same account. Due to the data being sensitive the security team has instructed you to ensure that the data traverses the VPC without being routed via the public Internet.

Which combination of actions would meet this requirement? (choose 2)

1. Create and configure an Amazon S3 VPC endpoint
2. Set up a NAT gateway in a private subnet to allow the Amazon RedShift cluster to access Amazon S3
3. Create a NAT gateway in a public subnet to allows the Amazon RedShift cluster to access Amazon S3
4. Create a cluster Security Group to allow the Amazon RedShift cluster to access Amazon S3
5. Enable Amazon RedShift Enhanced VPC routing


**Answer: 1,5**

**Explanation:**

- Amazon RedShift Enhanced VPC routing forces all COPY and UNLOAD traffic between clusters and data repositories through a VPC
- Implementing an S3 VPC endpoint will allow S3 to be accessed from other AWS services without traversing the public network. Amazon S3 uses the Gateway Endpoint type of VPC endpoint with which a target for a specified route is entered into the VPC route table and used for traffic destined to a supported AWS service
- Cluster Security Groups are used with RedShift on EC2-Classic VPCs, regular security groups are used in EC2-VPC
- A NAT Gateway is used to allow instances in a private subnet to access the Internet and is of no use in this situation

**References:**

https://docs.aws.amazon.com/redshift/latest/mgmt/enhanced-vpc-routing.html

https://digitalcloud.training/certification-training/aws-solutions-architect-associate/networking-and-content-delivery/amazon-vpc/

## 60. Question

Your company is opening a new office in the Asia Pacific region. Users in the new office will need to read data from an RDS database that is hosted in the U.S. To improve performance, you are planning to implement a Read Replica of the database in the Asia Pacific region. However, your Chief Security Officer (CSO) has explained to you that the company policy dictates that all data that leaves the U.S must be encrypted at rest. The master RDS DB is not currently encrypted.

What options are available to you? (choose 2)

1. You can create an encrypted Read Replica that is encrypted with a different key
2. You can create an encrypted Read Replica that is encrypted with the same key
3. You can use an ELB to provide an encrypted transport layer in front of the RDS DB
4. You can enable encryption for the master DB by creating a new DB from a snapshot with encryption enabled
5. You can enable encryption for the master DB through the management console

Answer: 1,4

Explanation:

- You cannot encrypt an existing DB, you need to create a snapshot, copy it, encrypt the copy, then build an encrypted DB from the snapshot
- You can encrypt your Amazon RDS instances and snapshots at rest by enabling the encryption option for your Amazon RDS DB instance
- Data that is encrypted at rest includes the underlying storage for a DB instance, its automated backups, Read Replicas, and snapshots
- A Read Replica of an Amazon RDS encrypted instance is also encrypted using the same key as the master instance when both are in the same region
- If the master and Read Replica are in different regions, you encrypt using the encryption key for that region
- You can't have an encrypted Read Replica of an unencrypted DB instance or an unencrypted Read Replica of an encrypted DB instance

References:

https://digitalcloud.training/certification-training/aws-solutions-architect-associate/database/amazon-rds/

https://docs.aws.amazon.com/AmazonRDS/latest/UserGuide/Overview.Encryption.html

## 61. Question

An application receives images uploaded by customers and stores them on Amazon S3. An AWS Lambda function then processes the images to add graphical elements. The processed images need to be available for users to download for 30 days, after which time they can be deleted. Processed images can be easily recreated from original images. The Original images need to be immediately available for 30 days and be accessible within 24 hours for another 90 days.

Which combination of Amazon S3 storage classes is most cost-effective for the original and processed images? (choose 2)

1. Store the original images in STANDARD for 30 days, transition to DEEP_ARCHIVE for 180 days, then expire the data
2. Store the processed images in ONEZONE_IA and then expire the data after 30 days

3. Store the processed images in STANDARD and then transition to GLACIER after 30 days
4. Store the original images in STANDARD_IA for 30 days and then transition to DEEP_ARCHIVE
5. Store the original images in STANDARD for 30 days, transition to GLACIER for 180 days, then expire the data

**Answer: 2,5**

**Explanation:**

- The key requirements for the original images are that they are immediately available for 30 days (STANDARD), available within 24 hours for 180 days (GLACIER) and then they are not needed (expire them).
- The key requirements for the processed images are that they are immediately available for 30 days (ONEZONE_IA as they can be recreated from the originals), and then are not needed (expire them).
- DEEP_ARCHIVE has a minimum storage duration of 180 days.
- There is no need to transition the processed images to GLACIER as are not needed after 30 days as they can be recreated if needed from the originals.

**References:**

https://docs.aws.amazon.com/AmazonS3/latest/dev/lifecycle-transition-general-considerations.html

https://aws.amazon.com/s3/storage-classes/

https://digitalcloud.training/certification-training/aws-solutions-architect-associate/storage/amazon-s3/

## 62. Question

**A web application is running on a fleet of Amazon EC2 instances using an Auto Scaling Group. It is desired that the CPU usage in the fleet is kept at 40%.**

**How should scaling be configured?**

1. Use a custom CloudWatch alarm to monitor CPU usage and notify the ASG using Amazon SNS
2. Use a simple scaling policy that launches instances when the average CPU hits 40%
3. Use a step scaling policy that uses the PercentChangeInCapacity value to adjust the group size as required
4. Use a target tracking policy that keeps the average aggregate CPU utilization at 40%

**Answer: 4**

**Explanation:**

- This is a perfect use case for a target tracking scaling policy. With target tracking scaling policies, you select a scaling metric and set a target value. In this case you can just set the target value to 40% average aggregate CPU utilization.
- A simple scaling policy will add instances when 40% CPU utilization is reached, but it is not designed to maintain 40% CPU utilization across the group.
- The step scaling policy makes scaling adjustments based on a number of factors. The PercentChangeInCapacity value increments or decrements the group size by a specified percentage. This does not relate to CPU utilization.
- You do not need to create a custom Amazon CloudWatch alarm as the ASG can scale using a policy based on CPU utilization using standard configuration.

**References:**

https://docs.aws.amazon.com/autoscaling/ec2/userguide/as-scaling-target-tracking.html

https://docs.aws.amazon.com/autoscaling/ec2/userguide/as-scaling-simple-step.html

https://digitalcloud.training/certification-training/aws-solutions-architect-associate/compute/aws-auto-scaling/

## 63. Question

A shared services VPC is being setup for use by several AWS accounts. An application needs to be securely shared from the shared services VPC. The solution should not allow consumers to connect to other instances in the VPC.

**How can this be setup with the least administrative effort? (choose 2)**

1. Create a Network Load Balancer (NLB)
2. Setup VPC peering between each AWS VPC
3. Configure security groups to restrict access
4. Use AWS PrivateLink to expose the application as an endpoint service
5. Use AWS ClassicLink to expose the application as an endpoint service

**Answer: 1,4**

**Explanation:**

- VPCs can be shared among multiple AWS accounts. Resources can then be shared amongst those accounts. However, to restrict access so that consumers cannot connect to other instances in the VPC the best solution is to use PrivateLink to create an endpoint for the application. The endpoint type will be an interface endpoint and it uses a NLB in the shared services VPC.
- ClassicLink allows you to link EC2-Classic instances to a VPC in your account, within the same region. This solution does not include EC2-Classic which is now deprecated (replaced by VPC).
- VPC peering could be used along with security groups to restrict access to the application and other instances in the VPC. However, this would be administratively difficult as you would need to ensure that you maintain the security groups as resources and addresses change.

**References:**

https://aws.amazon.com/about-aws/whats-new/2018/12/amazon-virtual-private-clouds-can-now-be-shared-with-other-aws-accounts/

https://aws.amazon.com/blogs/networking-and-content-delivery/vpc-sharing-a-new-approach-to-multiple-accounts-and-vpc-management/

https://d1.awsstatic.com/whitepapers/aws-privatelink.pdf

## 64. Question

An application running on Amazon EC2 needs to regularly download large objects from Amazon S3. How can performance be optimized for high-throughput use cases?

1. Issue parallel requests and use byte-range fetches
2. Use AWS Global Accelerator
3. Use Amazon S3 Transfer acceleration
4. Use Amazon CloudFront to cache the content

**Answer: 1**

**Explanation:**

- Using the Range HTTP header in a GET Object request, you can fetch a byte-range from an object, transferring only the specified portion. You can use concurrent connections to Amazon S3 to fetch different byte ranges from within the same object. This helps you achieve higher aggregate throughput versus a single whole-object request. Fetching smaller ranges of a large object also allows your application to improve retry times when requests are interrupted.
- Amazon S3 Transfer Acceleration is used for speeding up uploads of data to Amazon S3 by using the CloudFront network. It is not used for downloading data.
- Amazon CloudFront is used for caching content closer to users. In this case the EC2 instance needs to access the data so CloudFront is not a good solution (the edge location used by CloudFront may not be closer than the EC2 instance is to the S3 endpoint.
- AWS Global Accelerator is used for improving availability and performance for Amazon EC2 instances or Elastic Load Balancers (ALB and NLB). It is not used for improving Amazon S3 performance.

**References:**

https://digitalcloud.training/certification-training/aws-solutions-architect-associate/storage/amazon-s3/

https://docs.aws.amazon.com/AmazonS3/latest/dev/optimizing-performance-guidelines.html

https://docs.aws.amazon.com/AmazonS3/latest/dev/optimizing-performance-design-patterns.html

## 65. Question

A new application will run across multiple Amazon ECS tasks. Front-end application logic will process data and then pass that data to a back-end ECS task to perform further processing and write the data to a datastore. The Architect would like to reduce-interdependencies so failures do no impact other components.

**Which solution should the Architect use?**

1. Create an Amazon Kinesis Firehose delivery stream that delivers data to an Amazon S3 bucket, configure the front-end to write data to the stream and the back-end to read data from Amazon S3
2. Create an Amazon SQS queue and configure the front-end to add messages to the queue and the back-end to poll the queue for messages
3. Create an Amazon Kinesis Firehose delivery stream and configure the front-end to add data to the stream and the back-end to read data from the stream
4. Create an Amazon SQS queue that pushes messages to the back-end. Configure the front-end to add messages to the queue

**Answer: 2**

**Explanation:**

- This is a good use case for Amazon SQS. SQS is a service that is used for decoupling applications, thus reducing interdependencies, through a message bus. The front-end application can place messages on the queue and the back-end can then poll the queue for new messages. Please remember that Amazon SQS is pull-based (polling) not push-based (use SNS for push-based).
- Amazon Kinesis Firehose is used for streaming data. With Firehose the data is immediately loaded into a destination that can be Amazon S3, RedShift, Elasticsearch, or Splunk. This is not an ideal

use case for Firehose as this is not streaming data and there is no need to load data into an additional AWS service.

**References:**

https://digitalcloud.training/certification-training/aws-solutions-architect-associate/analytics/amazon-kinesis/

https://digitalcloud.training/certification-training/aws-solutions-architect-associate/application-integration/amazon-sqs/

https://docs.aws.amazon.com/AmazonECS/latest/developerguide/common_use_cases.html

# SET 3: PRACTICE QUESTIONS ONLY

*Or go directly to Set 3: Practice Questions, Answers & Explanations*

## 1. Question

Your Business Intelligence team use SQL tools to analyze data. What would be the best solution for performing queries on structured data that is being received at a high velocity?

1. EMR using Hive
2. Kinesis Firehose with RedShift
3. Kinesis Firehose with RDS
4. EMR running Apache Spark

## 2. Question

A Solutions Architect is migrating a small relational database into AWS. The database will run on an EC2 instance and the DB size is around 500 GB. The database is infrequently used with small amounts of requests spread across the day. The DB is a low priority and the Architect needs to lower the cost of the solution.

What is the MOST cost-effective storage type?

1. Amazon EBS Provisioned IOPS SSD
2. Amazon EBS Throughput Optimized HDD
3. Amazon EBS General Purpose SSD
4. Amazon EFS

## 3. Question

A Solutions Architect has been asked to improve the performance of a DynamoDB table. Latency is currently a few milliseconds and this needs to be reduced to microseconds whilst also scaling to millions of requests per second.

What is the BEST architecture to support this?

1. Reduce the number of Scan operations
2. Use CloudFront to cache the content
3. Create an ElastiCache Redis cluster
4. Create a DynamoDB Accelerator (DAX) cluster

## 4. Question

You are developing an application that uses Lambda functions. You need to store some sensitive data that includes credentials for accessing the database tier. You are planning to store this data as environment variables within Lambda. How can you ensure this sensitive information is properly secured?

1. There is no need to make any changes as all environment variables are encrypted by default with AWS Lambda
2. Use encryption helpers that leverage AWS Key Management Service to store the sensitive information as Ciphertext

3. This cannot be done, only the environment variables that relate to the Lambda function itself can be encrypted
4. Store the environment variables in an encrypted DynamoDB table and configure Lambda to retrieve them as required

## 5. Question

You have implemented API Gateway and enabled a cache for a specific stage. How can you control the cache to enhance performance and reduce load on back-end services?

1. Configure the throttling feature
2. Using CloudFront controls
3. Enable bursting
4. Using time-to-live (TTL) settings

## 6. Question

You are implementing an Elastic Load Balancer (ELB) for an application that will use encrypted communications. Which two types of security policies are supported by the Elastic Load Balancer for SSL negotiations between the ELB and clients? (choose 2)

1. ELB predefined Security policies
2. AES 256
3. Network ACLs
4. Security groups
5. Custom security policies

## 7. Question

A company is migrating an on-premises 10 TB MySQL database to AWS. The company expects the database to quadruple in size and the business requirement is that replicate lag must be kept under 100 milliseconds.

Which Amazon RDS engine meets these requirements?

1. Amazon Aurora
2. Oracle
3. Microsoft SQL Server
4. MySQL

## 8. Question

You have been asked to deploy a new High-Performance Computing (HPC) cluster. You need to create a design for the EC2 instances that ensures close proximity, low latency and high network throughput.

Which AWS features will help you to achieve this requirement whilst considering cost? (choose 2)

1. Use EC2 instances with Enhanced Networking
2. Use dedicated hosts
3. Launch I/O Optimized EC2 instances in one private subnet in an AZ
4. Use Placement groups
5. Use Provisioned IOPS EBS volumes

## 9. Question

Your company currently uses Puppet Enterprise for infrastructure and application management. You are looking to move some of your infrastructure onto AWS and would like to continue to use the same tools in the cloud. What AWS service provides a fully managed configuration management service that is compatible with Puppet Enterprise?

1. CloudFormation
2. OpsWorks
3. Elastic Beanstalk
4. CloudTrail

## 10. Question

You are a Solutions Architect for an insurance company. An application you manage is used to store photos and video files that relate to insurance claims. The application writes data using the iSCSI protocol to a storage array. The array currently holds 10TB of data and is approaching capacity.

Your manager has instructed you that he will not approve further capital expenditure for on-premises infrastructure. Therefore, you are planning to migrate data into the cloud. How can you move data into the cloud whilst retaining low-latency access to frequently accessed data on-premise using the iSCSI protocol?

1. Use an AWS Storage Gateway File Gateway in cached volume mode
2. Use an AWS Storage Gateway Virtual Tape Library
3. Use an AWS Storage Gateway Volume Gateway in cached volume mode
4. Use an AWS Storage Gateway Volume Gateway in stored volume mode

## 11. Question

You are a Solutions Architect at Digital Cloud Training. One of your clients is an online media company that attracts a large volume of users to their website each day. The media company are interested in analyzing the user's clickstream data so they can analyze user behavior in real-time and dynamically update advertising. This intelligent approach to advertising should help them to increase conversions.

What would you suggest as a solution to assist them with capturing and analyzing this data?

1. Update the application to write data to an SQS queue, and create an additional application component to analyze the data in the queue and update the website
2. Use EMR to process and analyze the data in real-time and Lambda to update the website based on the results
3. Use Kinesis Data Streams to process and analyze the clickstream data. Store the results in DynamoDB and create an application component that reads the data from the database and updates the website
4. Write the data directly to RedShift and use Business Intelligence tools to analyze the data

## 12. Question

A systems integration company that helps customers migrate into AWS repeatedly build large, standardized architectures using several AWS services. The Solutions Architects have documented the architectural blueprints for these solutions and are looking for a method of automating the provisioning of the resources.

**Which AWS service would satisfy this requirement?**

1. Elastic Beanstalk
2. AWS CloudFormation
3. AWS OpsWorks
4. AWS CodeDeploy

## 13. Question

A Solutions Architect is designing a static website that will use the zone apex of a DNS domain (e.g. example.com). The Architect wants to use the Amazon Route 53 service. Which steps should the Architect take to implement a scalable and cost-effective solution? (choose 2)

1. Host the website on an Amazon EC2 instance with ELB and Auto Scaling, and map a Route 53 Alias record to the ELB endpoint
2. Host the website using AWS Elastic Beanstalk, and map a Route 53 Alias record to the Beanstalk stack
3. Host the website on an Amazon EC2 instance, and map a Route 53 Alias record to the public IP address of the EC2 instance
4. Create a Route 53 hosted zone, and set the NS records of the domain to use Route 53 name servers
5. Serve the website from an Amazon S3 bucket, and map a Route 53 Alias record to the website endpoint

## 14. Question

A Solutions Architect is planning to run some Docker containers on Amazon ECS. The Architect needs to define some parameters for the containers. What application parameters can be defined in an ECS task definition? (choose 2)

1. The ELB node to be used to scale the task containers
2. The security group rules to apply
3. The ports that should be opened on the container instance for your application
4. The container images to use and the repositories in which they are located
5. The application configuration

## 15. Question

A major upcoming sales event is likely to result in heavy read traffic to a web application your company manages. As the Solutions Architect you have been asked for advice on how best to protect the database tier from the heavy load and ensure the user experience is not impacted.

The web application owner has also requested that the design be fault tolerant. The current configuration consists of a web application behind an ELB that uses Auto Scaling and an RDS MySQL database running in a multi-AZ configuration. As the database load is highly changeable the solution should allow elasticity by adding and removing nodes as required and should also be multi-threaded.

**What recommendations would you make?**

1. Deploy an ElastiCache Redis cluster with cluster mode disabled and multi-AZ with automatic failover
2. Deploy an ElastiCache Redis cluster with cluster mode enabled and multi-AZ with automatic failover
3. Deploy an ElastiCache Memcached cluster in multi-AZ mode in the same AZs as RDS

4.   Deploy an ElastiCache Memcached cluster in both AZs in which the RDS database is deployed

## 16. Question

An application currently stores all data on Amazon EBS volumes. All EBS volumes must be backed up durably across multiple Availability Zones.

What is the MOST resilient way to back up volumes?

1.   Create a script to copy data to an EC2 instance store
2.   Enable EBS volume encryption
3.   Mirror data across two EBS volumes
4.   Take regular EBS snapshots

## 17. Question

You work for Digital Cloud Training and have just created a number of IAM users in your AWS account. You need to ensure that the users are able to make API calls to AWS services. What else needs to be done?

1.   Enable Multi-Factor Authentication for the users
2.   Create a set of Access Keys for the users
3.   Create a group and add the users to it
4.   Set a password for each user

## 18. Question

A Solutions Architect is designing a workload that requires a high performance object-based storage system that must be shared with multiple Amazon EC2 instances.

Which AWS service delivers these requirements?

1.   Amazon S3
2.   Amazon EFS
3.   Amazon EBS
4.   Amazon ElastiCache

## 19. Question

A client from the agricultural sector has approached you for some advice around the collection of a large volume of data from sensors they have deployed around the country.

An application needs to collect data from over 100,000 sensors and each sensor will send around 1KB of data every minute. The data needs to then be stored in a durable, low latency data store. The client also needs historical data that is over 1 year old to be moved into a data warehouse where they can perform analytics using standard SQL queries.

What combination of AWS services would you recommend to the client? (choose 2)

1.   Use Amazon Elastic Map Reduce (EMR) for analytics
2.   Use Amazon RedShift for the analytics
3.   Use Amazon Kinesis data streams for data ingestion and enable extended data retention to store data for 1 year

4. Use Amazon Kinesis Data Firehose for data ingestion and configure a consumer to store data in Amazon DynamoDB
5. Use Amazon Kinesis Data Streams for data ingestion and configure a consumer to store data in Amazon DynamoDB

## 20. Question

An EC2 status check on an EBS volume is showing as *insufficient-data*. What is the most likely explanation?

1. The checks have failed on the volume
2. The checks require more information to be manually entered
3. The checks may still be in progress on the volume
4. The volume does not have enough data on it to check properly

## 21. Question

You run a two-tier application with a web tier that is behind an Internet-facing Elastic Load Balancer (ELB). You need to restrict access to the web tier to a specific list of public IP addresses.

What are two possible ways you can implement this requirement? (choose 2)

1. Configure a VPC NACL to allow web traffic from the list of IPs and deny all outbound traffic
2. Configure the VPC internet gateway to allow incoming traffic from these IP addresses
3. Configure the proxy protocol on the web servers and filter traffic based on IP address
4. Configure your ELB to send the X-forwarded for headers and the web servers to filter traffic based on the ELB's "X-forwarded-for" header
5. Configure the ELB security group to allow traffic only from the specific list of IPs

## 22. Question

An issue has been reported whereby Amazon EC2 instances are not being terminated from an Auto Scaling Group behind an ELB when traffic volumes are low. How can this be fixed?

1. Modify the scale down increment
2. Modify the scaling settings on the ELB
3. Modify the lower threshold settings on the ASG
4. Modify the upper threshold settings on the ASG

## 23. Question

A Solutions Architect is designing a solution for a financial application that will receive trading data in large volumes. What is the best solution for ingesting and processing a very large number of data streams in near real time?

1. Amazon EMR
2. Amazon Kinesis Data Streams
3. Amazon Redshift
4. Amazon Kinesis Firehose

## 24. Question

You have been asked to recommend the best AWS storage solution for a client. The client requires a storage solution that provide a mounted file system for a Big Data and Analytics application. The client's requirements include high throughput, low latency, read-after-write consistency and the ability to burst up to multiple GB/s for short periods of time.

Which AWS service can meet this requirement?

1. S3
2. DynamoDB
3. EBS
4. EFS

## 25. Question

A company runs a legacy application with a single-tier architecture on an Amazon EC2 instance. Disk I/O is low, with occasional small spikes during business hours. The company requires the instance to be stopped from 8pm to 8am daily.

Which storage option is MOST appropriate for this workload?

1. Amazon EBS Provisioned IOPS SSD (io1) storage
2. Amazon S3
3. Amazon EBS General Purpose SSD (gp2) storage
4. Amazon EC2 Instance Store storage

## 26. Question

An EC2 instance in an Auto Scaling group that has been reported as unhealthy has been marked for replacement. What is the process Auto Scaling uses to replace the instance? (choose 2)

1. Auto Scaling will send a notification to the administrator
2. Auto Scaling will terminate the existing instance before launching a replacement instance
3. If connection draining is enabled, Auto Scaling will wait for in-flight connections to complete or timeout
4. Auto Scaling has to perform rebalancing first, and then terminate the instance
5. Auto Scaling has to launch a replacement first before it can terminate the unhealthy instance

## 27. Question

You have an application running in ap-southeast that requires six EC2 instances running at all times.

With three Availability Zones available in that region (ap-southeast-2a, ap-southeast-2b, and ap-southeast-2c), which of the following deployments provides fault tolerance if any single Availability Zone in ap-southeast-2 becomes unavailable? (choose 2)

1. 2 EC2 instances in ap-southeast-2a, 2 EC2 instances in ap-southeast-2b, 2 EC2 instances in ap-southeast-2c
2. 3 EC2 instances in ap-southeast-2a, 3 EC2 instances in ap-southeast-2b, no EC2 instances in ap-southeast-2c
3. 4 EC2 instances in ap-southeast-2a, 2 EC2 instances in ap-southeast-2b, 2 EC2 instances in ap-southeast-2c

4.  6 EC2 instances in ap-southeast-2a, 6 EC2 instances in ap-southeast-2b, no EC2 instances in ap-southeast-2c
5.  3 EC2 instances in ap-southeast-2a, 3 EC2 instances in ap-southeast-2b, 3 EC2 instances in ap-southeast-2c

## 28. Question

For which of the following workloads should a Solutions Architect consider using Elastic Beanstalk? (choose 2)

1.  A management task run occasionally
2.  Caching content for Internet-based delivery
3.  A long running worker process
4.  A data lake
5.  A web application using Amazon RDS

## 29. Question

You need to create a file system that can be concurrently accessed by multiple EC2 instances within an AZ. The file system needs to support high throughput and the ability to burst. As the data that will be stored on the file system will be sensitive you need to ensure it is encrypted at rest and in transit.

What storage solution would you implement for the EC2 instances?

1.  Use the Elastic File System (EFS) and mount the file system using NFS v4.1
2.  Use the Elastic Block Store (EBS) and mount the file system at the block level
3.  Add EBS volumes to each EC2 instance and use an ELB to distribute data evenly between the volumes
4.  Add EBS volumes to each EC2 instance and configure data replication

## 30. Question

A Solutions Architect is designing a web page for event registrations and needs a managed service to send a text message to users every time users sign up for an event.

Which AWS service should the Architect use to achieve this?

1.  Amazon STS
2.  Amazon SQS
3.  AWS Lambda
4.  Amazon SNS

## 31. Question

A Solutions Architect is developing an application that will store and index large (>1 MB) JSON files. The data store must be highly available and latency must be consistently low even during times of heavy usage. Which service should the Architect use?

1.  AWS CloudFormation
2.  DynamoDB
3.  Amazon RedShift
4.  Amazon EFS

## 32. Question

An Architect is designing a serverless application that will accept images uploaded by users from around the world. The application will make API calls to back-end services and save the session state data of the user to a database.

Which combination of services would provide a solution that is cost-effective while delivering the least latency?

1. Amazon S3, API Gateway, AWS Lambda, Amazon RDS
2. Amazon CloudFront, API Gateway, Amazon S3, AWS Lambda, Amazon RDS
3. API Gateway, Amazon S3, AWS Lambda, DynamoDB
4. Amazon CloudFront, API Gateway, Amazon S3, AWS Lambda, DynamoDB

## 33. Question

A Solutions Architect is determining the best method for provisioning Internet connectivity for a data-processing application that will pull large amounts of data from an object storage system via the Internet. The solution must be redundant and have no constraints on bandwidth.

Which option satisfies these requirements?

1. Attach an Internet Gateway
2. Create a VPC endpoint
3. Use a NAT Gateway
4. Deploy NAT Instances in a public subnet

## 34. Question

The development team at your company have created a new mobile application that will be used by users to access confidential data. The developers have used Amazon Cognito for authentication, authorization, and user management. Due to the sensitivity of the data, there is a requirement to add another method of authentication in addition to a username and password.

You have been asked to recommend the best solution. What is your recommendation?

1. Enable multi-factor authentication (MFA) in IAM
2. Use multi-factor authentication (MFA) with a Cognito user pool
3. Integrate IAM with a user pool in Cognito
4. Integrate a third-party identity provider (IdP)

## 35. Question

You need to provide AWS Management Console access to a team of new application developers. The team members who perform the same role are assigned to a Microsoft Active Directory group and you have been asked to use Identity Federation and RBAC.

Which AWS services would you use to configure this access? (choose 2)

1. AWS IAM Groups
2. AWS Directory Service AD Connector
3. AWS IAM Users
4. AWS IAM Roles
5. AWS Directory Service Simple AD

## 36. Question

A critical database runs in your VPC for which availability is a concern. Which RDS DB instance events may force the DB to be taken offline during a maintenance window?

1. Selecting the Multi-AZ feature
2. Promoting a Read Replica
3. Security patching
4. Updating DB parameter groups

## 37. Question

You are putting together a design for a three-tier web application. The application tier requires a minimum of 6 EC2 instances to be running at all times. You need to provide fault tolerance to ensure that the failure of a single Availability Zone (AZ) will not affect application performance.

Which of the options below is the optimum solution to fulfill these requirements?

1. Create an ASG with 12 instances spread across 4 AZs behind an ELB
2. Create an ASG with 6 instances spread across 3 AZs behind an ELB
3. Create an ASG with 9 instances spread across 3 AZs behind an ELB
4. Create an ASG with 18 instances spread across 3 AZs behind an ELB

## 38. Question

You have a three-tier web application running on AWS that utilizes Route 53, ELB, Auto Scaling and RDS. One of the EC2 instances that is registered against the ELB fails a health check. What actions will the ELB take in this circumstance?

1. The ELB will terminate the instance that failed the health check
2. The ELB will stop sending traffic to the instance that failed the health check
3. The ELB will instruct Auto Scaling to terminate the instance and launch a replacement
4. The ELB will update Route 53 by removing any references to the instance

## 39. Question

A company runs a service on AWS to provide offsite backups for images on laptops and phones. The solution must support millions of customers, with thousands of images per customer. Images will be retrieved infrequently but must be available for retrieval immediately.

Which is the MOST cost-effective storage option that meets these requirements?

1. Amazon EFS
2. Amazon S3 Standard
3. Amazon S3 Standard-Infrequent Access
4. Amazon Glacier with expedited retrievals

## 40. Question

You are deploying an application on Amazon EC2 that must call AWS APIs. Which method of securely passing credentials to the application should you use?

1. Embed the API credentials into you application files
2. Assign IAM roles to the EC2 instances

3.  Store API credentials as an object in Amazon S3
4.  Store the API credentials on the instance using instance metadata

## 41. Question

A company is generating large datasets with millions of rows that must be summarized by column. Existing business intelligence tools will be used to build daily reports.

Which storage service meets the requirements?

1.  Amazon RedShift
2.  Amazon RDS
3.  Amazon ElastiCache
4.  Amazon DynamoDB

## 42. Question

A company runs a multi-tier application in an Amazon VPC. The application has an ELB Classic Load Balancer as the front end in a public subnet, and an Amazon EC2-based reverse proxy that performs content-based routing to two back end EC2 instances in a private subnet. The application is experiencing increasing load and the Solutions Architect is concerned that the reverse proxy and current back end setup will be insufficient.

Which actions should the Architect take to achieve a cost-effective solution that ensures the application automatically scales to meet the demand? (choose 2)

1.  Add Auto Scaling to the Amazon EC2 reverse proxy layer
2.  Add Auto Scaling to the Amazon EC2 back end fleet
3.  Use t3 burstable instance types for the back end fleet
4.  Replace both the front end and reverse proxy layers with an Application Load Balancer
5.  Replace the Amazon EC2 reverse proxy with an ELB internal Classic Load Balancer

## 43. Question

A new security mandate requires that all personnel data held in the cloud is encrypted at rest. Which two methods allow you to encrypt data stored in S3 buckets at rest cost-efficiently? (choose 2)

1.  Use AWS S3 server-side encryption with Key Management Service keys or Customer-provided keys
2.  Encrypt the data at the source using the client's CMK keys before transferring it to S3
3.  Use Multipart upload with SSL
4.  Make use of AWS S3 bucket policies to control access to the data at rest
5.  Use CloudHSM

## 44. Question

Your company has an on-premise LDAP directory service. As part of a gradual migration into AWS you would like to integrate the LDAP directory with AWS's Identity and Access Management (IAM) solutions so that existing users can authenticate against AWS services.

What method would you suggest using to enable this integration?

1.  Develop an on-premise custom identity provider (IdP) and use the AWS Security Token Service (STS) to provide temporary security credentials

2. Use SAML to develop a direct integration from the on-premise LDAP directory to the relevant AWS services
3. Create a policy in IAM that references users in the on-premise LDAP directory
4. Use AWS Simple AD and create a trust relationship with IAM

## 45. Question

You need to improve data security for your ElastiCache Redis cluster. How can you force users to enter a password before they are able to execute Redis commands?

1. Upload a key pair
2. Use Redis AUTH
3. Use a Cognito identity pool
4. Implement multi-factor authentication (MFA)

## 46. Question

A Kinesis consumer application is reading at a slower rate than expected. It has been identified that multiple consumer applications have total reads exceeding the per-shard limits. How can this situation be resolved?

1. Increase the number of shards in the Kinesis data stream
2. Implement API throttling to restrict the number of requests per-shard
3. Increase the number of read transactions per shard
4. Implement read throttling for the Kinesis data stream

## 47. Question

You are designing a solution on AWS that requires a file storage layer that can be shared between multiple EC2 instances. The storage should be highly-available and should scale easily.

Which AWS service can be used for this design?

1. Amazon S3
2. Amazon EFS
3. Amazon EC2 instance store
4. Amazon EBS

## 48. Question

You have been asked to take a snapshot of a non-root EBS volume that contains sensitive corporate data. You need to ensure you can capture all data that has been written to your Amazon EBS volume at the time the snapshot command is issued and are unable to pause any file writes to the volume long enough to take a snapshot.

What is the best way to take a consistent snapshot whilst minimizing application downtime?

1. Un-mount the EBS volume, take the snapshot, then re-mount it again
2. Take the snapshot while the EBS volume is attached and the instance is running
3. Stop the instance and take the snapshot
4. You can't take a snapshot for a non-root EBS volume

## 49. Question

You are working on a database migration plan from an on-premise data center that includes a variety of databases that are being used for diverse purposes. You are trying to map each database to the correct service in AWS.

Which of the below use cases are a good fit for DynamoDB (choose 2)

1. Complex queries and joins
2. Large amounts of dynamic data that require very low latency
3. Backup for on-premises Oracle DB
4. Migration from a Microsoft SQL relational database
5. Rapid ingestion of clickstream data


## 50. Question

You work as a System Administrator at Digital Cloud Training and your manager has asked you to investigate an EC2 web server hosting videos that is constantly running at over 80% CPU utilization. Which of the approaches below would you recommend to fix the issue?

1. Create a Launch Configuration from the instance using the CreateLaunchConfiguration action
2. Create a CloudFront distribution and configure the Amazon EC2 instance as the origin
3. Create an Elastic Load Balancer and register the EC2 instance to it
4. Create an Auto Scaling group from the instance using the CreateAutoScalingGroup action


## 51. Question

A Solutions Architect is designing a solution to store and archive corporate documents, and has determined that Amazon Glacier is the right solution. Data must be delivered within 10 minutes of a retrieval request.

Which features in Amazon Glacier can help meet this requirement?

1. Bulk retrieval
2. Expedited retrieval
3. Vault Lock
4. Standard retrieval


## 52. Question

A Solutions Architect is designing a mobile application that will capture receipt images to track expenses. The Architect wants to store the images on Amazon S3. However, uploading the images through the web server will create too much traffic.

What is the MOST efficient method to store images from a mobile application on Amazon S3?

1. Upload directly to S3 using a pre-signed URL
2. Upload to a second bucket, and have a Lambda event copy the image to the primary bucket
3. Expand the web server fleet with Spot instances to provide the resources to handle the images
4. Upload to a separate Auto Scaling Group of server behind an ELB Classic Load Balancer, and have the server instances write to the Amazon S3 bucket

## 53. Question

A company needs to deploy virtual desktops for its customers in an AWS VPC, and would like to leverage their existing on-premise security principles. AWS Workspaces will be used as the virtual desktop solution.

Which set of AWS services and features will meet the company's requirements?

1. A VPN connection, VPC NACLs and Security Groups
2. Amazon EC2, and AWS IAM
3. A VPN connection. AWS Directory Services
4. AWS Directory Service and AWS IAM

## 54. Question

An organization is considering ways to reduce administrative overhead and automate build processes. An Architect has suggested using CloudFormation. Which of the statements below are true regarding CloudFormation? (choose 2)

1. It provides visibility into user activity by recording actions taken on your account
2. It is used to collect and track metrics, collect and monitor log files, and set alarms
3. You pay for CloudFormation and the AWS resources created
4. Allows you to model your entire infrastructure in a text file
5. It provides a common language for you to describe and provision all the infrastructure resources in your cloud environment

## 55. Question

A legacy application running on-premises requires a Solutions Architect to be able to open a firewall to allow access to several Amazon S3 buckets. The Architect has a VPN connection to AWS in place.

Which option represents the simplest method for meeting this requirement?

1. Create an IAM role that allows access from the corporate network to Amazon S3
2. Configure IP whitelisting on the customer's gateway
3. Configure a proxy on Amazon EC2 and use an Amazon S3 VPC endpoint
4. Use Amazon API Gateway to do IP whitelisting

## 56. Question

You are planning to deploy a number of EC2 instances in your VPC. The EC2 instances will be deployed across several subnets and multiple AZs. What AWS feature can act as an instance-level firewall to control traffic between your EC2 instances?

1. AWS WAF
2. Security group
3. Route table
4. Network ACL

## 57. Question

You need a service that can provide you with control over which traffic to allow or block to your web applications by defining customizable web security rules. You need to block common attack patterns, such as SQL injection and cross-site scripting, as well as creating custom rules for your own applications.

**Which AWS service fits these requirements?**

1. Route 53
2. CloudFront
3. Security Groups
4. AWS WAF

## 58. Question

You would like to deploy an EC2 instance with enhanced networking. What are the pre-requisites for using enhanced networking? (choose 2)

1. Instances must be launched from a HVM AMI
2. Instances must be launched from a PV AMI
3. Instances must be launched in a VPC
4. Instances must be EBS backed, not Instance-store backed
5. Instances must be of T2 Micro type

## 59. Question

You have created an application in a VPC that uses a Network Load Balancer (NLB). The application will be offered in a service provider model for AWS principals in other accounts within the region to consume. Based on this model, what AWS service will be used to offer the service for consumption?

1. VPC Endpoint Services using AWS PrivateLink
2. API Gateway
3. IAM Role Based Access Control
4. Route 53

## 60. Question

Which service uses a simple text file to model and provision infrastructure resources, in an automated and secure manner?

1. OpsWorks
2. CloudFormation
3. Elastic Beanstalk
4. Simple Workflow Service

## 61. Question

An organization has a large amount of data on Windows (SMB) file shares in their on-premises data center. The organization would like to move data into Amazon S3. They would like to automate the migration of data over their AWS Direct Connect link.

**Which AWS service can assist them?**

1. AWS DataSync
2. AWS Snowball
3. AWS CloudFormation

4.   AWS Database Migration Service (DMS)

## 62. Question

An organization is extending a secure development environment into AWS. They have already secured the VPC including removing the Internet Gateway and setting up a Direct Connect connection.

What else needs to be done to add encryption?

1.   Setup a Virtual Private Gateway (VPG)
2.   Setup the Border Gateway Protocol (BGP) with encryption
3.   Configure an AWS Direct Connect Gateway
4.   Enable IPSec encryption on the Direct Connect connection

## 63. Question

An application running on an Amazon ECS container instance using the EC2 launch type needs permissions to write data to Amazon DynamoDB.

How can you assign these permissions only to the specific ECS task that is running the application?

1.   Modify the AmazonECSTaskExecutionRolePolicy policy to add permissions for DynamoDB
2.   Use a security group to allow outbound connections to DynamoDB and assign it to the container instance
3.   Create an IAM policy with permissions to DynamoDB and assign It to a task using the taskRoleArn parameter
4.   Create an IAM policy with permissions to DynamoDB and attach it to the container instance

## 64. Question

An Amazon RDS Read Replica is being deployed in a separate region. The master database is not encrypted but all data in the new region must be encrypted. How can this be achieved?

1.   Enable encryption using Key Management Service (KMS) when creating the cross-region Read Replica
2.   Encrypt a snapshot from the master DB instance, create a new encrypted master DB instance, and then create an encrypted cross-region Read Replica
3.   Encrypt a snapshot from the master DB instance, create an encrypted cross-region Read Replica from the snapshot
4.   Enabled encryption on the master DB instance, then create an encrypted cross-region Read Replica

## 65. Question

A legacy tightly-coupled High Performance Computing (HPC) application will be migrated to AWS. Which network adapter type should be used?

1.   Elastic Network Adapter (ENA)
2.   Elastic Fabric Adapter (EFA)
3.   Elastic IP Address
4.   Elastic Network Interface (ENI)

# SET 3: PRACTICE QUESTIONS, ANSWERS & EXPLANATIONS

## 1. Question

Your Business Intelligence team use SQL tools to analyze data. What would be the best solution for performing queries on structured data that is being received at a high velocity?

1. EMR using Hive
2. Kinesis Firehose with RedShift
3. Kinesis Firehose with RDS
4. EMR running Apache Spark

**Answer: 2**

**Explanation:**

- Kinesis Data Firehose is the easiest way to load streaming data into data stores and analytics tools. Firehose Destinations include: Amazon S3, Amazon Redshift, Amazon Elasticsearch Service, and Splunk
- Amazon Redshift is a fast, fully managed data warehouse that makes it simple and cost-effective to analyze all your data using standard SQL and existing Business Intelligence (BI) tools
- EMR is a hosted Hadoop framework and doesn't natively support SQL
- RDS is a transactional database and is not a supported Kinesis Firehose destination

**References:**

https://digitalcloud.training/certification-training/aws-solutions-architect-associate/analytics/amazon-kinesis/

## 2. Question

A Solutions Architect is migrating a small relational database into AWS. The database will run on an EC2 instance and the DB size is around 500 GB. The database is infrequently used with small amounts of requests spread across the day. The DB is a low priority and the Architect needs to lower the cost of the solution.

What is the MOST cost-effective storage type?

1. Amazon EBS Provisioned IOPS SSD
2. Amazon EBS Throughput Optimized HDD
3. Amazon EBS General Purpose SSD
4. Amazon EFS

**Answer: 2**

**Explanation:**

- Throughput Optimized HDD is the most cost-effective storage option and for a small DB with low traffic volumes it may be sufficient. Note that the volume must be at least 500 GB in size
- Provisioned IOPS SSD provides high performance but at a higher cost
- AWS recommend using General Purpose SSD rather than Throughput Optimized HDD for most use cases but it is more expensive

- The Amazon Elastic File System (EFS) is not an ideal storage solution for a database

**References:**

https://digitalcloud.training/certification-training/aws-solutions-architect-associate/compute/amazon-ebs/

## 3. Question

A Solutions Architect has been asked to improve the performance of a DynamoDB table. Latency is currently a few milliseconds and this needs to be reduced to microseconds whilst also scaling to millions of requests per second.

**What is the BEST architecture to support this?**

1. Reduce the number of Scan operations
2. Use CloudFront to cache the content
3. Create an ElastiCache Redis cluster
4. Create a DynamoDB Accelerator (DAX) cluster

**Answer: 4**

**Explanation:**

- Amazon DynamoDB Accelerator (DAX) is a fully managed, highly available, in-memory cache for DynamoDB that delivers up to a 10x performance improvement – from milliseconds to microseconds – even at millions of requests per second
- It is possible to use ElastiCache in front of DynamoDB, however this is not a supported architecture
- DynamoDB is not a supported origin for CloudFront
- Reducing the number of Scan operations on DynamoDB may improve performance but will not reduce latency to microseconds

**References:**

https://aws.amazon.com/dynamodb/dax/

## 4. Question

You are developing an application that uses Lambda functions. You need to store some sensitive data that includes credentials for accessing the database tier. You are planning to store this data as environment variables within Lambda. How can you ensure this sensitive information is properly secured?

1. There is no need to make any changes as all environment variables are encrypted by default with AWS Lambda
2. Use encryption helpers that leverage AWS Key Management Service to store the sensitive information as Ciphertext
3. This cannot be done, only the environment variables that relate to the Lambda function itself can be encrypted
4. Store the environment variables in an encrypted DynamoDB table and configure Lambda to retrieve them as required

**Answer: 2**

**Explanation:**

- Environment variables for Lambda functions enable you to dynamically pass settings to your function code and libraries, without making changes to your code. Environment variables are key-value pairs that you create and modify as part of your function configuration, using either the AWS Lambda Console, the AWS Lambda CLI or the AWS Lambda SDK. You can use environment variables to help libraries know what directory to install files in, where to store outputs, store connection and logging settings, and more

- When you deploy your Lambda function, all the environment variables you've specified are encrypted by default after, but not during, the deployment process. They are then decrypted automatically by AWS Lambda when the function is invoked. If you need to store sensitive information in an environment variable, we strongly suggest you encrypt that information before deploying your Lambda function. The Lambda console makes that easier for you by providing encryption helpers that leverage AWS Key Management Service to store that sensitive information as Ciphertext

- The environment variables are not encrypted throughout the entire process so there is a need to take action here. Storing the variables in an encrypted DynamoDB table is not necessary when you can use encryption helpers

**References:**

https://digitalcloud.training/certification-training/aws-solutions-architect-associate/compute/aws-lambda/

https://docs.aws.amazon.com/lambda/latest/dg/env_variables.html

## 5. Question

You have implemented API Gateway and enabled a cache for a specific stage. How can you control the cache to enhance performance and reduce load on back-end services?

1. Configure the throttling feature
2. Using CloudFront controls
3. Enable bursting
4. Using time-to-live (TTL) settings

**Answer: 4**

**Explanation:**

- Caches are provisioned for a specific stage of your APIs. Caching features include customisable keys and time-to-live (TTL) in seconds for your API data which enhances response times and reduces load on back-end services.

- You can throttle and monitor requests to protect your back-end, but the cache is used to reduce the load on the back-end.

- Bursting isn't an API Gateway feature that you can enable or disable.

- CloudFront is a bogus answer as even though it does have a cache of its own it won't help you to enhance the performance of the API Gateway cache.

**References:**

https://digitalcloud.training/certification-training/aws-solutions-architect-associate/networking-and-content-delivery/amazon-api-gateway/

## 6. Question

You are implementing an Elastic Load Balancer (ELB) for an application that will use encrypted communications. Which two types of security policies are supported by the Elastic Load Balancer for SSL negotiations between the ELB and clients? (choose 2)

1. ELB predefined Security policies
2. AES 256
3. Network ACLs
4. Security groups
5. Custom security policies

**Answer: 1,5**

**Explanation:**

- AWS recommend that you always use the default predefined security policy. When choosing a custom security policy you can select the ciphers and protocols (only for CLB)
- Security groups and network ACLs are security controls that apply to instances and subnets
- AES 256 is an encryption protocol, not a policy

**References:**

https://digitalcloud.training/certification-training/aws-solutions-architect-associate/compute/elastic-load-balancing/

## 7. Question

A company is migrating an on-premises 10 TB MySQL database to AWS. The company expects the database to quadruple in size and the business requirement is that replicate lag must be kept under 100 milliseconds.

Which Amazon RDS engine meets these requirements?

1. Amazon Aurora
2. Oracle
3. Microsoft SQL Server
4. MySQL

**Answer: 1**

**Explanation:**

- Aurora databases can scale up to 64 TB and Aurora replicas features millisecond latency
- All other RDS engines have a limit of 16 TiB maximum DB size and asynchronous replication typically takes seconds

**References:**

https://digitalcloud.training/certification-training/aws-solutions-architect-associate/database/amazon-rds/

https://docs.aws.amazon.com/AmazonRDS/latest/AuroraUserGuide/CHAP_Limits.html

## 8. Question

You have been asked to deploy a new High-Performance Computing (HPC) cluster. You need to create a design for the EC2 instances that ensures close proximity, low latency and high network throughput.

Which AWS features will help you to achieve this requirement whilst considering cost? (choose 2)

1. Use EC2 instances with Enhanced Networking
2. Use dedicated hosts
3. Launch I/O Optimized EC2 instances in one private subnet in an AZ
4. Use Placement groups
5. Use Provisioned IOPS EBS volumes

Answer: 1,4

Explanation:

- Placement groups are a logical grouping of instances in one of the following configurations:
    - Cluster—clusters instances into a low-latency group in a single AZ
    - Spread—spreads instances across underlying hardware (can span AZs)
- Placement groups are recommended for applications that benefit from low latency and high bandwidth and it s recommended to use an instance type that supports enhanced networking. Instances within a placement group can communicate with each other using private or public IP addresses
- I/O optimized instances and provisioned IOPS EBS volumes are more geared towards storage performance than network performance
- Dedicated hosts might ensure close proximity of instances but would not be cost efficient

References:

https://digitalcloud.training/certification-training/aws-solutions-architect-associate/compute/amazon-ec2/

## 9. Question

Your company currently uses Puppet Enterprise for infrastructure and application management. You are looking to move some of your infrastructure onto AWS and would like to continue to use the same tools in the cloud. What AWS service provides a fully managed configuration management service that is compatible with Puppet Enterprise?

1. CloudFormation
2. OpsWorks
3. Elastic Beanstalk
4. CloudTrail

Answer: 2

Explanation:

- The only service that would allow you to continue to use the same tools is OpsWorks. AWS OpsWorks is a configuration management service that provides managed instances of Chef and Puppet. OpsWorks lets you use Chef and Puppet to automate how servers are configured, deployed, and managed across your Amazon EC2 instances or on-premises compute environments.

**References:**

https://digitalcloud.training/certification-training/aws-solutions-architect-associate/management-tools/aws-opsworks/

https://docs.aws.amazon.com/opsworks/latest/userguide/welcome.html

## 10. Question

You are a Solutions Architect for an insurance company. An application you manage is used to store photos and video files that relate to insurance claims. The application writes data using the iSCSI protocol to a storage array. The array currently holds 10TB of data and is approaching capacity.

Your manager has instructed you that he will not approve further capital expenditure for on-premises infrastructure. Therefore, you are planning to migrate data into the cloud. How can you move data into the cloud whilst retaining low-latency access to frequently accessed data on-premise using the iSCSI protocol?

1. Use an AWS Storage Gateway File Gateway in cached volume mode
2. Use an AWS Storage Gateway Virtual Tape Library
3. Use an AWS Storage Gateway Volume Gateway in cached volume mode
4. Use an AWS Storage Gateway Volume Gateway in stored volume mode

**Answer: 3**

**Explanation:**

- The AWS Storage Gateway service enables hybrid storage between on-premises environments and the AWS Cloud. It provides low-latency performance by caching frequently accessed data on premises, while storing data securely and durably in Amazon cloud storage services
- AWS Storage Gateway supports three storage interfaces: file, volume, and tape
- File:
  - File gateway provides a virtual on-premises file server, which enables you to store and retrieve files as objects in Amazon S3
  - File gateway offers SMB or NFS-based access to data in Amazon S3 with local caching — the question asks for an iSCSI (block) storage solution so a file gateway is not the right solution
- Volume:
  - The volume gateway represents the family of gateways that support block-based volumes, previously referred to as gateway-cached and gateway-stored modes
  - Block storage – iSCSI based – the volume gateway is the correct solution choice as it provides iSCSI (block) storage which is compatible with the existing configuration
- Tape:
  - Used for backup with popular backup software
  - Each gateway is preconfigured with a media changer and tape drives. Supported by NetBackup, Backup Exec, Veeam etc.

**References:**

https://digitalcloud.training/certification-training/aws-solutions-architect-associate/storage/aws-storage-gateway/

## 11. Question

You are a Solutions Architect at Digital Cloud Training. One of your clients is an online media company that attracts a large volume of users to their website each day. The media company are interested in analyzing the user's clickstream data so they can analyze user behavior in real-time and dynamically update advertising. This intelligent approach to advertising should help them to increase conversions.

What would you suggest as a solution to assist them with capturing and analyzing this data?

1. Update the application to write data to an SQS queue, and create an additional application component to analyze the data in the queue and update the website
2. Use EMR to process and analyze the data in real-time and Lambda to update the website based on the results
3. Use Kinesis Data Streams to process and analyze the clickstream data. Store the results in DynamoDB and create an application component that reads the data from the database and updates the website
4. Write the data directly to RedShift and use Business Intelligence tools to analyze the data

Answer: 3

Explanation:

- This is an ideal use case for Kinesis Data Streams which can process and analyze the clickstream data. Kinesis Data Streams stores the results in a number of supported services which includes DynamoDB
- SQS does not provide a solution for analyzing the data
- RedShift is a data warehouse and good for analytics on structured data. It is not used for real time ingestion
- EMR utilizes a hosted Hadoop framework running on Amazon EC2 and Amazon S3 and is used for processing large quantities of data. It is not suitable for this solution

References:

https://digitalcloud.training/certification-training/aws-solutions-architect-associate/analytics/amazon-kinesis/

## 12. Question

A systems integration company that helps customers migrate into AWS repeatedly build large, standardized architectures using several AWS services. The Solutions Architects have documented the architectural blueprints for these solutions and are looking for a method of automating the provisioning of the resources.

Which AWS service would satisfy this requirement?

1. Elastic Beanstalk
2. AWS CloudFormation
3. AWS OpsWorks
4. AWS CodeDeploy

Answer: 2

Explanation:

- CloudFormation allows you to use a simple text file to model and provision, in an automated and secure manner, all the resources needed for your applications across all regions and accounts
- Elastic Beanstalk is a PaaS service that helps you to build and manage web applications
- AWS OpsWorks is a configuration management service that helps you build and operate highly dynamic applications, and propagate changes instantly
- AWS CodeDeploy is a deployment service that automates application deployments to Amazon EC2 instances, on-premises instances, or serverless Lambda functions

References:

https://digitalcloud.training/certification-training/aws-solutions-architect-associate/management-tools/aws-cloudformation/

## 13. Question

A Solutions Architect is designing a static website that will use the zone apex of a DNS domain (e.g. example.com). The Architect wants to use the Amazon Route 53 service. Which steps should the Architect take to implement a scalable and cost-effective solution? (choose 2)

1. Host the website on an Amazon EC2 instance with ELB and Auto Scaling, and map a Route 53 Alias record to the ELB endpoint
2. Host the website using AWS Elastic Beanstalk, and map a Route 53 Alias record to the Beanstalk stack
3. Host the website on an Amazon EC2 instance, and map a Route 53 Alias record to the public IP address of the EC2 instance
4. Create a Route 53 hosted zone, and set the NS records of the domain to use Route 53 name servers
5. Serve the website from an Amazon S3 bucket, and map a Route 53 Alias record to the website endpoint

Answer: 4,5

Explanation:

- To use Route 53 for an existing domain the Architect needs to change the NS records to point to the Amazon Route 53 name servers. This will direct name resolution to Route 53 for the domain name. The most cost-effective solution for hosting the website will be to use an Amazon S3 bucket. To do this you create a bucket using the same name as the domain name (e.g. example.com) and use a Route 53 Alias record to map to it
- Using an EC2 instance instead of an S3 bucket would be more costly so that rules out 2 options that explicitly mention EC2
- Elastic Beanstalk provisions EC2 instances so again this would be a more costly option

References:

https://docs.aws.amazon.com/AmazonS3/latest/dev/website-hosting-custom-domain-walkthrough.html

## 14. Question

A Solutions Architect is planning to run some Docker containers on Amazon ECS. The Architect needs to define some parameters for the containers. What application parameters can be defined in an ECS task definition? (choose 2)

1. The ELB node to be used to scale the task containers

2. The security group rules to apply
3. The ports that should be opened on the container instance for your application
4. The container images to use and the repositories in which they are located
5. The application configuration

**Answer: 3,4**

**Explanation:**

Some of the parameters you can specify in a task definition include:

- Which Docker images to use with the containers in your task
- How much CPU and memory to use with each container
- Whether containers are linked together in a task
- The Docker networking mode to use for the containers in your task
- What (if any) ports from the container are mapped to the host container instances
- Whether the task should continue if the container finished or fails
- The commands the container should run when it is started
- Environment variables that should be passed to the container when it starts
- Data volumes that should be used with the containers in the task
- IAM role the task should use for permissions

**References:**

https://digitalcloud.training/certification-training/aws-solutions-architect-associate/compute/amazon-ecs/

## 15. Question

A major upcoming sales event is likely to result in heavy read traffic to a web application your company manages. As the Solutions Architect you have been asked for advice on how best to protect the database tier from the heavy load and ensure the user experience is not impacted.

The web application owner has also requested that the design be fault tolerant. The current configuration consists of a web application behind an ELB that uses Auto Scaling and an RDS MySQL database running in a multi-AZ configuration. As the database load is highly changeable the solution should allow elasticity by adding and removing nodes as required and should also be multi-threaded.

**What recommendations would you make?**

1. Deploy an ElastiCache Redis cluster with cluster mode disabled and multi-AZ with automatic failover
2. Deploy an ElastiCache Redis cluster with cluster mode enabled and multi-AZ with automatic failover
3. Deploy an ElastiCache Memcached cluster in multi-AZ mode in the same AZs as RDS
4. Deploy an ElastiCache Memcached cluster in both AZs in which the RDS database is deployed

**Answer: 4**

**Explanation:**

- ElastiCache is a web service that makes it easy to deploy and run Memcached or Redis protocol-compliant server nodes in the cloud

- The in-memory caching provided by ElastiCache can be used to significantly improve latency and throughput for many read-heavy application workloads or compute-intensive workloads
- Memcached
  - Not persistent
  - Cannot be used as a data store
  - Supports large nodes with multiple cores or threads
  - Scales out and in, by adding and removing nodes
- Redis
  - Data is persistent
  - Can be used as a datastore
  - Not multi-threaded
  - Scales by adding shards, not nodes

**References:**

https://digitalcloud.training/certification-training/aws-solutions-architect-associate/database/amazon-elasticache/

https://docs.aws.amazon.com/AmazonElastiCache/latest/mem-ug/SelectEngine.html

## 16. Question

An application currently stores all data on Amazon EBS volumes. All EBS volumes must be backed up durably across multiple Availability Zones.

**What is the MOST resilient way to back up volumes?**

1. Create a script to copy data to an EC2 instance store
2. Enable EBS volume encryption
3. Mirror data across two EBS volumes
4. Take regular EBS snapshots

**Answer: 4**

**Explanation:**

1. EBS snapshots are stored in S3 and are therefore replicated across multiple locations
2. Enabling volume encryption would not increase resiliency
3. Instance stores are ephemeral (non-persistent) data stores so would not add any resilience
4. Mirroring data would provide resilience however both volumes would need to be mounted to the EC2 instance within the same AZ so you are not getting the redundancy required

**References:**

https://digitalcloud.training/certification-training/aws-solutions-architect-associate/compute/amazon-ebs/

## 17. Question

You work for Digital Cloud Training and have just created a number of IAM users in your AWS account. You need to ensure that the users are able to make API calls to AWS services. What else needs to be done?

1. Enable Multi-Factor Authentication for the users
2. Create a set of Access Keys for the users

3. Create a group and add the users to it
4. Set a password for each user

**Answer: 2**

**Explanation:**

- Access keys are a combination of an access key ID and a secret access key and you can assign two active access keys to a user at a time. These can be used to make programmatic calls to AWS when using the API in program code or at a command prompt when using the AWS CLI or the AWS PowerShell tools
- A password is needed for logging into the console but not for making API calls to AWS services. Similarly you don't need to create a group and add the users to it to provide access to make API calls to AWS services
- Multi-factor authentication can be used to control access to AWS service APIs but the question is not asking how to better secure the calls but just being able to make them

**References:**

https://digitalcloud.training/certification-training/aws-solutions-architect-associate/security-identity-compliance/aws-iam/

## 18. Question

A Solutions Architect is designing a workload that requires a high performance object-based storage system that must be shared with multiple Amazon EC2 instances.

**Which AWS service delivers these requirements?**

1. Amazon S3
2. Amazon EFS
3. Amazon EBS
4. Amazon ElastiCache

**Answer: 1**

**Explanation:**

- Amazon S3 is an object-based storage system. Though object storage systems aren't mounted and shared like filesystems or block based storage systems they can be shared by multiple instances as they allow concurrent access
- Amazon EFS is file-based storage system it is not object-based
- Amazon EBS is a block-based storage system it is not object-based
- Amazon ElastiCache is a database caching service

**References:**

https://digitalcloud.training/certification-training/aws-solutions-architect-associate/storage/amazon-s3/

## 19. Question

A client from the agricultural sector has approached you for some advice around the collection of a large volume of data from sensors they have deployed around the country.

An application needs to collect data from over 100,000 sensors and each sensor will send around 1KB of data every minute. The data needs to then be stored in a durable, low latency data store. The client also needs historical data that is over 1 year old to be moved into a data warehouse where they can perform analytics using standard SQL queries.

What combination of AWS services would you recommend to the client? (choose 2)

1. Use Amazon Elastic Map Reduce (EMR) for analytics
2. Use Amazon RedShift for the analytics
3. Use Amazon Kinesis data streams for data ingestion and enable extended data retention to store data for 1 year
4. Use Amazon Kinesis Data Firehose for data ingestion and configure a consumer to store data in Amazon DynamoDB
5. Use Amazon Kinesis Data Streams for data ingestion and configure a consumer to store data in Amazon DynamoDB

Answer: 2,5

Explanation:

- The key requirements are that historical data that data is recorded in a low latency, durable data store and then moved into a data warehouse when the data is over 1 year old for historical analytics. This is a good use case for using a Kinesis Data Streams producer for ingestion of the real-time data and then configuring a Kinesis Data Streams consumer to write the data to DynamoDB which is a low latency data store that can be used for holding the data for the first year
- Amazon Redshift is an ideal use case for storing longer term data and performing analytics on it. It is a fast, fully managed data warehouse that makes it simple and cost-effective to analyze all your data using standard SQL and existing Business Intelligence (BI) tools. RedShift is a SQL based data warehouse used for analytics applications
- You cannot configure DynamoDB as a destination in Amazon Kinesis Firehose. The options are S3, RedShift, Elasticsearch and Splunk
- When you have enabled extended data retention you can store data up to 7 days in Amazon Kinesis Data Streams – you cannot store it for 1 year
- Amazon EMR provides a managed Hadoop framework that makes it easy, fast, and cost-effective to process vast amounts of data across dynamically scalable Amazon EC2 instances. We're looking for a data warehouse in this solution so running up EC2 instances may not be cost-effective

References:

https://digitalcloud.training/certification-training/aws-solutions-architect-associate/database/amazon-dynamodb/

https://digitalcloud.training/certification-training/aws-solutions-architect-associate/database/amazon-redshift/

## 20. Question

An EC2 status check on an EBS volume is showing as *insufficient-data*. What is the most likely explanation?

1. The checks have failed on the volume
2. The checks require more information to be manually entered
3. The checks may still be in progress on the volume
4. The volume does not have enough data on it to check properly

**Answer: 3**

**Explanation:**

- The possible values are ok, impaired, warning, or insufficient-data. If all checks pass, the overall status of the volume is ok. If the check fails, the overall status is impaired. If the status is insufficient-data, then the checks may still be taking place on your volume at the time
- The checks do not require manual input and they have not failed or the status would be impaired. The volume does not need a certain amount of data on it to be checked properly

**References:**

https://digitalcloud.training/certification-training/aws-solutions-architect-associate/compute/amazon-ebs/

https://docs.aws.amazon.com/AWSEC2/latest/APIReference/API_DescribeVolumeStatus.html

## 21. Question

You run a two-tier application with a web tier that is behind an Internet-facing Elastic Load Balancer (ELB). You need to restrict access to the web tier to a specific list of public IP addresses.

What are two possible ways you can implement this requirement? (choose 2)

1. Configure a VPC NACL to allow web traffic from the list of IPs and deny all outbound traffic
2. Configure the VPC internet gateway to allow incoming traffic from these IP addresses
3. Configure the proxy protocol on the web servers and filter traffic based on IP address
4. Configure your ELB to send the X-forwarded for headers and the web servers to filter traffic based on the ELB's "X-forwarded-for" header
5. Configure the ELB security group to allow traffic only from the specific list of IPs

**Answer: 4,5**

**Explanation:**

- There are two methods you can use to restrict access from some known IP addresses. You can either use the ELB security group rules or you can configure the ELB to send the X-Forwarded For headers to the web servers. The web servers can then filter traffic using a local firewall such as iptables
- X-forwarded-for for HTTP/HTTPS carries the source IP/port information. X-forwarded-for only applies to L7. The ELB security group controls the ports and protocols that can reach the front-end listener
- Proxy protocol applies to layer 4 and is not configured on the web servers
- A NACL is applied at the subnet level and as they are stateless if you deny all outbound traffic return traffic will be blocked
- You cannot configure an Internet gateway to allow this traffic. Internet gateways are used for outbound Internet access from public subnets

**References:**

https://digitalcloud.training/certification-training/aws-solutions-architect-associate/compute/elastic-load-balancing/

## 22. Question

An issue has been reported whereby Amazon EC2 instances are not being terminated from an Auto Scaling Group behind an ELB when traffic volumes are low. How can this be fixed?

1. Modify the scale down increment
2. Modify the scaling settings on the ELB
3. Modify the lower threshold settings on the ASG
4. Modify the upper threshold settings on the ASG

Answer: 3

Explanation:

- The lower threshold may be set to high. With the lower threshold if the metric falls below this number for the breach duration, a scaling operation is triggered. If it's set too high you may find that your Auto Scaling group does not scale-in when required
- The upper threshold is the metric that, if the metric exceeds this number for the breach duration, a scaling operation is triggered. This would be adjusted when you need to change the behaviour of scale-out events
- You do not change scaling settings on an ELB, you change them on the Auto Scaling group
- The scale down increment defines the number of EC2 instances to remove when performing a scaling activity. This changes the number of instances that are removed but does not change the conditions in which they are removed which is the problem we need to solve here

References:

https://docs.aws.amazon.com/elasticbeanstalk/latest/dg/environments-cfg-autoscaling-triggers.html

## 23. Question

A Solutions Architect is designing a solution for a financial application that will receive trading data in large volumes. What is the best solution for ingesting and processing a very large number of data streams in near real time?

1. Amazon EMR
2. Amazon Kinesis Data Streams
3. Amazon Redshift
4. Amazon Kinesis Firehose

Answer: 2

Explanation:

- Kinesis Data Streams enables you to build custom applications that process or analyze streaming data for specialized needs. It enables real-time processing of streaming big data and can be used for rapidly moving data off data producers and then continuously processing the data. Kinesis Data Streams stores data for later processing by applications (key difference with Firehose which delivers data directly to AWS services)
- Kinesis Firehose can allow transformation of data and it then delivers data to supported services
- RedShift is a data warehouse solution used for analyzing data
- EMR is a hosted Hadoop framework that is used for analytics

References:

## 24. Question

You have been asked to recommend the best AWS storage solution for a client. The client requires a storage solution that provide a mounted file system for a Big Data and Analytics application. The client's requirements include high throughput, low latency, read-after-write consistency and the ability to burst up to multiple GB/s for short periods of time.

Which AWS service can meet this requirement?

1. S3
2. DynamoDB
3. EBS
4. EFS

**Answer: 4**

**Explanation:**

- EFS is a fully-managed service that makes it easy to set up and scale file storage in the Amazon Cloud. EFS is good for big data and analytics, media processing workflows, content management, web serving, home directories etc.. EFS uses the NFSv4.1 protocol which is a protocol for mounting file systems (similar to Microsoft's SMB)
- EBS is mounted as a block device not a file system
- S3 is object storage
- DynamoDB is a fully managed NoSQL database

**References:**

https://digitalcloud.training/certification-training/aws-solutions-architect-associate/storage/amazon-efs/

## 25. Question

A company runs a legacy application with a single-tier architecture on an Amazon EC2 instance. Disk I/O is low, with occasional small spikes during business hours. The company requires the instance to be stopped from 8pm to 8am daily.

Which storage option is MOST appropriate for this workload?

1. Amazon EBS Provisioned IOPS SSD (io1) storage
2. Amazon S3
3. Amazon EBS General Purpose SSD (gp2) storage
4. Amazon EC2 Instance Store storage

**Answer: 3**

**Explanation:**

- Amazon EBS General Purpose SSD is recommended for most workloads. This will provide enough performance and keep the costs lower than provisioned IOPS SSD
- Amazon EC2 instance store storage is not persistent so the data would be lost when the system is powered off each night

- The legacy application may not be able to write to object storage (Amazon S3)

References:

https://digitalcloud.training/certification-training/aws-solutions-architect-associate/compute/amazon-ebs/

## 26. Question

An EC2 instance in an Auto Scaling group that has been reported as unhealthy has been marked for replacement. What is the process Auto Scaling uses to replace the instance? (choose 2)

1. Auto Scaling will send a notification to the administrator
2. Auto Scaling will terminate the existing instance before launching a replacement instance
3. If connection draining is enabled, Auto Scaling will wait for in-flight connections to complete or timeout
4. Auto Scaling has to perform rebalancing first, and then terminate the instance
5. Auto Scaling has to launch a replacement first before it can terminate the unhealthy instance

Answer: 2,3

Explanation:

- If connection draining is enabled, Auto Scaling waits for in-flight requests to complete or timeout before terminating instances. Auto Scaling will terminate the existing instance before launching a replacement instance
- Auto Scaling does not send a notification to the administrator
- Unlike AZ rebalancing, termination of unhealthy instances happens first, then Auto Scaling attempts to launch new instances to replace terminated instances

References:

https://digitalcloud.training/certification-training/aws-solutions-architect-associate/compute/aws-auto-scaling/

## 27. Question

You have an application running in ap-southeast that requires six EC2 instances running at all times.

With three Availability Zones available in that region (ap-southeast-2a, ap-southeast-2b, and ap-southeast-2c), which of the following deployments provides fault tolerance if any single Availability Zone in ap-southeast-2 becomes unavailable? (choose 2)

1. 2 EC2 instances in ap-southeast-2a, 2 EC2 instances in ap-southeast-2b, 2 EC2 instances in ap-southeast-2c
2. 3 EC2 instances in ap-southeast-2a, 3 EC2 instances in ap-southeast-2b, no EC2 instances in ap-southeast-2c
3. 4 EC2 instances in ap-southeast-2a, 2 EC2 instances in ap-southeast-2b, 2 EC2 instances in ap-southeast-2c
4. 6 EC2 instances in ap-southeast-2a, 6 EC2 instances in ap-southeast-2b, no EC2 instances in ap-southeast-2c
5. 3 EC2 instances in ap-southeast-2a, 3 EC2 instances in ap-southeast-2b, 3 EC2 instances in ap-southeast-2c

**Answer: 4,5**

**Explanation:**

- This is a simple mathematical problem. Take note that the question asks that 6 instances must be available in the event that ANY SINGLE AZ becomes unavailable. There are only 2 options that fulfil these criteria

**References:**

https://digitalcloud.training/certification-training/aws-solutions-architect-associate/compute/amazon-ec2/

https://digitalcloud.training/certification-training/aws-solutions-architect-associate/networking-and-content-delivery/amazon-vpc/

## 28. Question

**For which of the following workloads should a Solutions Architect consider using Elastic Beanstalk? (choose 2)**

1. A management task run occasionally
2. Caching content for Internet-based delivery
3. A long running worker process
4. A data lake
5. A web application using Amazon RDS

**Answer: 3,5**

**Explanation:**

- A web application using RDS is a good fit as it includes multiple services and Elastic Beanstalk is an orchestration engine
- A data lake would not be a good fit for Elastic Beanstalk
- A Long running worker process is a good Elastic Beanstalk use case where it manages an SQS queue – again this is an example of multiple services being orchestrated
- Content caching would be a good use case for CloudFront
- A management task run occasionally might be a good fit for AWS Systems Manager Automation

**References:**

https://digitalcloud.training/certification-training/aws-solutions-architect-associate/compute/aws-elastic-beanstalk/

https://aws.amazon.com/elasticbeanstalk/faqs/

## 29. Question

**You need to create a file system that can be concurrently accessed by multiple EC2 instances within an AZ. The file system needs to support high throughput and the ability to burst. As the data that will be stored on the file system will be sensitive you need to ensure it is encrypted at rest and in transit.**

**What storage solution would you implement for the EC2 instances?**

1. Use the Elastic File System (EFS) and mount the file system using NFS v4.1
2. Use the Elastic Block Store (EBS) and mount the file system at the block level

3. Add EBS volumes to each EC2 instance and use an ELB to distribute data evenly between the volumes
4. Add EBS volumes to each EC2 instance and configure data replication

**Answer: 1**

**Explanation:**

- EFS is a fully-managed service that makes it easy to set up and scale file storage in the Amazon Cloud
- EFS uses the NFSv4.1 protocol
- Amazon EFS is designed to burst to allow high throughput levels for periods of time
- EFS offers the ability to encrypt data at rest and in transit

**References:**

https://digitalcloud.training/certification-training/aws-solutions-architect-associate/storage/amazon-efs/

## 30. Question

A Solutions Architect is designing a web page for event registrations and needs a managed service to send a text message to users every time users sign up for an event.

**Which AWS service should the Architect use to achieve this?**

1. Amazon STS
2. Amazon SQS
3. AWS Lambda
4. Amazon SNS

**Answer: 4**

**Explanation:**

- Amazon Simple Notification Service (SNS) is a web service that makes it easy to set up, operate, and send notifications from the cloud and supports notifications over multiple transports including HTTP/HTTPS, Email/Email-JSON, SQS and SMS
- Amazon Security Token Service (STS) is used for requesting temporary credentials
- Amazon Simple Queue Service (SQS) is a message queue used for decoupling application components
- Lambda is a serverless service that runs code in response to events/triggers

**References:**

https://digitalcloud.training/certification-training/aws-solutions-architect-associate/application-integration/amazon-sns/

## 31. Question

A Solutions Architect is developing an application that will store and index large (>1 MB) JSON files. The data store must be highly available and latency must be consistently low even during times of heavy usage. Which service should the Architect use?

1. AWS CloudFormation

2. DynamoDB
3. Amazon RedShift
4. Amazon EFS

**Answer: 4**

**Explanation:**

- EFS provides a highly-available data store with consistent low latencies and elasticity to scale as required
- RedShift is a data warehouse that is used for analyzing data using SQL
- DynamoDB is a low latency, highly available NoSQL DB. You can store JSON files up to 400KB in size in a DynamoDB table, for anything bigger you'd want to store a pointer to an object outside of the table
- CloudFormation is an orchestration tool and does not help with storing documents

**References:**

https://digitalcloud.training/certification-training/aws-solutions-architect-associate/storage/amazon-efs/

## 32. Question

An Architect is designing a serverless application that will accept images uploaded by users from around the world. The application will make API calls to back-end services and save the session state data of the user to a database.

Which combination of services would provide a solution that is cost-effective while delivering the least latency?

1. Amazon S3, API Gateway, AWS Lambda, Amazon RDS
2. Amazon CloudFront, API Gateway, Amazon S3, AWS Lambda, Amazon RDS
3. API Gateway, Amazon S3, AWS Lambda, DynamoDB
4. Amazon CloudFront, API Gateway, Amazon S3, AWS Lambda, DynamoDB

**Answer: 4**

**Explanation:**

- Amazon CloudFront caches content closer to users at Edge locations around the world. This is the lowest latency option for uploading content. API Gateway and AWS Lambda are present in all options. DynamoDB can be used for storing session state data
- The option that presents API Gateway first does not offer a front-end for users to upload content to
- Amazon RDS is not a serverless service so this option can be ruled out
- Amazon S3 alone will not provide the least latency for users around the world unless you have many buckets in different regions and a way of directing users to the closest bucket (such as Route 3 latency based routing). However, you would then need to manage replicating the data

**References:**

https://digitalcloud.training/certification-training/aws-solutions-architect-associate/networking-and-content-delivery/amazon-cloudfront/

https://aws.amazon.com/blogs/aws/amazon-cloudfront-content-uploads-post-put-other-methods/

## 33. Question

A Solutions Architect is determining the best method for provisioning Internet connectivity for a data-processing application that will pull large amounts of data from an object storage system via the Internet. The solution must be redundant and have no constraints on bandwidth.

Which option satisfies these requirements?

1. Attach an Internet Gateway
2. Create a VPC endpoint
3. Use a NAT Gateway
4. Deploy NAT Instances in a public subnet

Answer: 1

Explanation:

- Both a NAT gateway and an Internet gateway offer redundancy however the NAT gateway is limited to 45 Gbps whereas the IGW does not impose any limits
- A VPC endpoint is used to access public services from a VPC without traversing the Internet
- NAT instances are EC2 instances that are used, in a similar way to NAT gateways, by instances in private subnets to access the Internet. However they are not redundant and are limited in bandwidth

References:

https://digitalcloud.training/certification-training/aws-solutions-architect-associate/storage/amazon-s3/

## 34. Question

The development team at your company have created a new mobile application that will be used by users to access confidential data. The developers have used Amazon Cognito for authentication, authorization, and user management. Due to the sensitivity of the data, there is a requirement to add another method of authentication in addition to a username and password.

You have been asked to recommend the best solution. What is your recommendation?

1. Enable multi-factor authentication (MFA) in IAM
2. Use multi-factor authentication (MFA) with a Cognito user pool
3. Integrate IAM with a user pool in Cognito
4. Integrate a third-party identity provider (IdP)

Answer: 2

Explanation:

- You can use MFA with a Cognito user pool (not in IAM) and this satisfies the requirement.
- A user pool is a user directory in Amazon Cognito. With a user pool, your users can sign in to your web or mobile app through Amazon Cognito. Your users can also sign in through social identity providers like Facebook or Amazon, and through SAML identity providers
- Integrating IAM with a Cognito user pool or integrating a 3rd party IdP does not add another factor of authentication – "factors" include something you know (e.g. password), something you have (e.g. token device), and something you are (e.g. retina scan or fingerprint)

References:

## 35. Question

You need to provide AWS Management Console access to a team of new application developers. The team members who perform the same role are assigned to a Microsoft Active Directory group and you have been asked to use Identity Federation and RBAC.

Which AWS services would you use to configure this access? (choose 2)

1. AWS IAM Groups
2. AWS Directory Service AD Connector
3. AWS IAM Users
4. AWS IAM Roles
5. AWS Directory Service Simple AD

**Answer: 2,4**

**Explanation:**

- AD Connector is a directory gateway for redirecting directory requests to your on-premise Active Directory. AD Connector eliminates the need for directory synchronization and the cost and complexity of hosting a federation infrastructure and connects your existing on-premise AD to AWS. It is the best choice when you want to use an existing Active Directory with AWS services
- IAM Roles are created and then "assumed" by trusted entities and define a set of permissions for making AWS service requests. With IAM Roles you can delegate permissions to resources for users and services without using permanent credentials (e.g. user name and password)
- AWS Directory Service Simple AD is an inexpensive Active Directory-compatible service with common directory features. It is a fully cloud-based solution and does not integrate with an on-premises Active Directory service
- You map the groups in AD to IAM Roles, not IAM users or groups

**References:**

https://digitalcloud.training/certification-training/aws-solutions-architect-associate/security-identity-compliance/aws-directory-service/

## 36. Question

A critical database runs in your VPC for which availability is a concern. Which RDS DB instance events may force the DB to be taken offline during a maintenance window?

1. Selecting the Multi-AZ feature
2. Promoting a Read Replica
3. Security patching
4. Updating DB parameter groups

**Answer: 3**

**Explanation:**

- Maintenance windows are configured to allow DB instance modifications to take place such as scaling and software patching. Some operations require the DB instance to be taken offline briefly and this includes security patching
- Enabling Multi-AZ, promoting a Read Replica and updating DB parameter groups are not events that take place during a maintenance window

**References:**

https://digitalcloud.training/certification-training/aws-solutions-architect-associate/database/amazon-rds/


## 37. Question

You are putting together a design for a three-tier web application. The application tier requires a minimum of 6 EC2 instances to be running at all times. You need to provide fault tolerance to ensure that the failure of a single Availability Zone (AZ) will not affect application performance.

Which of the options below is the optimum solution to fulfill these requirements?

1. Create an ASG with 12 instances spread across 4 AZs behind an ELB
2. Create an ASG with 6 instances spread across 3 AZs behind an ELB
3. Create an ASG with 9 instances spread across 3 AZs behind an ELB
4. Create an ASG with 18 instances spread across 3 AZs behind an ELB


**Answer: 3**

**Explanation:**

- This is simply about numbers. You need 6 EC2 instances to be running even in the case of an AZ failure. The question asks for the "optimum" solution so you don't want to over provision. Remember that it takes time for EC2 instances to boot and applications to initialize so it may not be acceptable to have a reduced fleet of instances during this time, therefore you need enough that the minimum number of instances are running without interruption in the event of an AZ outage.

**References:**

https://digitalcloud.training/certification-training/aws-solutions-architect-associate/compute/aws-auto-scaling/

https://digitalcloud.training/certification-training/aws-solutions-architect-associate/compute/elastic-load-balancing/


## 38. Question

You have a three-tier web application running on AWS that utilizes Route 53, ELB, Auto Scaling and RDS. One of the EC2 instances that is registered against the ELB fails a health check. What actions will the ELB take in this circumstance?

1. The ELB will terminate the instance that failed the health check
2. The ELB will stop sending traffic to the instance that failed the health check
3. The ELB will instruct Auto Scaling to terminate the instance and launch a replacement
4. The ELB will update Route 53 by removing any references to the instance

**Answer: 2**

**Explanation:**

- The ELB will simply stop sending traffic to the instance as it has determined it to be unhealthy
- ELBs are not responsible for terminating EC2 instances.
- The ELB does not send instructions to the ASG, the ASG has its own health checks and can also use ELB health checks to determine the status of instances
- ELB does not update Route 53 records

**References:**

https://digitalcloud.training/certification-training/aws-solutions-architect-associate/compute/elastic-load-balancing/

## 39. Question

A company runs a service on AWS to provide offsite backups for images on laptops and phones. The solution must support millions of customers, with thousands of images per customer. Images will be retrieved infrequently but must be available for retrieval immediately.

Which is the MOST cost-effective storage option that meets these requirements?

1. Amazon EFS
2. Amazon S3 Standard
3. Amazon S3 Standard-Infrequent Access
4. Amazon Glacier with expedited retrievals

**Answer: 3**

**Explanation:**

- Amazon S3 Standard-Infrequent Access is the most cost-effective choice
- Amazon Glacier with expedited retrievals is fast (1-5 minutes) but not immediate
- Amazon EFS is a high-performance file system and not ideally suited to this scenario, it is also not the most cost-effective option
- Amazon S3 Standard provides immediate retrieval but is not less cost-effective compared to Standard-Infrequent access

**References:**

https://digitalcloud.training/certification-training/aws-solutions-architect-associate/storage/amazon-s3/

## 40. Question

You are deploying an application on Amazon EC2 that must call AWS APIs. Which method of securely passing credentials to the application should you use?

1. Embed the API credentials into you application files
2. Assign IAM roles to the EC2 instances
3. Store API credentials as an object in Amazon S3
4. Store the API credentials on the instance using instance metadata

**Answer: 2**

**Explanation:**

- Always use IAM roles when you can
- It is an AWS best practice not to store API credentials within applications, on file systems or on instances (such as in metadata).

**References:**

https://digitalcloud.training/certification-training/aws-solutions-architect-associate/security-identity-compliance/aws-iam/

## 41. Question

A company is generating large datasets with millions of rows that must be summarized by column. Existing business intelligence tools will be used to build daily reports.

**Which storage service meets the requirements?**

1. Amazon RedShift
2. Amazon RDS
3. Amazon ElastiCache
4. Amazon DynamoDB

**Answer: 1**

**Explanation:**

- Amazon RedShift uses columnar storage and is used for analyzing data using business intelligence tools (SQL)
- Amazon RDS is more suited to OLTP workloads rather than analytics workloads
- Amazon ElastiCache is an in-memory caching service
- Amazon DynamoDB is a fully managed NoSQL database service, it is not a columnar database

**References:**

https://digitalcloud.training/certification-training/aws-solutions-architect-associate/database/amazon-redshift/

## 42. Question

A company runs a multi-tier application in an Amazon VPC. The application has an ELB Classic Load Balancer as the front end in a public subnet, and an Amazon EC2-based reverse proxy that performs content-based routing to two back end EC2 instances in a private subnet. The application is experiencing increasing load and the Solutions Architect is concerned that the reverse proxy and current back end setup will be insufficient.

**Which actions should the Architect take to achieve a cost-effective solution that ensures the application automatically scales to meet the demand? (choose 2)**

1. Add Auto Scaling to the Amazon EC2 reverse proxy layer
2. Add Auto Scaling to the Amazon EC2 back end fleet
3. Use t3 burstable instance types for the back end fleet
4. Replace both the front end and reverse proxy layers with an Application Load Balancer
5. Replace the Amazon EC2 reverse proxy with an ELB internal Classic Load Balancer

**Answer: 2,4**

**Explanation:**

- Due to the reverse proxy being a bottleneck to scalability, we need to replace it with a solution that can perform content-based routing. This means we must use an ALB not a CLB as ALBs support path-based and host-based routing
- Auto Scaling should be added to the architecture so that the back end EC2 instances do not become a bottleneck. With Auto Scaling instances can be added and removed from the back end fleet as demand changes
- A Classic Load Balancer cannot perform content-based routing so cannot be used
- It is unknown how the reverse proxy can be scaled with Auto Scaling however using an ALB with content-based routing is a much better design as it scales automatically and is HA by default
- Burstable performance instances, which are T3 and T2 instances, are designed to provide a baseline level of CPU performance with the ability to burst to a higher level when required by your workload. CPU performance is not the constraint here and this would not be a cost-effective solution

**References:**

https://digitalcloud.training/certification-training/aws-solutions-architect-associate/compute/elastic-load-balancing/

https://digitalcloud.training/certification-training/aws-solutions-architect-associate/compute/aws-auto-scaling/

## 43. Question

**A new security mandate requires that all personnel data held in the cloud is encrypted at rest. Which two methods allow you to encrypt data stored in S3 buckets at rest cost-efficiently? (choose 2)**

1. Use AWS S3 server-side encryption with Key Management Service keys or Customer-provided keys
2. Encrypt the data at the source using the client's CMK keys before transferring it to S3
3. Use Multipart upload with SSL
4. Make use of AWS S3 bucket policies to control access to the data at rest
5. Use CloudHSM

**Answer: 1,2**

**Explanation:**

- When using S3 encryption your data is always encrypted at rest and you can choose to use KMS managed keys or customer-provided keys. If you encrypt the data at the source and transfer it in an encrypted state it will also be encrypted in-transit
- With client side encryption data is encrypted on the client side and transferred in an encrypted state and with server-side encryption data is encrypted by S3 before it is written to disk (data is decrypted when it is downloaded)
- You can use bucket policies to control encryption of data that is uploaded but use of encryption is not stated in the answer given. Simply using bucket policies to control access to the data does not meet the security mandate that data must be encrypted
- Multipart upload helps with uploading large files but does not encrypt your data
- CloudHSM can be used to encrypt data but as a dedicated service it is charged on an hourly basis and is less cost-efficient compared to S3 encryption or encrypting the data at the source.

## 44. Question

Your company has an on-premise LDAP directory service. As part of a gradual migration into AWS you would like to integrate the LDAP directory with AWS's Identity and Access Management (IAM) solutions so that existing users can authenticate against AWS services.

What method would you suggest using to enable this integration?

1.  Develop an on-premise custom identity provider (IdP) and use the AWS Security Token Service (STS) to provide temporary security credentials
2.  Use SAML to develop a direct integration from the on-premise LDAP directory to the relevant AWS services
3.  Create a policy in IAM that references users in the on-premise LDAP directory
4.  Use AWS Simple AD and create a trust relationship with IAM

Answer: 1

Explanation:

-   The AWS Security Token Service (STS) is a web service that enables you to request temporary, limited-privilege credentials for IAM users or for users that you authenticate (federated users). If your identity store is not compatible with SAML 2.0, then you can build a custom identity broker application to perform a similar function. The broker application authenticates users, requests temporary credentials for users from AWS, and then provides them to the user to access AWS resources
-   You cannot create trust relationships between SimpleAD and IAM
-   You cannot use references in an IAM policy to an on-premise AD
-   SAML may not be supported by the on-premise LDAP directory so you would need to develop a custom IdP and use STS

References:

https://digitalcloud.training/certification-training/aws-solutions-architect-associate/security-identity-compliance/aws-iam/

https://docs.aws.amazon.com/IAM/latest/UserGuide/id_roles_common-scenarios_federated-users.html

## 45. Question

You need to improve data security for your ElastiCache Redis cluster. How can you force users to enter a password before they are able to execute Redis commands?

1.  Upload a key pair
2.  Use Redis AUTH
3.  Use a Cognito identity pool
4.  Implement multi-factor authentication (MFA)

Answer: 2

Explanation:

- Using Redis AUTH command can improve data security by requiring the user to enter a password before they are granted permission to execute Redis commands on a password-protected Redis server
- You cannot use MFA with ElastiCache
- Key pairs are used with EC2 instances, not ElastiCache

**References:**

https://docs.aws.amazon.com/AmazonElastiCache/latest/red-ug/auth.html


## 46. Question

A Kinesis consumer application is reading at a slower rate than expected. It has been identified that multiple consumer applications have total reads exceeding the per-shard limits. How can this situation be resolved?

1. Increase the number of shards in the Kinesis data stream
2. Implement API throttling to restrict the number of requests per-shard
3. Increase the number of read transactions per shard
4. Implement read throttling for the Kinesis data stream


**Answer: 1**

**Explanation:**

- In a case where multiple consumer applications have total reads exceeding the per-shard limits, you need to increase the number of shards in the Kinesis data stream
- Read throttling is enabled by default for Kinesis data streams. If you're still experiencing performance issues you must increase the number of shards
- You cannot increase the number of read transactions per shard
- API throttling is used to throttle API requests it is not responsible and cannot be used for throttling Get requests in a Kinesis stream

**References:**

https://docs.aws.amazon.com/streams/latest/dev/troubleshooting-consumers.html#consumer-app-reading-slower

https://docs.aws.amazon.com/streams/latest/dev/kinesis-record-processor-additional-considerations.html

https://digitalcloud.training/certification-training/aws-solutions-architect-associate/analytics/amazon-kinesis/


## 47. Question

You are designing a solution on AWS that requires a file storage layer that can be shared between multiple EC2 instances. The storage should be highly-available and should scale easily.

**Which AWS service can be used for this design?**

1. Amazon S3
2. Amazon EFS
3. Amazon EC2 instance store
4. Amazon EBS

**Answer: 2**

**Explanation:**

- Amazon Elastic File Service (EFS) allows concurrent access from many EC2 instances and is mounted over NFS which is a file-level protocol
- An Amazon Elastic Block Store (EBS) volume can only be attached to a single instance and cannot be shared
- Amazon S3 is an object storage system that is accessed via REST API not file-level protocols. It cannot be attached to EC2 instances
- An EC2 instance store is an ephemeral storage volume that is local to the server on which the instances runs and is not persistent. It is accessed via block protocols and also cannot be shared between instances

**References:**

https://digitalcloud.training/certification-training/aws-solutions-architect-associate/storage/amazon-efs/

## 48. Question

You have been asked to take a snapshot of a non-root EBS volume that contains sensitive corporate data. You need to ensure you can capture all data that has been written to your Amazon EBS volume at the time the snapshot command is issued and are unable to pause any file writes to the volume long enough to take a snapshot.

What is the best way to take a consistent snapshot whilst minimizing application downtime?

1. Un-mount the EBS volume, take the snapshot, then re-mount it again
2. Take the snapshot while the EBS volume is attached and the instance is running
3. Stop the instance and take the snapshot
4. You can't take a snapshot for a non-root EBS volume

**Answer: 1**

**Explanation:**

- The key facts here are that whilst minimizing application downtime you need to take a consistent snapshot and are unable to pause writes long enough to do so. Therefore the best option is to unmount the EBS volume and take the snapshot. This will be much faster than shutting down the instance, taking the snapshot, and then starting it back up again
- Snapshots capture a point-in-time state of an instance and are stored on S3. To take a consistent snapshot writes must be stopped (paused) until the snapshot is complete – if not possible the volume needs to be detached, or if it's an EBS root volume the instance must be stopped
- If you take the snapshot with the EBS volume attached you may not get a fully consistent snapshot. Though stopping the instance and taking a snapshot will ensure the snapshot if fully consistent the requirement is that you minimize application downtime. You can take snapshots of any EBS volume

**References:**

https://digitalcloud.training/certification-training/aws-solutions-architect-associate/compute/amazon-ebs/

## 49. Question

You are working on a database migration plan from an on-premise data center that includes a variety of databases that are being used for diverse purposes. You are trying to map each database to the correct service in AWS.

Which of the below use cases are a good fit for DynamoDB (choose 2)

1. Complex queries and joins
2. Large amounts of dynamic data that require very low latency
3. Backup for on-premises Oracle DB
4. Migration from a Microsoft SQL relational database
5. Rapid ingestion of clickstream data

**Answer: 2,5**

**Explanation:**

- Amazon Dynamo DB is a fully managed NoSQL database service that provides fast and predictable performance with seamless scalability that provides low read and write latency. Because of its performance profile and the fact that it is a NoSQL type of database, DynamoDB is good for rapidly ingesting clickstream data
- You should use a relational database such as RDS when you need to do complex queries and joins. Microsoft SQL and Oracle DB are both relational databases so DynamoDB is not a good backup target or migration destination for these types of DB

**References:**

https://digitalcloud.training/certification-training/aws-solutions-architect-associate/database/amazon-dynamodb/

## 50. Question

You work as a System Administrator at Digital Cloud Training and your manager has asked you to investigate an EC2 web server hosting videos that is constantly running at over 80% CPU utilization. Which of the approaches below would you recommend to fix the issue?

1. Create a Launch Configuration from the instance using the CreateLaunchConfiguration action
2. Create a CloudFront distribution and configure the Amazon EC2 instance as the origin
3. Create an Elastic Load Balancer and register the EC2 instance to it
4. Create an Auto Scaling group from the instance using the CreateAutoScalingGroup action

**Answer: 2**

**Explanation:**

- Using the CloudFront content delivery network (CDN) would offload the processing from the EC2 instance as the videos would be cached and accessed without hitting the EC2 instance
- CloudFront is a web service that gives businesses and web application developers an easy and cost-effective way to distribute content with low latency and high data transfer speeds. CloudFront is a good choice for distribution of frequently accessed static content that benefits from edge delivery—like popular website images, videos, media files or software downloads. An origin is the origin of the files that the CDN will distribute. Origins can be either an S3 bucket, an EC2 instance, and Elastic Load Balancer, or Route53) – can also be external (non-AWS)

- Using CloudFront is preferable to using an Auto Scaling group to launch more instances as it is designed for caching content and would provide the best user experience
- Creating an ELB will not help unless there a more instances to distributed the load to

**References:**

https://digitalcloud.training/certification-training/aws-solutions-architect-associate/networking-and-content-delivery/amazon-cloudfront/

## 51. Question

A Solutions Architect is designing a solution to store and archive corporate documents, and has determined that Amazon Glacier is the right solution. Data must be delivered within 10 minutes of a retrieval request.

Which features in Amazon Glacier can help meet this requirement?

1. Bulk retrieval
2. Expedited retrieval
3. Vault Lock
4. Standard retrieval

**Answer: 2**

**Explanation:**

- Expedited retrieval enables access to data in 1-5 minutes
- Bulk retrievals allow cost-effective access to significant amounts of data in 5-12 hours
- Standard retrievals typically complete in 3-5 hours
- Vault Lock allows you to easily deploy and enforce compliance controls on individual Glacier vaults via a lockable policy (Vault Lock policy)

**References:**

https://digitalcloud.training/certification-training/aws-solutions-architect-associate/storage/amazon-s3/

https://docs.aws.amazon.com/amazonglacier/latest/dev/downloading-an-archive-two-steps.html

## 52. Question

A Solutions Architect is designing a mobile application that will capture receipt images to track expenses. The Architect wants to store the images on Amazon S3. However, uploading the images through the web server will create too much traffic.

What is the MOST efficient method to store images from a mobile application on Amazon S3?

1. Upload directly to S3 using a pre-signed URL
2. Upload to a second bucket, and have a Lambda event copy the image to the primary bucket
3. Expand the web server fleet with Spot instances to provide the resources to handle the images
4. Upload to a separate Auto Scaling Group of server behind an ELB Classic Load Balancer, and have the server instances write to the Amazon S3 bucket

**Answer: 1**

**Explanation:**

- Uploading using a pre-signed URL allows you to upload the object without having any AWS security credentials/permissions. Pre-signed URLs can be generated programmatically and anyone who receives a valid pre-signed URL can then programmatically upload an object. This solution bypasses the web server avoiding any performance bottlenecks
- Uploading to a second bucket (through the web server) does not solve the issue of the web server being the bottleneck
- Using Auto Scaling, ELB and fleets of EC2 instances (including Spot instances) is not the most efficient solution to the problem

**References:**

https://docs.aws.amazon.com/AmazonS3/latest/dev/PresignedUrlUploadObject.html

https://digitalcloud.training/certification-training/aws-solutions-architect-associate/storage/amazon-s3/


## 53. Question

A company needs to deploy virtual desktops for its customers in an AWS VPC, and would like to leverage their existing on-premise security principles. AWS Workspaces will be used as the virtual desktop solution.

**Which set of AWS services and features will meet the company's requirements?**

1. A VPN connection, VPC NACLs and Security Groups
2. Amazon EC2, and AWS IAM
3. A VPN connection. AWS Directory Services
4. AWS Directory Service and AWS IAM


**Answer: 3**

**Explanation:**

- A security principle is an individual identity such as a user account within a directory. The AWS Directory service includes: Active Directory Service for Microsoft Active Directory, Simple AD, AD Connector. One of these services may be ideal depending on detailed requirements. The Active Directory Service for Microsoft AD and AD Connector both require a VPN or Direct Connect connection
- A VPN with NACLs and security groups will not deliver the required solution. AWS Directory Service with IAM or EC2 with IAM are also not sufficient for leveraging on-premise security principles. You must have a VPN

**References:**

https://digitalcloud.training/certification-training/aws-solutions-architect-associate/security-identity-compliance/aws-directory-service/


## 54. Question

An organization is considering ways to reduce administrative overhead and automate build processes. An Architect has suggested using CloudFormation. Which of the statements below are true regarding CloudFormation? (choose 2)

1. It provides visibility into user activity by recording actions taken on your account
2. It is used to collect and track metrics, collect and monitor log files, and set alarms
3. You pay for CloudFormation and the AWS resources created

4. Allows you to model your entire infrastructure in a text file
5. It provides a common language for you to describe and provision all the infrastructure resources in your cloud environment

**Answer: 4,5**

**Explanation:**

- CloudFormation allows you to model your infrastructure in a text file using a common language. You can then provision those resources using CloudFormation and only ever pay for the resources created. It provides a common language for you to describe and provision all the infrastructure resources in your cloud environment
- You do not pay for CloudFormation, only the resources created
- CloudWatch is used to collect and track metrics, collect and monitor log files, and set alarm
- CloudTrail provides visibility into user activity by recording actions taken on your account

**References:**

https://digitalcloud.training/certification-training/aws-solutions-architect-associate/management-tools/aws-cloudformation/

# 55. Question

A legacy application running on-premises requires a Solutions Architect to be able to open a firewall to allow access to several Amazon S3 buckets. The Architect has a VPN connection to AWS in place.

**Which option represents the simplest method for meeting this requirement?**

1. Create an IAM role that allows access from the corporate network to Amazon S3
2. Configure IP whitelisting on the customer's gateway
3. Configure a proxy on Amazon EC2 and use an Amazon S3 VPC endpoint
4. Use Amazon API Gateway to do IP whitelisting

**Answer: 1**

**Explanation:**

- The solutions architect can create an IAM role that provides access to the required S3 buckets. With the on-premises firewall opened to allow outbound access to S3 (over HTTPS), a secure connection can be made and the files can be uploaded. This is the simplest solution. You can use a condition in the IAM role that restricts access to a list of source IP addresses (your on-premise routed IPs)
- Configuring a proxy on EC2 and using a VPC endpoint is not the simplest solution
- API Gateway is not suitable for performing IP whitelisting
- You cannot perform IP whitelisting on a VPN customer gateway

**References:**

https://digitalcloud.training/certification-training/aws-solutions-architect-associate/storage/amazon-s3/

https://docs.aws.amazon.com/AmazonS3/latest/dev/example-bucket-policies.html#example-bucket-policies-use-case-3

## 56. Question

You are planning to deploy a number of EC2 instances in your VPC. The EC2 instances will be deployed across several subnets and multiple AZs. What AWS feature can act as an instance-level firewall to control traffic between your EC2 instances?

1. AWS WAF
2. Security group
3. Route table
4. Network ACL

**Answer: 2**

**Explanation:**

- Network ACL's function at the subnet level
- Route tables are not firewalls
- Security groups act like a firewall at the instance level
- Specifically, security groups operate at the network interface level
- AWS WAF is a web application firewall and does not work at the instance level

**References:**

https://digitalcloud.training/certification-training/aws-solutions-architect-associate/networking-and-content-delivery/amazon-vpc/

## 57. Question

You need a service that can provide you with control over which traffic to allow or block to your web applications by defining customizable web security rules. You need to block common attack patterns, such as SQL injection and cross-site scripting, as well as creating custom rules for your own applications.

Which AWS service fits these requirements?

1. Route 53
2. CloudFront
3. Security Groups
4. AWS WAF

**Answer: 4**

**Explanation:**

- AWS WAF is a web application firewall that helps detect and block malicious web requests targeted at your web applications. AWS WAF allows you to create rules that can help protect against common web exploits like SQL injection and cross-site scripting. With AWS WAF you first identify the resource (either an Amazon CloudFront distribution or an Application Load Balancer) that you need to protect. You then deploy the rules and filters that will best protect your applications
- The other services listed do not enable you to create custom web security rules that can block known malicious attacks

**References:**

https://aws.amazon.com/waf/details/

## 58. Question

You would like to deploy an EC2 instance with enhanced networking. What are the pre-requisites for using enhanced networking? (choose 2)

1. Instances must be launched from a HVM AMI
2. Instances must be launched from a PV AMI
3. Instances must be launched in a VPC
4. Instances must be EBS backed, not Instance-store backed
5. Instances must be of T2 Micro type

**Answer: 1.3**

**Explanation:**

- AWS currently supports enhanced networking capabilities using SR-IOV which provides direct access to network adapters, provides higher performance (packets-per-second) and lower latency. You must launch an HVM AMI with the appropriate drivers and it is only available for certain instance types and only supported in VPC
- You cannot use enhanced networking with instances launched from a PV AMI. There is not restriction on EBS vs Instance Store backed VMs and instances do not need to be T2 Micros

**References:**

https://digitalcloud.training/certification-training/aws-solutions-architect-associate/compute/amazon-ec2/

## 59. Question

You have created an application in a VPC that uses a Network Load Balancer (NLB). The application will be offered in a service provider model for AWS principals in other accounts within the region to consume. Based on this model, what AWS service will be used to offer the service for consumption?

1. VPC Endpoint Services using AWS PrivateLink
2. API Gateway
3. IAM Role Based Access Control
4. Route 53

**Answer: 1**

**Explanation:**

- An Interface endpoint uses AWS PrivateLink and is an elastic network interface (ENI) with a private IP address that serves as an entry point for traffic destined to a supported service
- Using PrivateLink you can connect your VPC to supported AWS services, services hosted by other AWS accounts (VPC endpoint services), and supported AWS Marketplace partner services

**References:**

https://digitalcloud.training/certification-training/aws-solutions-architect-associate/networking-and-content-delivery/amazon-vpc/

## 60. Question

Which service uses a simple text file to model and provision infrastructure resources, in an automated and secure manner?

1. OpsWorks
2. CloudFormation
3. Elastic Beanstalk
4. Simple Workflow Service

**Answer: 2**

**Explanation:**

- AWS CloudFormation is a service that gives developers and businesses an easy way to create a collection of related AWS resources and provision them in an orderly and predictable fashion. CloudFormation can be used to provision a broad range of AWS resources. Think of CloudFormation as deploying infrastructure as code
- Elastic Beanstalk is a PaaS solution for deploying and managing applications
- SWF helps developers build, run, and scale background jobs that have parallel or sequential steps
- OpsWorks is a configuration management service that provides managed instances of Chef and Puppet

**References:**

https://digitalcloud.training/certification-training/aws-solutions-architect-associate/management-tools/aws-cloudformation/

## 61. Question

An organization has a large amount of data on Windows (SMB) file shares in their on-premises data center. The organization would like to move data into Amazon S3. They would like to automate the migration of data over their AWS Direct Connect link.

Which AWS service can assist them?

1. AWS DataSync
2. AWS Snowball
3. AWS CloudFormation
4. AWS Database Migration Service (DMS)

**Answer: 1**

**Explanation:**

- AWS DataSync can be used to move large amounts of data online between on-premises storage and Amazon S3 or Amazon Elastic File System (Amazon EFS). DataSync eliminates or automatically handles many of these tasks, including scripting copy jobs, scheduling and monitoring transfers, validating data, and optimizing network utilization. The source datastore can be Server Message Block (SMB) file servers.
- AWS Database Migration Service (DMS) is used for migrating databases, not data on file shares.
- AWS CloudFormation can be used for automating infrastructure provisioning. This is not the best use case for CloudFormation as DataSync is designed specifically for this scenario.

- AWS Snowball is a hardware device that is used for migrating data into AWS. The organization plan to use their Direct Connect link for migrating data rather than sending it in via a physical device. Also, Snowball will not automate the migration.

**References:**

https://digitalcloud.training/certification-training/aws-solutions-architect-associate/migration/aws-datasync/

https://aws.amazon.com/datasync/faqs/

## 62. Question

An organization is extending a secure development environment into AWS. They have already secured the VPC including removing the Internet Gateway and setting up a Direct Connect connection.

**What else needs to be done to add encryption?**

1.  Setup a Virtual Private Gateway (VPG)
2.  Setup the Border Gateway Protocol (BGP) with encryption
3.  Configure an AWS Direct Connect Gateway
4.  Enable IPSec encryption on the Direct Connect connection

**Answer: 1**

**Explanation:**

- A VPG is used to setup an AWS VPN which you can use in combination with Direct Connect to encrypt all data that traverses the Direct Connect link. This combination provides an IPsec-encrypted private connection that also reduces network costs, increases bandwidth throughput, and provides a more consistent network experience than internet-based VPN connections.
- There is no option to enable IPSec encryption on the Direct Connect connection.
- The BGP protocol is not used to enable encryption for Direct Connect, it is used for routing.
- An AWS Direct Connect Gateway is used to connect to VPCs across multiple AWS regions. It is not involved with encryption

**References:**

https://docs.aws.amazon.com/whitepapers/latest/aws-vpc-connectivity-options/aws-direct-connect-plus-vpn-network-to-amazon.html

https://docs.aws.amazon.com/directconnect/latest/UserGuide/direct-connect-gateways-intro.html

## 63. Question

An application running on an Amazon ECS container instance using the EC2 launch type needs permissions to write data to Amazon DynamoDB.

**How can you assign these permissions only to the specific ECS task that is running the application?**

1.  Modify the AmazonECSTaskExecutionRolePolicy policy to add permissions for DynamoDB
2.  Use a security group to allow outbound connections to DynamoDB and assign it to the container instance
3.  Create an IAM policy with permissions to DynamoDB and assign It to a task using the taskRoleArn parameter
4.  Create an IAM policy with permissions to DynamoDB and attach it to the container instance

**Answer: 3**

**Explanation:**

- To specify permissions for a specific task on Amazon ECS you should use IAM Roles for Tasks. The permissions policy can be applied to tasks when creating the task definition, or by using an IAM task role override using the AWS CLI or SDKs. The taskRoleArn parameter is used to specify the policy.
- You should not apply the permissions to the container instance as they will then apply to all tasks running on the instance as well as the instance itself.
- Though you will need a security group to allow outbound connections to DynamoDB, the question is asking how to assign permissions to write data to DynamoDB and a security group cannot provide those permissions.
- The AmazonECSTaskExecutionRolePolicy policy is the Task Execution IAM Role. This is used by the container agent to be able to pull container images, write log file etc.

**References:**

https://docs.aws.amazon.com/AmazonECS/latest/developerguide/task-iam-roles.html

https://digitalcloud.training/certification-training/aws-solutions-architect-associate/compute/amazon-ecs/

## 64. Question

An Amazon RDS Read Replica is being deployed in a separate region. The master database is not encrypted but all data in the new region must be encrypted. How can this be achieved?

1. Enable encryption using Key Management Service (KMS) when creating the cross-region Read Replica
2. Encrypt a snapshot from the master DB instance, create a new encrypted master DB instance, and then create an encrypted cross-region Read Replica
3. Encrypt a snapshot from the master DB instance, create an encrypted cross-region Read Replica from the snapshot
4. Enabled encryption on the master DB instance, then create an encrypted cross-region Read Replica

**Answer: 2**

**Explanation:**

- You cannot create an encrypted Read Replica from an unencrypted master DB instance. You also cannot enable encryption after launch time for the master DB instance. Therefore, you must create a new master DB by taking a snapshot of the existing DB, encrypting it, and then creating the new DB from the snapshot. You can then create the encrypted cross-region Read Replica of the master DB.
- All other options will not work dues to the limitations explained above.

**References:**

https://digitalcloud.training/certification-training/aws-solutions-architect-associate/database/amazon-rds/

https://docs.aws.amazon.com/AmazonRDS/latest/UserGuide/USER_ReadRepl.html

https://docs.aws.amazon.com/AmazonRDS/latest/UserGuide/Overview.Encryption.html

## 65. Question

A legacy tightly-coupled High Performance Computing (HPC) application will be migrated to AWS. Which network adapter type should be used?

1. Elastic Network Adapter (ENA)
2. Elastic Fabric Adapter (EFA)
3. Elastic IP Address
4. Elastic Network Interface (ENI)

**Answer: 2**

**Explanation:**

- An Elastic Fabric Adapter is an AWS Elastic Network Adapter (ENA) with added capabilities. The EFA lets you apply the scale, flexibility, and elasticity of the AWS Cloud to tightly-coupled HPC apps. It is ideal for tightly coupled app as it uses the Message Passing Interface (MPI).
- The ENI is a basic type of adapter and is not the best choice for this use case.
- The ENA, which provides Enhanced Networking, does provide high bandwidth and low inter-instance latency but it does not support the features for a tightly-coupled app that the EFA does.

**References:**

https://aws.amazon.com/blogs/aws/now-available-elastic-fabric-adapter-efa-for-tightly-coupled-hpc-workloads/

https://digitalcloud.training/certification-training/aws-solutions-architect-associate/compute/amazon-ec2/

# SET 4: PRACTICE QUESTIONS ONLY

*Or go directly to Set 4: Practice Questions, Answers & Explanations*

## 1. Question

In your AWS VPC, you need to add a new subnet that will allow you to host a total of 20 EC2 instances.

Which of the following IPv4 CIDR blocks can you use for this scenario?

1. 172.0.0.0/30
2. 172.0.0.0/27
3. 172.0.0.0/28
4. 172.0.0.0/29

## 2. Question

You have a requirement to perform a large-scale testing operation that will assess the ability of your application to scale. You are planning on deploying a large number of c3.2xlarge instances with several PIOPS EBS volumes attached to each. You need to ensure you don't run into any problems with service limits. What are the service limits you need to be aware of in this situation?

1. 20 On-Demand EC2 instances and 100,000 aggregate PIOPS per account
2. 20 On-Demand EC2 instances and 100,000 aggregate PIOPS per region
3. 20 On-Demand EC2 instances and 300 TiB of aggregate PIOPS volume storage per region
4. 20 On-Demand EC2 instances and 300 TiB of aggregate PIOPS volume storage per account

## 3. Question

You are discussing EC2 with a colleague and need to describe the differences between EBS-backed instances and Instance store-backed instances. Which of the statements below would be valid descriptions? (choose 2)

1. For both types of volume rebooting the instances will result in data loss
2. On an EBS-backed instance, the default action is for the root EBS volume to be deleted upon termination
3. By default, root volumes for both types will be retained on termination unless you configured otherwise
4. EBS volumes can be detached and reattached to other EC2 instances
5. Instance store volumes can be detached and reattached to other EC2 instances

## 4. Question

You are creating a series of environments within a single VPC. You need to implement a system of categorization that allows for identification of EC2 resources by business unit, owner, or environment.

Which AWS feature allows you to do this?

1. Metadata
2. Parameters
3. Tags
4. Custom filters

## 5. Question

Your manager is interested in reducing operational overhead and cost and heard about "serverless" computing at a conference he recently attended. He has asked you if AWS provide any services that the company can leverage. Which services from the list below would you tell him about? (choose 2)

1. API Gateway
2. EC2
3. EMR
4. ECS
5. Lambda

## 6. Question

An application you are designing will gather data from a website hosted on an EC2 instance and write the data to an S3 bucket. The application will use API calls to interact with the EC2 instance and S3 bucket.

Which Amazon S3 access control method will be the the MOST operationally efficient? (choose 2)

1. Grant AWS Management Console access
2. Create an IAM policy
3. Create a bucket policy
4. Use key pairs
5. Grant programmatic access

## 7. Question

You are designing the disk configuration for an EC2 instance. The instance will be running an application that requires heavy read/write IOPS. You need to provision a single volume that is 500 GiB in size and needs to support 20,000 IOPS.

What EBS volume type will you select?

1. EBS General Purpose SSD in a RAID 1 configuration
2. EBS General Purpose SSD
3. EBS Provisioned IOPS SSD
4. EBS Throughput Optimized HDD

## 8. Question

An Auto Scaling group is configured with the default termination policy. The group spans multiple Availability Zones and each AZ has the same number of instances running.

A scale in event needs to take place, what is the first step in evaluating which instances to terminate?

1. Select instances that use the oldest launch configuration
2. Select instances randomly
3. Select the newest instance in the group
4. Select instances that are closest to the next billing hour

## 9. Question

You need to connect from your office to a Linux instance that is running in a public subnet in your VPC using the Internet. Which of the following items are required to enable this access? (choose 2)

1. A bastion host
2. A Public or Elastic IP address on the EC2 instance
3. A NAT Gateway
4. An IPSec VPN
5. An Internet Gateway attached to the VPC and route table attached to the public subnet pointing to it

## 10. Question

A customer has a public-facing web application hosted on a single Amazon Elastic Compute Cloud (EC2) instance serving videos directly from an Amazon S3 bucket. Which of the following will restrict third parties from directly accessing the video assets in the bucket?

1. Use a bucket policy to only allow the public IP address of the Amazon EC2 instance hosting the customer website
2. Use a bucket policy to only allow referrals from the main website URL
3. Launch the website Amazon EC2 instance using an IAM role that is authorized to access the videos
4. Restrict access to the bucket to the public CIDR range of the company locations

## 11. Question

You are a Solutions Architect for a pharmaceutical company. The company uses a strict process for release automation that involves building and testing services in 3 separate VPCs. A peering topology is configured with VPC-A peered with VPC-B and VPC-B peered with VPC-C. The development team wants to modify the process so that they can release code directly from VPC-A to VPC-C.

How can this be accomplished?

1. Update VPC-As route table with an entry using the VPC peering as a target
2. Create a new VPC peering connection between VPC-A and VPC-C
3. Update VPC-Bs route table with peering targets for VPC-A and VPC-C and enable route propagation
4. Update the CIDR blocks to match to enable inter-VPC routing

## 12. Question

You have an Amazon RDS Multi-AZ deployment across two availability zones. An outage of the availability zone in which the primary RDS DB instance is running occurs. What actions will take place in this circumstance? (choose 2)

1. A manual failover of the DB instance will need to be initiated using Reboot with failover
2. Due to the loss of network connectivity the process to switch to the standby replica cannot take place
3. The primary DB instance will switch over automatically to the standby replica
4. A failover will take place once the connection draining timer has expired
5. The failover mechanism automatically changes the DNS record of the DB instance to point to the standby DB instance

## 13. Question

You need to record connection information from clients using an ELB. When enabling the Proxy Protocol with an ELB to carry connection information from the source requesting the connection, what prerequisites apply? (choose 2)

1. Confirm that your load balancer is configured to include the X-Forwarded-For request header
2. Confirm that your instances are on-demand instances
3. Confirm that your back-end listeners are configured for TCP and front-end listeners are configured for TCP
4. Confirm that your load balancer is not behind a proxy server with Proxy Protocol enabled
5. Confirm that your load balancer is using HTTPS listeners

## 14. Question

You have been assigned the task of moving some sensitive documents into the AWS cloud. You need to ensure that the security of the documents is maintained. Which AWS features can help ensure that the sensitive documents cannot be read even if they are compromised? (choose 2)

1. EBS encryption with Customer Managed Keys
2. S3 Server-Side Encryption
3. S3 cross region replication
4. IAM Access Policy
5. EBS snapshots

## 15. Question

An Auto Scaling Group is unable to respond quickly enough to load changes resulting in lost messages from another application tier. The messages are typically around 128KB in size.

What is the best design option to prevent the messages from being lost?

1. Use larger EC2 instance sizes
2. Launch an Elastic Load Balancer
3. Store the messages on an SQS queue
4. Store the messages on Amazon S3

## 16. Question

There is a problem with an EC2 instance that was launched by AWS Auto Scaling. The EC2 status checks have reported that the instance is "Impaired". What action will AWS Auto Scaling take?

1. It will mark the instance for termination, terminate it, and then launch a replacement
2. Auto Scaling will wait for 300 seconds to give the instance a chance to recover
3. It will launch a new instance immediately and then mark the impaired one for replacement
4. Auto Scaling performs its own status checks and does not integrate with EC2 status checks

## 17. Question

You're trying to explain to a colleague typical use cases where you can use the Simple Workflow Service (SWF). Which of the scenarios below would be valid? (choose 2)

1. For web applications that require content delivery networks

2. Sending notifications via SMS when an EC2 instance reaches a certain threshold
3. Providing a reliable, highly-scalable, hosted queue for storing messages in transit between EC2 instances
4. Managing a multi-step and multi-decision checkout process for a mobile application
5. Coordinating business process workflows across distributed application components

## 18. Question

You work for a systems integrator running a platform that stores medical records. The government security policy mandates that patient data that contains personally identifiable information (PII) must be encrypted at all times, both at rest and in transit. You are using Amazon S3 to back up data into the AWS cloud.

How can you ensure the medical records are properly secured? (choose 2)

1. Before uploading the data to S3 over HTTPS, encrypt the data locally using your own encryption keys
2. Upload the data using CloudFront with an EC2 origin
3. Attach an encrypted EBS volume to an EC2 instance
4. Enable Server Side Encryption with S3 managed keys on an S3 bucket using AES-128
5. Enable Server Side Encryption with S3 managed keys on an S3 bucket using AES-256

## 19. Question

You are a Solutions Architect for Digital Cloud Training. A client is migrating a large amount of data that their customers access onto the AWS cloud. The client is located in Australia and most of their customers will be accessing the data from within Australia. The customer has asked you for some advice about S3 buckets.

Which of the following statements would be good advice? (choose 2)

1. To reduce latency and improve performance, create the buckets in the Asia Pacific (Sydney) region
2. S3 is a global service so it doesn't matter where you create your buckets
3. S3 is a universal namespace so bucket names must be unique globally
4. Buckets can be renamed after they have been created
5. S3 buckets have a limit on the number of objects you can store in them

## 20. Question

An application has been deployed in a private subnet within your VPC and an ELB will be used to accept incoming connections. You need to setup the configuration for the listeners on the ELB. When using a Classic Load Balancer, which of the following combinations of listeners support the proxy protocol? (choose 2)

1. Front-End – TCP & Back-End – TCP
2. Front-End – SSL & Back-End – SSL
3. Front-End – SSL & Back-End – TCP
4. Front-End – HTTP & Back-End SSL
5. Front-End – TCP & Back-End SSL

## 21. Question

You created a second ENI (eth1) interface when launching an EC2 instance. You would like to terminate the instance and have not made any changes.

**What will happen to the attached ENIs?**

1. eth1 will be terminated, but eth0 will persist
2. Both eth0 and eth1 will be terminated with the instance
3. eth1 will persist but eth0 will be terminated
4. Both eth0 and eth1 will persist

## 22. Question

An application that you manage uses a combination of Reserved and On-Demand instances to handle typical load. The application involves performing analytics on a set of data and you need to temporarily deploy a large number of EC2 instances. You only need these instances to be available for a short period of time until the analytics job is completed.

**If job completion is not time-critical what is likely to be the MOST cost-effective choice of EC2 instance type to use for this requirement?**

1. Use Reserved instances
2. Use On-Demand instances
3. Use Spot instances
4. Use dedicated hosts

## 23. Question

A health club is developing a mobile fitness app that allows customers to upload statistics and view their progress. Amazon Cognito is being used for authentication, authorization and user management and users will sign-in with Facebook IDs.

**In order to securely store data in DynamoDB, the design should use temporary AWS credentials. What feature of Amazon Cognito is used to obtain temporary credentials to access AWS services?**

1. SAML Identity Providers
2. Identity Pools
3. User Pools
4. Key Pairs

## 24. Question

A membership website your company manages has become quite popular and is gaining members quickly. The website currently runs on EC2 instances with one web server instance and one DB instance running MySQL. You are concerned about the lack of high-availability in the current architecture.

**What can you do to easily enable HA without making major changes to the architecture?**

1. Install MySQL on an EC2 instance in another AZ and enable replication
2. Install MySQL on an EC2 instance in the same AZ and enable replication
3. Enable Multi-AZ for the MySQL instance
4. Create a Read Replica in another AZ

## 25. Question

You are a Developer working for Digital Cloud Training. You are planning to write some code that creates a URL that lets users who sign in to your organization's network securely access the AWS Management Console. The URL will include a sign-in token that you get from AWS that authenticates the user to AWS. You are using Microsoft Active Directory Federation Services as your identity provider (IdP) which is compatible with SAML 2.0.

Which of the steps below will you need to include when developing your custom identity broker? (choose 2)

1. Generate a pre-signed URL programmatically using the AWS SDK for Java or the AWS SDK for .NET
2. Delegate access to the IdP through the "Configure Provider" wizard in the IAM console
3. Assume an IAM Role through the console or programmatically with the AWS CLI, Tools for Windows PowerShell or API
4. Call the AWS federation endpoint and supply the temporary security credentials to request a sign-in token
5. Call the AWS Security Token Service (AWS STS) AssumeRole or GetFederationToken API operations to obtain temporary security credentials for the user

## 26. Question

You need to create an EBS volume to mount to an existing EC2 instance for an application that will be writing structured data to the volume. The application vendor suggests that the performance of the disk should be up to 3 IOPS per GB. You expect the capacity of the volume to grow to 2TB.

Taking into account cost effectiveness, which EBS volume type would you select?

1. Provisioned IOPS (Io1)
2. General Purpose (GP2)
3. Throughput Optimized HDD (ST1)
4. Cold HDD (SC1)

## 27. Question

Your manager has asked you to explain the benefits of using IAM groups. Which of the below statements are valid benefits? (choose 2)

1. Provide the ability to create custom permission policies
2. Enables you to attach IAM permission policies to more than one user at a time
3. Groups let you specify permissions for multiple users, which can make it easier to manage the permissions for those users
4. Provide the ability to nest groups to create an organizational hierarchy
5. You can restrict access to the subnets in your VPC

## 28. Question

You are designing solutions that will utilize CloudFormation templates and your manager has asked how much extra will it cost to use CloudFormation to deploy resources?

1. CloudFormation is charged per hour of usage
2. Amazon charge a flat fee for each time you use CloudFormation

3. There is no additional charge for AWS CloudFormation, you only pay for the AWS resources that are created
4. The cost is based on the size of the template

## 29. Question

An important application you manage uses an Elastic Load Balancer (ELB) to distribute incoming requests amongst a fleet of EC2 instances. You need to ensure any operational issues are identified. Which of the statements below are correct about monitoring of an ELB? (choose 2)

1. CloudWatch metrics can be logged to an S3 bucket
2. Access logs are enabled by default
3. CloudTrail can be used to capture application logs
4. Access logs can identify requester, IP, and request type
5. Information is sent to CloudWatch every minute if there are active requests

## 30. Question

You have created a new VPC and setup an Auto Scaling Group to maintain a desired count of 2 EC2 instances. The security team has requested that the EC2 instances be located in a private subnet. To distribute load, you have to also setup an Internet-facing Application Load Balancer (ALB).

With your security team's wishes in mind what else needs to be done to get this configuration to work? (choose 2)

1. Attach an Internet Gateway to the private subnets
2. Add an Elastic IP address to each EC2 instance in the private subnet
3. Add a NAT gateway to the private subnet
4. Associate the public subnets with the ALB
5. For each private subnet create a corresponding public subnet in the same AZ

## 31. Question

A Solutions Architect is creating a design for a multi-tiered serverless application. Which two services form the application facing services from the AWS serverless infrastructure? (choose 2)

1. Amazon ECS
2. API Gateway
3. Elastic Load Balancer
4. AWS Cognito
5. AWS Lambda

## 32. Question

An application you manage stores encrypted data in S3 buckets. You need to be able to query the encrypted data using SQL queries and write the encrypted results back the S3 bucket. As the data is sensitive you need to implement fine-grained control over access to the S3 bucket.

What combination of services represent the BEST options support these requirements? (choose 2)

1. Use bucket ACLs to restrict access to the bucket
2. Use IAM policies to restrict access to the bucket
3. Use AWS Glue to extract the data, analyze it, and load it back to the S3 bucket

4.  Use Athena for querying the data and writing the results back to the bucket
5.  Use the AWS KMS API to query the encrypted data, and the S3 API for writing the results

## 33. Question

A new application you are designing will store data in an Amazon Aurora MySQL DB. You are looking for a way to enable inter-region disaster recovery capabilities with fast replication and fast failover. Which of the following options is the BEST solution?

1.  Use Amazon Aurora Global Database
2.  Enable Multi-AZ for the Aurora DB
3.  Create a cross-region Aurora Read Replica
4.  Create an EBS backup of the Aurora volumes and use cross-region replication to copy the snapshot

## 34. Question

You are putting together a design for a web-facing application. The application will be run on EC2 instances behind ELBs in multiple regions in an active/passive configuration. The website address the application runs on is digitalcloud.training. You will be using Route 53 to perform DNS resolution for the application.

How would you configure Route 53 in this scenario based on AWS best practices? (choose 2)

1.  Use a Failover Routing Policy
2.  Connect the ELBs using CNAME records
3.  Use a Weighted Routing Policy
4.  Set Evaluate Target Health to "No" for the primary
5.  Connect the ELBs using Alias records

## 35. Question

You recently noticed that your Network Load Balancer (NLB) in one of your VPCs is not distributing traffic evenly between EC2 instances in your AZs. There are an odd number of EC2 instances spread across two AZs. The NLB is configured with a TCP listener on port 80 and is using active health checks.

What is the most likely problem?

1.  NLB can only load balance within a single AZ
2.  There is no HTTP listener
3.  Health checks are failing in one AZ due to latency
4.  Cross-zone load balancing is disabled

## 36. Question

You are a Solutions Architect at Digital Cloud Training. A new client who has not used cloud computing has asked you to explain how AWS works. The client wants to know what service is provided that will provide a virtual network infrastructure that loosely resembles a traditional data center but has the capacity to scale more easily?

1.  Elastic Load Balancing
2.  Elastic Compute Cloud
3.  Direct Connect
4.  Virtual Private Cloud

## 37. Question

You manage an application that uses Auto Scaling. Recently there have been incidents of multiple scaling events in an hour and you are looking at methods of stabilizing the Auto Scaling Group. Select the statements below that are correct with regards to the Auto Scaling cooldown period? (choose 2)

1. The default value is 600 seconds
2. It ensures that the Auto Scaling group terminates the EC2 instances that are least busy
3. It ensures that before the Auto Scaling group scales out, the EC2 instances can apply system updates
4. The default value is 300 seconds
5. It ensures that the Auto Scaling group does not launch or terminate additional EC2 instances before the previous scaling activity takes effect

## 38. Question

An application you manage in your VPC uses an Auto Scaling Group that spans 3 AZs and there are currently 4 EC2 instances running in the group. What actions will Auto Scaling take, by default, if it needs to terminate an EC2 instance? (choose 2)

1. Wait for the cooldown period and then terminate the instance that has been running the longest
2. Randomly select one of the 3 AZs, and then terminate an instance in that AZ
3. Terminate an instance in the AZ which currently has 2 running EC2 instances
4. Send an SNS notification, if configured to do so
5. Terminate the instance with the least active network connections. If multiple instances meet this criterion, one will be randomly selected

## 39. Question

You are creating a CloudFormation template that will provision a new EC2 instance and new EBS volume. What do you need to specify to associate the block store with the instance?

1. Both the EC2 logical ID and the EBS logical ID
2. The EC2 logical ID
3. Both the EC2 physical ID and the EBS physical ID
4. The EC2 physical ID

## 40. Question

You regularly launch EC2 instances manually from the console and want to streamline the process to reduce administrative overhead. Which feature of EC2 allows you to store settings such as AMI ID, instance type, key pairs and Security Groups?

1. Run Command
2. Launch Templates
3. Launch Configurations
4. Placement Groups

## 41. Question

You are configuring Route 53 for a customer's website. Their web servers are behind an Internet-facing ELB. What record set would you create to point the customer's DNS zone apex record at the ELB?

1. Create an A record that is an Alias, and select the ELB DNS as a target
2. Create a PTR record pointing to the DNS name of the load balancer
3. Create an A record pointing to the DNS name of the load balancer
4. Create a CNAME record that is an Alias, and select the ELB DNS as a target

## 42. Question

An Auto Scaling Group in which you have four EC2 instances running is becoming heavily loaded. The instances are using the m4.large instance type and the CPUs are hitting 80%. Due to licensing constraints you don't want to add additional instances to the ASG so you are planning to upgrade to the m4.xlarge instance type instead. You need to make the change immediately but don't want to terminate the existing instances.

How can you perform the change without causing the ASG to launch new instances? (choose 2)

1. Edit the existing launch configuration and specify the new instance type
2. On the ASG suspend the Auto Scaling process until you have completed the change
3. Stop each instance and change its instance type. Start the instance again
4. Change the instance type and then restart the instance
5. Create a new launch configuration with the new instance type specified

## 43. Question

An issue has been raised to you whereby a client is concerned about the permissions assigned to his containerized applications. The containers are using the EC2 launch type. The current configuration uses the container instance's IAM roles for assigning permissions to the containerized applications.

The client has asked if it's possible to implement more granular permissions so that some applications can be assigned more restrictive permissions?

1. This can be achieved using IAM roles for tasks, and splitting the containers according to the permissions required to different task definition profiles
2. This can be achieved by configuring a resource-based policy for each application
3. This cannot be changed as IAM roles can only be linked to container instances
4. This can only be achieved using the Fargate launch type

## 44. Question

You are putting together the design for a new retail website for a high-profile company. The company has previously been the victim of targeted distributed denial-of-service (DDoS) attacks and have requested that you ensure the design includes mitigation techniques.

Which of the following are the BEST techniques to help ensure the availability of the services is not compromised in an attack? (choose 2)

1. Use CloudFront for distributing both static and dynamic content
2. Use Spot instances to reduce the cost impact in case of attack
3. Configure Auto Scaling with a high maximum number of instances to ensure it can scale accordingly
4. Use encryption on your EBS volumes
5. Use Placement Groups to ensure high bandwidth and low latency

## 45. Question

A Solutions Architect is creating the business process workflows associated with an order fulfilment system. What AWS service can assist with coordinating tasks across distributed application components?

1. Amazon SNS
2. Amazon SWF
3. Amazon SQS
4. Amazon STS

## 46. Question

A Solutions Architect has setup a VPC with a public subnet and a VPN-only subnet. The public subnet is associated with a custom route table that has a route to an Internet Gateway. The VPN-only subnet is associated with the main route table and has a route to a virtual private gateway.

The Architect has created a new subnet in the VPC and launched an EC2 instance in it. However, the instance cannot connect to the Internet. What is the MOST likely reason?

1. The subnet has been automatically associated with the main route table which does not have a route to the Internet
2. The new subnet has not been associated with a route table
3. The Internet Gateway is experiencing connectivity problems
4. There is no NAT Gateway available in the new subnet so Internet connectivity is not possible

## 47. Question

You need to run a production batch process quickly that will use several EC2 instances. The process cannot be interrupted and must be completed within a short time period.

What is likely to be the MOST cost-effective choice of EC2 instance type to use for this requirement?

1. Flexible instances
2. Spot instances
3. Reserved instances
4. On-demand instances

## 48. Question

An Amazon CloudWatch alarm recently notified you that the load on a DynamoDB table you are running is getting close to the provisioned capacity for writes. The DynamoDB table is part of a two-tier customer-facing application and is configured using provisioned capacity. You are concerned about what will happen if the limit is reached but need to wait for approval to increase the WriteCapacityUnits value assigned to the table.

What will happen if the limit for the provisioned capacity for writes is reached?

1. The requests will succeed, and an HTTP 200 status code will be returned
2. The requests will be throttled, and fail with an HTTP 503 code (Service Unavailable)
3. The requests will be throttled, and fail with an HTTP 400 code (Bad Request) and a ProvisionedThroughputExceededException
4. DynamoDB scales automatically so there's no need to worry

## 49. Question

A new application you are deploying uses Docker containers. You are creating a design for an ECS cluster to host the application. Which statements about ECS clusters are correct? (choose 2)

1. ECS Clusters are a logical grouping of container instances that you can place tasks on
2. Each container instance may be part of multiple clusters at a time
3. Clusters can contain tasks using the Fargate and EC2 launch type
4. Clusters can contain a single container instance type
5. Clusters are AZ specific

## 50. Question

A Solutions Architect is designing a three-tier web application that includes an Auto Scaling group of Amazon EC2 Instances running behind an ELB Classic Load Balancer. The security team requires that all web servers must be accessible only through the Elastic Load Balancer and that none of the web servers are directly accessible from the Internet. How should the Architect meet these requirements?

1. Install a Load Balancer on an Amazon EC2 instance
2. Configure the web servers' security group to deny traffic from the Internet
3. Create an Amazon CloudFront distribution in front of the Elastic Load Balancer
4. Configure the web tier security group to allow only traffic from the Elastic Load Balancer

## 51. Question

You are building a new Elastic Container Service (ECS) cluster. The ECS instances are running the EC2 launch type and you would like to enable load balancing to distributed connections to the tasks running on the cluster. You would like the mapping of ports to be performed dynamically and will need to route to different groups of servers based on the path in the requested URL. Which AWS service would you choose to fulfil these requirements?

1. Classic Load Balancer
2. ECS Services
3. Network Load Balancer
4. Application Load Balancer

## 52. Question

You have created a VPC with private and public subnets and will be deploying a new mySQL database server running on an EC2 instance. According to AWS best practice, which subnet should you deploy the database server into?

1. The private subnet
2. The public subnet
3. It doesn't matter
4. The subnet that is mapped to the primary AZ in the region

## 53. Question

You just attempted to restart a stopped EC2 instance and it immediately changed from a pending state to a terminated state. What are the most likely explanations? (choose 2)

1. AWS does not currently have enough available On-Demand capacity to service your request
2. You've reached your EBS volume limit
3. The AMI is unsupported
4. You have reached the limit on the number of instances that you can launch in a region
5. An EBS snapshot is corrupt

## 54. Question

Your organization has a data lake on S3 and you need to find a solution for performing in-place queries of the data assets in the data lake. The requirement is to perform both data discovery and SQL querying, and complex queries from a large number of concurrent users using BI tools.

What is the BEST combination of AWS services to use in this situation? (choose 2)

1. AWS Lambda for the complex queries
2. Amazon Athena for the ad hoc SQL querying
3. RedShift Spectrum for the complex queries
4. AWS Glue for the ad hoc SQL querying

## 55. Question

You have been asked to come up with a solution for providing single sign-on to existing staff in your company who manage on-premise web applications and now need access to the AWS management console to manage resources in the AWS cloud.

Which product combinations provide the best solution to achieve this requirement?

1. Use IAM and Amazon Cognito
2. Use your on-premise LDAP directory with IAM
3. Use IAM and MFA
4. Use the AWS Secure Token Service (STS) and SAML

## 56. Question

An EC2 instance in an Auto Scaling Group is having some issues that are causing the ASG to launch new instances based on the dynamic scaling policy. You need to troubleshoot the EC2 instance and prevent the ASG from launching new instances temporarily.

What is the best method to accomplish this? (choose 2)

1. Remove the EC2 instance from the Target Group
2. Disable the dynamic scaling policy
3. Place the EC2 instance that is experiencing issues into the Standby state
4. Disable the launch configuration associated with the EC2 instance
5. Suspend the scaling processes responsible for launching new instances

## 57. Question

To increase the resiliency of your RDS DB instance, you decided to enable Multi-AZ. Where will the new standby RDS instance be created?

1. You must specify the location when configuring Multi-AZ
2. In another subnet within the same AZ

3. In the same AWS Region but in a different AZ for high availability
4. In a different AWS Region to protect against Region failures

## 58. Question

Your Systems Administrators currently use Chef for configuration management of on-premise servers. Which AWS service will provide a fully-managed configuration management service that will allow you to use your existing Chef cookbooks?

1. Elastic Beanstalk
2. OpsWorks for Chef Automate
3. Opsworks Stacks
4. CloudFormation

## 59. Question

You would like to store a backup of an Amazon EBS volume on Amazon S3. What is the easiest way of achieving this?

1. Use SWF to automatically create a backup of your EBS volumes and then upload them to an S3 bucket
2. Write a custom script to automatically copy your data to an S3 bucket
3. Create a snapshot of the volume
4. You don't need to do anything, EBS volumes are automatically backed up by default

## 60. Question

When using throttling controls with API Gateway what happens when request submissions exceed the steady-state request rate and burst limits?

1. The requests will be buffered in a cache until the load reduces
2. API Gateway fails the limit-exceeding requests and returns "429 Too Many Requests" error responses to the client
3. API Gateway drops the requests and does not return a response to the client
4. API Gateway fails the limit-exceeding requests and returns "500 Internal Server Error" error responses to the client

## 61. Question

Health related data in Amazon S3 needs to be frequently accessed for up to 90 days. After that time the data must be retained for compliance reasons for seven years and is rarely accessed.

Which storage classes should be used?

1. Store data in STANDARD for 90 days then transition the data to DEEP_ARCHIVE
2. Store data in INTELLIGENT_TIERING for 90 days then transition to STANDARD_IA
3. Store data in STANDARD for 90 days then expire the data
4. Store data in STANDARD for 90 days then transition to REDUCED_REDUNDANCY

## 62. Question

A manual script that runs a few times a week and completes within 10 minutes needs to be replaced with an automated solution. Which of the following options should an Architect use?

1. Use AWS CloudFormation
2. Use AWS Lambda
3. Use a cron job on an Amazon EC2 instance
4. Use AWS Batch

## 63. Question

A high-performance file system is required for a financial modelling application. The data set will be stored on Amazon S3 and the storage solution must have seamless integration so objects can be accessed as files.

Which storage solution should be used?

1. Amazon FSx for Windows File Server
2. Amazon FSx for Lustre
3. Amazon Elastic File System (EFS)
4. Amazon Elastic Block Store (EBS)

## 64. Question

Amazon EC2 instances in a development environment run between 9am and 5pm Monday-Friday. Production instances run 24/7. Which pricing models should be used? (choose 2)

1. Use Spot instances for the development environment
2. Use scheduled reserved instances for the development environment
3. Use Reserved instances for the production environment
4. Use Reserved instances for the development environment
5. Use On-Demand instances for the production environment

## 65. Question

An High Performance Computing (HPC) application needs storage that can provide 135,000 IOPS. The storage layer is replicated across all instances in a cluster.

What is the optimal storage solution that provides the required performance and is cost-effective?

1. Use Amazon EC2 Enhanced Networking with an EBS HDD Throughput Optimized volume
2. Use Amazon S3 with byte-range fetch
3. Use Amazon Instance Store
4. Use Amazon EBS Provisioned IOPS volume with 135,000 IOPS

# SET 4: PRACTICE QUESTIONS, ANSWERS & EXPLANATIONS

## 1. Question

In your AWS VPC, you need to add a new subnet that will allow you to host a total of 20 EC2 instances.

Which of the following IPv4 CIDR blocks can you use for this scenario?

1. 172.0.0.0/30
2. 172.0.0.0/27
3. 172.0.0.0/28
4. 172.0.0.0/29

**Answer: 2**

**Explanation:**

- When you create a VPC, you must specify an IPv4 CIDR block for the VPC
- The allowed block size is between a /16 netmask (65,536 IP addresses) and /28 netmask (16 IP addresses)
- The CIDR block must not overlap with any existing CIDR block that's associated with the VPC
- A /27 subnet mask provides 32 addresses
- The first four IP addresses and the last IP address in each subnet CIDR block are not available for you to use, and cannot be assigned to an instance
- The following list shows total addresses for different subnet masks: /32 = 1 ; /31 = 2 ; /30 = 4 ; /29 = 8 ; /28 = 16 ; /27 = 32

**References:**

https://digitalcloud.training/certification-training/aws-solutions-architect-associate/networking-and-content-delivery/amazon-vpc/

## 2. Question

You have a requirement to perform a large-scale testing operation that will assess the ability of your application to scale. You are planning on deploying a large number of c3.2xlarge instances with several PIOPS EBS volumes attached to each. You need to ensure you don't run into any problems with service limits. What are the service limits you need to be aware of in this situation?

1. 20 On-Demand EC2 instances and 100,000 aggregate PIOPS per account
2. 20 On-Demand EC2 instances and 100,000 aggregate PIOPS per region
3. 20 On-Demand EC2 instances and 300 TiB of aggregate PIOPS volume storage per region
4. 20 On-Demand EC2 instances and 300 TiB of aggregate PIOPS volume storage per account

**Answer: 3**

**Explanation:**

- You are limited to running up to a total of 20 On-Demand instances across the instance family, purchasing 20 Reserved Instances, and requesting Spot Instances per your dynamic spot limit per region (by default)

- You are limited to an aggregate of 300 TiB of aggregate PIOPS volumes per region and 300,000 aggregate PIOPS

**References:**

https://digitalcloud.training/certification-training/aws-solutions-architect-associate/compute/amazon-ec2/

https://digitalcloud.training/certification-training/aws-solutions-architect-associate/compute/amazon-ebs/

## 3. Question

You are discussing EC2 with a colleague and need to describe the differences between EBS-backed instances and Instance store-backed instances. Which of the statements below would be valid descriptions? (choose 2)

1. For both types of volume rebooting the instances will result in data loss
2. On an EBS-backed instance, the default action is for the root EBS volume to be deleted upon termination
3. By default, root volumes for both types will be retained on termination unless you configured otherwise
4. EBS volumes can be detached and reattached to other EC2 instances
5. Instance store volumes can be detached and reattached to other EC2 instances

**Answer: 2,4**

**Explanation:**

- On an EBS-backed instance, the default action is for the root EBS volume to be deleted upon termination
- EBS volumes can be detached and reattached to other EC2 instances
- Instance store volumes cannot be detached and reattached to other EC2 instances
- When rebooting the instances for both types data will not be lost
- By default, root volumes for both types will be deleted on termination unless you configured otherwise

**References:**

https://digitalcloud.training/certification-training/aws-solutions-architect-associate/compute/amazon-ebs/

## 4. Question

You are creating a series of environments within a single VPC. You need to implement a system of categorization that allows for identification of EC2 resources by business unit, owner, or environment.

Which AWS feature allows you to do this?

1. Metadata
2. Parameters
3. Tags
4. Custom filters

**Answer: 3**

**Explanation:**

- A tag is a label that you assign to an AWS resource. Each tag consists of a key and an optional value, both of which you define. Tags enable you to categorize your AWS resources in different ways, for example, by purpose, owner, or environment
- Instance metadata is data about your instance that you can use to configure or manage the running instance
- Parameters and custom filters are not used for categorization

**References:**

https://digitalcloud.training/certification-training/aws-solutions-architect-associate/compute/amazon-ec2/

## 5. Question

Your manager is interested in reducing operational overhead and cost and heard about "serverless" computing at a conference he recently attended. He has asked you if AWS provide any services that the company can leverage. Which services from the list below would you tell him about? (choose 2)

1. API Gateway
2. EC2
3. EMR
4. ECS
5. Lambda

**Answer: 1,5**

**Explanation:**

AWS Serverless services include (but not limited to):

- API Gateway
- Lambda
- S3
- DynamoDB
- SNS
- SQS
- Kinesis

EMR, EC2 and ECS all use compute instances running on Amazon EC2 so are not serverless

**References:**

https://aws.amazon.com/serverless/

## 6. Question

An application you are designing will gather data from a website hosted on an EC2 instance and write the data to an S3 bucket. The application will use API calls to interact with the EC2 instance and S3 bucket.

Which Amazon S3 access control method will be the the MOST operationally efficient? (choose 2)

1. Grant AWS Management Console access
2. Create an IAM policy
3. Create a bucket policy
4. Use key pairs
5. Grant programmatic access

**Answer: 2,5**

**Explanation:**

- Policies are documents that define permissions and can be applied to users, groups and roles. Policy documents are written in JSON (key value pair that consists of an attribute and a value)
- Within an IAM policy you can grant either programmatic access or AWS Management Console access to Amazon S3 resources
- Key pairs are used for access to EC2 instances; a bucket policy would not assist with access control with EC2 and granting management console access will not assist the application which is making API calls to the services

**References:**

https://digitalcloud.training/certification-training/aws-solutions-architect-associate/security-identity-compliance/aws-iam/

https://digitalcloud.training/certification-training/aws-solutions-architect-associate/storage/amazon-s3/

## 7. Question

You are designing the disk configuration for an EC2 instance. The instance will be running an application that requires heavy read/write IOPS. You need to provision a single volume that is 500 GiB in size and needs to support 20,000 IOPS.

**What EBS volume type will you select?**

1. EBS General Purpose SSD in a RAID 1 configuration
2. EBS General Purpose SSD
3. EBS Provisioned IOPS SSD
4. EBS Throughput Optimized HDD

**Answer: 3**

**Explanation:**

- This is simply about understanding the performance characteristics of the different EBS volume types. The only EBS volume type that supports over 10,000 IOPS is Provisioned IOPS SSD
- SSD, General Purpose – GP2
- Baseline of 3 IOPS per GiB with a minimum of 100 IOPS
- Burst up to 3000 IOPS for volumes >= 334GB)
- SSD, Provisioned IOPS – I01
- More than 10,000 IOPS
- Up to 32000 IOPS per volume
- Up to 50 IOPS per GiB
- HDD, Throughput Optimized – (ST1)

- Throughput measured in MB/s, and includes the ability to burst up to 250 MB/s per TB, with a baseline throughput of 40 MB/s per TB and a maximum throughput of 500 MB/s per volume
- HDD, Cold – (SC1)
- Lowest cost storage – cannot be a boot volume
- These volumes can burst up to 80 MB/s per TB, with a baseline throughput of 12 MB/s per TB and a maximum throughput of 250 MB/s per volume
- HDD, Magnetic – Standard – cheap, infrequently accessed storage – lowest cost storage that can be a boot volume

**References:**

https://digitalcloud.training/certification-training/aws-solutions-architect-associate/compute/amazon-ebs/

## 8. Question

An Auto Scaling group is configured with the default termination policy. The group spans multiple Availability Zones and each AZ has the same number of instances running.

A scale in event needs to take place, what is the first step in evaluating which instances to terminate?

1. Select instances that use the oldest launch configuration
2. Select instances randomly
3. Select the newest instance in the group
4. Select instances that are closest to the next billing hour

**Answer: 1**

**Explanation:**

- Using the default termination policy, when there are even number of instances in multiple AZs, Auto Scaling will first select the instances with the oldest launch configuration, and if multiple instances share the oldest launch configuration, AS then selects the instances that are closest to the next billing hour
- Please see the AWS article linked below for more details on the termination process

**References:**

https://docs.aws.amazon.com/autoscaling/ec2/userguide/as-instance-termination.html

## 9. Question

You need to connect from your office to a Linux instance that is running in a public subnet in your VPC using the Internet. Which of the following items are required to enable this access? (choose 2)

1. A bastion host
2. A Public or Elastic IP address on the EC2 instance
3. A NAT Gateway
4. An IPSec VPN
5. An Internet Gateway attached to the VPC and route table attached to the public subnet pointing to it

**Answer: 2,5**

**Explanation:**

- A public subnet is a subnet that has an Internet Gateway attached and "Enable auto-assign public IPv4 address" enabled. Instances require a public IP or Elastic IP address. It is also necessary to have the subnet route table updated to point to the Internet Gateway and security groups and network ACLs must be configured to allow the SSH traffic on port 22
- A bastion host can be used to access instances in private subnets but is not required for instances in public subnets
- A NAT Gateway allows instances in private subnets to access the Internet, it is not used for remote access
- An IPSec VPN is not required to connect to an instance in a public subnet

**References:**

https://digitalcloud.training/certification-training/aws-solutions-architect-associate/networking-and-content-delivery/amazon-vpc/


## 10. Question

A customer has a public-facing web application hosted on a single Amazon Elastic Compute Cloud (EC2) instance serving videos directly from an Amazon S3 bucket. Which of the following will restrict third parties from directly accessing the video assets in the bucket?

1. Use a bucket policy to only allow the public IP address of the Amazon EC2 instance hosting the customer website
2. Use a bucket policy to only allow referrals from the main website URL
3. Launch the website Amazon EC2 instance using an IAM role that is authorized to access the videos
4. Restrict access to the bucket to the public CIDR range of the company locations


**Answer: 2**

**Explanation:**

- To allow read access to the S3 video assets from the public-facing web application, you can add a bucket policy that allows s3:GetObject permission with a condition, using the aws:referer key, that the get request must originate from specific webpages. This is a good answer as it fully satisfies the objective of ensuring the that EC2 instance can access the videos but direct access to the videos from other sources is prevented.
- You can use condition statements in a bucket policy to restrict access via IP address. However, using the referrer condition in a bucket policy is preferable as it is a best practice to use DNS names / URLs instead of hard-coding IPs whenever possible
- Restricting access to the bucket to the public CIDR range of the company locations will stop third-parties from accessing the bucket however it will also stop the EC2 instance from accessing the bucket and the question states that the EC2 instance is serving the files directly
- Launching the EC2 instance with an IAM role that is authorized to access the videos is only half a solution as you would also need to create a bucket policy that specifies that the IAM role is granted access

**References:**

https://docs.aws.amazon.com/AmazonS3/latest/dev/example-bucket-policies.html#example-bucket-policies-use-case-4

## 11. Question

You are a Solutions Architect for a pharmaceutical company. The company uses a strict process for release automation that involves building and testing services in 3 separate VPCs. A peering topology is configured with VPC-A peered with VPC-B and VPC-B peered with VPC-C. The development team wants to modify the process so that they can release code directly from VPC-A to VPC-C.

How can this be accomplished?

1. Update VPC-As route table with an entry using the VPC peering as a target
2. Create a new VPC peering connection between VPC-A and VPC-C
3. Update VPC-Bs route table with peering targets for VPC-A and VPC-C and enable route propagation
4. Update the CIDR blocks to match to enable inter-VPC routing

Answer: 2

Explanation:

- It is not possible to use transitive peering relationships with VPC peering and therefore you must create an additional VPC peering connection between VPC-A and VPC-C
- You must update route tables to configure routing however updating VPC-As route table alone will not lead to the desired result without first creating the additional peering connection
- Route propagation cannot be used to extend VPC peering connections
- You cannot have matching (overlapping) CIDR blocks with VPC peering

References:

https://digitalcloud.training/certification-training/aws-solutions-architect-associate/networking-and-content-delivery/amazon-vpc/

## 12. Question

You have an Amazon RDS Multi-AZ deployment across two availability zones. An outage of the availability zone in which the primary RDS DB instance is running occurs. What actions will take place in this circumstance? (choose 2)

1. A manual failover of the DB instance will need to be initiated using Reboot with failover
2. Due to the loss of network connectivity the process to switch to the standby replica cannot take place
3. The primary DB instance will switch over automatically to the standby replica
4. A failover will take place once the connection draining timer has expired
5. The failover mechanism automatically changes the DNS record of the DB instance to point to the standby DB instance

Answer: 3,5

Explanation:

- Multi-AZ RDS creates a replica in another AZ and synchronously replicates to it (DR only)
- A failover may be triggered in the following circumstances:
- Loss of primary AZ or primary DB instance failure
- Loss of network connectivity on primary
- Compute (EC2) unit failure on primary
- Storage (EBS) unit failure on primary

- The primary DB instance is changed
- Patching of the OS on the primary DB instance
- Manual failover (reboot with failover selected on primary)
- During failover RDS automatically updates configuration (including DNS endpoint) to use the second node
- The process to failover is not reliant on network connectivity as it is designed for fault tolerance
  - Connection draining timers are applicable to ELBs not RDS
  - You do not need to manually failover the DB instance, multi-AZ has an automatic process as outlined above

**References:**

https://digitalcloud.training/certification-training/aws-solutions-architect-associate/database/amazon-rds/

## 13. Question

You need to record connection information from clients using an ELB. When enabling the Proxy Protocol with an ELB to carry connection information from the source requesting the connection, what prerequisites apply? (choose 2)

1. Confirm that your load balancer is configured to include the X-Forwarded-For request header
2. Confirm that your instances are on-demand instances
3. Confirm that your back-end listeners are configured for TCP and front-end listeners are configured for TCP
4. Confirm that your load balancer is not behind a proxy server with Proxy Protocol enabled
5. Confirm that your load balancer is using HTTPS listeners

**Answer: 3,4**

**Explanation:**

- Proxy protocol for TCP/SSL carries the source (client) IP/port information. The Proxy Protocol header helps you identify the IP address of a client when you have a load balancer that uses TCP for back-end connections. You need to ensure the client doesn't go through a proxy or there will be multiple proxy headers. You also need to ensure the EC2 instance's TCP stack can process the extra information
- The back-end and front-end listeners must be configured for TCP
- HTTPS listeners do not carry proxy protocol information (use the X-Forwarded-For header instead)
- It doesn't matter what type of pricing model you're using for EC2 (e.g. on-demand, reserved etc.)
- X-Forwarded-For is a different protocol that operates at layer 7 whereas proxy protocol operates at layer 4

**References:**

https://digitalcloud.training/certification-training/aws-solutions-architect-associate/compute/elastic-load-balancing/

https://docs.aws.amazon.com/elasticloadbalancing/latest/classic/using-elb-listenerconfig-quickref.html

## 14. Question

You have been assigned the task of moving some sensitive documents into the AWS cloud. You need to ensure that the security of the documents is maintained. Which AWS features can help ensure that the sensitive documents cannot be read even if they are compromised? (choose 2)

1. EBS encryption with Customer Managed Keys
2. S3 Server-Side Encryption
3. S3 cross region replication
4. IAM Access Policy
5. EBS snapshots

**Answer: 1,2**

**Explanation:**

- It is not specified what types of documents are being moved into the cloud or what services they will be placed on. Therefore, we can assume that options include S3 and EBS. To prevent the documents from being read if they are compromised, we need to encrypt them. Both of these services provide native encryption functionality to ensure security of the sensitive documents. With EBS you can use KMS-managed or customer-managed encryption keys. With S3 you can use client-side or server-side encryption

- IAM access policies can be used to control access but if the documents are somehow compromised, they will not stop the documents from being read. For this we need encryption, and IAM access policies are not used for controlling encryption

- EBS snapshots are used for creating a point-in-time backup or data. They do maintain the encryption status of the data from the EBS volume but are not used for actually encrypting the data in the first place

- S3 cross-region replication can be used for fault tolerance but does not apply any additional security to the data

**References:**

https://digitalcloud.training/certification-training/aws-solutions-architect-associate/compute/amazon-ebs/

https://digitalcloud.training/certification-training/aws-solutions-architect-associate/storage/amazon-s3/

## 15. Question

An Auto Scaling Group is unable to respond quickly enough to load changes resulting in lost messages from another application tier. The messages are typically around 128KB in size.

What is the best design option to prevent the messages from being lost?

1. Use larger EC2 instance sizes
2. Launch an Elastic Load Balancer
3. Store the messages on an SQS queue
4. Store the messages on Amazon S3

**Answer: 3**

**Explanation:**

- In this circumstance the ASG cannot launch EC2 instances fast enough. You need to be able to store the messages somewhere so they don't get lost whilst the EC2 instances are launched. This is a classic use case for decoupling and SQS is designed for exactly this purpose
- Amazon Simple Queue Service (Amazon SQS) is a web service that gives you access to message queues that store messages waiting to be processed. SQS offers a reliable, highly-scalable, hosted queue for storing messages in transit between computers. An SQS queue can be used to create distributed/decoupled applications
- Storing the messages on S3 is potentially feasible but SQS is the preferred solution as it is designed for decoupling. If the messages are over 256KB and therefore cannot be stored in SQS, you may want to consider using S3 and it can be used in combination with SQS by using the Amazon SQS Extended Client Library for Java
- An ELB can help to distribute incoming connections to the back-end EC2 instances however if the ASG is not scaling fast enough then there aren't enough resources for the ELB to distributed traffic to

**References:**

https://digitalcloud.training/certification-training/aws-solutions-architect-associate/application-integration/amazon-sqs/

## 16. Question

There is a problem with an EC2 instance that was launched by AWS Auto Scaling. The EC2 status checks have reported that the instance is "Impaired". What action will AWS Auto Scaling take?

1. It will mark the instance for termination, terminate it, and then launch a replacement
2. Auto Scaling will wait for 300 seconds to give the instance a chance to recover
3. It will launch a new instance immediately and then mark the impaired one for replacement
4. Auto Scaling performs its own status checks and does not integrate with EC2 status checks

**Answer: 1**

**Explanation:**

- If any health check returns an unhealthy status the instance will be terminated. Unlike AZ rebalancing, termination of unhealthy instances happens first, then Auto Scaling attempts to launch new instances to replace terminated instances
- AS will not launch a new instance immediately as it always terminates unhealthy instance before launching a replacement
- Auto Scaling does not wait for 300 seconds, once the health check has failed the configured number of times the instance will be terminated
- Auto Scaling does integrate with EC2 status checks as well as having its own status checks

**References:**

https://digitalcloud.training/certification-training/aws-solutions-architect-associate/compute/aws-auto-scaling/

## 17. Question

You're trying to explain to a colleague typical use cases where you can use the Simple Workflow Service (SWF). Which of the scenarios below would be valid? (choose 2)

1. For web applications that require content delivery networks
2. Sending notifications via SMS when an EC2 instance reaches a certain threshold
3. Providing a reliable, highly-scalable, hosted queue for storing messages in transit between EC2 instances
4. Managing a multi-step and multi-decision checkout process for a mobile application
5. Coordinating business process workflows across distributed application components

**Answer: 4,5**

**Explanation:**

- Amazon Simple Workflow Service (SWF) is a web service that makes it easy to coordinate work across distributed application components
- SWF enables applications for a range of use cases, including media processing, web application back-ends, business process workflows, and analytics pipelines, to be designed as a coordination of tasks
- You should use Amazon SNS for sending SMS messages
- You should use CloudFront if you need a CDN
- Yo should use SQS for storing messages in a queue

**References:**

https://digitalcloud.training/certification-training/aws-solutions-architect-associate/application-integration/amazon-swf/

## 18. Question

**You work for a systems integrator running a platform that stores medical records. The government security policy mandates that patient data that contains personally identifiable information (PII) must be encrypted at all times, both at rest and in transit. You are using Amazon S3 to back up data into the AWS cloud.**

**How can you ensure the medical records are properly secured? (choose 2)**

1. Before uploading the data to S3 over HTTPS, encrypt the data locally using your own encryption keys
2. Upload the data using CloudFront with an EC2 origin
3. Attach an encrypted EBS volume to an EC2 instance
4. Enable Server Side Encryption with S3 managed keys on an S3 bucket using AES-128
5. Enable Server Side Encryption with S3 managed keys on an S3 bucket using AES-256

**Answer: 1,5**

**Explanation:**

- When data is stored in an encrypted state it is referred to as encrypted "at rest" and when it is encrypted as it is being transferred over a network it is referred to as encrypted "in transit". You can securely upload/download your data to Amazon S3 via SSL endpoints using the HTTPS protocol (In Transit – SSL/TLS). You have the option of encrypting the data locally before it is uploaded or uploading using SSL/TLS so it is secure in transit and encrypting on the Amazon S3 side using S3 managed keys. The S3 managed keys will be AES-256 (not AES-128) bit keys

- Uploading data using CloudFront with an EC2 origin or using an encrypted EBS volume attached to an EC2 instance is not a solution to this problem as your company wants to backup these records onto S3 (not EC2/EBS)

**References:**

https://digitalcloud.training/certification-training/aws-solutions-architect-associate/storage/amazon-s3/

## 19. Question

You are a Solutions Architect for Digital Cloud Training. A client is migrating a large amount of data that their customers access onto the AWS cloud. The client is located in Australia and most of their customers will be accessing the data from within Australia. The customer has asked you for some advice about S3 buckets.

**Which of the following statements would be good advice? (choose 2)**

1. To reduce latency and improve performance, create the buckets in the Asia Pacific (Sydney) region
2. S3 is a global service so it doesn't matter where you create your buckets
3. S3 is a universal namespace so bucket names must be unique globally
4. Buckets can be renamed after they have been created
5. S3 buckets have a limit on the number of objects you can store in them

**Answer: 1,3**

**Explanation:**

- For better performance, lower latency and lower costs the buckets should be created in the region that is closest to the client's customers
- S3 is a universal namespace so names must be unique globally
- Bucket names cannot be changed after they have been created
- An S3 bucket is created within a region and all replicated copies of the data stay within the region unless you explicitly configure cross-region replication
- There is no limit on the number of objects you can store in an S3 bucket

**References:**

https://digitalcloud.training/certification-training/aws-solutions-architect-associate/storage/amazon-s3/

## 20. Question

An application has been deployed in a private subnet within your VPC and an ELB will be used to accept incoming connections. You need to setup the configuration for the listeners on the ELB. When using a Classic Load Balancer, which of the following combinations of listeners support the proxy protocol? (choose 2)

1. Front-End – TCP & Back-End – TCP
2. Front-End – SSL & Back-End – SSL
3. Front-End – SSL & Back-End – TCP
4. Front-End – HTTP & Back-End SSL
5. Front-End – TCP & Back-End SSL

**Answer: 1,3**

**Explanation:**

- The proxy protocol only applies to L4 and the back-end listener must be TCP for proxy protocol
- When using the proxy protocol the front-end listener can be either TCP or SSL
- The X-forwarded-for header only applies to L7
- Proxy protocol for TCP/SSL carries the source (client) IP/port information. The Proxy Protocol header helps you identify the IP address of a client when you have a load balancer that uses TCP for back-end connection

**References:**

https://digitalcloud.training/certification-training/aws-solutions-architect-associate/compute/elastic-load-balancing/

https://docs.aws.amazon.com/elasticloadbalancing/latest/classic/using-elb-listenerconfig-quickref.html


## 21. Question

You created a second ENI (eth1) interface when launching an EC2 instance. You would like to terminate the instance and have not made any changes.

What will happen to the attached ENIs?

1. eth1 will be terminated, but eth0 will persist
2. Both eth0 and eth1 will be terminated with the instance
3. eth1 will persist but eth0 will be terminated
4. Both eth0 and eth1 will persist


**Answer: 3**

**Explanation:**

- By default, Eth0 is the only Elastic Network Interface (ENI) created with an EC2 instance when launched. You can add additional interfaces to EC2 instances (number dependent on instances family/type). Default interfaces are terminated with instance termination. Manually added interfaces are not terminated by default

**References:**

https://digitalcloud.training/certification-training/aws-solutions-architect-associate/compute/amazon-ec2/


## 22. Question

An application that you manage uses a combination of Reserved and On-Demand instances to handle typical load. The application involves performing analytics on a set of data and you need to temporarily deploy a large number of EC2 instances. You only need these instances to be available for a short period of time until the analytics job is completed.

If job completion is not time-critical what is likely to be the MOST cost-effective choice of EC2 instance type to use for this requirement?

1. Use Reserved instances
2. Use On-Demand instances
3. Use Spot instances
4. Use dedicated hosts

**Answer: 3**

**Explanation:**

- The key requirements here are that you need to temporarily deploy a large number of instances, can tolerate an delay (not time-critical), and need the most economical solution. In this case Spot instances are likely to be the most economical solution. You must be able to tolerate delays if using Spot instances as if the market price increases your instances will be terminated and you may have to wait for the price to lower back to your budgeted allowance.
- On-demand is good for temporary deployments when you cannot tolerate any delays (instances being terminated by AWS). It is likely to be more expensive than Spot however so if delays can be tolerated it is not the best solution
- Reserved instances are used for longer more stable requirements where you can get a discount for a fixed 1 or 3 year term. This pricing model is not good for temporary requirements
- An EC2 Dedicated Host is a physical server with EC2 instance capacity fully dedicated to your use. They are much more expensive than on-demand or Spot instances and are used for use cases such as bringing your own socket-based software licences to AWS or for compliance reasons

**References:**

https://digitalcloud.training/certification-training/aws-solutions-architect-associate/compute/amazon-ec2/

## 23. Question

A health club is developing a mobile fitness app that allows customers to upload statistics and view their progress. Amazon Cognito is being used for authentication, authorization and user management and users will sign-in with Facebook IDs.

In order to securely store data in DynamoDB, the design should use temporary AWS credentials. What feature of Amazon Cognito is used to obtain temporary credentials to access AWS services?

1. SAML Identity Providers
2. Identity Pools
3. User Pools
4. Key Pairs

**Answer: 2**

**Explanation:**

- With an identity pool, users can obtain temporary AWS credentials to access AWS services, such as Amazon S3 and DynamoDB
- A user pool is a user directory in Amazon Cognito. With a user pool, users can sign in to web or mobile apps through Amazon Cognito, or federate through a third-party identity provider (IdP)
- SAML Identity Providers are supported IDPs for identity pools but cannot be used for gaining temporary credentials for AWS services
- Key pairs are used in Amazon EC2 for access to instances

**References:**

https://digitalcloud.training/certification-training/aws-solutions-architect-associate/storage/amazon-s3/

## 24. Question

A membership website your company manages has become quite popular and is gaining members quickly. The website currently runs on EC2 instances with one web server instance and one DB instance running MySQL. You are concerned about the lack of high-availability in the current architecture.

What can you do to easily enable HA without making major changes to the architecture?

1. Install MySQL on an EC2 instance in another AZ and enable replication
2. Install MySQL on an EC2 instance in the same AZ and enable replication
3. Enable Multi-AZ for the MySQL instance
4. Create a Read Replica in another AZ

**Answer: 1**

**Explanation:**

- If you are installing MySQL on an EC2 instance you cannot enable read replicas or multi-AZ. Instead you would need to use Amazon RDS with a MySQL DB engine to use these features
- Migrating to RDS would entail a major change to the architecture so is not really feasible. In this example it will therefore be easier to use the native HA features of MySQL rather than to migrate to RDS. You would want to place the second MySQL DB instance in another AZ to enable high availability and fault tolerance

**References:**

https://digitalcloud.training/certification-training/aws-solutions-architect-associate/compute/amazon-ec2/

https://digitalcloud.training/certification-training/aws-solutions-architect-associate/database/amazon-rds/

## 25. Question

You are a Developer working for Digital Cloud Training. You are planning to write some code that creates a URL that lets users who sign in to your organization's network securely access the AWS Management Console. The URL will include a sign-in token that you get from AWS that authenticates the user to AWS. You are using Microsoft Active Directory Federation Services as your identity provider (IdP) which is compatible with SAML 2.0.

Which of the steps below will you need to include when developing your custom identity broker? (choose 2)

1. Generate a pre-signed URL programmatically using the AWS SDK for Java or the AWS SDK for .NET
2. Delegate access to the IdP through the "Configure Provider" wizard in the IAM console
3. Assume an IAM Role through the console or programmatically with the AWS CLI, Tools for Windows PowerShell or API
4. Call the AWS federation endpoint and supply the temporary security credentials to request a sign-in token
5. Call the AWS Security Token Service (AWS STS) AssumeRole or GetFederationToken API operations to obtain temporary security credentials for the user

**Answer: 4,5**

**Explanation:**

- The aim of this solution is to create a single sign-on solution that enables users signed in to the organization's Active Directory service to be able to connect to AWS resources. When developing a custom identity broker you use the AWS STS service.
- The AWS Security Token Service (STS) is a web service that enables you to request temporary, limited-privilege credentials for IAM users or for users that you authenticate (federated users). The steps performed by the custom identity broker to sign users into the AWS management console are:

1. Verify that the user is authenticated by your local identity system
2. Call the AWS Security Token Service (AWS STS) AssumeRole or GetFederationToken API operations to obtain temporary security credentials for the user
3. Call the AWS federation endpoint and supply the temporary security credentials to request a sign-in token
4. Construct a URL for the console that includes the token
5. Give the URL to the user or invoke the URL on the user's behalf

- You cannot generate a pre-signed URL for this purpose using SDKs, delegate access through the IAM console os directly assume IAM roles.

**References:**

https://digitalcloud.training/certification-training/aws-solutions-architect-associate/security-identity-compliance/aws-iam/

https://docs.aws.amazon.com/IAM/latest/UserGuide/id_roles_providers_enable-console-custom-url.html

## 26. Question

You need to create an EBS volume to mount to an existing EC2 instance for an application that will be writing structured data to the volume. The application vendor suggests that the performance of the disk should be up to 3 IOPS per GB. You expect the capacity of the volume to grow to 2TB.

Taking into account cost effectiveness, which EBS volume type would you select?

1. Provisioned IOPS (Io1)
2. General Purpose (GP2)
3. Throughput Optimized HDD (ST1)
4. Cold HDD (SC1)

**Answer: 2**

**Explanation:**

- SSD, General Purpose (GP2) provides enough IOPS to support this requirement and is the most economical option that does. Using Provisioned IOPS would be more expensive and the other two options do not provide an SLA for IOPS
- More information on the volume types:
  - SSD, General Purpose (GP2) provides 3 IOPS per GB up to 16,000 IOPS. Volume size is 1 GB to 16 TB
  - Provisioned IOPS (Io1) provides the IOPS you assign up to 50 IOPS per GiB and up to 64,000 IOPS per volume. Volume size is 4 GB to 16TB

- Throughput Optimized HDD (ST1) provides up to 500 IOPS per volume but does not provide an SLA for IOPS
- Cold HDD (SC1) provides up to 250 IOPS per volume but does not provide an SLA for IOPS

**References:**

https://digitalcloud.training/certification-training/aws-solutions-architect-associate/compute/amazon-ebs/

https://docs.aws.amazon.com/AWSEC2/latest/UserGuide/EBSVolumeTypes.html?icmpid=docs_ec2_console

## 27. Question

**Your manager has asked you to explain the benefits of using IAM groups. Which of the below statements are valid benefits? (choose 2)**

1. Provide the ability to create custom permission policies
2. Enables you to attach IAM permission policies to more than one user at a time
3. Groups let you specify permissions for multiple users, which can make it easier to manage the permissions for those users
4. Provide the ability to nest groups to create an organizational hierarchy
5. You can restrict access to the subnets in your VPC

**Answer: 2,3**

**Explanation:**

- Groups are collections of users and have policies attached to them. A group is not an identity and cannot be identified as a principal in an IAM policy. Use groups to assign permissions to users. Use the principal of least privilege when assigning permissions. You cannot nest groups (groups within groups)
- You cannot use groups to restrict access to subnet in your VPC
- Custom permission policies are created using IAM policies. These are then attached to users, groups or roles

**References:**

https://digitalcloud.training/certification-training/aws-solutions-architect-associate/security-identity-compliance/aws-iam/

## 28. Question

**You are designing solutions that will utilize CloudFormation templates and your manager has asked how much extra will it cost to use CloudFormation to deploy resources?**

1. CloudFormation is charged per hour of usage
2. Amazon charge a flat fee for each time you use CloudFormation
3. There is no additional charge for AWS CloudFormation, you only pay for the AWS resources that are created
4. The cost is based on the size of the template

**Answer: 3**

**Explanation:**

- There is no additional charge for AWS CloudFormation. You pay for AWS resources (such as Amazon EC2 instances, Elastic Load Balancing load balancers, etc.) created using AWS CloudFormation in the same manner as if you created them manually. You only pay for what you use, as you use it; there are no minimum fees and no required upfront commitments
- There is no flat fee, per hour usage costs or charges applicable to templates

**References:**

https://digitalcloud.training/certification-training/aws-solutions-architect-associate/management-tools/aws-cloudformation/

## 29. Question

An important application you manage uses an Elastic Load Balancer (ELB) to distribute incoming requests amongst a fleet of EC2 instances. You need to ensure any operational issues are identified. Which of the statements below are correct about monitoring of an ELB? (choose 2)

1. CloudWatch metrics can be logged to an S3 bucket
2. Access logs are enabled by default
3. CloudTrail can be used to capture application logs
4. Access logs can identify requester, IP, and request type
5. Information is sent to CloudWatch every minute if there are active requests

**Answer: 4,5**

**Explanation:**

- Information is sent by the ELB to CloudWatch every 1 minute when requests are active. Can be used to trigger SNS notifications
- Access Logs are disabled by default. Includes information about the clients (not included in CloudWatch metrics) including identifying the requester, IP, request type etc. Access logs can be optionally stored and retained in S3
- CloudWatch metrics for ELB cannot be logged directly to an S3 bucket. Instead you should use ELB access logs
- CloudTrail is used to capture API calls to the ELB and logs can be stored in an S3 bucket

**References:**

https://digitalcloud.training/certification-training/aws-solutions-architect-associate/compute/elastic-load-balancing/

## 30. Question

You have created a new VPC and setup an Auto Scaling Group to maintain a desired count of 2 EC2 instances. The security team has requested that the EC2 instances be located in a private subnet. To distribute load, you have to also setup an Internet-facing Application Load Balancer (ALB).

With your security team's wishes in mind what else needs to be done to get this configuration to work? (choose 2)

1. Attach an Internet Gateway to the private subnets

2. Add an Elastic IP address to each EC2 instance in the private subnet
3. Add a NAT gateway to the private subnet
4. Associate the public subnets with the ALB
5. For each private subnet create a corresponding public subnet in the same AZ

**Answer: 4,5**

**Explanation:**

- ELB nodes have public IPs and route traffic to the private IP addresses of the EC2 instances. You need one public subnet in each AZ where the ELB is defined and the private subnets are located
- Attaching an Internet gateway (which is done at the VPC level, not the subnet level) or a NAT gateway will not assist as these are both used for outbound communications which is not the goal here
- ELBs talk to the private IP addresses of the EC2 instances so adding an Elastic IP address to the instance won't help. Additionally Elastic IP addresses are used in public subnets to allow Internet access via an Internet Gateway

**References:**

https://digitalcloud.training/certification-training/aws-solutions-architect-associate/compute/elastic-load-balancing/

https://aws.amazon.com/premiumsupport/knowledge-center/public-load-balancer-private-ec2/

## 31. Question

**A Solutions Architect is creating a design for a multi-tiered serverless application. Which two services form the application facing services from the AWS serverless infrastructure? (choose 2)**

1. Amazon ECS
2. API Gateway
3. Elastic Load Balancer
4. AWS Cognito
5. AWS Lambda

**Answer: 2,5**

**Explanation:**

- The only application services here are API Gateway and Lambda and these are considered to be serverless services
- ECS provides the platform for running containers and uses Amazon EC2 instances
- ELB provides distribution of incoming network connections and also uses Amazon EC2 instances
- AWS Cognito is used for providing authentication services for web and mobile apps

**References:**

https://aws.amazon.com/serverless/

## 32. Question

An application you manage stores encrypted data in S3 buckets. You need to be able to query the encrypted data using SQL queries and write the encrypted results back the S3 bucket. As the data is sensitive you need to implement fine-grained control over access to the S3 bucket.

What combination of services represent the BEST options support these requirements? (choose 2)

1. Use bucket ACLs to restrict access to the bucket
2. Use IAM policies to restrict access to the bucket
3. Use AWS Glue to extract the data, analyze it, and load it back to the S3 bucket
4. Use Athena for querying the data and writing the results back to the bucket
5. Use the AWS KMS API to query the encrypted data, and the S3 API for writing the results

Answer: 2,4

Explanation:

- Athena also allows you to easily query encrypted data stored in Amazon S3 and write encrypted results back to your S3 bucket. Both, server-side encryption and client-side encryption are supported
- With IAM policies, you can grant IAM users fine-grained control to your S3 buckets, and is preferable to using bucket ACLs
- AWS Glue is an ETL service and is not used for querying and analyzing data in S3
- The AWS KMS API can be used for encryption purposes, however it cannot perform analytics so is not suitable

References:

https://aws.amazon.com/athena/

https://digitalcloud.training/certification-training/aws-solutions-architect-associate/security-identity-compliance/aws-iam/

## 33. Question

A new application you are designing will store data in an Amazon Aurora MySQL DB. You are looking for a way to enable inter-region disaster recovery capabilities with fast replication and fast failover. Which of the following options is the BEST solution?

1. Use Amazon Aurora Global Database
2. Enable Multi-AZ for the Aurora DB
3. Create a cross-region Aurora Read Replica
4. Create an EBS backup of the Aurora volumes and use cross-region replication to copy the snapshot

Answer: 1

Explanation:

- Amazon Aurora Global Database is designed for globally distributed applications, allowing a single Amazon Aurora database to span multiple AWS regions. It replicates your data with no impact on database performance, enables fast local reads with low latency in each region, and provides disaster recovery from region-wide outages. Aurora Global Database uses storage-based replication with typical latency of less than 1 second, using dedicated infrastructure that leaves your database fully available to serve application workloads. In the unlikely event of a regional degradation or outage, one of the secondary regions can be promoted to full read/write capabilities in less than 1 minute.

- You can create an Amazon Aurora MySQL DB cluster as a Read Replica in a different AWS Region than the source DB cluster. Taking this approach can improve your disaster recovery capabilities, let you scale read operations into an AWS Region that is closer to your users, and make it easier to migrate from one AWS Region to another. However, this solution would not provide the fast storage replication and fast failover capabilities of the Aurora Global Database and is therefore not the best option
- Enabling Multi-AZ for the Aurora DB would provide AZ-level resiliency within the region not across regions
- Though you can take a DB snapshot and replicate it across regions, it does not provide an automated solution and it would not enable fast failover

**References:**

https://digitalcloud.training/certification-training/aws-solutions-architect-associate/database/amazon-rds/

https://docs.aws.amazon.com/AmazonRDS/latest/UserGuide/Aurora.Replication.html

## 34. Question

You are putting together a design for a web-facing application. The application will be run on EC2 instances behind ELBs in multiple regions in an active/passive configuration. The website address the application runs on is digitalcloud.training. You will be using Route 53 to perform DNS resolution for the application.

How would you configure Route 53 in this scenario based on AWS best practices? (choose 2)

1. Use a Failover Routing Policy
2. Connect the ELBs using CNAME records
3. Use a Weighted Routing Policy
4. Set Evaluate Target Health to "No" for the primary
5. Connect the ELBs using Alias records

**Answer: 1,5**

**Explanation:**

- The failover routing policy is used for active/passive configurations. Alias records can be used to map the domain apex (digitalcloud.training) to the Elastic Load Balancers.
- Weighted routing is not an active/passive routing policy. All records are active and the traffic is distributed according to the weighting
- You cannot use CNAME records for the domain apex record, you must use Alias records
- For Evaluate Target Health choose Yes for your primary record and choose No for your secondary record. For your primary record choose Yes for Associate with Health Check. Then for Health Check to Associate select the health check that you created for your primary resource

**References:**

https://digitalcloud.training/certification-training/aws-solutions-architect-associate/networking-and-content-delivery/amazon-route-53/

## 35. Question

You recently noticed that your Network Load Balancer (NLB) in one of your VPCs is not distributing traffic evenly between EC2 instances in your AZs. There are an odd number of EC2 instances spread across two AZs. The NLB is configured with a TCP listener on port 80 and is using active health checks.

What is the most likely problem?

1. NLB can only load balance within a single AZ
2. There is no HTTP listener
3. Health checks are failing in one AZ due to latency
4. Cross-zone load balancing is disabled

Answer: 4

Explanation:

- Without cross-zone load balancing enabled, the NLB will distribute traffic 50/50 between AZs. As there are an odd number of instances across the two AZs some instances will not receive any traffic. Therefore enabling cross-zone load balancing will ensure traffic is distributed evenly between available instances in all AZs
- If health checks fail this will cause the NLB to stop sending traffic to these instances. However, the health check packets are very small and it is unlikely that latency would be the issue within a region
- Listeners are used to receive incoming connections. An NLB listens on TCP not on HTTP therefore having no HTTP listener is not the issue here
- An NLB can load balance across multiple AZs just like the other ELB types

References:

https://digitalcloud.training/certification-training/aws-solutions-architect-associate/compute/elastic-load-balancing/

## 36. Question

You are a Solutions Architect at Digital Cloud Training. A new client who has not used cloud computing has asked you to explain how AWS works. The client wants to know what service is provided that will provide a virtual network infrastructure that loosely resembles a traditional data center but has the capacity to scale more easily?

1. Elastic Load Balancing
2. Elastic Compute Cloud
3. Direct Connect
4. Virtual Private Cloud

Answer: 4

Explanation:

- Amazon VPC lets you provision a logically isolated section of the Amazon Web Services (AWS) cloud where you can launch AWS resources in a virtual network that you define. It is analogous to having your own DC inside AWS and provides complete control over the virtual networking environment including selection of IP ranges, creation of subnets, and configuration of route tables and gateways. A VPC is logically isolated from other VPCs on AWS

- Elastic Load Balancing automatically distributes incoming application traffic across multiple targets, such as Amazon EC2 instances, containers, IP addresses, and Lambda functions
- Amazon Elastic Compute Cloud (Amazon EC2) is a web service that provides secure, resizable compute capacity in the cloud
- AWS Direct Connect is a cloud service solution that makes it easy to establish a dedicated network connection from your premises to AWS

**References:**

https://digitalcloud.training/certification-training/aws-solutions-architect-associate/networking-and-content-delivery/amazon-vpc/

## 37. Question

**You manage an application that uses Auto Scaling. Recently there have been incidents of multiple scaling events in an hour and you are looking at methods of stabilizing the Auto Scaling Group. Select the statements below that are correct with regards to the Auto Scaling cooldown period? (choose 2)**

1. The default value is 600 seconds
2. It ensures that the Auto Scaling group terminates the EC2 instances that are least busy
3. It ensures that before the Auto Scaling group scales out, the EC2 instances can apply system updates
4. The default value is 300 seconds
5. It ensures that the Auto Scaling group does not launch or terminate additional EC2 instances before the previous scaling activity takes effect

**Answer: 4,5**

**Explanation:**

- The cooldown period is a configurable setting for your Auto Scaling group that helps to ensure that it doesn't launch or terminate additional instances before the previous scaling activity takes effect
- The default cooldown period is applied when you create your Auto Scaling group
- The default value is 300 seconds
- You can configure the default cooldown period when you create the Auto Scaling group, using the AWS Management Console, the create-auto-scaling-group command (AWS CLI), or the CreateAutoScalingGroup API operation

**References:**

https://digitalcloud.training/certification-training/aws-solutions-architect-associate/compute/aws-auto-scaling/

https://docs.aws.amazon.com/autoscaling/ec2/userguide/Cooldown.html

## 38. Question

**An application you manage in your VPC uses an Auto Scaling Group that spans 3 AZs and there are currently 4 EC2 instances running in the group. What actions will Auto Scaling take, by default, if it needs to terminate an EC2 instance? (choose 2)**

1. Wait for the cooldown period and then terminate the instance that has been running the longest
2. Randomly select one of the 3 AZs, and then terminate an instance in that AZ
3. Terminate an instance in the AZ which currently has 2 running EC2 instances

4. Send an SNS notification, if configured to do so
5. Terminate the instance with the least active network connections. If multiple instances meet this criterion, one will be randomly selected

**Answer: 3,4**

**Explanation:**

- Auto Scaling can perform rebalancing when it finds that the number of instances across AZs is not balanced. Auto Scaling rebalances by launching new EC2 instances in the AZs that have fewer instances first, only then will it start terminating instances in AZs that had more instances
- Auto Scaling can be configured to send an SNS email when:
  - An instance is launched
  - An instance is terminated
  - An instance fails to launch
  - An instance fails to terminate
- Auto Scaling does not terminate the instance that has been running the longest
- Auto Scaling will only terminate an instance randomly after it has first gone through several other selection steps. Please see the AWS article below for detailed information on the process

**References:**

https://digitalcloud.training/certification-training/aws-solutions-architect-associate/compute/aws-auto-scaling/

https://docs.aws.amazon.com/autoscaling/ec2/userguide/as-instance-termination.html

## 39. Question

You are creating a CloudFormation template that will provision a new EC2 instance and new EBS volume. What do you need to specify to associate the block store with the instance?

1. Both the EC2 logical ID and the EBS logical ID
2. The EC2 logical ID
3. Both the EC2 physical ID and the EBS physical ID
4. The EC2 physical ID

**Answer: 1**

**Explanation:**

- Logical IDs are used to reference resources within the template
- Physical IDs identify resources outside of AWS CloudFormation templates, but only after the resources have been created

**References:**

https://docs.aws.amazon.com/AWSCloudFormation/latest/UserGuide/resources-section-structure.html

https://digitalcloud.training/certification-training/aws-solutions-architect-associate/management-tools/aws-cloudformation/

## 40. Question

You regularly launch EC2 instances manually from the console and want to streamline the process to reduce administrative overhead. Which feature of EC2 allows you to store settings such as AMI ID, instance type, key pairs and Security Groups?

1. Run Command
2. Launch Templates
3. Launch Configurations
4. Placement Groups

**Answer: 2**

**Explanation:**

- Launch templates enable you to store launch parameters so that you do not have to specify them every time you launch an instance. When you launch an instance using the Amazon EC2 console, an AWS SDK, or a command line tool, you can specify the launch template to use
- Launch Configurations are used with Auto Scaling Groups
- Run Command automates common administrative tasks, and lets you perform ad hoc configuration changes at scale
- You can launch or start instances in a placement group, which determines how instances are placed on underlying hardware

**References:**

https://docs.aws.amazon.com/AWSEC2/latest/UserGuide/ec2-launch-templates.html

## 41. Question

You are configuring Route 53 for a customer's website. Their web servers are behind an Internet-facing ELB. What record set would you create to point the customer's DNS zone apex record at the ELB?

1. Create an A record that is an Alias, and select the ELB DNS as a target
2. Create a PTR record pointing to the DNS name of the load balancer
3. Create an A record pointing to the DNS name of the load balancer
4. Create a CNAME record that is an Alias, and select the ELB DNS as a target

**Answer: 1**

**Explanation:**

- An Alias record can be used for resolving apex or naked domain names (e.g. example.com). You can create an A record that is an Alias that uses the customer's website zone apex domain name and map it to the ELB DNS name
- A CNAME record can't be used for resolving apex or naked domain names
- A standard A record maps the DNS domain name to the IP address of a resource. You cannot obtain the IP of the ELB so you must use an Alias record which maps the DNS domain name of the customer's website to the ELB DNS name (rather than its IP)
- PTR records are reverse lookup records where you use the IP to find the DNS name

**References:**

## 42. Question

An Auto Scaling Group in which you have four EC2 instances running is becoming heavily loaded. The instances are using the m4.large instance type and the CPUs are hitting 80%. Due to licensing constraints you don't want to add additional instances to the ASG so you are planning to upgrade to the m4.xlarge instance type instead. You need to make the change immediately but don't want to terminate the existing instances.

How can you perform the change without causing the ASG to launch new instances? (choose 2)

1. Edit the existing launch configuration and specify the new instance type
2. On the ASG suspend the Auto Scaling process until you have completed the change
3. Stop each instance and change its instance type. Start the instance again
4. Change the instance type and then restart the instance
5. Create a new launch configuration with the new instance type specified

Answer: 2,3

Explanation:

- When you resize an instance, you must select an instance type that is compatible with the configuration of the instance. You must stop your Amazon EBS–backed instance before you can change its instance type
- You can suspend and then resume one or more of the scaling processes for your Auto Scaling group. Suspending scaling processes can be useful when you want to investigate a configuration problem or other issue with your web application and then make changes to your application, without invoking the scaling processes
- You do not need to create a new launch configuration and you cannot edit an existing launch configuration
- You cannot change an instance type without first stopping the instance

References:

https://digitalcloud.training/certification-training/aws-solutions-architect-associate/compute/aws-auto-scaling/

https://docs.aws.amazon.com/AWSEC2/latest/UserGuide/ec2-instance-resize.html

## 43. Question

An issue has been raised to you whereby a client is concerned about the permissions assigned to his containerized applications. The containers are using the EC2 launch type. The current configuration uses the container instance's IAM roles for assigning permissions to the containerized applications.

The client has asked if it's possible to implement more granular permissions so that some applications can be assigned more restrictive permissions?

1. This can be achieved using IAM roles for tasks, and splitting the containers according to the permissions required to different task definition profiles
2. This can be achieved by configuring a resource-based policy for each application
3. This cannot be changed as IAM roles can only be linked to container instances

4. This can only be achieved using the Fargate launch type

**Answer: 1**

**Explanation:**

- With IAM roles for Amazon ECS tasks, you can specify an IAM role that can be used by the containers in a task. Using this feature you can achieve the required outcome by using IAM roles for tasks and splitting the containers according to the permissions required to different task profiles.
- The solution can be achieved whether using the EC2 or Fargate launch types
- Amazon ECS does not support IAM resource-based policies

**References:**

https://digitalcloud.training/certification-training/aws-solutions-architect-associate/compute/amazon-ecs/

https://docs.aws.amazon.com/AmazonECS/latest/userguide/task-iam-roles.html

https://docs.aws.amazon.com/IAM/latest/UserGuide/reference_aws-services-that-work-with-iam.html

## 44. Question

You are putting together the design for a new retail website for a high-profile company. The company has previously been the victim of targeted distributed denial-of-service (DDoS) attacks and have requested that you ensure the design includes mitigation techniques.

Which of the following are the BEST techniques to help ensure the availability of the services is not compromised in an attack? (choose 2)

1. Use CloudFront for distributing both static and dynamic content
2. Use Spot instances to reduce the cost impact in case of attack
3. Configure Auto Scaling with a high maximum number of instances to ensure it can scale accordingly
4. Use encryption on your EBS volumes
5. Use Placement Groups to ensure high bandwidth and low latency

**Answer: 1,3**

**Explanation:**

- CloudFront distributes traffic across multiple edge locations and filters requests to ensure that only valid HTTP(S) requests will be forwarded to backend hosts. CloudFront also supports geoblocking, which you can use to prevent requests from particular geographic locations from being served
- ELB automatically distributes incoming application traffic across multiple targets, such as Amazon Elastic Compute Cloud (Amazon EC2) instances, containers, and IP addresses, and multiple Availability Zones, which minimizes the risk of overloading a single resource
- ELB, like CloudFront, only supports valid TCP requests, so DDoS attacks such as UDP and SYN floods are not able to reach EC2 instances
- ELB also offers a single point of management and can serve as a line of defense between the internet and your backend, private EC2 instances

- Auto Scaling helps to maintain a desired count of EC2 instances running at all times and setting a high maximum number of instances allows your fleet to grow and absorb some of the impact of the attack
- RDS supports several scenarios for deploying DB instances in private and public facing configurations
- CloudWatch can be used to setup alerts for when metrics reach unusual levels. High network in traffic may indicate a DDoS attack
- Encrypting EBS volumes does not help in a DDoS attack as the attack is targeted at reducing availability rather than compromising data
- Spot instances may reduce the cost (depending on the current Spot price) however the questions asks us to focus on availability not cost

**References:**

https://digitalcloud.training/certification-training/aws-solutions-architect-associate/networking-and-content-delivery/amazon-cloudfront/

https://digitalcloud.training/certification-training/aws-solutions-architect-associate/compute/elastic-load-balancing/

https://digitalcloud.training/certification-training/aws-solutions-architect-associate/database/amazon-rds/

https://aws.amazon.com/answers/networking/aws-ddos-attack-mitigation/

https://docs.aws.amazon.com/waf/latest/developerguide/tutorials-ddos-cross-service.html

https://docs.aws.amazon.com/AmazonRDS/latest/UserGuide/USER_VPC.Scenarios.html

## 45. Question

A Solutions Architect is creating the business process workflows associated with an order fulfilment system. What AWS service can assist with coordinating tasks across distributed application components?

1. Amazon SNS
2. Amazon SWF
3. Amazon SQS
4. Amazon STS

**Answer: 2**

**Explanation:**

- Amazon Simple Workflow Service (SWF) is a web service that makes it easy to coordinate work across distributed application components. SWF enables applications for a range of use cases, including media processing, web application back-ends, business process workflows, and analytics pipelines, to be designed as a coordination of tasks
- Amazon Security Token Service (STS) is used for requesting temporary credentials
- Amazon Simple Queue Service (SQS) is a message queue used for decoupling application components
- Amazon Simple Notification Service (SNS) is a web service that makes it easy to set up, operate, and send notifications from the cloud
- SNS supports notifications over multiple transports including HTTP/HTTPS, Email/Email-JSON, SQS and SMS

**References:**

https://digitalcloud.training/certification-training/aws-solutions-architect-associate/application-integration/amazon-swf/

## 46. Question

A Solutions Architect has setup a VPC with a public subnet and a VPN-only subnet. The public subnet is associated with a custom route table that has a route to an Internet Gateway. The VPN-only subnet is associated with the main route table and has a route to a virtual private gateway.

The Architect has created a new subnet in the VPC and launched an EC2 instance in it. However, the instance cannot connect to the Internet. What is the MOST likely reason?

1. The subnet has been automatically associated with the main route table which does not have a route to the Internet
2. The new subnet has not been associated with a route table
3. The Internet Gateway is experiencing connectivity problems
4. There is no NAT Gateway available in the new subnet so Internet connectivity is not possible

**Answer: 1**

**Explanation:**

- When you create a new subnet, it is automatically associated with the main route table. Therefore, the EC2 instance will not have a route to the Internet. The Architect should associate the new subnet with the custom route table
- NAT Gateways are used for connecting EC2 instances in private subnets to the Internet. This is a valid reason for a private subnet to not have connectivity, however in this case the Architect is attempting to use an Internet Gateway
- Subnets are always associated to a route table when created
- Internet Gateways are highly-available so it's unlikely that IGW connectivity is the issue

**References:**

https://docs.aws.amazon.com/vpc/latest/userguide/VPC_Route_Tables.html

## 47. Question

You need to run a production batch process quickly that will use several EC2 instances. The process cannot be interrupted and must be completed within a short time period.

What is likely to be the MOST cost-effective choice of EC2 instance type to use for this requirement?

1. Flexible instances
2. Spot instances
3. Reserved instances
4. On-demand instances

**Answer: 4**

**Explanation:**

- The key requirements here are that you need to deploy several EC2 instances quickly to run the batch process and you must ensure that the job completes. The on-demand pricing model is the best for this ad-hoc requirement as though spot pricing may be cheaper you cannot afford to risk that the instances are terminated by AWS when the market price increases
- Spot instances provide a very low hourly compute cost and are good when you have flexible start and end times. They are often used for use cases such as grid computing and high-performance computing (HPC)
- Reserved instances are used for longer more stable requirements where you can get a discount for a fixed 1 or 3 year term. This pricing model is not good for temporary requirements
- There is no such thing as a "flexible instance"

**References:**

https://digitalcloud.training/certification-training/aws-solutions-architect-associate/compute/amazon-ec2/


## 48. Question

An Amazon CloudWatch alarm recently notified you that the load on a DynamoDB table you are running is getting close to the provisioned capacity for writes. The DynamoDB table is part of a two-tier customer-facing application and is configured using provisioned capacity. You are concerned about what will happen if the limit is reached but need to wait for approval to increase the WriteCapacityUnits value assigned to the table.

What will happen if the limit for the provisioned capacity for writes is reached?

1. The requests will succeed, and an HTTP 200 status code will be returned
2. The requests will be throttled, and fail with an HTTP 503 code (Service Unavailable)
3. The requests will be throttled, and fail with an HTTP 400 code (Bad Request) and a ProvisionedThroughputExceededException
4. DynamoDB scales automatically so there's no need to worry


**Answer: 3**

**Explanation:**

- DynamoDB can throttle requests that exceed the provisioned throughput for a table. When a request is throttled it fails with an HTTP 400 code (Bad Request) and a ProvisionedThroughputExceeded exception (not a 503 or 200 status code)
- When using the provisioned capacity pricing model DynamoDB does not automatically scale. DynamoDB can automatically scale when using the new on-demand capacity mode, however this is not configured for this database

**References:**

https://digitalcloud.training/certification-training/aws-solutions-architect-associate/database/amazon-dynamodb/


## 49. Question

A new application you are deploying uses Docker containers. You are creating a design for an ECS cluster to host the application. Which statements about ECS clusters are correct? (choose 2)

1. ECS Clusters are a logical grouping of container instances that you can place tasks on

2. Each container instance may be part of multiple clusters at a time
3. Clusters can contain tasks using the Fargate and EC2 launch type
4. Clusters can contain a single container instance type
5. Clusters are AZ specific

**Answer: 1,3**

**Explanation:**

- ECS Clusters are a logical grouping of container instances the you can place tasks on
- Clusters can contain tasks using BOTH the Fargate and EC2 launch type
- Each container instance may only be part of one cluster at a time
- Clusters are region specific
- For clusters with the EC2 launch type clusters can contain different container instance types

**References:**

https://digitalcloud.training/certification-training/aws-solutions-architect-associate/compute/amazon-ecs/

## 50. Question

**A Solutions Architect is designing a three-tier web application that includes an Auto Scaling group of Amazon EC2 Instances running behind an ELB Classic Load Balancer. The security team requires that all web servers must be accessible only through the Elastic Load Balancer and that none of the web servers are directly accessible from the Internet. How should the Architect meet these requirements?**

1. Install a Load Balancer on an Amazon EC2 instance
2. Configure the web servers' security group to deny traffic from the Internet
3. Create an Amazon CloudFront distribution in front of the Elastic Load Balancer
4. Configure the web tier security group to allow only traffic from the Elastic Load Balancer

**Answer: 4**

**Explanation:**

- The web servers must be kept private so they will be not have public IP addresses. The ELB is Internet-facing so it will be publicly accessible via it's DNS address (and corresponding public IP). To restrict web servers to be accessible only through the ELB you can configure the web tier security group to allow only traffic from the ELB. You would normally do this by adding the ELBs security group to the rule on the web tier security group
- This scenario is using an ELB Classic Load Balancer and these cannot be installed on EC2 instances (at least not by you, in reality all ELBs are actually running on EC2 instances but these are transparent to the AWS end user)
- You cannot create deny rules in security groups
- CloudFront distributions are used for caching content to improve performance for users on the Internet. They are not security devices to be used for restricting access to EC2 instances

**References:**

https://digitalcloud.training/certification-training/aws-solutions-architect-associate/compute/elastic-load-balancing/

## 51. Question

You are building a new Elastic Container Service (ECS) cluster. The ECS instances are running the EC2 launch type and you would like to enable load balancing to distributed connections to the tasks running on the cluster. You would like the mapping of ports to be performed dynamically and will need to route to different groups of servers based on the path in the requested URL. Which AWS service would you choose to fulfil these requirements?

1. Classic Load Balancer
2. ECS Services
3. Network Load Balancer
4. Application Load Balancer

**Answer: 4**

**Explanation:**

- An ALB allows containers to use dynamic host port mapping so that multiple tasks from the same service are allowed on the same container host – the CLB and NLB do not offer this
- An ALB can also route requests based on the content of the request in the host field: host-based or path-based

**References:**

https://digitalcloud.training/certification-training/aws-solutions-architect-associate/compute/elastic-load-balancing/

https://aws.amazon.com/premiumsupport/knowledge-center/dynamic-port-mapping-ecs/

https://docs.aws.amazon.com/elasticloadbalancing/latest/application/tutorial-load-balancer-routing.html

## 52. Question

You have created a VPC with private and public subnets and will be deploying a new mySQL database server running on an EC2 instance. According to AWS best practice, which subnet should you deploy the database server into?

1. The private subnet
2. The public subnet
3. It doesn't matter
4. The subnet that is mapped to the primary AZ in the region

**Answer: 1**

**Explanation:**

- AWS best practice is to deploy databases into private subnets wherever possible. You can then deploy your web front-ends into public subnets and configure these, or an additional application tier to write data to the database
- Public subnets are typically used for web front-ends as they are directly accessible from the Internet. It is preferable to launch your database in a private subnet
- There is no such thing as a "primary" Availability Zone (AZ). All AZs are essentially created equal and your subnets map 1:1 to a single AZ

References:

https://digitalcloud.training/certification-training/aws-solutions-architect-associate/networking-and-content-delivery/amazon-vpc/

## 53. Question

You just attempted to restart a stopped EC2 instance and it immediately changed from a pending state to a terminated state. What are the most likely explanations? (choose 2)

1. AWS does not currently have enough available On-Demand capacity to service your request
2. You've reached your EBS volume limit
3. The AMI is unsupported
4. You have reached the limit on the number of instances that you can launch in a region
5. An EBS snapshot is corrupt

Answer: 2,5

Explanation:

- The following are a few reasons why an instance might immediately terminate:
    - You've reached your EBS volume limit
    - An EBS snapshot is corrupt
    - The root EBS volume is encrypted and you do not have permissions to access the KMS key for decryption
    - The instance store-backed AMI that you used to launch the instance is missing a required part (an image.part.xx file)
- It is possible that an instance type is not supported by an AMI and this can cause an "UnsupportedOperation" client error. However, in this case the instance was previously running (it is in a stopped state) so it is unlikely that this is the issue
- If AWS does not have capacity available a InsufficientInstanceCapacity error will be generated when you try to launch a new instance or restart a stopped instance
- If you've reached the limit on the number of instances you can launch in a region you get an InstanceLimitExceeded error when you try to launch a new instance or restart a stopped instance

References:

https://docs.aws.amazon.com/AWSEC2/latest/UserGuide/troubleshooting-launch.html

## 54. Question

Your organization has a data lake on S3 and you need to find a solution for performing in-place queries of the data assets in the data lake. The requirement is to perform both data discovery and SQL querying, and complex queries from a large number of concurrent users using BI tools.

What is the BEST combination of AWS services to use in this situation? (choose 2)

1. AWS Lambda for the complex queries
2. Amazon Athena for the ad hoc SQL querying
3. RedShift Spectrum for the complex queries
4. AWS Glue for the ad hoc SQL querying

Answer: 2,3

**Explanation:**

- Performing in-place queries on a data lake allows you to run sophisticated analytics queries directly on the data in S3 without having to load it into a data warehouse
- You can use both Athena and Redshift Spectrum against the same data assets. You would typically use Athena for ad hoc data discovery and SQL querying, and then use Redshift Spectrum for more complex queries and scenarios where a large number of data lake users want to run concurrent BI and reporting workloads
- AWS Lambda is a serverless technology for running functions, it is not the best solution for running analytics queries
- AWS Glue is an ETL service

**References:**

https://docs.aws.amazon.com/aws-technical-content/latest/building-data-lakes/in-place-querying.html

https://aws.amazon.com/redshift/

https://aws.amazon.com/athena/


## 55. Question

You have been asked to come up with a solution for providing single sign-on to existing staff in your company who manage on-premise web applications and now need access to the AWS management console to manage resources in the AWS cloud.

**Which product combinations provide the best solution to achieve this requirement?**

1. Use IAM and Amazon Cognito
2. Use your on-premise LDAP directory with IAM
3. Use IAM and MFA
4. Use the AWS Secure Token Service (STS) and SAML


**Answer: 4**

**Explanation:**

- Single sign-on using federation allows users to login to the AWS console without assigning IAM credentials
- The AWS Security Token Service (STS) is a web service that enables you to request temporary, limited-privilege credentials for IAM users or for users that you authenticate (such as federated users from an on-premise directory)
- Federation (typically Active Directory) uses SAML 2.0 for authentication and grants temporary access based on the users AD credentials. The user does not need to be a user in IAM
- You cannot use your on-premise LDAP directory with IAM, you must use federation
- Enabling multi-factor authentication (MFA) for IAM is not a federation solution
- Amazon Cognito is used for authenticating users to web and mobile apps not for providing single sign-on between on-premises directories and the AWS management console

**References:**

https://digitalcloud.training/certification-training/aws-solutions-architect-associate/security-identity-compliance/aws-iam/

## 56. Question

An EC2 instance in an Auto Scaling Group is having some issues that are causing the ASG to launch new instances based on the dynamic scaling policy. You need to troubleshoot the EC2 instance and prevent the ASG from launching new instances temporarily.

What is the best method to accomplish this? (choose 2)

1.  Remove the EC2 instance from the Target Group
2.  Disable the dynamic scaling policy
3.  Place the EC2 instance that is experiencing issues into the Standby state
4.  Disable the launch configuration associated with the EC2 instance
5.  Suspend the scaling processes responsible for launching new instances

**Answer: 3,5**

**Explanation:**

- You can suspend and then resume one or more of the scaling processes for your Auto Scaling group. This can be useful when you want to investigate a configuration problem or other issue with your web application and then make changes to your application, without invoking the scaling processes. You can manually move an instance from an ASG and put it in the standby state

- Instances in standby state are still managed by Auto Scaling, are charged as normal, and do not count towards available EC2 instance for workload/application use. Auto scaling does not perform health checks on instances in the standby state. Standby state can be used for performing updates/changes/troubleshooting etc. without health checks being performed or replacement instances being launched

- You do not need to disable the dynamic scaling policy, you can just suspend it as previously described

- You cannot disable the launch configuration and you can't modify a launch configuration after you've created it

- Target Groups are features of ELB (specifically ALB/NLB). Removing the instance from the target group will stop the ELB from sending connections to it but will not stop Auto Scaling from launching new instances while you are troubleshooting it

**References:**

https://digitalcloud.training/certification-training/aws-solutions-architect-associate/compute/aws-auto-scaling/

## 57. Question

To increase the resiliency of your RDS DB instance, you decided to enable Multi-AZ. Where will the new standby RDS instance be created?

1.  You must specify the location when configuring Multi-AZ
2.  In another subnet within the same AZ
3.  In the same AWS Region but in a different AZ for high availability
4.  In a different AWS Region to protect against Region failures

**Answer: 3**

**Explanation:**

- Multi-AZ RDS creates a replica in another AZ within the same region and synchronously replicates to it (DR only). You cannot choose which AZ in the region will be chosen to create the standby DB instance

**References:**

https://digitalcloud.training/certification-training/aws-solutions-architect-associate/database/amazon-rds/

## 58. Question

Your Systems Administrators currently use Chef for configuration management of on-premise servers. Which AWS service will provide a fully-managed configuration management service that will allow you to use your existing Chef cookbooks?

1. Elastic Beanstalk
2. OpsWorks for Chef Automate
3. Opsworks Stacks
4. CloudFormation

**Answer: 2**

**Explanation:**

- AWS OpsWorks is a configuration management service that provides managed instances of Chef and Puppet. AWS OpsWorks for Chef Automate is a fully-managed configuration management service that hosts Chef Automate, a suite of automation tools from Chef for configuration management, compliance and security, and continuous deployment. OpsWorks for Chef Automate is completely compatible with tooling and cookbooks from the Chef community and automatically registers new nodes with your Chef server
- AWS OpsWorks Stacks lets you manage applications and servers on AWS and on-premises and uses Chef Solo. The question does not require the managed solution on AWS to manage on-premises resources, just to use existing cookbooks so this is not the preferred solution
- Elastic Beanstalk and CloudFormation are not able to build infrastructure using Chef cookbooks

**References:**

https://digitalcloud.training/certification-training/aws-solutions-architect-associate/management-tools/aws-opsworks/

## 59. Question

You would like to store a backup of an Amazon EBS volume on Amazon S3. What is the easiest way of achieving this?

1. Use SWF to automatically create a backup of your EBS volumes and then upload them to an S3 bucket
2. Write a custom script to automatically copy your data to an S3 bucket
3. Create a snapshot of the volume
4. You don't need to do anything, EBS volumes are automatically backed up by default

**Answer: 3**

**Explanation:**

- Snapshots capture a point-in-time state of an instance. Snapshots of Amazon EBS volumes are stored on S3 by design so you only need to take a snapshot and it will automatically be stored on Amazon S3
- EBS volumes are not automatically backed up using snapshots. You need to manually take a snapshot or you can use Amazon Data Lifecycle Manager (Amazon DLM) to automate the creation, retention, and deletion of snapshots
- This is not a good use case for Amazon SWF

**References:**

https://digitalcloud.training/certification-training/aws-solutions-architect-associate/compute/amazon-ebs/

## 60. Question

When using throttling controls with API Gateway what happens when request submissions exceed the steady-state request rate and burst limits?

1. The requests will be buffered in a cache until the load reduces
2. API Gateway fails the limit-exceeding requests and returns "429 Too Many Requests" error responses to the client
3. API Gateway drops the requests and does not return a response to the client
4. API Gateway fails the limit-exceeding requests and returns "500 Internal Server Error" error responses to the client

**Answer: 2**

**Explanation:**

- You can throttle and monitor requests to protect your backend. Resiliency through throttling rules based on the number of requests per second for each HTTP method (GET, PUT). Throttling can be configured at multiple levels including Global and Service Call
- When request submissions exceed the steady-state request rate and burst limits, API Gateway fails the limit-exceeding requests and returns 429 Too Many Requests error responses to the client

**References:**

https://digitalcloud.training/certification-training/aws-solutions-architect-associate/networking-and-content-delivery/amazon-api-gateway/

https://docs.aws.amazon.com/apigateway/latest/developerguide/api-gateway-request-throttling.html

## 61. Question

Health related data in Amazon S3 needs to be frequently accessed for up to 90 days. After that time the data must be retained for compliance reasons for seven years and is rarely accessed.

Which storage classes should be used?

1. Store data in STANDARD for 90 days then transition the data to DEEP_ARCHIVE
2. Store data in INTELLIGENT_TIERING for 90 days then transition to STANDARD_IA
3. Store data in STANDARD for 90 days then expire the data
4. Store data in STANDARD for 90 days then transition to REDUCED_REDUNDANCY

**Answer: 1**

**Explanation:**

- In this case the data is frequently accessed so must be stored in standard for the first 90 days. After that the data is still to be kept for compliance reasons but is rarely accessed so is a good use case for DEEP_ARCHIVE
- You cannot transition from INTELLIGENT_TIERING to STANDARD_IA
- You cannot transition from any storage class to REDUCED_REDUNDANCY
- Expiring the data is not possible as it must be retained for compliance

**References:**

https://docs.aws.amazon.com/AmazonS3/latest/dev/lifecycle-transition-general-considerations.html

https://digitalcloud.training/certification-training/aws-solutions-architect-associate/storage/amazon-s3/

## 62. Question

A manual script that runs a few times a week and completes within 10 minutes needs to be replaced with an automated solution. Which of the following options should an Architect use?

1. Use AWS CloudFormation
2. Use AWS Lambda
3. Use a cron job on an Amazon EC2 instance
4. Use AWS Batch

**Answer: 2**

**Explanation:**

- AWS Lambda has a maximum execution time of 900 seconds (15 minutes). Therefore the script will complete within this time. AWS Lambda is the best solution as you don't need to run any instances (it's serverless) and therefore you will pay only for the execution time.
- AWS Batch is used for running large numbers of batch computing jobs on AWS. AWS Batch dynamically provisions the EC2 instances. This is not a good solution for an ad-hoc use case such as this one where you just need to run a single script a few times a week.
- Cron Jobs are used for scheduling tasks to run on Linux instances. They are used for automating maintenance and administration. This is a workable solution for running a script but does require the instance to be running all the time. Also, AWS prefer you to use services such as AWS Lambda for centralized control and administration.
- AWS CloudFormation is used for launching infrastructure. You can use scripts with AWS CloudFormation but its more about running scripts related to infrastructure provisioning.

**References:**

https://digitalcloud.training/certification-training/aws-solutions-architect-associate/compute/aws-lambda/

## 63. Question

A high-performance file system is required for a financial modelling application. The data set will be stored on Amazon S3 and the storage solution must have seamless integration so objects can be accessed as files.

Which storage solution should be used?

1. Amazon FSx for Windows File Server
2. Amazon FSx for Lustre
3. Amazon Elastic File System (EFS)
4. Amazon Elastic Block Store (EBS)

Answer: 2

Explanation:

- Amazon FSx for Lustre provides a high-performance file system optimized for fast processing of workloads such as machine learning, high performance computing (HPC), video processing, financial modeling, and electronic design automation (EDA). Amazon FSx works natively with Amazon S3, letting you transparently access your S3 objects as files on Amazon FSx to run analyses for hours to months.
- Amazon FSx for Windows File Server provides a fully managed native Microsoft Windows file system so you can easily move your Windows-based applications that require shared file storage to AWS. This solution integrates with Windows file shares, not with Amazon S3.
- EFS and EBS are not good use cases for this solution. Neither storage solution is capable of presenting Amazon S3 objects as files to the application.

References:

https://digitalcloud.training/certification-training/aws-solutions-architect-associate/storage/amazon-fsx/

https://aws.amazon.com/fsx/

## 64. Question

Amazon EC2 instances in a development environment run between 9am and 5pm Monday-Friday. Production instances run 24/7. Which pricing models should be used? (choose 2)

1. Use Spot instances for the development environment
2. Use scheduled reserved instances for the development environment
3. Use Reserved instances for the production environment
4. Use Reserved instances for the development environment
5. Use On-Demand instances for the production environment

Answer: 2,3

Explanation:

- Scheduled Instances are a good choice for workloads that do not run continuously but do run on a regular schedule. This is ideal for the development environment
- Reserved instances are a good choice for workloads that run continuously. This is a good option for the production environment

- Spot Instances are a cost-effective choice if you can be flexible about when your applications run and if your applications can be interrupted. Spot instances are not suitable for the development environment as important work may be interrupted.
- There is no long-term commitment required when you purchase On-Demand Instances. However, you do not get any discount and therefore this is the most expensive option.

**References:**

https://docs.aws.amazon.com/AWSEC2/latest/WindowsGuide/instance-purchasing-options.html

https://digitalcloud.training/certification-training/aws-solutions-architect-associate/compute/amazon-ec2/


## 65. Question

An High Performance Computing (HPC) application needs storage that can provide 135,000 IOPS. The storage layer is replicated across all instances in a cluster.

What is the optimal storage solution that provides the required performance and is cost-effective?

1. Use Amazon EC2 Enhanced Networking with an EBS HDD Throughput Optimized volume
2. Use Amazon S3 with byte-range fetch
3. Use Amazon Instance Store
4. Use Amazon EBS Provisioned IOPS volume with 135,000 IOPS


**Answer: 3**

**Explanation:**

- Instance stores offer very high performance and low latency. As long as you can afford to lose an instance, i.e. you are replicating your data, these can be a good solution for high performance/low latency requirements. Also, the cost of instance stores is included in the instance charges so it can also be more cost-effective than EBS Provisioned IOPS.
- In the case of a HPC cluster that replicates data between nodes you don't necessarily need a shared storage solution such as Amazon EBS Provisioned IOPS – this would also be a more expensive solution as the Instance Store is included in the cost of the HPC instance.
- Amazon S3 is not a solution for this HPC application as in this case it will require block-based storage to provide the required IOPS.
- Enhanced networking provides higher bandwidth and lower latency and is implemented using an Elastic Network Adapter (ENA). However, using an ENA with an HDD Throughput Optimized volume is not recommended and the volume will not provide the performance required for this use case.

**References:**

https://digitalcloud.training/certification-training/aws-solutions-architect-associate/compute/amazon-ec2/

https://digitalcloud.training/certification-training/aws-solutions-architect-associate/compute/amazon-ebs/

https://docs.aws.amazon.com/AWSEC2/latest/UserGuide/InstanceStorage.html

# SET 5: PRACTICE QUESTIONS ONLY

*Or go directly to Set 5: Practice Questions, Answers & Explanations*

## 1. Question

A Solutions Architect is designing the messaging and streaming layers of a serverless application. The messaging layer will manage communications between components and the streaming layer will manage real-time analysis and processing of streaming data.

The Architect needs to select the most appropriate AWS services for these functions. Which services should be used for the messaging and streaming layers? (choose 2)

1. Use Amazon Kinesis for collecting, processing and analyzing real-time streaming data
2. Use Amazon EMR for collecting, processing and analyzing real-time streaming data
3. Use Amazon SNS for providing a fully managed messaging service
4. Use Amazon SWF for providing a fully managed messaging service
5. Use Amazon CloudTrail for collecting, processing and analyzing real-time streaming data

## 2. Question

You are using CloudWatch to monitor the performance of AWS Lambda. Which metrics does Lambda track? (choose 2)

1. Latency per request
2. Total number of connections
3. Total number of transactions
4. Total number of requests
5. Number of users

## 3. Question

The financial institution you are working for stores large amounts of historical transaction records. There are over 25TB of records and your manager has decided to move them into the AWS Cloud. You are planning to use Snowball as copying the data would take too long. Which of the statements below are true regarding Snowball? (choose 2)

1. Can be used with multipart upload
2. Snowball can import to S3 but cannot export from S3
3. Snowball can be used for migration on-premise to on-premise
4. Petabyte scale data transport solution for transferring data into or out of AWS
5. Uses a secure storage device for physical transportation

## 4. Question

A three-tier application running in your VPC uses Auto Scaling for maintaining a desired count of EC2 instances. One of the EC2 instances just reported an EC2 Status Check status of Impaired. Once this information is reported to Auto Scaling, what action will be taken?

1. The impaired instance will be terminated, then a replacement will be launched
2. A new instance will immediately be launched, then the impaired instance will be terminated

3. Auto Scaling must verify with the ELB status checks before taking any action
4. Auto Scaling waits for the health check grace period and then terminates the instance

## 5. Question

You just created a new subnet in your VPC and have launched an EC2 instance into it. You are trying to directly access the EC2 instance from the Internet and cannot connect. Which steps should you take to troubleshoot the issue? (choose 2)

1. Check that you can ping the instance from another subnet
2. Check that Security Group has a rule for outbound traffic
3. Check that the route table associated with the subnet has an entry for an Internet Gateway
4. Check that there is a NAT Gateway configured for the subnet
5. Check that the instance has a public IP address

## 6. Question

You are creating a design for a two-tier application with a MySQL RDS back-end. The performance requirements of the database tier are hard to quantify until the application is running and you are concerned about right-sizing the database.

What methods of scaling are possible after the MySQL RDS database is deployed? (choose 2)

1. Horizontal scaling for read and write by enabling Multi-Master RDS DB
2. Horizontal scaling for write capacity by enabling Multi-AZ
3. Horizontal scaling for read capacity by creating a read-replica
4. Vertical scaling for read and write by using Transfer Acceleration
5. Vertical scaling for read and write by choosing a larger instance size

## 7. Question

Your company has multiple AWS accounts for each environment (Prod, Dev, Test etc.). You would like to copy an EBS snapshot from DEV to PROD. The snapshot is from an EBS volume that was encrypted with a custom key.

What steps do you need to take to share the encrypted EBS snapshot with the Prod account? (choose 2)

1. Share the custom key used to encrypt the volume
2. Modify the permissions on the encrypted snapshot to share it with the Prod account
3. Use CloudHSM to distribute the encryption keys use to encrypt the volume
4. Make a copy of the EBS volume and unencrypt the data in the process
5. Create a snapshot of the unencrypted volume and share it with the Prod account

## 8. Question

A Solutions Architect is designing the compute layer of a serverless application. The compute layer will manage requests from external systems, orchestrate serverless workflows, and execute the business logic.

The Architect needs to select the most appropriate AWS services for these functions. Which services should be used for the compute layer? (choose 2)

1. Use Amazon ECS for executing the business logic
2. Use AWS CloudFormation for orchestrating serverless workflows
3. Use Amazon API Gateway with AWS Lambda for executing the business logic
4. Use AWS Elastic Beanstalk for executing the business logic
5. Use AWS Step Functions for orchestrating serverless workflows

## 9. Question

You are building a small web application running on EC2 that will be serving static content. The user base is spread out globally and speed is important. Which AWS service can deliver the best user experience cost-effectively and reduce the load on the web server?

1. Amazon CloudFront
2. Amazon EBS volume
3. Amazon RedShift
4. Amazon S3

## 10. Question

You are developing a multi-tier application that includes loosely-coupled, distributed application components and need to determine a method of sending notifications instantaneously. Using SNS which transport protocols are supported? (choose 2)

1. FTP
2. AWS Lambda
3. Amazon SWF
4. HTTPS
5. Email-JSON

## 11. Question

You are a developer at Digital Cloud Training. An application stack you are building needs a message bus to decouple the application components from each other. The application will generate up to 300 messages per second without using batching. You need to ensure that a message is only delivered once and duplicates are not introduced into the queue. It is not necessary to maintain the order of the messages.

Which SQS queue type will you use?

1. Standard queues
2. Long polling queues
3. FIFO queues
4. Auto Scaling queues

## 12. Question

AWS Regions provide multiple, physically separated and isolated _____ which are connected with low latency, high throughput, and highly redundant networking. Select the missing term from the options below.

1. Subnets
2. Facilities

3. Edge Locations
4. Availability Zones

## 13. Question

The application development team in your company have created a new application written in .NET. You are looking for a way to easily deploy the application whilst maintaining full control of the underlying resources.

**Which PaaS service provided by AWS would suit this requirement?**

1. CloudFront
2. Elastic Beanstalk
3. CloudFormation
4. EC2 Placement Groups

## 14. Question

You work for a large multinational retail company. The company has a large presence in AWS in multiple regions. You have established a new office and need to implement a high-bandwidth, low-latency connection to multiple VPCs in multiple regions within the same account. The VPCs each have unique CIDR ranges.

**What would be the optimum solution design using AWS technology? (choose 2)**

1. Create a Direct Connect gateway, and create private VIFs to each region
2. Configure AWS VPN CloudHub
3. Provision an MPLS network
4. Implement a Direct Connect connection to the closest AWS region
5. Implement Direct Connect connections to each AWS region

## 15. Question

A client has requested a design for a fault tolerant database that can failover between AZs. You have decided to use RDS in a multi-AZ configuration. What type of replication will the primary database use to replicate to the standby instance?

1. Asynchronous replication
2. Continuous replication
3. Scheduled replication
4. Synchronous replication

## 16. Question

Using the VPC wizard, you have selected the option "VPC with Public and Private Subnets and Hardware VPN access". Which of the statements below correctly describe the configuration that will be created? (choose 2)

1. A NAT gateway will be created for the private subnet
2. One subnet will be connected to your corporate data center using an IPSec VPN tunnel
3. A physical VPN device will be allocated to your VPC
4. A peering connection will be made between the public and private subnets
5. A virtual private gateway will be created

## 17. Question

A three-tier web application that you deployed in your VPC has been experiencing heavy load on the DB tier. The DB tier uses RDS MySQL in a multi-AZ configuration. Customers have been complaining about poor response times and you have been asked to find a solution. During troubleshooting you discover that the DB tier is experiencing high read contention during peak hours of the day.

What are two possible options you could use to offload some of the read traffic from the DB to resolve the performance issues? (choose 2)

1. Deploy ElastiCache in each AZ
2. Migrate to DynamoDB
3. Use an ELB to distribute load between RDS instances
4. Use a larger RDS instance size
5. Add RDS read replicas in each AZ

## 18. Question

A company is deploying new services on EC2 and needs to determine which instance types to use with what type of attached storage. Which of the statements about Instance store-backed and EBS-backed instances is true?

1. EBS-backed instances can be stopped and restarted
2. Instance-store backed instances can be stopped and restarted
3. Instance-store backed instances can only be terminated
4. EBS-backed instances cannot be restarted

## 19. Question

An application you manage regularly uploads files from an EC2 instance to S3. The files can be a couple of GB in size and sometimes the uploads are slower than you would like resulting in poor upload times. What method can be used to increase throughput and speed things up?

1. Randomize the object names when uploading
2. Use Amazon S3 multipart upload
3. Upload the files using the S3 Copy SDK or REST API
4. Turn off versioning on the destination bucket

## 20. Question

You need to create a file system that can be concurrently accessed by multiple EC2 instances within an AZ. The file system needs to support high throughput and the ability to burst. As the data that will be stored on the file system will be sensitive you need to ensure it is encrypted at rest and in transit.

Which storage solution would you implement for the EC2 instances?

1. Add EBS volumes to each EC2 instance and use an ELB to distribute data evenly between the volumes
2. Add EBS volumes to each EC2 instance and configure data replication
3. Use the Elastic File System (EFS) and mount the file system using NFS v4.1
4. Use the Elastic Block Store (EBS) and mount the file system at the block level

## 21. Question

A Solutions Architect needs a storage solution for a fleet of Linux web application servers. The solution should provide a file system interface and be able to support millions of files. Which AWS service should the Architect choose?

1. Amazon ElastiCache
2. Amazon S3
3. Amazon EBS
4. Amazon EFS

## 22. Question

You are running an application on EC2 instances in a private subnet of your VPC. You would like to connect the application to Amazon API Gateway. For security reasons, you need to ensure that no traffic traverses the Internet and need to ensure all traffic uses private IP addresses only.

How can you achieve this?

1. Create a public VIF on a Direct Connect connection
2. Create a NAT gateway
3. Create a private API using an interface VPC endpoint
4. Add the API gateway to the subnet the EC2 instances are located in

## 23. Question

You have just initiated the creation of a snapshot of an EBS volume and the snapshot process is currently in operation. Which of the statements below is true regarding the operations that are possible while the snapshot process in running?

1. The volume cannot be used until the snapshot completes
2. The volume can be used in write-only mode while the snapshot is in progress
3. The volume can be used in read-only mode while the snapshot is in progress
4. The volume can be used as normal while the snapshot is in progress

## 24. Question

An EC2 instance on which you are running a video on demand web application has been experiencing high CPU utilization. You would like to take steps to reduce the impact on the EC2 instance and improve performance for consumers. Which of the steps below would help?

1. Create a CloudFront distribution and configure a custom origin pointing at the EC2 instance
2. Create a CloudFront RTMP distribution and point it at the EC2 instance
3. Use ElastiCache as the web front-end and forward connections to EC2 for cache misses
4. Create an ELB and place it in front of the EC2 instance

## 25. Question

A new application that you rolled out recently runs on Amazon EC2 instances and uses API Gateway and Lambda. Your company is planning on running an advertising campaign that will likely result in significant hits to the application after each ad is run.

You're concerned about the impact this may have on your application and would like to put in place some controls to limit the number of requests per second that hit the application.

**What controls will you implement in this situation?**

1. Enable caching on the API Gateway and specify a size in gigabytes
2. API Gateway and Lambda scale automatically to handle any load so there's no need to implement controls
3. Enable Lambda continuous scaling
4. Implement throttling rules on the API Gateway

## 26. Question

The development team in your company have created a Python application running on ECS containers with the Fargate launch type. You have created an ALB with a Target Group that routes incoming connections to the ECS-based application. The application will be used by consumers who will authenticate using federated OIDC compliant Identity Providers such as Google and Facebook. You would like to securely authenticate the users on the front-end before they access the authenticated portions of the application.

**How can this be done on the ALB?**

1. This cannot be done on an ALB; you'll need to authenticate users on the back-end with AWS Single Sign-On (SSO) integration
2. This cannot be done on an ALB; you'll need to use another layer in front of the ALB
3. This can be done on the ALB by creating an authentication action on a listener rule that configures an Amazon Cognito user pool with the social IdP
4. The only option is to use SAML with Amazon Cognito on the ALB

## 27. Question

A new department will begin using AWS services in your account and you need to create an authentication and authorization strategy. Select the correct statements regarding IAM groups? (choose 2)

1. IAM groups can be used to group EC2 instances
2. IAM groups can be nested up to 4 levels
3. IAM groups can be used to assign permissions to users
4. An IAM group is not an identity and cannot be identified as a principal in an IAM policy
5. IAM groups can temporarily assume a role to take on permissions for a specific task

## 28. Question

A systems integration consultancy regularly deploys and manages infrastructure services for customers on AWS. The SysOps team are facing challenges in tracking changes that are made to the infrastructure services and rolling back when problems occur.

**Which of the approaches below would BEST assist the SysOps team?**

1. Use AWS Systems Manager to manage all updates to the infrastructure services
2. Use Trusted Advisor to record updates made to the infrastructure services
3. Use CloudFormation templates to deploy and manage the infrastructure services
4. Use CodeDeploy to manage version control for the infrastructure services

## 29. Question

A company runs several web applications on AWS that experience a large amount of traffic. An Architect is considering adding a caching service to one of the most popular web applications. What are two advantages of using ElastiCache? (choose 2)

1. Decoupling application components
2. Can be used for storing session state data
3. Caching query results for improved performance
4. Low latency network connectivity
5. Multi-region HA

## 30. Question

An application you manage runs a number of components using a micro-services architecture. Several ECS container instances in your ECS cluster are displaying as disconnected. The ECS instances were created from the Amazon ECS-Optimized AMI. What steps might you take to troubleshoot the issue? (choose 2)

1. Verify that the container instances have the container agent installed
2. Verify that the IAM instance profile has the necessary permissions
3. Verify that the instances have the correct IAM group applied
4. Verify that the container agent is running on the container instances
5. Verify that the container instances are using the Fargate launch type

## 31. Question

You are using encryption with several AWS services and are looking for a solution for secure storage of the keys. Which AWS service provides a hardware-based storage solution for cryptographic keys?

1. Virtual Private Cloud (VPC)
2. Key Management Service (KMS)
3. Public Key Infrastructure (PKI)
4. CloudHSM

## 32. Question

You are concerned that you may be getting close to some of the default service limits for several AWS services. Which AWS tool can be used to display current usage and limits?

1. AWS Systems Manager
2. AWS Trusted Advisor
3. AWS Dashboard
4. AWS CloudWatch

## 33. Question

The development team in a media organization is moving their SDLC processes into the AWS Cloud. Which AWS service is primarily used for software version control?

1. CodeCommit
2. CodeStar

3. CloudHSM
4. Step Functions

## 34. Question

Your operations team would like to be notified if an RDS database exceeds certain metric thresholds. They have asked you how this could be automated?

1. Create a CloudWatch alarm and associate an SQS queue with it that delivers a message to SES
2. Setup an RDS alarm and associate an SNS topic with it that sends an email
3. Create a CloudTrail alarm and configure a notification event to send an SMS
4. Create a CloudWatch alarm and associate an SNS topic with it that sends an email notification

## 35. Question

You are a Solutions Architect at Digital Cloud Training. In your VPC you have a mixture of EC2 instances in production and non-production environments. You need to devise a way to segregate access permissions to different sets of users for instances in different environments.

How can this be achieved? (choose 2)

1. Attach an Identity Provider (IdP) and delegate access to the instances to the relevant groups
2. Create an IAM policy with a conditional statement that matches the environment variables
3. Create an IAM policy that grants access to any instances with the specific tag and attach to the users and groups
4. Add an environment variable to the instances using user data
5. Add a specific tag to the instances you want to grant the users or groups access to

## 36. Question

You are a Solutions Architect at Digital Cloud Training. You have just completed the implementation of a 2-tier web application for a client. The application uses EC2 instances, ELB and Auto Scaling across two subnets. After deployment you notice that only one subnet has EC2 instances running in it. What might be the cause of this situation?

1. Cross-zone load balancing is not enabled on the ELB
2. The AMI is missing from the ASG's launch configuration
3. The Auto Scaling Group has not been configured with multiple subnets
4. The ELB is configured as an internal-only load balancer

## 37. Question

The AWS Acceptable Use Policy describes permitted and prohibited behavior on AWS and includes descriptions of prohibited security violations and network abuse. According to the policy, what is AWS's position on penetration testing?

1. AWS do not allow any form of penetration testing
2. AWS allow penetration testing by customers on their own VPC resources
3. AWS allow penetration for some resources without prior authorization
4. AWS allow penetration testing for all resources

## 38. Question

A Solutions Architect is creating a design for a multi-tiered web application. The application will use multiple AWS services and must be designed with elasticity and high-availability in mind.

Which architectural best practices should be followed to reduce interdependencies between systems? (choose 2)

1. Enable automatic scaling for storage and databases
2. Implement service discovery using static IP addresses
3. Enable graceful failure through AWS Auto Scaling
4. Implement well-defined interfaces using a relational database
5. Implement asynchronous integration using Amazon SQS queues

## 39. Question

An event in CloudTrail is the record of an activity in an AWS account. What are the two types of events that can be logged in CloudTrail? (choose 2)

1. Data Events which are also known as data plane operations
2. System Events which are also known as instance level operations
3. Management Events which are also known as control plane operations
4. Platform Events which are also known as hardware level operations

## 40. Question

You would like to provide some elasticity for your RDS DB. You are considering read replicas and are evaluating the features. Which of the following statements are applicable when using RDS read replicas? (choose 2)

1. You cannot have more than four instances involved in a replication chain
2. Replication is synchronous
3. It is possible to have read-replicas of read-replicas
4. You cannot specify the AZ the read replica is deployed in
5. During failover RDS automatically updates configuration (including DNS endpoint) to use the second node

## 41. Question

A solutions architect is building a scalable and fault tolerant web architecture and is evaluating the benefits of the Elastic Load Balancing (ELB) service. Which statements are true regarding ELBs? (select 2)

1. Multiple subnets per AZ can be enabled for each ELB
2. Both types of ELB route traffic to the public IP addresses of EC2 instances
3. For public facing ELBs you must have one public subnet in each AZ where the ELB is defined
4. Internal-only load balancers require an Internet gateway
5. Internet facing ELB nodes have public IPs

## 42. Question

There is new requirement for a database that will store a large number of records for an online store. You are evaluating the use of DynamoDB. Which of the following are AWS best practices for DynamoDB? (choose 2)

1. Use separate local secondary indexes for each item
2. Store objects larger than 400KB in S3 and use pointers in DynamoDB
3. Store more frequently and less frequently accessed data in separate tables
4. Use for BLOB data use cases
5. Use large files

## 43. Question

A Solutions Architect needs to migrate an Oracle database running on RDS onto Amazon RedShift to improve performance and reduce cost. What combination of tasks using AWS services should be followed to execute the migration? (choose 2)

1. Configure API Gateway to extract, transform and load the data into RedShift
2. Migrate the database using the AWS Database Migration Service (DMS)
3. Enable log shipping from the Oracle database to RedShift
4. Take a snapshot of the Oracle database and restore the snapshot onto RedShift
5. Convert the schema using the AWS Schema Conversion Tool

## 44. Question

An application running in your on-premise data center writes data to a MySQL database. You are re-architecting the application and plan to move the database layer into the AWS cloud on RDS. You plan to keep the application running in your on-premise data center.

What do you need to do to connect the application to the RDS database via the Internet? (choose 2)

1. Create a DB subnet group that is publicly accessible
2. Configure an NAT Gateway and attach the RDS database
3. Choose to make the RDS instance publicly accessible and place it in a public subnet
4. Create a security group allowing access from your public IP to the RDS instance and assign to the RDS instance
5. Select a public IP within the DB subnet group to assign to the RDS instance

## 45. Question

A new financial platform has been re-architected to use Docker containers in a micro-services architecture. The new architecture will be implemented on AWS and you have been asked to recommend the solution configuration. For operational reasons, it will be necessary to access the operating system of the instances on which the containers run.

Which solution delivery option will you select?

1. ECS with a default cluster
2. ECS with the Fargate launch type
3. EKS with Kubernetes managed infrastructure
4. ECS with the EC2 launch type

## 46. Question

You are using encrypted Amazon Elastic Block Store (EBS) volumes with your instances in EC2. A security administrator has asked how encryption works with EBS. Which statements are correct? (choose 2)

1. Data is only encrypted at rest
2. Data in transit between an instance and an encrypted volume is also encrypted
3. You cannot mix encrypted with unencrypted volumes on an instance
4. Encryption is supported on all Amazon EBS volume types
5. Volumes created from encrypted snapshots are unencrypted

## 47. Question

Which AWS service does API Gateway integrate with to enable users from around the world to achieve the lowest possible latency for API requests and responses?

1. S3 Transfer Acceleration
2. Direct Connect
3. CloudFront
4. Lambda

## 48. Question

You are trying to decide on the best data store to use for a new project. The requirements are that the data store is schema-less, supports strongly consistent reads, and stores data in tables, indexed by a primary key.

Which AWS data store would you use?

1. Amazon S3
2. Amazon RDS
3. Amazon DynamoDB
4. Amazon RedShift

## 49. Question

You are a Solutions Architect at Digital Cloud Training. One of your customers runs an application on-premise that stores large media files. The data is mounted to different servers using either the SMB or NFS protocols. The customer is having issues with scaling the storage infrastructure on-premise and is looking for a way to offload the data set into the cloud whilst retaining a local cache for frequently accessed content.

Which of the following is the best solution?

1. Establish a VPN and use the Elastic File System (EFS)
2. Use the AWS Storage Gateway File Gateway
3. Create a script that migrates infrequently used data to S3 using multi-part upload
4. Use the AWS Storage Gateway Volume Gateway in cached volume mode

## 50. Question

You are trying to clean up your unused EBS volumes and snapshots to save some space and cost. How many of the most recent snapshots of an EBS volume need to be maintained to guarantee that you can recreate the full EBS volume from the snapshot?

1. The oldest snapshot, as this references data in all other snapshots
2. You must retain all snapshots as the process is incremental and therefore data is required from each snapshot
3. Two snapshots, the oldest and most recent snapshots
4. Only the most recent snapshot. Snapshots are incremental, but the deletion process will ensure that no data is lost

## 51. Question

The development team at Digital Cloud Training have created a new web-based application that will soon be launched. The application will utilize 20 EC2 instances for the web front-end. Due to concerns over latency, you will not be using an ELB but still want to load balance incoming connections across multiple EC2 instances. You will be using Route 53 for the DNS service and want to implement health checks to ensure instances are available.

What two Route 53 configuration options are available that could be individually used to ensure connections reach multiple web servers in this configuration? (choose 2)

1. Use Route 53 multivalue answers to return up to 8 records with each DNS query
2. Use Route 53 simple load balancing which will return records in a round robin fashion
3. Use Route 53 Alias records to resolve using the zone apex
4. Use Route 53 weighted records and give equal weighting to all 20 EC2 instances
5. Use Route 53 failover routing in an active-passive configuration

## 52. Question

You have setup multi-factor authentication (MFA) for your root account according to AWS best practices and configured it to work with Google Authenticator on your smart phone. Unfortunately, your smart phone has been lost. What are the options available to access your account as the root user?

1. You will need to contact AWS support to request that the MFA device is deactivated and have your password reset
2. On the AWS sign-in with authentication device web page, choose to sign in using alternative factors of authentication and use the verification email and code to sign in
3. Unfortunately, you will no longer be able to access this account as the root user
4. Get a user with administrative privileges in your AWS account to deactivate the MFA device assigned to the root account

## 53. Question

The development team in your organization would like to start leveraging AWS services. They have asked you what AWS service can be used to quickly deploy and manage applications in the AWS Cloud? The developers would like the ability to simply upload applications and have AWS handle the deployment details of capacity provisioning, load balancing, auto-scaling, and application health monitoring. What AWS service would you recommend?

1. EC2
2. OpsWorks
3. Auto Scaling
4. Elastic Beanstalk

## 54. Question

A Solutions Architect is creating a solution for an application that must be deployed on Amazon EC2 hosts that are dedicated to the client. Instance placement must be automatic and billing should be per instance.

Which type of EC2 deployment model should be used?

1. Reserved Instance
2. Dedicated Instance
3. Dedicated Host
4. Cluster Placement Group

## 55. Question

A client has made some updates to their web application. The application uses an Auto Scaling Group to maintain a group of several EC2 instances. The application has been modified and a new AMI must be used for launching any new instances.

What do you need to do to add the new AMI?

1. Suspend Auto Scaling and replace the existing AMI
2. Create a new target group that uses a new launch configuration with the new AMI
3. Create a new launch configuration that uses the AMI and update the ASG to use the new launch configuration
4. Modify the existing launch configuration to add the new AMI

## 56. Question

A Solutions Architect is designing an application stack that will be highly elastic. Which AWS services can be used that don't require you to make any capacity decisions upfront? (choose 2)

1. AWS Lambda
2. DynamoDB
3. Amazon EC2
4. Amazon Kinesis Firehose
5. Amazon RDS

## 57. Question

A Solutions Architect is creating a design for an online gambling application that will process thousands of records. Which AWS service makes it easy to collect, process, and analyze real-time, streaming data?

1. S3
2. Kinesis Data Streams
3. RedShift
4. EMR

## 58. Question

You are developing some code that uses a Lambda function and you would like to enable the function to connect to an ElastiCache cluster within a VPC that you own. What VPC-specific information must you include in your function to enable this configuration? (choose 2)

1. VPC Subnet IDs
2. VPC Peering IDs
3. VPC Route Table IDs
4. VPC Logical IDs
5. VPC Security Group IDs

## 59. Question

You are a Solutions Architect for Digital Cloud Training. A client has asked for some assistance in selecting the best database for a specific requirement. The database will be used for a data warehouse solution and the data will be stored in a structured format. The client wants to run complex analytics queries using business intelligence tools.

Which AWS database service will you recommend?

1. Amazon RDS
2. Amazon Aurora
3. Amazon RedShift
4. Amazon DynamoDB

## 60. Question

A company is moving some unstructured data into AWS and a Solutions Architect has created a bucket named "contosocustomerdata" in the ap-southeast-2 region. Which of the following bucket URLs would be valid for accessing the bucket? (choose 2)

1. https://s3.ap-southeast-2.amazonaws.com/contosocustomerdata
2. https://s3.amazonaws.com/contosocustomerdata
3. https://s3-ap-southeast-2.amazonaws.com.contosocustomerdata
4. https://contosocustomerdata.s3.amazonaws.com
5. https://amazonaws.s3-ap-southeast-2.com/contosocustomerdata

## 61. Question

An organization is creating a new storage solution and needs to ensure that Amazon S3 objects that are deleted are immediately restorable for up to 30 days. After 30 days the objects should be retained for a further 180 days and be restorable within 24 hours.

The solution should be operationally simple and cost-effective. How can these requirements be achieved? (choose 2)

1. Create a lifecycle rule to transition non-current versions to GLACIER after 30 days, and then expire the objects after 180 days
2. Enable object versioning on the Amazon S3 bucket that will contain the objects
3. Create a lifecycle rule to transition non-current versions to STANDARD_IA after 30 days, and then expire the objects after 180 days
4. Enable cross-region replication (CRR) for the Amazon S3 bucket that will contain the objects

5. Enable multi-factor authentication (MFA) delete protection

## 62. Question

A company wishes to restrict access to their Amazon DynamoDB table to specific, private source IP addresses from their VPC. What should be done to secure access to the table?

1. Create the Amazon DynamoDB table in the VPC
2. Create an interface VPC endpoint in the VPC with an Elastic Network Interface (ENI)
3. Create an AWS VPN connection to the Amazon DynamoDB endpoint
4. Create a gateway VPC endpoint and add an entry to the route table

## 63. Question

An application running on Amazon EC2 needs to asynchronously invoke an AWS Lambda function to perform data processing. The services should be decoupled.

Which service can be used to decouple the compute services?

1. Amazon MQ
2. Amazon SNS
3. Amazon SQS
4. Amazon Step Functions

## 64. Question

An Amazon RDS PostgreSQL database is configured as Multi-AZ. You need to scale read performance. What is the most cost-effective solution?

1. Configure the application to read from the Multi-AZ standby instance
2. Deploy a Read Replica in a different AZ to the master DB instance
3. Create an ElastiCache cluster in front of the RDS DB instance
4. Deploy a Read Replica in the same AZ as the master DB instance

## 65. Question

An AWS Organization has an OU with multiple member accounts in it. The company needs to restrict the ability to launch only specific Amazon EC2 instance types. How can this policy be applied across the accounts with the least effort?

1. Create an IAM policy to deny launching all but the specific instance types
2. Create an SCP with a deny rule that denies all but the specific instance types
3. Use AWS Resource Access Manager to control which launch types can be used
4. Create an SCP with an allow rule that allows launching the specific instance types

# SET 5: PRACTICE QUESTIONS, ANSWERS & EXPLANATIONS

## 1. Question

A Solutions Architect is designing the messaging and streaming layers of a serverless application. The messaging layer will manage communications between components and the streaming layer will manage real-time analysis and processing of streaming data.

The Architect needs to select the most appropriate AWS services for these functions. Which services should be used for the messaging and streaming layers? (choose 2)

1. Use Amazon Kinesis for collecting, processing and analyzing real-time streaming data
2. Use Amazon EMR for collecting, processing and analyzing real-time streaming data
3. Use Amazon SNS for providing a fully managed messaging service
4. Use Amazon SWF for providing a fully managed messaging service
5. Use Amazon CloudTrail for collecting, processing and analyzing real-time streaming data

**Answer: 1,3**

**Explanation:**

- Amazon Kinesis makes it easy to collect, process, and analyze real-time streaming data. With Amazon Kinesis Analytics, you can run standard SQL or build entire streaming applications using SQL
- Amazon Simple Notification Service (Amazon SNS) provides a fully managed messaging service for pub/sub patterns using asynchronous event notifications and mobile push notifications for microservices, distributed systems, and serverless applications
- Amazon Elastic Map Reduce runs on EC2 instances so is not serverless
- Amazon Simple Workflow Service is used for executing tasks not sending messages
- Amazon CloudTrail is used for recording API activity on your account

**References:**

https://digitalcloud.training/certification-training/aws-solutions-architect-associate/analytics/amazon-kinesis/

https://digitalcloud.training/certification-training/aws-solutions-architect-associate/application-integration/amazon-sns/

## 2. Question

You are using CloudWatch to monitor the performance of AWS Lambda. Which metrics does Lambda track? (choose 2)

1. Latency per request
2. Total number of connections
3. Total number of transactions
4. Total number of requests
5. Number of users

**Answer: 1,4**

**Explanation:**

- Lambda automatically monitors Lambda functions and reports metrics through CloudWatch.
- Lambda tracks the number of requests, the latency per request, and the number of requests resulting in an error
- You can view the request rates and error rates using the AWS Lambda Console, the CloudWatch console, and other AWS resources

**References:**

https://digitalcloud.training/certification-training/aws-solutions-architect-associate/compute/aws-lambda/

## 3. Question

The financial institution you are working for stores large amounts of historical transaction records. There are over 25TB of records and your manager has decided to move them into the AWS Cloud. You are planning to use Snowball as copying the data would take too long. Which of the statements below are true regarding Snowball? (choose 2)

1. Can be used with multipart upload
2. Snowball can import to S3 but cannot export from S3
3. Snowball can be used for migration on-premise to on-premise
4. Petabyte scale data transport solution for transferring data into or out of AWS
5. Uses a secure storage device for physical transportation

**Answer: 4,5**

**Explanation:**

- Snowball is a petabyte scale data transport solution for transferring data into or out of AWS. It uses a secure storage device for physical transportation
- The AWS Snowball Client is software that is installed on a local computer and is used to identify, compress, encrypt, and transfer data. It uses 256-bit encryption (managed with the AWS KMS) and tamper-resistant enclosures with TPM
- Snowball can import to S3 or export from S3
- Snowball cannot be used with multipart upload
- You cannot use Snowball for migration between on-premise data centers

**References:**

https://digitalcloud.training/certification-training/aws-solutions-architect-associate/migration/aws-snowball/

## 4. Question

A three-tier application running in your VPC uses Auto Scaling for maintaining a desired count of EC2 instances. One of the EC2 instances just reported an EC2 Status Check status of Impaired. Once this information is reported to Auto Scaling, what action will be taken?

1. The impaired instance will be terminated, then a replacement will be launched
2. A new instance will immediately be launched, then the impaired instance will be terminated
3. Auto Scaling must verify with the ELB status checks before taking any action
4. Auto Scaling waits for the health check grace period and then terminates the instance

**Answer: 1**

**Explanation:**

- By default Auto Scaling uses EC2 status checks
- Unlike AZ rebalancing, termination of unhealthy instances happens first, then Auto Scaling attempts to launch new instances to replace terminated instances
- Auto Scaling does not wait for the health check grace period or verify with ELB before taking any action

**References:**

https://digitalcloud.training/certification-training/aws-solutions-architect-associate/compute/aws-auto-scaling/

## 5. Question

You just created a new subnet in your VPC and have launched an EC2 instance into it. You are trying to directly access the EC2 instance from the Internet and cannot connect. Which steps should you take to troubleshoot the issue? (choose 2)

1. Check that you can ping the instance from another subnet
2. Check that Security Group has a rule for outbound traffic
3. Check that the route table associated with the subnet has an entry for an Internet Gateway
4. Check that there is a NAT Gateway configured for the subnet
5. Check that the instance has a public IP address

**Answer: 3,5**

**Explanation:**

- Public subnets are subnets that have:
  - "Auto-assign public IPv4 address" set to "Yes"
  - The subnet route table has an attached Internet Gateway
- A NAT Gateway is used for providing outbound Internet access for EC2 instances in private subnets
- Checking you can ping from another subnet does not relate to being able to access the instance remotely as it uses different protocols and a different network path
- Security groups are stateful and do not need a rule for outbound traffic. For this solution you would only need to create an inbound rule that allows the relevant protocol

**References:**

https://digitalcloud.training/certification-training/aws-solutions-architect-associate/networking-and-content-delivery/amazon-vpc/

## 6. Question

You are creating a design for a two-tier application with a MySQL RDS back-end. The performance requirements of the database tier are hard to quantify until the application is running and you are concerned about right-sizing the database.

What methods of scaling are possible after the MySQL RDS database is deployed? (choose 2)

1. Horizontal scaling for read and write by enabling Multi-Master RDS DB

2. Horizontal scaling for write capacity by enabling Multi-AZ
3. Horizontal scaling for read capacity by creating a read-replica
4. Vertical scaling for read and write by using Transfer Acceleration
5. Vertical scaling for read and write by choosing a larger instance size

**Answer: 3,5**

**Explanation:**

- Relational databases can scale vertically (e.g. upgrading to a larger RDS DB instance)
- For read-heavy use cases, you can scale horizontally using read replicas
- There is no such thing as a Multi-Master MySQL RDS DB (there is for Aurora)
- You cannot scale write capacity by enabling Multi-AZ as only one DB is active and can be written to
- Transfer Acceleration is a feature of S3 for fast uploads of objects

**References:**

https://aws.amazon.com/architecture/well-architected/

https://digitalcloud.training/certification-training/aws-solutions-architect-associate/database/amazon-rds/

## 7. Question

Your company has multiple AWS accounts for each environment (Prod, Dev, Test etc.). You would like to copy an EBS snapshot from DEV to PROD. The snapshot is from an EBS volume that was encrypted with a custom key.

What steps do you need to take to share the encrypted EBS snapshot with the Prod account? (choose 2)

1. Share the custom key used to encrypt the volume
2. Modify the permissions on the encrypted snapshot to share it with the Prod account
3. Use CloudHSM to distribute the encryption keys use to encrypt the volume
4. Make a copy of the EBS volume and unencrypt the data in the process
5. Create a snapshot of the unencrypted volume and share it with the Prod account

**Answer: 1,2**

**Explanation:**

- When an EBS volume is encrypted with a custom key you must share the custom key with the PROD account. You also need to modify the permissions on the snapshot to share it with the PROD account. The PROD account must copy the snapshot before they can then create volumes from the snapshot
- You cannot share encrypted volumes created using a default CMK key and you cannot change the CMK key that is used to encrypt a volume
- CloudHSM is used for key management and storage but not distribution
- You do not need to decrypt the data as there is a workable solution that keeps the data secure at all times

**References:**

## 8. Question

A Solutions Architect is designing the compute layer of a serverless application. The compute layer will manage requests from external systems, orchestrate serverless workflows, and execute the business logic.

The Architect needs to select the most appropriate AWS services for these functions. Which services should be used for the compute layer? (choose 2)

1. Use Amazon ECS for executing the business logic
2. Use AWS CloudFormation for orchestrating serverless workflows
3. Use Amazon API Gateway with AWS Lambda for executing the business logic
4. Use AWS Elastic Beanstalk for executing the business logic
5. Use AWS Step Functions for orchestrating serverless workflows

**Answer: 3,5**

**Explanation:**

- With Amazon API Gateway, you can run a fully managed REST API that integrates with Lambda to execute your business logic and includes traffic management, authorization and access control, monitoring, and API versioning
- AWS Step Functions orchestrates serverless workflows including coordination, state, and function chaining as well as combining long-running executions not supported within Lambda execution limits by breaking into multiple steps or by calling workers running on Amazon Elastic Compute Cloud (Amazon EC2) instances or on-premises
- The Amazon Elastic Container Service (ECS) is not a serverless application stack, containers run on EC2 instances
- AWS CloudFormation and Elastic Beanstalk are orchestrators that are used for describing and provisioning resources not actually performing workflow functions within the application

**References:**

https://aws.amazon.com/step-functions/

https://digitalcloud.training/certification-training/aws-solutions-architect-associate/networking-and-content-delivery/amazon-api-gateway/

## 9. Question

You are building a small web application running on EC2 that will be serving static content. The user base is spread out globally and speed is important. Which AWS service can deliver the best user experience cost-effectively and reduce the load on the web server?

1. Amazon CloudFront
2. Amazon EBS volume
3. Amazon RedShift
4. Amazon S3

**Answer: 1**

**Explanation:**

- This is a good use case for CloudFront as the user base is spread out globally and CloudFront can cache the content closer to users and also reduce the load on the web server running on EC2
- Amazon S3 is very cost-effective however a bucket is located in a single region and therefore performance is
- EBS is not the most cost-effective storage solution and the data would be located in a single region to latency could be an issue
- Amazon RedShift is a data warehouse and is not suitable in this solution

**References:**

https://digitalcloud.training/certification-training/aws-solutions-architect-associate/storage/amazon-s3/

## 10. Question

You are developing a multi-tier application that includes loosely-coupled, distributed application components and need to determine a method of sending notifications instantaneously. Using SNS which transport protocols are supported? (choose 2)

1. FTP
2. AWS Lambda
3. Amazon SWF
4. HTTPS
5. Email-JSON

**Answer: 4,5**

**Explanation:**

Note that the questions asks you which <u>transport</u> protocols are supported, NOT which <u>subscribers</u> – therefore Lambda is not supported

SNS supports notifications over multiple transport protocols:

- HTTP/HTTPS – subscribers specify a URL as part of the subscription registration
- Email/Email-JSON – messages are sent to registered addresses as email (text-based or JSON-object)
- SQS – users can specify an SQS standard queue as the endpoint
- SMS – messages are sent to registered phone numbers as SMS text messages

**References:**

https://digitalcloud.training/certification-training/aws-solutions-architect-associate/application-integration/amazon-sns/

## 11. Question

You are a developer at Digital Cloud Training. An application stack you are building needs a message bus to decouple the application components from each other. The application will generate up to 300 messages per second without using batching. You need to ensure that a message is only delivered once and duplicates are not introduced into the queue. It is not necessary to maintain the order of the messages.

**Which SQS queue type will you use?**

1. Standard queues
2. Long polling queues
3. FIFO queues
4. Auto Scaling queues

**Answer: 3**

**Explanation:**

- The key fact you need to consider here is that duplicate messages cannot be introduced into the queue. For this reason alone you must use a FIFO queue. The statement about it not being necessary to maintain the order of the messages is meant to confuse you, as that might lead you to think you can use a standard queue, but standard queues don't guarantee that duplicates are not introduced into the queue
- FIFO (first-in-first-out) queues preserve the exact order in which messages are sent and received – note that this is not required in the question but exactly once processing is. FIFO queues provide exactly-once processing, which means that each message is delivered once and remains available until a consumer processes it and deletes it
- Standard queues provide a loose-FIFO capability that attempts to preserve the order of messages. Standard queues provide at-least-once delivery, which means that each message is delivered at least once
- Long polling is configuration you can apply to a queue, it is not a queue type
- There is no such thing as an Auto Scaling queue

**References:**

https://digitalcloud.training/certification-training/aws-solutions-architect-associate/application-integration/amazon-sqs/

## 12. Question

AWS Regions provide multiple, physically separated and isolated _____ which are connected with low latency, high throughput, and highly redundant networking. Select the missing term from the options below.

1. Subnets
2. Facilities
3. Edge Locations
4. Availability Zones

**Answer: 4**

**Explanation:**

- Availability Zones are distinct locations that are engineered to be isolated from failures in other Availability Zones and are connected with low latency, high throughput, and highly redundant networking

- Subnets are created within availability zones (AZs). Each subnet must reside entirely within one Availability Zone and cannot span zones
- Each AZ is located in one or more data centers (facilities)
- An Edge Location is a CDN endpoint for CloudFront

**References:**

https://digitalcloud.training/certification-training/aws-solutions-architect-associate/networking-and-content-delivery/amazon-vpc/

https://docs.aws.amazon.com/AWSEC2/latest/UserGuide/using-regions-availability-zones.html

## 13. Question

The application development team in your company have created a new application written in .NET. You are looking for a way to easily deploy the application whilst maintaining full control of the underlying resources.

Which PaaS service provided by AWS would suit this requirement?

1. CloudFront
2. Elastic Beanstalk
3. CloudFormation
4. EC2 Placement Groups

**Answer: 2**

**Explanation:**

- AWS Elastic Beanstalk can be used to quickly deploy and manage applications in the AWS Cloud. Developers upload applications and Elastic Beanstalk handles the deployment details of capacity provisioning, load balancing, auto-scaling, and application health monitoring. It is considered to be a Platform as a Service (PaaS) solution and allows full control of the underlying resources
- CloudFront is a content delivery network for caching content to improve performance
- CloudFormation uses templates to provision infrastructure
- EC2 Placement Groups are used to control how instances are launched to enable low-latency connectivity or to be spread across distinct hardware

**References:**

https://digitalcloud.training/certification-training/aws-solutions-architect-associate/compute/aws-elastic-beanstalk/

## 14. Question

You work for a large multinational retail company. The company has a large presence in AWS in multiple regions. You have established a new office and need to implement a high-bandwidth, low-latency connection to multiple VPCs in multiple regions within the same account. The VPCs each have unique CIDR ranges.

What would be the optimum solution design using AWS technology? (choose 2)

1. Create a Direct Connect gateway, and create private VIFs to each region
2. Configure AWS VPN CloudHub
3. Provision an MPLS network

4. Implement a Direct Connect connection to the closest AWS region
5. Implement Direct Connect connections to each AWS region

**Answer: 1,4**

**Explanation:**

- You should implement an AWS Direct Connect connection to the closest region. You can then use Direct Connect gateway to create private virtual interfaces (VIFs) to each AWS region. Direct Connect gateway provides a grouping of Virtual Private Gateways (VGWs) and Private Virtual Interfaces (VIFs) that belong to the same AWS account and enables you to interface with VPCs in any AWS Region (except AWS China Region). You can share a private virtual interface to interface with more than one Virtual Private Cloud (VPC) reducing the number of BGP sessions required
- You do not need to implement multiple Direct Connect connections to each region. This would be a more expensive option as you would need to pay for an international private connection
- AWS VPN CloudHub is not the best solution as you have been asked to implement high-bandwidth, low-latency connections and VPN uses the Internet so is not reliable
- An MPLS network could be used to create a network topology that gets you closer to AWS in each region but you would still need use Direct Connect or VPN for the connectivity into AWS. Also, the question states that you should use AWS technology and MPLS is not offered as a service by AWS

**References:**

https://digitalcloud.training/certification-training/aws-solutions-architect-associate/networking-and-content-delivery/aws-direct-connect/

## 15. Question

**A client has requested a design for a fault tolerant database that can failover between AZs. You have decided to use RDS in a multi-AZ configuration. What type of replication will the primary database use to replicate to the standby instance?**

1. Asynchronous replication
2. Continuous replication
3. Scheduled replication
4. Synchronous replication

**Answer: 4**

**Explanation:**

- Multi-AZ RDS creates a replica in another AZ and synchronously replicates to it (DR only). Multi-AZ deployments for the MySQL, MariaDB, Oracle and PostgreSQL engines utilize synchronous physical replication. Multi-AZ deployments for the SQL Server engine use synchronous logical replication (SQL Server-native Mirroring technology)
- Asynchronous replication is used by RDS for Read Replicas
- Scheduled and continuous replication are not replication types that are supported by RDS

**References:**

https://digitalcloud.training/certification-training/aws-solutions-architect-associate/database/amazon-rds/

## 16. Question

Using the VPC wizard, you have selected the option "VPC with Public and Private Subnets and Hardware VPN access". Which of the statements below correctly describe the configuration that will be created? (choose 2)

1. A NAT gateway will be created for the private subnet
2. One subnet will be connected to your corporate data center using an IPSec VPN tunnel
3. A physical VPN device will be allocated to your VPC
4. A peering connection will be made between the public and private subnets
5. A virtual private gateway will be created

**Answer: 2,5**

**Explanation:**

- The configuration for this scenario includes a virtual private cloud (VPC) with a public subnet and a private subnet, and a virtual private gateway to enable communication with your own network over an IPsec VPN tunnel
- Review the scenario described in the AWS article below for more information

**References:**

https://digitalcloud.training/certification-training/aws-solutions-architect-associate/networking-and-content-delivery/amazon-vpc/

https://docs.aws.amazon.com/AmazonVPC/latest/UserGuide/VPC_Scenario3.html

## 17. Question

A three-tier web application that you deployed in your VPC has been experiencing heavy load on the DB tier. The DB tier uses RDS MySQL in a multi-AZ configuration. Customers have been complaining about poor response times and you have been asked to find a solution. During troubleshooting you discover that the DB tier is experiencing high read contention during peak hours of the day.

What are two possible options you could use to offload some of the read traffic from the DB to resolve the performance issues? (choose 2)

1. Deploy ElastiCache in each AZ
2. Migrate to DynamoDB
3. Use an ELB to distribute load between RDS instances
4. Use a larger RDS instance size
5. Add RDS read replicas in each AZ

**Answer: 1,5**

**Explanation:**

- ElastiCache is a web service that makes it easy to deploy and run Memcached or Redis protocol-compliant server nodes in the cloud. The in-memory caching provided by ElastiCache can be used to significantly improve latency and throughput for many read-heavy application workloads or compute-intensive workloads
- Read replicas are used for read heavy DBs and replication is asynchronous. They are for workload sharing and offloading and are created from a snapshot of the master instance
- Moving from a relational DB to a NoSQL DB (DynamoDB) is unlikely to be a viable solution

- Using a larger instance size may alleviate the problems the question states that the solution should offload reads from the main DB, read replicas can do this

References:

https://digitalcloud.training/certification-training/aws-solutions-architect-associate/database/amazon-elasticache/

https://digitalcloud.training/certification-training/aws-solutions-architect-associate/database/amazon-rds/

## 18. Question

A company is deploying new services on EC2 and needs to determine which instance types to use with what type of attached storage. Which of the statements about Instance store-backed and EBS-backed instances is true?

1. EBS-backed instances can be stopped and restarted
2. Instance-store backed instances can be stopped and restarted
3. Instance-store backed instances can only be terminated
4. EBS-backed instances cannot be restarted

Answer: 1

Explanation:

- EBS-backed means the root volume is an EBS volume and storage is persistent whereas instance store-backed means the root volume is an instance store volume and storage is not persistent
- On an EBS-backed instance, the default action is for the root EBS volume to be deleted upon termination
- EBS backed instances can be stopped. You will not lose the data on this instance if it is stopped (persistent)
- EBS volumes can be detached and reattached to other EC2 instances
- EBS volume root devices are launched from AMI's that are backed by EBS snapshots
- Instance store volumes are sometimes called Ephemeral storage (non-persistent)
- Instance store volumes cannot be stopped. If the underlying host fails the data will be lost
- Instance store volume root devices are created from AMI templates stored on S3
- Instance store volumes cannot be detached/reattached
- When rebooting the instances for both types data will not be lost
- By default, both root volumes will be deleted on termination unless you configured otherwise

References:

https://digitalcloud.training/certification-training/aws-solutions-architect-associate/compute/amazon-ebs/

## 19. Question

An application you manage regularly uploads files from an EC2 instance to S3. The files can be a couple of GB in size and sometimes the uploads are slower than you would like resulting in poor upload times. What method can be used to increase throughput and speed things up?

1. Randomize the object names when uploading
2. Use Amazon S3 multipart upload

3. Upload the files using the S3 Copy SDK or REST API
4. Turn off versioning on the destination bucket

**Answer: 2**

**Explanation:**

- Multipart upload can be used to speed up uploads to S3. Multipart upload uploads objects in parts independently, in parallel and in any order. It is performed using the S3 Multipart upload API and is recommended for objects of 100MB or larger. It can be used for objects from 5MB up to 5TB and must be used for objects larger than 5GB
- Randomizing object names provides no value in this context, random prefixes are used for intensive read requests
- Copy is used for copying, moving and renaming objects within S3 not for uploading to S3
- Turning off versioning will not speed up the upload

**References:**

https://digitalcloud.training/certification-training/aws-solutions-architect-associate/storage/amazon-s3/

## 20. Question

You need to create a file system that can be concurrently accessed by multiple EC2 instances within an AZ. The file system needs to support high throughput and the ability to burst. As the data that will be stored on the file system will be sensitive you need to ensure it is encrypted at rest and in transit.

Which storage solution would you implement for the EC2 instances?

1. Add EBS volumes to each EC2 instance and use an ELB to distribute data evenly between the volumes
2. Add EBS volumes to each EC2 instance and configure data replication
3. Use the Elastic File System (EFS) and mount the file system using NFS v4.1
4. Use the Elastic Block Store (EBS) and mount the file system at the block level

**Answer: 3**

**Explanation:**

- EFS is a fully-managed service that makes it easy to set up and scale file storage in the Amazon Cloud. EFS file systems are mounted using the NFSv4.1 protocol. EFS is designed to burst to allow high throughput levels for periods of time. EFS also offers the ability to encrypt data at rest and in transit
- EBS is a block-level storage system not a file-level storage system. You cannot connect to a single EBS volume concurrently from multiple EC2 instances
- Adding EBS volumes to each instance and configuring data replication is not the best solution for this scenario and there is no native capability within AWS for performing the replication. Some 3rd party data management software does use this model however
- You cannot use an ELB to distribute data between EBS volumes

**References:**

https://digitalcloud.training/certification-training/aws-solutions-architect-associate/storage/amazon-efs/

## 21. Question

A Solutions Architect needs a storage solution for a fleet of Linux web application servers. The solution should provide a file system interface and be able to support millions of files. Which AWS service should the Architect choose?

1. Amazon ElastiCache
2. Amazon S3
3. Amazon EBS
4. Amazon EFS

**Answer: 4**

**Explanation:**

- The Amazon Elastic File System (EFS) is the only storage solution in the list that provides a file system interface. It also supports millions of files as requested
- Amazon S3 is an object storage solution and does not provide a file system interface
- Amazon EBS provides a block storage interface
- Amazon ElastiCache is an in-memory caching solution for databases

**References:**

https://digitalcloud.training/certification-training/aws-solutions-architect-associate/storage/amazon-efs/

## 22. Question

You are running an application on EC2 instances in a private subnet of your VPC. You would like to connect the application to Amazon API Gateway. For security reasons, you need to ensure that no traffic traverses the Internet and need to ensure all traffic uses private IP addresses only.

**How can you achieve this?**

1. Create a public VIF on a Direct Connect connection
2. Create a NAT gateway
3. Create a private API using an interface VPC endpoint
4. Add the API gateway to the subnet the EC2 instances are located in

**Answer: 3**

**Explanation:**

- An Interface endpoint uses AWS PrivateLink and is an elastic network interface (ENI) with a private IP address that serves as an entry point for traffic destined to a supported service. Using PrivateLink you can connect your VPC to supported AWS services, services hosted by other AWS accounts (VPC endpoint services), and supported AWS Marketplace partner services
- You do not need to implement Direct Connect and create a public VIF. Public IP addresses are used in public VIFs and the question requests that only private addresses are used
- You cannot add API Gateway to the subnet the EC2 instances are in, it is a public service with a public endpoint
- NAT Gateways are used to provide Internet access for EC2 instances in private subnets so are of no use in this solution

**References:**

## 23. Question

You have just initiated the creation of a snapshot of an EBS volume and the snapshot process is currently in operation. Which of the statements below is true regarding the operations that are possible while the snapshot process in running?

1. The volume cannot be used until the snapshot completes
2. The volume can be used in write-only mode while the snapshot is in progress
3. The volume can be used in read-only mode while the snapshot is in progress
4. The volume can be used as normal while the snapshot is in progress

### Answer: 4

### Explanation:

- You can take a snapshot of an EBS volume while the instance is running and it does not cause any outage of the volume so it can continue to be used as normal. However, the advice is that to take consistent snapshots writes to the volume should be stopped. For non-root EBS volumes this can entail taking the volume offline (detaching the volume with the instance still running), and for root EBS volumes it entails shutting down the instance

### References:

https://digitalcloud.training/certification-training/aws-solutions-architect-associate/compute/amazon-ebs/

https://docs.aws.amazon.com/AWSEC2/latest/UserGuide/ebs-creating-snapshot.html

## 24. Question

An EC2 instance on which you are running a video on demand web application has been experiencing high CPU utilization. You would like to take steps to reduce the impact on the EC2 instance and improve performance for consumers. Which of the steps below would help?

1. Create a CloudFront distribution and configure a custom origin pointing at the EC2 instance
2. Create a CloudFront RTMP distribution and point it at the EC2 instance
3. Use ElastiCache as the web front-end and forward connections to EC2 for cache misses
4. Create an ELB and place it in front of the EC2 instance

### Answer: 1

### Explanation:

- This is a good use case for CloudFront which is a content delivery network (CDN) that caches content to improve performance for users who are consuming the content. This will take the load off of the EC2 instances as CloudFront has a cached copy of the video files. An origin is the origin of the files that the CDN will distribute. Origins can be either an S3 bucket, an EC2 instance, and Elastic Load Balancer, or Route 53 – can also be external (non-AWS)
- ElastiCache cannot be used as an Internet facing web front-end
- For RTMP CloudFront distributions files must be stored in an S3 bucket

- Placing an ELB in front of a single EC2 instance does not help to reduce load

References:

https://digitalcloud.training/certification-training/aws-solutions-architect-associate/networking-and-content-delivery/amazon-cloudfront/

## 25. Question

A new application that you rolled out recently runs on Amazon EC2 instances and uses API Gateway and Lambda. Your company is planning on running an advertising campaign that will likely result in significant hits to the application after each ad is run.

You're concerned about the impact this may have on your application and would like to put in place some controls to limit the number of requests per second that hit the application.

What controls will you implement in this situation?

1. Enable caching on the API Gateway and specify a size in gigabytes
2. API Gateway and Lambda scale automatically to handle any load so there's no need to implement controls
3. Enable Lambda continuous scaling
4. Implement throttling rules on the API Gateway

Answer: 4

Explanation:

- The key requirement is that you need to limit the number of requests per second that hit the application. This can only be done by implementing throttling rules on the API Gateway. Throttling enables you to throttle the number of requests to your API which in turn means less traffic will be forwarded to your application server
- Caching can improve performance but does not limit the amount of requests coming in
- API Gateway and Lambda both scale up to their default limits however the bottleneck is with the application server running on EC2 which may not be able to scale to keep up with demand
- Lambda continuous scaling does not resolve the scalability concerns with the EC2 application server

References:

https://digitalcloud.training/certification-training/aws-solutions-architect-associate/networking-and-content-delivery/amazon-api-gateway/

https://docs.aws.amazon.com/apigateway/latest/developerguide/api-gateway-request-throttling.html

## 26. Question

The development team in your company have created a Python application running on ECS containers with the Fargate launch type. You have created an ALB with a Target Group that routes incoming connections to the ECS-based application. The application will be used by consumers who will authenticate using federated OIDC compliant Identity Providers such as Google and Facebook. You would like to securely authenticate the users on the front-end before they access the authenticated portions of the application.

How can this be done on the ALB?

1. This cannot be done on an ALB; you'll need to authenticate users on the back-end with AWS Single Sign-On (SSO) integration
2. This cannot be done on an ALB; you'll need to use another layer in front of the ALB
3. This can be done on the ALB by creating an authentication action on a listener rule that configures an Amazon Cognito user pool with the social IdP
4. The only option is to use SAML with Amazon Cognito on the ALB

**Answer: 3**

**Explanation:**

- ALB supports authentication from OIDC compliant identity providers such as Google, Facebook and Amazon. It is implemented through an authentication action on a listener rule that integrates with Amazon Cognito to create user pools
- SAML can be used with Amazon Cognito but this is not the only option

**References:**

https://digitalcloud.training/certification-training/aws-solutions-architect-associate/compute/elastic-load-balancing/

https://aws.amazon.com/blogs/aws/built-in-authentication-in-alb/

## 27. Question

A new department will begin using AWS services in your account and you need to create an authentication and authorization strategy. Select the correct statements regarding IAM groups? (choose 2)

1. IAM groups can be used to group EC2 instances
2. IAM groups can be nested up to 4 levels
3. IAM groups can be used to assign permissions to users
4. An IAM group is not an identity and cannot be identified as a principal in an IAM policy
5. IAM groups can temporarily assume a role to take on permissions for a specific task

**Answer: 3,4**

**Explanation:**

- Groups are collections of users and have policies attached to them
- A group is not an identity and cannot be identified as a principal in an IAM policy
- Use groups to assign permissions to users
- IAM groups cannot be used to group EC2 instances
- Only users and services can assume a role to take on permissions (not groups)

**References:**

https://digitalcloud.training/certification-training/aws-solutions-architect-associate/security-identity-compliance/aws-iam/

## 28. Question

A systems integration consultancy regularly deploys and manages infrastructure services for customers on AWS. The SysOps team are facing challenges in tracking changes that are made to the infrastructure services and rolling back when problems occur.

**Which of the approaches below would BEST assist the SysOps team?**

1. Use AWS Systems Manager to manage all updates to the infrastructure services
2. Use Trusted Advisor to record updates made to the infrastructure services
3. Use CloudFormation templates to deploy and manage the infrastructure services
4. Use CodeDeploy to manage version control for the infrastructure services

**Answer: 3**

**Explanation:**

- When you provision your infrastructure with AWS CloudFormation, the AWS CloudFormation template describes exactly what resources are provisioned and their settings. Because these templates are text files, you simply track differences in your templates to track changes to your infrastructure, similar to the way developers control revisions to source code. For example, you can use a version control system with your templates so that you know exactly what changes were made, who made them, and when. If at any point you need to reverse changes to your infrastructure, you can use a previous version of your template.
- AWS Systems Manager gives you visibility and control of your infrastructure on AWS. Systems Manager provides a unified user interface so you can view operational data from multiple AWS services and allows you to automate operational tasks across your AWS resources. However, CloudFormation would be the preferred method of maintaining the state of the overall architecture.
- AWS CodeDeploy is a deployment service that automates application (not infrastructure) deployments to Amazon EC2 instances, on-premises instances, or serverless Lambda functions. This would be a good fit if we were talking about an application environment where code changes need to be managed but not for infrastructure services.
- AWS Trusted Advisor is an online resource to help you reduce cost, increase performance, and improve security by optimizing your AWS environment, Trusted Advisor provides real time guidance to help you provision your resources following AWS best practices.

**References:**

https://aws.amazon.com/cloudformation/resources/

## 29. Question

A company runs several web applications on AWS that experience a large amount of traffic. An Architect is considering adding a caching service to one of the most popular web applications. What are two advantages of using ElastiCache? (choose 2)

1. Decoupling application components
2. Can be used for storing session state data
3. Caching query results for improved performance
4. Low latency network connectivity
5. Multi-region HA

**Answer: 2,3**

**Explanation:**

- The in-memory caching provided by ElastiCache can be used to significantly improve latency and throughput for many read-heavy application workloads or compute-intensive workloads
- Elasticache can also be used for storing session state
- You cannot enable multi-region HA with ElastiCache
- ElastiCache is a caching service, not a network service so it is not responsible for providing low-latency network connectivity
- Amazon SQS is used for decoupling application components

**References:**

https://digitalcloud.training/certification-training/aws-solutions-architect-associate/database/amazon-elasticache/

## 30. Question

An application you manage runs a number of components using a micro-services architecture. Several ECS container instances in your ECS cluster are displaying as disconnected. The ECS instances were created from the Amazon ECS-Optimized AMI. What steps might you take to troubleshoot the issue? (choose 2)

1. Verify that the container instances have the container agent installed
2. Verify that the IAM instance profile has the necessary permissions
3. Verify that the instances have the correct IAM group applied
4. Verify that the container agent is running on the container instances
5. Verify that the container instances are using the Fargate launch type

**Answer: 2,4**

**Explanation:**

- The ECS container agent is included in the Amazon ECS optimized AMI and can also be installed on any EC2 instance that supports the ECS specification (only supported on EC2 instances). Therefore, you know don't need to verify that the agent is installed
- You need to verify that the installed agent is running and that the IAM instance profile has the necessary permissions applied. You apply IAM roles (instance profile) to EC2 instances, not groups
- This example is based on the EC2 launch type not the Fargate launch type. With Fargate the infrastructure is managed for you by AWS
- Troubleshooting steps for containers include:

    - Verify that the Docker daemon is running on the container instance

    - Verify that the Docker Container daemon is running on the container instance

    - Verify that the container agent is running on the container instance

    - Verify that the IAM instance profile has the necessary permissions

**References:**

https://digitalcloud.training/certification-training/aws-solutions-architect-associate/compute/amazon-ecs/

https://aws.amazon.com/premiumsupport/knowledge-center/ecs-agent-disconnected/

## 31. Question

You are using encryption with several AWS services and are looking for a solution for secure storage of the keys. Which AWS service provides a hardware-based storage solution for cryptographic keys?

1. Virtual Private Cloud (VPC)
2. Key Management Service (KMS)
3. Public Key Infrastructure (PKI)
4. CloudHSM

**Answer: 4**

**Explanation:**

- AWS CloudHSM is a cloud-based hardware security module (HSM) that allows you to easily add secure key storage and high-performance crypto operations to your AWS applications
- CloudHSM is a managed service that automates time-consuming administrative tasks, such as hardware provisioning, software patching, high availability, and backups
- CloudHSM is one of several AWS services, including AWS Key Management Service (KMS), which offer a high level of security for your cryptographic keys
- KMS provides an easy, cost-effective way to manage encryption keys on AWS that meets the security needs for the majority of customer data
- A VPC is a logical networking construct within an AWS account
- PKI is a term used to describe the whole infrastructure responsible for the usage of public key cryptography

**References:**

https://aws.amazon.com/cloudhsm/details/

## 32. Question

You are concerned that you may be getting close to some of the default service limits for several AWS services. Which AWS tool can be used to display current usage and limits?

1. AWS Systems Manager
2. AWS Trusted Advisor
3. AWS Dashboard
4. AWS CloudWatch

**Answer: 2**

**Explanation:**

- Trusted Advisor is an online resource to help you reduce cost, increase performance, and improve security by optimizing your AWS environment. Trusted Advisor provides real time guidance to help you provision your resources following AWS best practices. AWS Trusted Advisor offers a Service Limits check (in the Performance category) that displays your usage and limits for some aspects of some services
- AWS CloudWatch is used for performance monitoring not displaying usage limits
- AWS Systems Manager gives you visibility and control of your infrastructure on AWS. Systems Manager provides a unified user interface so you can view operational data from multiple AWS services and allows you to automate operational tasks across your AWS resources

- There is no service known as "AWS Dashboard"

**References:**

https://docs.aws.amazon.com/general/latest/gr/aws_service_limits.html

## 33. Question

The development team in a media organization is moving their SDLC processes into the AWS Cloud. Which AWS service is primarily used for software version control?

1. CodeCommit
2. CodeStar
3. CloudHSM
4. Step Functions

**Answer: 1**

**Explanation:**

- AWS CodeCommit is a fully-managed source control service that hosts secure Git-based repositories
- AWS CodeStar enables you to quickly develop, build, and deploy applications on AWS
- AWS CloudHSM is a cloud-based hardware security module (HSM) that enables you to easily generate and use your own encryption keys on the AWS Cloud
- AWS Step Functions lets you coordinate multiple AWS services into serverless workflows so you can build and update apps quickly

**References:**

https://aws.amazon.com/codecommit/

## 34. Question

Your operations team would like to be notified if an RDS database exceeds certain metric thresholds. They have asked you how this could be automated?

1. Create a CloudWatch alarm and associate an SQS queue with it that delivers a message to SES
2. Setup an RDS alarm and associate an SNS topic with it that sends an email
3. Create a CloudTrail alarm and configure a notification event to send an SMS
4. Create a CloudWatch alarm and associate an SNS topic with it that sends an email notification

**Answer: 4**

**Explanation:**

- You can create a CloudWatch alarm that watches a single CloudWatch metric or the result of a math expression based on CloudWatch metrics. The alarm performs one or more actions based on the value of the metric or expression relative to a threshold over a number of time periods. The action can be an Amazon EC2 action, an Amazon EC2 Auto Scaling action, or a notification sent to an Amazon SNS topic. SNS can be configured to send an email notification
- CloudTrail is used for auditing API access, not for performance monitoring
- CloudWatch performs performance monitoring so you don't setup alarms in RDS itself

- You cannot associate an SQS queue with a CloudWatch alarm

**References:**

https://digitalcloud.training/certification-training/aws-solutions-architect-associate/management-tools/amazon-cloudwatch/

## 35. Question

You are a Solutions Architect at Digital Cloud Training. In your VPC you have a mixture of EC2 instances in production and non-production environments. You need to devise a way to segregate access permissions to different sets of users for instances in different environments.

How can this be achieved? (choose 2)

1. Attach an Identity Provider (IdP) and delegate access to the instances to the relevant groups
2. Create an IAM policy with a conditional statement that matches the environment variables
3. Create an IAM policy that grants access to any instances with the specific tag and attach to the users and groups
4. Add an environment variable to the instances using user data
5. Add a specific tag to the instances you want to grant the users or groups access to

**Answer: 3,5**

**Explanation:**

- You can use the condition checking in IAM policies to look for a specific tag. IAM checks that the tag attached to the principal making the request matches the specified key name and value
- You cannot achieve this outcome using environment variables stored in user data and conditional statements in a policy. You must use an IAM policy that grants access to instances based on the tag
- You cannot use an IdP for this solution

**References:**

https://aws.amazon.com/premiumsupport/knowledge-center/iam-ec2-resource-tags/

https://docs.aws.amazon.com/IAM/latest/UserGuide/reference_policies_condition-keys.html

## 36. Question

You are a Solutions Architect at Digital Cloud Training. You have just completed the implementation of a 2-tier web application for a client. The application uses EC2 instances, ELB and Auto Scaling across two subnets. After deployment you notice that only one subnet has EC2 instances running in it. What might be the cause of this situation?

1. Cross-zone load balancing is not enabled on the ELB
2. The AMI is missing from the ASG's launch configuration
3. The Auto Scaling Group has not been configured with multiple subnets
4. The ELB is configured as an internal-only load balancer

**Answer: 3**

**Explanation:**

- You can specify which subnets Auto Scaling will launch new instances into. Auto Scaling will try to distribute EC2 instances evenly across AZs. If only one subnet has EC2 instances running in it the first thing to check is that you have added all relevant subnets to the configuration
- The type of ELB deployed is not relevant here as Auto Scaling is responsible for launching instances into subnets whereas ELB is responsible for distributing connections to the instances
- Cross-zone load balancing is an ELB feature and ELB is not the issue here as it is not responsible for launching instances into subnets
- If the AMI was missing from the launch configuration no instances would be running

**References:**

https://digitalcloud.training/certification-training/aws-solutions-architect-associate/compute/aws-auto-scaling/

## 37. Question

**The AWS Acceptable Use Policy describes permitted and prohibited behavior on AWS and includes descriptions of prohibited security violations and network abuse. According to the policy, what is AWS's position on penetration testing?**

1. AWS do not allow any form of penetration testing
2. AWS allow penetration testing by customers on their own VPC resources
3. AWS allow penetration for some resources without prior authorization
4. AWS allow penetration testing for all resources

**Answer: 3**

**Explanation:**

- AWS customers are welcome to carry out security assessments or penetration tests against their AWS infrastructure without prior approval for 8 services. Please check the AWS link below for the latest information.
- There is a limited set of resources on which penetration testing can be performed.
- Note of caution: AWS used to require authorization for all penetration testing and this was changed in early 2019 – the exam may or may not reflect this.

**References:**

https://digitalcloud.training/certification-training/aws-certified-cloud-practitioner/cloud-security/

https://aws.amazon.com/security/penetration-testing/

## 38. Question

**A Solutions Architect is creating a design for a multi-tiered web application. The application will use multiple AWS services and must be designed with elasticity and high-availability in mind.**

**Which architectural best practices should be followed to reduce interdependencies between systems? (choose 2)**

1. Enable automatic scaling for storage and databases
2. Implement service discovery using static IP addresses
3. Enable graceful failure through AWS Auto Scaling
4. Implement well-defined interfaces using a relational database

5. Implement asynchronous integration using Amazon SQS queues

**Answer: 3,5**

**Explanation:**

- Asynchronous integration – this is another form of loose coupling where an interaction does not need an immediate response (think SQS queue or Kinesis)
- Graceful failure – build applications such that they handle failure in a graceful manner (reduce the impact of failure and implement retries). Auto Scaling helps to reduce the impact of failure by launching replacement instances
- Well-defined interfaces – reduce interdependencies in a system by enabling interaction only through specific, technology-agnostic interfaces (e.g. RESTful APIs). A relational database is not an example of a well-defined interface
- Service discovery – disparate resources must have a way of discovering each other without prior knowledge of the network topology. Usually DNS names and a method of resolution are preferred over static IP addresses which need to be hardcoded somewhere
- Though automatic scaling for storage and database provides scalability (not necessarily elasticity), it does not reduce interdependencies between systems

**References:**

https://aws.amazon.com/architecture/well-architected/


## 39. Question

**An event in CloudTrail is the record of an activity in an AWS account. What are the two types of events that can be logged in CloudTrail? (choose 2)**

1. Data Events which are also known as data plane operations
2. System Events which are also known as instance level operations
3. Management Events which are also known as control plane operations
4. Platform Events which are also known as hardware level operations

**Answer: 1,3**

**Explanation:**

Trails can be configured to log Data events and management events:

- Data events: These events provide insight into the resource operations performed on or within a resource. These are also known as data plane operations
- Management events: Management events provide insight into management operations that are performed on resources in your AWS account. These are also known as control plane operations. Management events can also include non-API events that occur in your account

**References:**

https://digitalcloud.training/certification-training/aws-solutions-architect-associate/management-tools/aws-cloudtrail/

https://docs.aws.amazon.com/awscloudtrail/latest/userguide/logging-management-and-data-events-with-cloudtrail.html

## 40. Question

You would like to provide some elasticity for your RDS DB. You are considering read replicas and are evaluating the features. Which of the following statements are applicable when using RDS read replicas? (choose 2)

1. You cannot have more than four instances involved in a replication chain
2. Replication is synchronous
3. It is possible to have read-replicas of read-replicas
4. You cannot specify the AZ the read replica is deployed in
5. During failover RDS automatically updates configuration (including DNS endpoint) to use the second node

**Answer: 1,3**

**Explanation:**

- Multi-AZ utilizes failover and DNS endpoint updates, not read replicas
- Read replicas are used for read heavy DBs and replication is asynchronous
- You can have read replicas of read replicas for MySQL and MariaDB but not for PostgreSQL
- You cannot have more than four instances involved in a replication chain
- You can specify the AZ the read replica is deployed in

**References:**

https://digitalcloud.training/certification-training/aws-solutions-architect-associate/database/amazon-rds/

## 41. Question

A solutions architect is building a scalable and fault tolerant web architecture and is evaluating the benefits of the Elastic Load Balancing (ELB) service. Which statements are true regarding ELBs? (select 2)

1. Multiple subnets per AZ can be enabled for each ELB
2. Both types of ELB route traffic to the public IP addresses of EC2 instances
3. For public facing ELBs you must have one public subnet in each AZ where the ELB is defined
4. Internal-only load balancers require an Internet gateway
5. Internet facing ELB nodes have public IPs

**Answer: 3,5**

**Explanation:**

- Internet facing ELB nodes have public IPs
- Both types of ELB route traffic to the private IP addresses of EC2 instances
- For public facing ELBs you must have one public subnet in each AZ where the ELB is defined
- Internal-only load balancers do not require an Internet gateway
- Only 1 subnet per AZ can be enabled for each ELB

**References:**

https://digitalcloud.training/certification-training/aws-solutions-architect-associate/compute/elastic-load-balancing/

## 42. Question

There is new requirement for a database that will store a large number of records for an online store. You are evaluating the use of DynamoDB. Which of the following are AWS best practices for DynamoDB? (choose 2)

1. Use separate local secondary indexes for each item
2. Store objects larger than 400KB in S3 and use pointers in DynamoDB
3. Store more frequently and less frequently accessed data in separate tables
4. Use for BLOB data use cases
5. Use large files

**Answer: 2,3**

**Explanation:**

DynamoDB best practices include:

- Keep item sizes small
- If you are storing serial data in DynamoDB that will require actions based on data/time use separate tables for days, weeks, months
- Store more frequently and less frequently accessed data in separate tables
- If possible, compress larger attribute values
- Store objects larger than 400KB in S3 and use pointers (S3 Object ID) in DynamoDB

**References:**

https://digitalcloud.training/certification-training/aws-solutions-architect-associate/database/amazon-dynamodb/

## 43. Question

A Solutions Architect needs to migrate an Oracle database running on RDS onto Amazon RedShift to improve performance and reduce cost. What combination of tasks using AWS services should be followed to execute the migration? (choose 2)

1. Configure API Gateway to extract, transform and load the data into RedShift
2. Migrate the database using the AWS Database Migration Service (DMS)
3. Enable log shipping from the Oracle database to RedShift
4. Take a snapshot of the Oracle database and restore the snapshot onto RedShift
5. Convert the schema using the AWS Schema Conversion Tool

**Answer: 2,5**

**Explanation:**

- Convert the data warehouse schema and code from the Oracle database running on RDS using the AWS Schema Conversion Tool (AWS SCT) then migrate data from the Oracle database to Amazon Redshift using the AWS Database Migration Service (AWS DMS)
- API Gateway is not used for ETL functions
- Log shipping, or snapshots are not supported migration methods from RDS to RedShift

**References:**

https://aws.amazon.com/getting-started/projects/migrate-oracle-to-amazon-redshift/

## 44. Question

An application running in your on-premise data center writes data to a MySQL database. You are re-architecting the application and plan to move the database layer into the AWS cloud on RDS. You plan to keep the application running in your on-premise data center.

What do you need to do to connect the application to the RDS database via the Internet? (choose 2)

1. Create a DB subnet group that is publicly accessible
2. Configure an NAT Gateway and attach the RDS database
3. Choose to make the RDS instance publicly accessible and place it in a public subnet
4. Create a security group allowing access from your public IP to the RDS instance and assign to the RDS instance
5. Select a public IP within the DB subnet group to assign to the RDS instance

Answer: 3,4

Explanation:

- When you create the RDS instance, you need to select the option to make it publicly accessible. A security group will need to be created and assigned to the RDS instance to allow access from the public IP address of your application (or firewall)
- NAT Gateways are used for enabling Internet connectivity for EC2 instances in private subnets
- A DB subnet group is a collection of subnets (typically private) that you create in a VPC and that you then designate for your DB instance. The DB subnet group cannot be made publicly accessible, even if the subnets are public subnets, it is the RDS DB that must be configured to be publicly accessible

References:

https://digitalcloud.training/certification-training/aws-solutions-architect-associate/database/amazon-rds/

https://docs.aws.amazon.com/AmazonRDS/latest/UserGuide/USER_VPC.Scenarios.html#USER_VPC.Scenario4

## 45. Question

A new financial platform has been re-architected to use Docker containers in a micro-services architecture. The new architecture will be implemented on AWS and you have been asked to recommend the solution configuration. For operational reasons, it will be necessary to access the operating system of the instances on which the containers run.

Which solution delivery option will you select?

1. ECS with a default cluster
2. ECS with the Fargate launch type
3. EKS with Kubernetes managed infrastructure
4. ECS with the EC2 launch type

Answer: 4

Explanation:

- Amazon Elastic Container Service (ECS) is a highly scalable, high performance container management service that supports Docker containers and allows you to easily run applications on a managed cluster of Amazon EC2 instances
- The EC2 Launch Type allows you to run containers on EC2 instances that you manage so you will be able to access the operating system instances
- The Fargate Launch Type is a serverless infrastructure managed by AWS so you do not have access to the operating system of the EC2 instances that the container platform runs on
- The EKS service is a managed Kubernetes service that provides a fully-managed control plane so you would not have access to the EC2 instances that the platform runs on
- ECS with a default cluster is an incorrect answer, you need to choose the launch type to ensure you get the access required, not the cluster configuration

**References:**

https://digitalcloud.training/certification-training/aws-solutions-architect-associate/compute/amazon-ecs/

## 46. Question

You are using encrypted Amazon Elastic Block Store (EBS) volumes with your instances in EC2. A security administrator has asked how encryption works with EBS. Which statements are correct? (choose 2)

1. Data is only encrypted at rest
2. Data in transit between an instance and an encrypted volume is also encrypted
3. You cannot mix encrypted with unencrypted volumes on an instance
4. Encryption is supported on all Amazon EBS volume types
5. Volumes created from encrypted snapshots are unencrypted

**Answer: 2,4**

**Explanation:**

- All EBS types support encryption and all instance families now support encryption
- Not all instance types support encryption
- Data in transit between an instance and an encrypted volume is also encrypted (data is encrypted in trans
- You can have encrypted an unencrypted EBS volumes attached to an instance at the same time
- Snapshots of encrypted volumes are encrypted automatically
- EBS volumes restored from encrypted snapshots are encrypted automatically
- EBS volumes created from encrypted snapshots are also encrypted

**References:**

https://digitalcloud.training/certification-training/aws-solutions-architect-associate/compute/amazon-ebs/

## 47. Question

Which AWS service does API Gateway integrate with to enable users from around the world to achieve the lowest possible latency for API requests and responses?

1. S3 Transfer Acceleration

2. Direct Connect
3. CloudFront
4. Lambda

**Answer: 3**

**Explanation:**

- CloudFront is used as the public endpoint for API Gateway and provides reduced latency and distributed denial of service protection through the use of CloudFront
- Direct Connect provides a private network into AWS from your data center
- S3 Transfer Acceleration is not used with API Gateway, it is used to accelerate uploads of S3 objects
- Lambda is not used to reduce latency for API requests

**References:**

https://digitalcloud.training/certification-training/aws-solutions-architect-associate/networking-and-content-delivery/amazon-api-gateway/

## 48. Question

You are trying to decide on the best data store to use for a new project. The requirements are that the data store is schema-less, supports strongly consistent reads, and stores data in tables, indexed by a primary key.

**Which AWS data store would you use?**

1. Amazon S3
2. Amazon RDS
3. Amazon DynamoDB
4. Amazon RedShift

**Answer: 3**

**Explanation:**

- Amazon Dynamo DB is a fully managed NoSQL (schema-less) database service that provides fast and predictable performance with seamless scalability. Provides two read models: eventually consistent reads (Default) and strongly consistent reads. DynamoDB stores structured data in tables, indexed by a primary key
- Amazon S3 is an object store and stores data in buckets, not tables
- Amazon RDS is a relational (has a schema) database service used for transactional purposes
- Amazon RedShift is a relational (has a schema) database service used for analytics

**References:**

https://digitalcloud.training/certification-training/aws-solutions-architect-associate/database/amazon-dynamodb/

## 49. Question

You are a Solutions Architect at Digital Cloud Training. One of your customers runs an application on-premise that stores large media files. The data is mounted to different servers using either the SMB or

NFS protocols. The customer is having issues with scaling the storage infrastructure on-premise and is looking for a way to offload the data set into the cloud whilst retaining a local cache for frequently accessed content.

**Which of the following is the best solution?**

1. Establish a VPN and use the Elastic File System (EFS)
2. Use the AWS Storage Gateway File Gateway
3. Create a script that migrates infrequently used data to S3 using multi-part upload
4. Use the AWS Storage Gateway Volume Gateway in cached volume mode

**Answer: 2**

**Explanation:**

- File gateway provides a virtual on-premises file server, which enables you to store and retrieve files as objects in Amazon S3. It can be used for on-premises applications, and for Amazon EC2-resident applications that need file storage in S3 for object based workloads. Used for flat files only, stored directly on S3. File gateway offers SMB or NFS-based access to data in Amazon S3 with local caching
- The AWS Storage Gateway Volume Gateway in cached volume mode is a block-based (not file-based) solution so you cannot mount the storage with the SMB or NFS protocols With Cached Volume mode – the entire dataset is stored on S3 and a cache of the most frequently accessed data is cached on-site
- You could mount EFS over a VPN but it would not provide you a local cache of the data
- Creating a script the migrates infrequently used data to S3 is possible but that data would then not be indexed on the primary filesystem so you wouldn't have a method of retrieving it without developing some code to pull it back from S3. This is not the best solution

**References:**

https://digitalcloud.training/certification-training/aws-solutions-architect-associate/storage/aws-storage-gateway/

## 50. Question

You are trying to clean up your unused EBS volumes and snapshots to save some space and cost. How many of the most recent snapshots of an EBS volume need to be maintained to guarantee that you can recreate the full EBS volume from the snapshot?

1. The oldest snapshot, as this references data in all other snapshots
2. You must retain all snapshots as the process is incremental and therefore data is required from each snapshot
3. Two snapshots, the oldest and most recent snapshots
4. Only the most recent snapshot. Snapshots are incremental, but the deletion process will ensure that no data is lost

**Answer: 4**

**Explanation:**

- Snapshots capture a point-in-time state of an instance. If you make periodic snapshots of a volume, the snapshots are incremental, which means that only the blocks on the device that have changed after your last snapshot are saved in the new snapshot

- Even though snapshots are saved incrementally, the snapshot deletion process is designed so that you need to retain only the most recent snapshot in order to restore the volume

**References:**

https://digitalcloud.training/certification-training/aws-solutions-architect-associate/compute/amazon-ebs/

https://docs.aws.amazon.com/AWSEC2/latest/UserGuide/ebs-deleting-snapshot.html

## 51. Question

The development team at Digital Cloud Training have created a new web-based application that will soon be launched. The application will utilize 20 EC2 instances for the web front-end. Due to concerns over latency, you will not be using an ELB but still want to load balance incoming connections across multiple EC2 instances. You will be using Route 53 for the DNS service and want to implement health checks to ensure instances are available.

What two Route 53 configuration options are available that could be individually used to ensure connections reach multiple web servers in this configuration? (choose 2)

1. Use Route 53 multivalue answers to return up to 8 records with each DNS query
2. Use Route 53 simple load balancing which will return records in a round robin fashion
3. Use Route 53 Alias records to resolve using the zone apex
4. Use Route 53 weighted records and give equal weighting to all 20 EC2 instances
5. Use Route 53 failover routing in an active-passive configuration

**Answer: 1,4**

**Explanation:**

- The key requirement here is that you can load balance incoming connections to a series of EC2 instances using Route 53 AND the solution must support health checks. With multi-value answers Route 53 responds with up to eight health records (per query) that are selected at random The weighted record type is similar to simple but you can specify a weight per IP address. You create records that have the same name and type and assign each record a relative weight. In this case you could assign multiple records the same weight and Route 53 will essentially round robin between the records
- We cannot use the simple record type as it does not support health checks
- Alias records let you route traffic to selected AWS resources, such as CloudFront distributions and Amazon S3 buckets. They do not provide equal distribution to multiple endpoints or multi-value answers
- Failover routing with an active-passive configuration puts some resources in a standby state. In this case, it would be preferable to use active-active but this option is not presented

**References:**

https://digitalcloud.training/certification-training/aws-solutions-architect-associate/networking-and-content-delivery/amazon-route-53/

## 52. Question

You have setup multi-factor authentication (MFA) for your root account according to AWS best practices and configured it to work with Google Authenticator on your smart phone. Unfortunately,

**your smart phone has been lost. What are the options available to access your account as the root user?**

1. You will need to contact AWS support to request that the MFA device is deactivated and have your password reset
2. On the AWS sign-in with authentication device web page, choose to sign in using alternative factors of authentication and use the verification email and code to sign in
3. Unfortunately, you will no longer be able to access this account as the root user
4. Get a user with administrative privileges in your AWS account to deactivate the MFA device assigned to the root account

**Answer: 2**

**Explanation:**

- Multi-factor authentication (MFA) can be enabled/enforced for the AWS account and for individual users under the account. MFA uses an authentication device that continually generates random, six-digit, single-use authentication codes
- If your AWS account root user multi-factor authentication (MFA) device is lost, damaged, or not working, you can sign in using alternative methods of authentication. This means that if you can't sign in with your MFA device, you can sign in by verifying your identity using the email and phone that are registered with your account
- There is a resolution to this problem as described above and you do not need to raise a support request with AWS to deactivate the device and reset your password
- An administrator can deactivate the MFA device but this does not enable you to access the account as the root user, you must sign in using alternative factors of authentication

**References:**

https://digitalcloud.training/certification-training/aws-solutions-architect-associate/security-identity-compliance/aws-iam/

https://docs.aws.amazon.com/IAM/latest/UserGuide/id_credentials_mfa_lost-or-broken.html

## 53. Question

The development team in your organization would like to start leveraging AWS services. They have asked you what AWS service can be used to quickly deploy and manage applications in the AWS Cloud? The developers would like the ability to simply upload applications and have AWS handle the deployment details of capacity provisioning, load balancing, auto-scaling, and application health monitoring. What AWS service would you recommend?

1. EC2
2. OpsWorks
3. Auto Scaling
4. Elastic Beanstalk

**Answer: 4**

**Explanation:**

- Whenever you hear about developers uploading code/applications think Elastic Beanstalk.AWS Elastic Beanstalk can be used to quickly deploy and manage applications in the AWS Cloud. Developers upload applications and Elastic Beanstalk handles the deployment details of capacity provisioning, load balancing, auto-scaling, and application health monitoring. It is considered to be a Platform as a Service (PaaS) solution and supports Java, .NET, PHP, Node.js, Python, Ruby, Go, and Docker web applications

- If you use EC2 you must manage the deployment yourself, AWS will not handle the deployment, capacity provisioning etc.
- Auto Scaling does not assist with deployment of applications
- OpsWorks provides a managed Chef or Puppet infrastructure. You can define how to deploy and configure infrastructure but it does not give you the ability to upload application code and have the service deploy the application for you

**References:**

https://digitalcloud.training/certification-training/aws-solutions-architect-associate/compute/aws-elastic-beanstalk/

## 54. Question

A Solutions Architect is creating a solution for an application that must be deployed on Amazon EC2 hosts that are dedicated to the client. Instance placement must be automatic and billing should be per instance.

**Which type of EC2 deployment model should be used?**

1. Reserved Instance
2. Dedicated Instance
3. Dedicated Host
4. Cluster Placement Group

**Answer: 2**

**Explanation:**

- Dedicated Instances are Amazon EC2 instances that run in a VPC on hardware that's dedicated to a single customer. Your Dedicated instances are physically isolated at the host hardware level from instances that belong to other AWS accounts. Dedicated instances allow automatic instance placement and billing is per instance
- An Amazon EC2 Dedicated Host is a physical server with EC2 instance capacity fully dedicated to your use. Dedicated Hosts can help you address compliance requirements and reduce costs by allowing you to use your existing server-bound software licenses. With dedicated hosts billing is on a per-host basis (not per instance)
- Reserved instances are a method of reducing cost by committing to a fixed contract term of 1 or 3 years
- A Cluster Placement Group determines how instances are placed on underlying hardware to enable low-latency connectivity

**References:**

https://digitalcloud.training/certification-training/aws-solutions-architect-associate/compute/amazon-ec2/

https://aws.amazon.com/ec2/dedicated-hosts/

## 55. Question

A client has made some updates to their web application. The application uses an Auto Scaling Group to maintain a group of several EC2 instances. The application has been modified and a new AMI must be used for launching any new instances.

What do you need to do to add the new AMI?

1. Suspend Auto Scaling and replace the existing AMI
2. Create a new target group that uses a new launch configuration with the new AMI
3. Create a new launch configuration that uses the AMI and update the ASG to use the new launch configuration
4. Modify the existing launch configuration to add the new AMI

Answer: 3

Explanation:

- A launch configuration is the template used to create new EC2 instances and includes parameters such as instance family, instance type, AMI, key pair and security groups
- You cannot edit a launch configuration once defined. In this case you can create a new launch configuration that uses the new AMI and any new instances that are launched by the ASG will use the new AMI
- Suspending scaling processes can be useful when you want to investigate a configuration problem or other issue with your web application and then make changes to your application, without invoking the scaling processes. It is not useful in this situation
- A target group is a concept associated with an ELB not Auto Scaling

References:

https://digitalcloud.training/certification-training/aws-solutions-architect-associate/compute/amazon-ebs/

## 56. Question

A Solutions Architect is designing an application stack that will be highly elastic. Which AWS services can be used that don't require you to make any capacity decisions upfront? (choose 2)

1. AWS Lambda
2. DynamoDB
3. Amazon EC2
4. Amazon Kinesis Firehose
5. Amazon RDS

Answer: 1,4

Explanation:

- With Kinesis Data Firehose, you only pay for the amount of data you transmit through the service, and if applicable, for data format conversion. There is no minimum fee or setup cost
- AWS Lambda lets you run code without provisioning or managing servers. You pay only for the compute time you consume – there is no charge when your code is not running
- With Amazon EC2 you need to select your instance sizes and number of instances
- With RDS you need to select the instance size for the DB

- With DynamoDB you need to specify the read/write capacity of the DB

**References:**

https://digitalcloud.training/certification-training/aws-solutions-architect-associate/compute/aws-lambda/

https://digitalcloud.training/certification-training/aws-solutions-architect-associate/analytics/amazon-kinesis/

## 57. Question

A Solutions Architect is creating a design for an online gambling application that will process thousands of records. Which AWS service makes it easy to collect, process, and analyze real-time, streaming data?

1. S3
2. Kinesis Data Streams
3. RedShift
4. EMR

**Answer: 2**

**Explanation:**

- Amazon Kinesis makes it easy to collect, process, and analyze real-time, streaming data so you can get timely insights and react quickly to new information. Kinesis Data Streams enables you to build custom applications that process or analyze streaming data for specialized needs. Kinesis Data Streams enables real-time processing of streaming big data and is used for rapidly moving data off data producers and then continuously processing the data
- Amazon S3 is an object store and does not have any native functionality for collecting, processing or analyzing streaming data
- RedShift is a data warehouse that can be used for storing data in a columnar structure for later analysis. It is not however used for streaming data
- Amazon EMR provides a managed Hadoop framework that makes it easy, fast, and cost-effective to process vast amounts of data across dynamically scalable Amazon EC2 instances. It does not collect streaming data

**References:**

https://digitalcloud.training/certification-training/aws-solutions-architect-associate/analytics/amazon-kinesis/

## 58. Question

You are developing some code that uses a Lambda function and you would like to enable the function to connect to an ElastiCache cluster within a VPC that you own. What VPC-specific information must you include in your function to enable this configuration? (choose 2)

1. VPC Subnet IDs
2. VPC Peering IDs
3. VPC Route Table IDs
4. VPC Logical IDs
5. VPC Security Group IDs

**Answer: 1,5**

**Explanation:**

- To enable your Lambda function to access resources inside your private VPC, you must provide additional VPC-specific configuration information that includes VPC subnet IDs and security group IDs. AWS Lambda uses this information to set up elastic network interfaces (ENIs) that enable your function
- Please see the AWS article linked below for more details on the requirements

**References:**

https://digitalcloud.training/certification-training/aws-solutions-architect-associate/compute/aws-lambda/

https://docs.aws.amazon.com/lambda/latest/dg/vpc.html


## 59. Question

You are a Solutions Architect for Digital Cloud Training. A client has asked for some assistance in selecting the best database for a specific requirement. The database will be used for a data warehouse solution and the data will be stored in a structured format. The client wants to run complex analytics queries using business intelligence tools.

**Which AWS database service will you recommend?**

1. Amazon RDS
2. Amazon Aurora
3. Amazon RedShift
4. Amazon DynamoDB


**Answer: 3**

**Explanation:**

- Amazon Redshift is a fast, fully managed data warehouse that makes it simple and cost-effective to analyze all your data using standard SQL and existing Business Intelligence (BI) tools. RedShift is a SQL based data warehouse used for analytics applications. RedShift is an Online Analytics Processing (OLAP) type of DB. RedShift is used for running complex analytic queries against petabytes of structured data, using sophisticated query optimization, columnar storage on high-performance local disks, and massively parallel query execution
- Amazon RDS does store data in a structured format but it is not a data warehouse. The primary use case for RDS is as a transactional database (not an analytics database)
- Amazon DynamoDB is not a structured database (schema-less / NoSQL) and is not a data warehouse solution
- Amazon Aurora is a type of RDS database so is also not suitable for a data warehouse use case

**References:**

https://digitalcloud.training/certification-training/aws-solutions-architect-associate/database/amazon-redshift/

### 60. Question

A company is moving some unstructured data into AWS and a Solutions Architect has created a bucket named "contosocustomerdata" in the ap-southeast-2 region. Which of the following bucket URLs would be valid for accessing the bucket? (choose 2)

1. https://s3.ap-southeast-2.amazonaws.com/contosocustomerdata
2. https://s3.amazonaws.com/contosocustomerdata
3. https://s3-ap-southeast-2.amazonaws.com.contosocustomerdata
4. https://contosocustomerdata.s3.amazonaws.com
5. https://amazonaws.s3-ap-southeast-2.com/contosocustomerdata

Answer: 1,4

Explanation:

- AWS supports S3 URLs in the format of https://<bucket>.s3.amazonaws.com/<object> (virtual host style addressing) and https://s3.<region>.amazonaws.com/<bucket>/<object>

References:

https://docs.aws.amazon.com/AmazonS3/latest/dev/UsingBucket.html

### 61. Question

An organization is creating a new storage solution and needs to ensure that Amazon S3 objects that are deleted are immediately restorable for up to 30 days. After 30 days the objects should be retained for a further 180 days and be restorable within 24 hours.

The solution should be operationally simple and cost-effective. How can these requirements be achieved? (choose 2)

1. Create a lifecycle rule to transition non-current versions to GLACIER after 30 days, and then expire the objects after 180 days
2. Enable object versioning on the Amazon S3 bucket that will contain the objects
3. Create a lifecycle rule to transition non-current versions to STANDARD_IA after 30 days, and then expire the objects after 180 days
4. Enable cross-region replication (CRR) for the Amazon S3 bucket that will contain the objects
5. Enable multi-factor authentication (MFA) delete protection

Answer: 1,2

Explanation:

- Object Versioning is a means of keeping multiple variants of an object in the same Amazon S3 bucket. When you delete an object in a versioning enabled bucket the object is not deleted, a delete marker is added and the object is considered "non-current". In this case we can then transition the non-current versions to GLACIER after 30 days (as we need immediate recoverability for 30 days), and then expire the object after 180 days as they are no longer required to be recoverable.
- Multi-factor authentication (MFA) delete is a way of adding an extra layer of security to prevent accidental deletion. That's not what we're looking to do here. We don't want to add any additional operational elements, we just need the ability to restore if we accidentally delete something.

- Cross-region replication (CRR) is used for replicating the entire bucket to another region. This provide disaster recovery and a full additional copy of data. This is not the most cost-effective solution as you have 2 full copies of your data. However, deletions are not replicated so it does provide protection from deleting objects.
- Transitioning to STANDARD_IA is less cost-effective than transitioning to GLACIER. As we only need recoverability within 24 hours GLACIER is the best option.

**References:**

https://d0.awsstatic.com/whitepapers/protecting-s3-against-object-deletion.pdf

https://digitalcloud.training/certification-training/aws-solutions-architect-associate/storage/amazon-s3/


## 62. Question

A company wishes to restrict access to their Amazon DynamoDB table to specific, private source IP addresses from their VPC. What should be done to secure access to the table?

1. Create the Amazon DynamoDB table in the VPC
2. Create an interface VPC endpoint in the VPC with an Elastic Network Interface (ENI)
3. Create an AWS VPN connection to the Amazon DynamoDB endpoint
4. Create a gateway VPC endpoint and add an entry to the route table


**Answer: 4**

**Explanation:**

- There are two different types of VPC endpoint: interface endpoint, and gateway endpoint. With an interface endpoint you use an ENI in the VPC. With a gateway endpoint you configure your route table to point to the endpoint. Amazon S3 and DynamoDB use gateway endpoints. This solution means that all traffic will go through the VPC endpoint straight to DynamoDB using private IP addresses.
- As mentioned above, an interface endpoint is not used for DynamoDB, you must use a gateway endpoint.
- You cannot create a DynamoDB table in a VPC, to connect securely using private addresses you should use a gateway endpoint instead.
- You cannot create an AWS VPN connection to the Amazon DynamoDB endpoint.

**References:**

https://docs.amazonaws.cn/en_us/vpc/latest/userguide/vpc-endpoints-ddb.html

https://aws.amazon.com/premiumsupport/knowledge-center/iam-restrict-calls-ip-addresses/

https://aws.amazon.com/blogs/aws/new-vpc-endpoints-for-dynamodb/

https://digitalcloud.training/certification-training/aws-solutions-architect-associate/networking-and-content-delivery/amazon-vpc/


## 63. Question

An application running on Amazon EC2 needs to asynchronously invoke an AWS Lambda function to perform data processing. The services should be decoupled.

Which service can be used to decouple the compute services?

1.  Amazon MQ
2.  Amazon SNS
3.  Amazon SQS
4.  Amazon Step Functions

**Answer: 2**

**Explanation:**

*   You can use a Lambda function to process Amazon Simple Notification Service notifications. Amazon SNS supports Lambda functions as a target for messages sent to a topic. This solution decouples the Amazon EC2 application from Lambda and ensures the Lambda function is invoked.
*   You cannot invoke a Lambda function using Amazon SQS. Lambda can be configured to poll a queue, as SQS is pull-based, but it is not push-based like SNS which is what this solution is looking for.
*   Amazon MQ is similar to SQS but is used for existing applications that are being migrated into AWS. SQS should be used for new applications being created in the cloud.
*   Amazon Step Functions is a workflow service. It is not the best solution for this scenario.

**References:**

https://docs.aws.amazon.com/lambda/latest/dg/with-sns.html

https://digitalcloud.training/certification-training/aws-solutions-architect-associate/compute/aws-lambda/

https://digitalcloud.training/certification-training/aws-solutions-architect-associate/application-integration/amazon-sns/

https://aws.amazon.com/sns/features/

## 64. Question

An Amazon RDS PostgreSQL database is configured as Multi-AZ. You need to scale read performance. What is the most cost-effective solution?

1.  Configure the application to read from the Multi-AZ standby instance
2.  Deploy a Read Replica in a different AZ to the master DB instance
3.  Create an ElastiCache cluster in front of the RDS DB instance
4.  Deploy a Read Replica in the same AZ as the master DB instance

**Answer: 4**

**Explanation:**

*   The best option is to deploy a read replica. For PostgreSQL the read replica cannot be in another AZ. This solution will allow scaling of read performance and is the most cost-effective option that works.
*   You can combine Read Replicas with Multi-AZ for MySQL and MariaDB. However, PostgreSQL is not currently supported.
*   ElastiCache can assist with caching read requests but is not the most cost-effective option here.

**References:**

https://digitalcloud.training/certification-training/aws-solutions-architect-associate/database/amazon-rds/

https://aws.amazon.com/about-aws/whats-new/2018/01/amazon-rds-read-replicas-now-support-multi-az-deployments/

## 65. Question

An AWS Organization has an OU with multiple member accounts in it. The company needs to restrict the ability to launch only specific Amazon EC2 instance types. How can this policy be applied across the accounts with the least effort?

1. Create an IAM policy to deny launching all but the specific instance types
2. Create an SCP with a deny rule that denies all but the specific instance types
3. Use AWS Resource Access Manager to control which launch types can be used
4. Create an SCP with an allow rule that allows launching the specific instance types

Answer:2

Explanation:

- To apply the restrictions across multiple member accounts you must use a Service Control Policy (SCP) in the AWS Organization. The way you would do this is to create a deny rule that applies to anything that does not equal the specific instance type you want to allow.
- With IAM you need to apply the policy within each account rather than centrally so this would require much more effort.
- AWS Resource Access Manager (RAM) is a service that enables you to easily and securely share AWS resources with any AWS account or within your AWS Organization. It is not used for restricting access or permissions.

References:

https://docs.aws.amazon.com/organizations/latest/userguide/orgs_manage_policies_example-scps.html#example-ec2-instances

https://digitalcloud.training/certification-training/aws-solutions-architect-associate/management-tools/aws-organizations/

# SET 6: PRACTICE QUESTIONS ONLY

*Or go directly to Set 6: Practice Questions, Answers & Explanations*

## 1. Question

You are putting together an architecture for a new VPC on AWS. Your on-premise data center will be connected to the VPC by a hardware VPN and has public and VPN-only subnets. The security team has requested that traffic hitting public subnets on AWS that's destined to on-premise applications must be directed over the VPN to the corporate firewall.

**How can this be achieved?**

1. In the public subnet route table, add a route for your remote network and specify the virtual private gateway as the target
2. Configure a NAT Gateway and configure all traffic to be directed via the virtual private gateway
3. In the VPN-only subnet route table, add a route that directs all Internet traffic to the virtual private gateway
4. In the public subnet route table, add a route for your remote network and specify the customer gateway as the target

## 2. Question

A development team are creating a Continuous Integration and Continuous Delivery (CI/CD) toolchain on the AWS cloud. The team currently use Jenkins X and Kubernetes on-premise and are looking to utilize the same services in the AWS cloud.

**What AWS service can provide a managed container platform that is MOST similar to their current CI/CD toolchain?**

1. AWS CodePipeline
2. Amazon EKS
3. Amazon ECS
4. AWS Lambda

## 3. Question

A customer is deploying services in a hybrid cloud model. The customer has mandated that data is transferred directly between cloud data centers, bypassing ISPs.

**Which AWS service can be used to enable hybrid cloud connectivity?**

1. IPSec VPN
2. Amazon Route 53
3. AWS Direct Connect
4. Amazon VPC

## 4. Question

A web application you manage receives order processing information from customers and places the messages on an SQS queue. A fleet of EC2 instances are configured to pick up the messages, process them, and store the results in a DynamoDB table. The current configuration has been resulting in a large number of empty responses to ReceiveMessage requests. You would like to update the configuration to eliminate empty responses to reduce operational overhead. How can this be done?

1. Use a Standard queue to provide at-least-once delivery, which means that each message is delivered at least once
2. Use a FIFO (first-in-first-out) queue to preserve the exact order in which messages are sent and received
3. Configure Short Polling to eliminate empty responses by reducing the length of time a connection request remains open
4. Configure Long Polling to eliminate empty responses by allowing Amazon SQS to wait until a message is available in a queue before sending a response

## 5. Question

Your company runs a web-based application that uses EC2 instances for the web front-end and RDS for the database back-end. The web application writes transaction log files to an S3 bucket and the quantity of files is becoming quite large. You have determined that it is acceptable to retain the most recent 60 days of log files and permanently delete the rest. What can you do to enable this to happen automatically?

1. Use an S3 lifecycle policy to move the log files that are more than 60 days old to the GLACIER storage class
2. Write a Ruby script that checks the age of objects and deletes any that are more than 60 days old
3. Use an S3 lifecycle policy with object expiration configured to automatically remove objects that are more than 60 days old
4. Use an S3 bucket policy that deletes objects that are more than 60 days old

## 6. Question

You have created an Auto Scaling Group (ASG) that has launched several EC2 instances running Linux. The ASG was created using the CLI. You want to ensure that you do not pay for monitoring. What needs to be done to ensure that monitoring is free of charge?

1. The launch configuration will have been created with basic monitoring enabled which is free of charge so you do not need to do anything
2. The launch configuration will have been created with detailed monitoring enabled which is chargeable. You will need to change the settings on the launch configuration
3. The launch configuration will have been created with detailed monitoring enabled which is chargeable. You will need to recreate the launch configuration with basic monitoring enabled
4. The launch configuration will have been created with detailed monitoring enabled which is chargeable. You will need to modify the settings on the ASG

## 7. Question

You have associated a new launch configuration to your Auto Scaling Group (ASG) which runs a fleet of EC2 instances. The new launch configuration changes monitoring from detailed to basic. There are a couple of CloudWatch alarms configured on the ASG which monitor every 60 seconds. There is a mismatch in frequency of metric reporting between these configuration settings, what will be the result?

1. The EC2 metrics will be updated automatically to match the frequency of the alarms and send updates every 60 seconds

2. The alarm state will be immediately set to INSUFFICIENT_DATA
3. If you do not update your alarms to match the five-minute period, they continue to check for statistics every minute and might find no data available for as many as four out of every five periods
4. The ASG will automatically update the frequency of the alarms to 300 seconds to match the EC2 monitoring in the launch configuration

## 8. Question

You need to run a PowerShell script on a fleet of EC2 instances running Microsoft Windows. The instances have already been launched in your VPC. What tool can be run from the AWS Management Console that will run the script on all target EC2 instances?

1. AWS CodeDeploy
2. AWS OpsWorks
3. Run Command
4. AWS Config

## 9. Question

You are using the Elastic Container Service (ECS) to run a number of containers using the EC2 launch type. To gain more control over scheduling containers you have decided to utilize Blox to integrate a third-party scheduler. The third-party scheduler will use the StartTask API to place tasks on specific container instances. What type of ECS scheduler will you need to use to enable this configuration?

1. Cron Scheduler
2. ECS Scheduler
3. Custom Scheduler
4. Service Scheduler

## 10. Question

You need to run a production process that will use several EC2 instances and run constantly on an ongoing basis. The process cannot be interrupted or restarted without issue. Which EC2 pricing model would be best for this workload?

1. Reserved instances
2. Spot instances
3. On-demand instances
4. Flexible instances

## 11. Question

You have recently enabled Access Logs on your Application Load Balancer (ALB). One of your colleagues would like to process the log files using a hosted Hadoop service. What configuration changes and services can be leveraged to deliver this requirement?

1. Configure Access Logs to be delivered to S3 and use Kinesis for processing the log files
2. Configure Access Logs to be delivered to DynamoDB and use EMR for processing the log files
3. Configure Access Logs to be delivered to S3 and use EMR for processing the log files
4. Configure Access Logs to be delivered to EC2 and install Hadoop for processing the log files

## 12. Question

You created a new IAM user account for a temporary employee who recently joined the company. The user does not have permissions to perform any actions, which statement is true about newly created users in IAM?

1. They are created with user privileges
2. They are created with full permissions
3. They are created with limited permissions
4. They are created with no permissions

## 13. Question

In your VPC you have several EC2 instances that have been running for some time. You have logged into an instance and need to determine a few pieces of information including what IAM role is assigned, the instance ID and the names of the security groups that are assigned to the instance.

From the options below, what would be a source of this information?

1. Parameters
2. Tags
3. Metadata
4. User data

## 14. Question

The application development team in your company have developed a Java application and saved the source code in a .war file. They would like to run the application on AWS resources and are looking for a service that can handle the provisioning and management of the underlying resources it will run on.

What AWS service would allow the developers to upload the Java source code file and provide capacity provisioning and infrastructure management?

1. AWS CodeDeploy
2. AWS Elastic Beanstalk
3. AWS CloudFormation
4. AWS OpsWorks

## 15. Question

You have launched an EC2 instance into a VPC. You need to ensure that instances have both a private and public DNS hostname. Assuming you did not change any settings during creation of the VPC, how will DNS hostnames be assigned by default? (choose 2)

1. In a default VPC instances will be assigned a private but not a public DNS hostname
2. In a non-default VPC instances will be assigned a public and private DNS hostname
3. In a non-default VPC instances will be assigned a private but not a public DNS hostname
4. In all VPCs instances no DNS hostnames will be assigned
5. In a default VPC instances will be assigned a public and private DNS hostname

## 16. Question

A Solutions Architect has created a VPC and is in the process of formulating the subnet design. The VPC will be used to host a two-tier application that will include Internet facing web servers, and internal-only DB servers. Zonal redundancy is required.

How many subnets are required to support this requirement?

1. 1 subnet
2. 2 subnets
3. 6 subnets
4. 4 subnets

## 17. Question

A security officer has requested that all data associated with a specific customer is encrypted. The data resides on Elastic Block Store (EBS) volumes. Which of the following statements about using EBS encryption are correct? (choose 2)

1. Not all EBS types support encryption
2. Data in transit between an instance and an encrypted volume is also encrypted
3. All attached EBS volumes must share the same encryption state
4. There is no direct way to change the encryption state of a volume
5. All instance types support encryption

## 18. Question

You have just created a new security group in your VPC. You have not yet created any rules. Which of the statements below are correct regarding the default state of the security group? (choose 2)

1. There are is an inbound rule that allows traffic from the Internet Gateway
2. There is an inbound rule allowing traffic from the Internet to port 22 for management
3. There is an outbound rule allowing traffic to the Internet Gateway
4. There is an outbound rule that allows all traffic to all IP addresses
5. There are no inbound rules and traffic will be implicitly denied

## 19. Question

You are running a database on an EC2 instance in your VPC. The load on the DB is increasing and you have noticed that the performance has been impacted. Which of the options below would help to increase storage performance? (choose 2)

1. Use EBS optimized instances
2. Use HDD, Cold (SC1) EBS volumes
3. Use Provisioned IOPS (I01) EBS volumes
4. Use a larger instance size within the instance family
5. Create a RAID 1 array from multiple EBS volumes

## 20. Question

One of you clients has asked for assistance with a performance issue they are experiencing. The client has a fleet of EC2 instances behind an Elastic Load Balancer (ELB) that are a mixture of c4.2xlarge instance types and c5.large instances. The load on the CPUs on the c5.large instances has been very high, often hitting 100% utilization, whereas the c4.2xlarge instances have been performing well. The client has asked for advice on the most cost-effective way to resolve the performance problems?

1. Add more c5.large instances to spread the load more evenly
2. Change the configuration to use only c4.2xlarge instance types
3. Add all of the instances into a Placement Group
4. Enable the weighted routing policy on the ELB and

## 21. Question

A large quantity of data that is rarely accessed is being archived onto Amazon Glacier. Your CIO wants to understand the resilience of the service. Which of the statements below is correct about Amazon Glacier storage? (choose 2)

1. Data is replicated globally
2. Provides 99.999999999% durability of archives
3. Data is resilient in the event of one entire region destruction
4. Provides 99.9% availability of archives
5. Data is resilient in the event of one entire Availability Zone destruction

## 22. Question

An EC2 instance you manage is generating very high packets-per-second and performance of the application stack is being impacted. You have been asked for a resolution to the issue that results in improved performance from the EC2 instance. What would you suggest?

1. Configure a RAID 1 array from multiple EBS volumes
2. Create a placement group and put the EC2 instance in it
3. Use enhanced networking
4. Add multiple Elastic IP addresses to the instance

## 23. Question

One of your EC2 instances that is behind an Elastic Load Balancer (ELB) is in the process of being de-registered. Which ELB feature can be used to allow existing connections to close cleanly?

1. Sticky Sessions
2. Deletion Protection
3. Proxy Protocol
4. Connection Draining

## 24. Question

Your manager has asked you to explain some of the security features available in the AWS cloud. How can you describe the function of Amazon CloudHSM?

1. It is a firewall for use with web applications
2. It can be used to generate, use and manage encryption keys in the cloud
3. It provides server-side encryption for S3 objects
4. It is a Public Key Infrastructure (PKI)

## 25. Question

One of your clients has multiple VPCs that are peered with each other. The client would like to use a single Elastic Load Balancer (ELB) to route traffic to multiple EC2 instances in peered VPCs within the same region. Is this possible?

1. This is not possible with ELB, you would need to use Route 53
2. This is possible using the Network Load Balancer (NLB) and Application Load Balancer (ALB) if using IP addresses as targets
3. This is possible using the Classic Load Balancer (CLB) if using Instance IDs
4. No, the instances that an ELB routes traffic to must be in the same VPC

## 26. Question

An application you manage runs a series of EC2 instances with a web application behind an Application Load Balancer (ALB). You are updating the configuration with a health check and need to select the protocol to use. What options are available to you? (choose 2)

1. HTTP
2. TCP
3. ICMP
4. SSL
5. HTTPS

## 27. Question

You have just created a new Network ACL in your VPC. You have not yet created any rules. Which of the statements below are correct regarding the default state of the Network ACL? (choose 2)

1. There is a default outbound rule denying all traffic
2. There is a default outbound rule allowing traffic to the Internet Gateway
3. There is a default inbound rule allowing traffic from the VPC CIDR block
4. There is a default outbound rule allowing all traffic
5. There is a default inbound rule denying all traffic

## 28. Question

You are trying to SSH into an EC2 instance running Linux but cannot connect. The EC2 instance has been launched in a public subnet with an Internet Gateway. Upon investigation you have verified that the instance has a public IP address and that the route table does reference the Internet Gateway correctly. What else needs to be checked to enable connectivity?

1. Check that there is a Bastion Host in the subnet and connect to it first
2. Check that the subnet CIDR block is referenced properly in the route table
3. Check that the VPN is configured correctly
4. Check that the Security Groups and Network ACLs have the correct rules configured

## 29. Question

You launched an EBS-backed EC2 instance into your VPC. A requirement has come up for some high-performance ephemeral storage and so you would like to add an instance-store backed volume. How can you add the new instance store volume?

1. You can specify the instance store volumes for your instance only when you launch an instance
2. You can use a block device mapping to specify additional instance store volumes when you launch your instance, or you can attach additional instance store volumes after your instance is running
3. You must use an Elastic Network Adapter (ENA) to add instance store volumes. First, attach an ENA, and then attach the instance store volume
4. You must shutdown the instance in order to be able to add the instance store volume

## 30. Question

You are creating a CloudFormation Stack that will create EC2 instances that will record log files to an S3 bucket. When creating the template which optional section is used to return the name of the S3 bucket?

1. Resources
2. Parameters
3. Outputs
4. Mappings

## 31. Question

Your company has started using the AWS CloudHSM for secure key storage. A recent administrative error resulted in the loss of credentials to access the CloudHSM. You need access to data that was encrypted using keys stored on the hardware security module. How can you recover the keys that are no longer accessible?

1. There is no way to recover your keys if you lose your credentials
2. Reset the CloudHSM device and create a new set of credentials
3. Log a case with AWS support and they will use MFA to recover the credentials
4. Restore a snapshot of the CloudHSM

## 32. Question

A development team needs to run up a few lab servers on a weekend for a new project. The servers will need to run uninterrupted for a few hours. Which EC2 pricing option would be most suitable?

1. Spot
2. Reserved
3. On-Demand
4. Dedicated Instances

## 33. Question

You are a Solutions Architect at Digital Cloud Training. A client has asked you for some advice about how they can capture detailed information about all HTTP requests that are processed by their Internet facing Application Load Balancer (ALB). The client requires information on the requester, IP address, and request type for analyzing traffic patterns to better understand their customer base.

What would you recommend to the client?

1. Use CloudTrail to capture all API calls made to the ALB
2. Enable Access Logs and store the data on S3
3. Configure metrics in CloudWatch for the ALB

4.  Enable EC2 detailed monitoring

## 34. Question

You are planning to launch a fleet of EC2 instances running Linux. As part of the launch you would like to install some application development frameworks and custom software onto the instances. The installation will be initiated using some scripts you have written. What feature allows you to specify the scripts so you can install the software during the EC2 instance launch?

1.  Run Command
2.  User Data
3.  Metadata
4.  AWS Config

## 35. Question

An application you manage uses RDS in a multi-AZ configuration as the database back-end. There is a failure of the primary DB instance. Which of the following statements are correct in relation to the process RDS uses to failover to the standby DB instance? (choose 2)

1.  The failover mechanism automatically moves the Elastic IP address of the instance to the standby DB instance
2.  Multi-AZ uses synchronous replication; therefore, the failover is instantaneous
3.  Failover times are typically 60-120 seconds
4.  The failover mechanism automatically changes the DNS record of the DB instance to point to the standby DB instance

## 36. Question

A Solutions Architect is designing the system monitoring and deployment layers of a serverless application. The system monitoring layer will manage system visibility through recording logs and metrics and the deployment layer will deploy the application stack and manage workload changes through a release management process.

The Architect needs to select the most appropriate AWS services for these functions. Which services and frameworks should be used for the system monitoring and deployment layers? (choose 2)

1.  Use AWS SAM to package, test, and deploy the serverless application stack
2.  Use AWS X-Ray to package, test, and deploy the serverless application stack
3.  Use AWS Lambda to package, test, and deploy the serverless application stack
4.  Use Amazon CloudWatch for consolidating system and application logs and monitoring custom metrics
5.  Use Amazon CloudTrail for consolidating system and application logs and monitoring custom metrics

## 37. Question

You need to upload a large (2GB) file to an S3 bucket. What is the recommended way to upload a single large file to an S3 bucket?

1.  Use AWS Import/Export
2.  Use Multipart Upload

3. Use a single PUT request to upload the large file
4. Use Amazon Snowball

## 38. Question

You are using a series of Spot instances that process messages from an SQS queue and store results in a DynamoDB table. Shortly after picking up a message from the queue AWS terminated the Spot instance. The Spot instance had not finished processing the message. What will happen to the message?

1. The results may be duplicated in DynamoDB as the message will likely be processed multiple times
2. The message will be lost as it would have been deleted from the queue when processed
3. The message will remain in the queue and be immediately picked up by another instance
4. The message will become available for processing again after the visibility timeout expires

## 39. Question

A DynamoDB table you manage has a variable load, ranging from sustained heavy usage some days, to only having small spikes on others. The load is 80% read and 20% write. The provisioned throughput capacity has been configured to account for the heavy load to ensure throttling does not occur.

You have been asked to find a solution for saving cost. What would be the most efficient and cost-effective solution?

1. Create a CloudWatch alarm that notifies you of increased/decreased load, and manually adjust the provisioned throughput
2. Create a DynamoDB Auto Scaling scaling policy
3. Create a CloudWatch alarm that triggers an AWS Lambda function that adjusts the provisioned throughput
4. Use DynamoDB DAX to increase the performance of the database

## 40. Question

A financial services company regularly runs an analysis of the day's transaction costs, execution reporting, and market performance. The company currently uses third-party commercial software for provisioning, managing, monitoring, and scaling the computing jobs which utilize a large fleet of EC2 instances.

The company is seeking to reduce costs and utilize AWS services. Which AWS service could be used in place of the third-party software?

1. Amazon Lex
2. Amazon Athena
3. AWS Systems Manager
4. AWS Batch

## 41. Question

One of the applications you manage receives a high traffic load between 7:30am and 9:30am daily. The application uses an Auto Scaling Group (ASG) to maintain 3 EC2 instances most of the time but during the peak period requires 6 EC2 instances. How can you configure ASG to perform a regular scale-out event at 7:30am and a scale-in event at 9:30am daily to account for the peak load?

1. Use a Simple scaling policy
2. Use a Scheduled scaling policy
3. Use a Step scaling policy
4. Use a Dynamic scaling policy

## 42. Question

A large multi-national client has requested a design for a multi-region database. The master database will be in the EU (Frankfurt) region and databases will be located in 4 other regions to service local read traffic. The database should be a managed service including the replication.

The solution should be cost-effective and secure. Which AWS service can deliver these requirements?

1. RDS with cross-region Read Replicas
2. RDS with Multi-AZ
3. ElastiCache with Redis and clustering mode enabled
4. EC2 instances with EBS replication

## 43. Question

You have just created a new AWS account and selected the Asia Pacific (Sydney) region. Within the default VPC there is a default security group. What settings are configured within this security group by default? (choose 2)

1. There is an outbound rule that allows all traffic to all addresses
2. There is an outbound rule that allows traffic to the VPC router
3. There is an outbound rule that allows all traffic to the security group itself
4. There is an inbound rule that allows all traffic from any address
5. There is an inbound rule that allows all traffic from the security group itself

## 44. Question

You are running an Auto Scaling Group (ASG) with an Elastic Load Balancer (ELB) and a fleet of EC2 instances. Health checks are configured on the ASG to use EC2 status checks. The ELB has determined that an EC2 instance is unhealthy and has removed it from service. However, you noticed that the instance is still running and has not been terminated by the ASG.

What would be an explanation for this behavior?

1. The ELB health check type has not been selected for the ASG and so it is unaware that the instance has been determined to be unhealthy by the ELB and has been removed from service
2. Connection draining is enabled and the ASG is waiting for in-flight requests to complete
3. The health check grace period has not yet expired
4. The ASG is waiting for the cooldown timer to expire before terminating the instance

## 45. Question

A developer is writing code for AWS Lambda and is looking to automate the release process. Which AWS services can be used to automate the release process of Lambda applications? (choose 2)

1. AWS Glue
2. AWS OpsWorks
3. AWS CodeDeploy

4. AWS Cognito
5. AWS CodePipeline

## 46. Question

When using the MySQL database with AWS RDS, features such as Point-In-Time restore and snapshot restore require a recoverable storage engine. Which storage engine must be used to enable these features?

1. Memory
2. MyISAM
3. InnoDB
4. Federated

## 47. Question

One of your clients is transitioning their web presence into the AWS cloud. As part of the migration the client will be running a web application both on-premises and in AWS for a period of time. During the period of co-existence the client would like 80% of the traffic to hit the AWS-based web servers and 20% to be directed to the on-premises web servers.

What method can you use to distribute traffic as requested?

1. Use Route 53 with a simple routing policy
2. Use Route 53 with a weighted routing policy and configure the respective weights
3. Use an Application Load Balancer to distribute traffic based on IP address
4. Use a Network Load Balancer to distribute traffic based on Instance ID

## 48. Question

A government agency is using CloudFront for a web application that receives personally identifiable information (PII) from citizens. What feature of CloudFront applies an extra level of encryption at CloudFront edge locations to ensure the PII data is secured end-to-end?

1. Origin access identity
2. Field-level encryption
3. Object invalidation
4. RTMP distribution

## 49. Question

An application is generating a large amount of clickstream events data that is being stored on S3. The business needs to understand customer behaviour and want to run complex analytics queries against the data.

Which AWS service can be used for this requirement?

1. Amazon Kinesis Firehose
2. Amazon RDS
3. Amazon Neptune
4. Amazon RedShift

## 50. Question

You need to setup a distribution method for some static files. The requests will be mainly GET requests and you are expecting a high volume of GETs often exceeding 2000 per second. The files are currently stored in an S3 bucket. According to AWS best practices, what can you do to optimize performance?

1. Integrate CloudFront with S3 to cache the content
2. Use cross-region replication to spread the load across regions
3. Use ElastiCache to cache the content
4. Use S3 Transfer Acceleration

## 51. Question

An RDS database is experiencing heavy read traffic. You are planning on creating read replicas. When using Amazon RDS with Read Replicas, which of the deployment options below are valid? (choose 2)

1. Cross-Continent
2. Within an Availability Zone
3. Cross-subnet
4. Cross-Availability Zone
5. Cross-Facility

## 52. Question

You are planning on using AWS Auto Scaling to ensure that you have the correct number of Amazon EC2 instances available to handle the load for your applications. Which of the following statements is correct about Auto Scaling? (choose 2)

1. Auto Scaling is a region-specific service
2. Auto Scaling can span multiple AZs within the same AWS region
3. Auto Scaling is charged by the hour when registered
4. You create collections of EC2 instances, called Launch Groups
5. Auto Scaling relies on Elastic Load Balancing

## 53. Question

As a Solutions Architect at Digital Cloud Training you are helping a client to design a multi-tier web application architecture. The client has requested that the architecture provide low-latency connectivity between all servers and be resilient across multiple locations. The client uses Microsoft SQL Server for existing databases. The client has a limited budget for staff costs and does not need to access the underlying operating system

What would you recommend as the most efficient solution?

1. Amazon RDS with Microsoft SQL Server
2. Amazon EC2 instances with Microsoft SQL Server and data replication within an AZ
3. Amazon RDS with Microsoft SQL Server in a Multi-AZ configuration
4. Amazon EC2 instances with Microsoft SQL Server and data replication between two different AZs

## 54. Question

A company is investigating ways to analyze and process large amounts of data in the cloud faster, without needing to load or transform the data in a data warehouse. The data resides in Amazon S3.

Which AWS services would allow the company to query the data in place? (choose 2)

1. Amazon RedShift Spectrum
2. Amazon Elasticsearch
3. Amazon Kinesis Data Streams
4. Amazon SWF
5. Amazon S3 Select

## 55. Question

You work as an Enterprise Architect for a global organization which employs 20,000 people. The company is growing at around 5% per annum. The company strategy is to increasingly adopt AWS cloud services. There is an existing Microsoft Active Directory (AD) service that is used as the on-premise identity and access management system. You want to enable users to authenticate using their existing identities and access AWS resources (including the AWS Management Console) using single sign-on (SSO).

What is the simplest way to enable SSO to the AWS management console using the existing domain?

1. Launch a large AWS Directory Service AD Connector to proxy all authentication back to your on-premise AD service for authentication
2. Use a large AWS Simple AD in AWS
3. Launch an Enterprise Edition AWS Active Directory Service for Microsoft Active Directory and setup trust relationships with your on-premise domain
4. Install a Microsoft Active Directory Domain Controller on AWS and add it into your existing on-premise domain

## 56. Question

One of the departments in your company has been generating a large amount of data on S3 and you are considering the increasing costs of hosting it. You have discussed the matter with the department head and he explained that data older than 90 days is rarely accessed but must be retained for several years. If this data does need to be accessed at least 24 hours notice will be provided.

How can you optimize the costs associated with storage of this data whilst ensuring it is accessible if required?

1. Use S3 lifecycle policies to move data to GLACIER after 90 days
2. Implement archival software that automatically moves the data to tape
3. Select the older data and manually migrate it to GLACIER
4. Use S3 lifecycle policies to move data to the STANDARD_IA storage class

## 57. Question

You need to launch a series of EC2 instances with multiple attached volumes by modifying the block device mapping. Which block device can be specified in a block device mapping to be used with an EC2 instance? (choose 2)

1. EFS volume

2. Snapshot
3. S3 bucket
4. Instance store volume
5. EBS volume

## 58. Question

Some data has become corrupt in an RDS database you manage. You are planning to use point-in-time restore to recover the data to the last known good configuration. Which of the following statements is correct about restoring an RDS database to a specific point-in-time? (choose 2)

1. The database restore overwrites the existing database
2. The default DB security group is applied to the new DB instance
3. You can restore up to the last 1 minute
4. Custom DB security groups are applied to the new DB instance
5. You can restore up to the last 5 minutes

## 59. Question

You are designing the disk configuration for an EC2 instance. The instance needs to support a MapReduce process that requires high throughput for a large dataset with large I/O sizes. You need to provision the most cost-effective storage solution option.

What EBS volume type will you select?

1. EBS General Purpose SSD in a RAID 1 configuration
2. EBS Throughput Optimized HDD
3. EBS Provisioned IOPS SSD
4. EBS General Purpose SSD

## 60. Question

A company is deploying a new two-tier web application that uses EC2 web servers and a DynamoDB database backend. An Internet facing ELB distributes connections between the web servers.

The Solutions Architect has created a security group for the web servers and needs to create a security group for the ELB. What rules should be added? (choose 2)

1. Add an Inbound rule that allows HTTP/HTTPS, and specify the source as 0.0.0.0/32
2. Add an Outbound rule that allows ALL TCP, and specify the destination as the Internet Gateway
3. Add an Inbound rule that allows HTTP/HTTPS, and specify the source as 0.0.0.0/0
4. Add an Outbound rule that allows HTTP/HTTPS, and specify the destination as the web server security group
5. Add an Outbound rule that allows HTTP/HTTPS, and specify the destination as VPC CIDR

## 61. Question

A High Performance Computing (HPC) application will be migrated to AWS. The application requires low network latency and high throughput between nodes and will be deployed in a single AZ.

How should the application be deployed for best inter-node performance?

1. Behind a Network Load Balancer (NLB)

2. In a partition placement group
3. In a cluster placement group
4. In a spread placement group

## 62. Question

A web application is deployed in multiple regions behind an ELB Application Load Balancer. You need deterministic routing to the closest region and automatic failover. Traffic should traverse the AWS global network for consistent performance.

**How can this be achieved?**

1. Use a CloudFront distribution with multiple custom origins in each region and configure for high availability
2. Create a Route 53 Alias record for each ALB and configure a latency-based routing policy
3. Place an EC2 Proxy in front of the ALB and configure automatic failover
4. Configure AWS Global Accelerator and configure the ALBs as targets

## 63. Question

An application on Amazon Elastic Container Service (ECS) performs data processing in two parts. The second part takes much longer to complete. How can an Architect decouple the data processing from the backend application component?

1. Process both parts using the same ECS task. Create an Amazon Kinesis Firehose stream
2. Process each part using a separate ECS task. Create an Amazon SQS queue
3. Create an Amazon DynamoDB table and save the output of the first part to the table
4. Process each part using a separate ECS task. Create an Amazon SNS topic and send a notification when the processing completes

## 64. Question

A new relational database is being deployed on AWS. The performance requirements are unknown. Which database service does not require you to make capacity decisions upfront?

1. Amazon RDS
2. Amazon ElastiCache
3. Amazon Aurora Serverless
4. Amazon DynamoDB

## 65. Question

The database tier of a web application is running on a Windows server on-premises. The database is a Microsoft SQL Server database. The application owner would like to migrate the database to an Amazon RDS instance.

**How can the migration be executed with minimal administrative effort and downtime?**

1. Use AWS DataSync to migrate the data from the database to Amazon S3. Use AWS Database Migration Service (DMS) to migrate the database to RDS
2. Use the AWS Database Migration Service (DMS) to directly migrate the database to RDS. Use the Schema Conversion Tool (SCT) to enable conversion from Microsoft SQL Server to Amazon RDS
3. Use the AWS Database Migration Service (DMS) to directly migrate the database to RDS

4. Use the AWS Server Migration Service (SMS) to migrate the server to Amazon EC2. Use AWS Database Migration Service (DMS) to migrate the database to RDS

# SET 6: PRACTICE QUESTIONS, ANSWERS & EXPLANATIONS

## 1. Question

You are putting together an architecture for a new VPC on AWS. Your on-premise data center will be connected to the VPC by a hardware VPN and has public and VPN-only subnets. The security team has requested that traffic hitting public subnets on AWS that's destined to on-premise applications must be directed over the VPN to the corporate firewall.

How can this be achieved?

1. In the public subnet route table, add a route for your remote network and specify the virtual private gateway as the target
2. Configure a NAT Gateway and configure all traffic to be directed via the virtual private gateway
3. In the VPN-only subnet route table, add a route that directs all Internet traffic to the virtual private gateway
4. In the public subnet route table, add a route for your remote network and specify the customer gateway as the target

Answer: 1

Explanation:

- Route tables determine where network traffic is directed. In your route table, you must add a route for your remote network and specify the virtual private gateway as the target. This enables traffic from your VPC that's destined for your remote network to route via the virtual private gateway and over one of the VPN tunnels. You can enable route propagation for your route table to automatically propagate your network routes to the table for you
- You must select the virtual private gateway (AWS side of the VPN) not the customer gateway (customer side of the VPN) in the target in the route table
- NAT Gateways are used to enable Internet access for EC2 instances in private subnets, they cannot be used to direct traffic to VPG
- You must create the route table rule in the route table attached to the public subnet, not the VPN-only subnet

References:

https://docs.aws.amazon.com/vpc/latest/userguide/VPC_VPN.html

## 2. Question

A development team are creating a Continuous Integration and Continuous Delivery (CI/CD) toolchain on the AWS cloud. The team currently use Jenkins X and Kubernetes on-premise and are looking to utilize the same services in the AWS cloud.

What AWS service can provide a managed container platform that is MOST similar to their current CI/CD toolchain?

1. AWS CodePipeline
2. Amazon EKS
3. Amazon ECS
4. AWS Lambda

**Answer: 2**

**Explanation:**

- Amazon EKS is AWS' managed Kubernetes offering, which enables you to focus on building applications, while letting AWS handle managing Kubernetes and the underlying cloud infrastructure
- Amazon Elastic Container Service (ECS) does not use Kubernetes so it is not the most similar product
- AWS Lambda is a serverless service that executes code as functions
- AWS CodePipeline is a fully managed continuous delivery service that helps you automate your release pipelines for fast and reliable application and infrastructure updates. It is not a container platform

**References:**

https://aws.amazon.com/eks/

# 3. Question

A customer is deploying services in a hybrid cloud model. The customer has mandated that data is transferred directly between cloud data centers, bypassing ISPs.

Which AWS service can be used to enable hybrid cloud connectivity?

1. IPSec VPN
2. Amazon Route 53
3. AWS Direct Connect
4. Amazon VPC

**Answer: 3**

**Explanation:**

- With AWS Direct Connect, you can connect to all your AWS resources in an AWS Region, transfer your business-critical data directly from your datacenter, office, or colocation environment into and from AWS, bypassing your Internet service provider and removing network congestion
- Amazon Route 53 is a highly available and scalable cloud Domain Name System (DNS) web service
- An IPSec VPN can be used to connect to AWS however it does not bypass the ISPs or Internet
- Amazon Virtual Private Cloud (Amazon VPC) enables you to launch AWS resources into a virtual network that you've defined

**References:**

https://digitalcloud.training/certification-training/aws-solutions-architect-associate/networking-and-content-delivery/aws-direct-connect/

# 4. Question

A web application you manage receives order processing information from customers and places the messages on an SQS queue. A fleet of EC2 instances are configured to pick up the messages, process them, and store the results in a DynamoDB table. The current configuration has been resulting in a large number of empty responses to ReceiveMessage requests. You would like to update the configuration to eliminate empty responses to reduce operational overhead. How can this be done?

1. Use a Standard queue to provide at-least-once delivery, which means that each message is delivered at least once
2. Use a FIFO (first-in-first-out) queue to preserve the exact order in which messages are sent and received
3. Configure Short Polling to eliminate empty responses by reducing the length of time a connection request remains open
4. Configure Long Polling to eliminate empty responses by allowing Amazon SQS to wait until a message is available in a queue before sending a response

**Answer: 4**

**Explanation:**

- The correct answer is to use Long Polling which will eliminate empty responses by allowing Amazon SQS to wait until a message is available in a queue before sending a response
- The problem does not relate to the order in which the messages are processed in and there are no concerns over messages being delivered more than once so it doesn't matter whether you use a FIFO or standard queue
- Long Polling:
    - Uses fewer requests and reduces cost
    - Eliminates false empty responses by querying all servers
    - SQS waits until a message is available in the queue before sending a response
    - Requests contain at least one of the available messages up to the maximum number of messages specified in the ReceiveMessage action
    - Shouldn't be used if your application expects an immediate response to receive message calls
    - ReceiveMessageWaitTime is set to a non-zero value (up to 20 seconds)
    - Same charge per million requests as short polling
- Changing the queue type would not assist in this situation
- Short Polling:
    - Does not wait for messages to appear in the queue
    - It queries only a subset of the available servers for messages (based on weighted random execution)
    - Short polling is the default
    - ReceiveMessageWaitTime is set to 0
    - More requests are used, which implies higher cost

**References:**

https://digitalcloud.training/certification-training/aws-solutions-architect-associate/application-integration/amazon-sqs/

https://docs.aws.amazon.com/AWSSimpleQueueService/latest/SQSDeveloperGuide/sqs-long-polling.html

## 5. Question

Your company runs a web-based application that uses EC2 instances for the web front-end and RDS for the database back-end. The web application writes transaction log files to an S3 bucket and the quantity of files is becoming quite large. You have determined that it is acceptable to retain the most recent 60 days of log files and permanently delete the rest. What can you do to enable this to happen automatically?

1. Use an S3 lifecycle policy to move the log files that are more than 60 days old to the GLACIER storage class
2. Write a Ruby script that checks the age of objects and deletes any that are more than 60 days old
3. Use an S3 lifecycle policy with object expiration configured to automatically remove objects that are more than 60 days old
4. Use an S3 bucket policy that deletes objects that are more than 60 days old

**Answer: 3**

**Explanation:**

- Moving logs to Glacier may save cost but the questions requests that the files are permanently deleted
- Object Expiration allows you to schedule removal of your objects after a defined time period
- Using Object Expiration rules to schedule periodic removal of objects eliminates the need to build processes to identify objects for deletion and submit delete requests to Amazon S3

**References:**

https://aws.amazon.com/about-aws/whats-new/2011/12/27/amazon-s3-announces-object-expiration/

https://aws.amazon.com/about-aws/whats-new/2011/12/27/amazon-s3-announces-object-expiration/

## 6. Question

You have created an Auto Scaling Group (ASG) that has launched several EC2 instances running Linux. The ASG was created using the CLI. You want to ensure that you do not pay for monitoring. What needs to be done to ensure that monitoring is free of charge?

1. The launch configuration will have been created with basic monitoring enabled which is free of charge so you do not need to do anything
2. The launch configuration will have been created with detailed monitoring enabled which is chargeable. You will need to change the settings on the launch configuration
3. The launch configuration will have been created with detailed monitoring enabled which is chargeable. You will need to recreate the launch configuration with basic monitoring enabled
4. The launch configuration will have been created with detailed monitoring enabled which is chargeable. You will need to modify the settings on the ASG

**Answer: 3**

**Explanation:**

- Basic monitoring sends EC2 metrics to CloudWatch about ASG instances every 5 minutes
- Detailed can be enabled and sends metrics every 1 minute (chargeable)
- When the launch configuration is created from the CLI detailed monitoring of EC2 instances is enabled by default

- You cannot edit a launch configuration once defined
- If you want to change your launch configuration you have to create a new one, make the required changes, and use that with your auto scaling groups

**References:**

https://digitalcloud.training/certification-training/aws-solutions-architect-associate/compute/aws-auto-scaling/

## 7. Question

**You have associated a new launch configuration to your Auto Scaling Group (ASG) which runs a fleet of EC2 instances. The new launch configuration changes monitoring from detailed to basic. There are a couple of CloudWatch alarms configured on the ASG which monitor every 60 seconds. There is a mismatch in frequency of metric reporting between these configuration settings, what will be the result?**

1. The EC2 metrics will be updated automatically to match the frequency of the alarms and send updates every 60 seconds
2. The alarm state will be immediately set to INSUFFICIENT_DATA
3. If you do not update your alarms to match the five-minute period, they continue to check for statistics every minute and might find no data available for as many as four out of every five periods
4. The ASG will automatically update the frequency of the alarms to 300 seconds to match the EC2 monitoring in the launch configuration

**Answer: 3**

**Explanation:**

- If you have an Auto Scaling group and need to change which type of monitoring is enabled for your Auto Scaling instances, you must create a new launch configuration and update the Auto Scaling group to use this launch configuration. After that, the instances that the Auto Scaling group launches will use the updated monitoring type
- If you have CloudWatch alarms associated with your Auto Scaling group, use the put-metric-alarm command to update each alarm so that its period matches the monitoring type (300 seconds for basic monitoring and 60 seconds for detailed monitoring). If you change from detailed monitoring to basic monitoring but do not update your alarms to match the five-minute period, they continue to check for statistics every minute and might find no data available for as many as four out of every five periods

**References:**

https://docs.aws.amazon.com/autoscaling/ec2/userguide/as-instance-monitoring.html#as-group-metrics

## 8. Question

**You need to run a PowerShell script on a fleet of EC2 instances running Microsoft Windows. The instances have already been launched in your VPC. What tool can be run from the AWS Management Console that will run the script on all target EC2 instances?**

1. AWS CodeDeploy
2. AWS OpsWorks
3. Run Command

4. AWS Config

**Answer: 3**

**Explanation:**

- Run Command is designed to support a wide range of enterprise scenarios including installing software, running ad hoc scripts or Microsoft PowerShell commands, configuring Windows Update settings, and more. Run Command can be used to implement configuration changes across Windows instances on a consistent yet ad hoc basis and is accessible from the AWS Management Console, the AWS Command Line Interface (CLI), the AWS Tools for Windows PowerShell, and the AWS SDKs
- AWS OpsWorks provides instances of managed Puppet and Chef
- AWS Config is a service that enables you to assess, audit, and evaluate the configurations of your AWS resources. It is not used for ad-hoc script execution
- AWS CodeDeploy is a deployment service that automates application deployments to Amazon EC2 instances, on-premises instances, serverless Lambda functions, or Amazon ECS services

**References:**

https://aws.amazon.com/blogs/aws/new-ec2-run-command-remote-instance-management-at-scale/

## 9. Question

You are using the Elastic Container Service (ECS) to run a number of containers using the EC2 launch type. To gain more control over scheduling containers you have decided to utilize Blox to integrate a third-party scheduler. The third-party scheduler will use the StartTask API to place tasks on specific container instances. What type of ECS scheduler will you need to use to enable this configuration?

1. Cron Scheduler
2. ECS Scheduler
3. Custom Scheduler
4. Service Scheduler

**Answer: 3**

**Explanation:**

- Amazon ECS provides a service scheduler (for long-running tasks and applications), the ability to run tasks manually (for batch jobs or single run tasks), with Amazon ECS placing tasks on your cluster for you. The service scheduler is ideally suited for long running stateless services and applications. Amazon ECS allows you to create your own schedulers that meet the needs of your business, or to leverage third party schedulers
- Custom schedulers use the StartTask API operation to place tasks on specific container instances within your cluster. Custom schedulers are only compatible with tasks using the EC2 launch type. If you are using the Fargate launch type for your tasks, the StartTask API does not work
- Blox is an open-source project that gives you more control over how your containerized applications run on Amazon ECS. Blox enables you to build schedulers and integrate third-party schedulers with Amazon ECS while leveraging Amazon ECS to fully manage and scale your clusters
- A cron scheduler is used in UNIX/Linux but is not a type of ECS scheduler
- A service scheduler is not a type of third-party scheduler

**References:**

https://digitalcloud.training/certification-training/aws-solutions-architect-associate/compute/amazon-ecs/

https://docs.aws.amazon.com/AmazonECS/latest/developerguide/scheduling_tasks.html

## 10. Question

You need to run a production process that will use several EC2 instances and run constantly on an ongoing basis. The process cannot be interrupted or restarted without issue. Which EC2 pricing model would be best for this workload?

1. Reserved instances
2. Spot instances
3. On-demand instances
4. Flexible instances

Answer: 1

Explanation:

- In this scenario for a stable process that will run constantly on an ongoing basis RIs will be the most affordable solution
- RIs provide you with a significant discount (up to 75%) compared to On-Demand instance pricing. You have the flexibility to change families, OS types, and tenancies while benefitting from RI pricing when you use Convertible RIs
- Spot is more suited to short term jobs that can afford to be interrupted and offer the lowest price of all options
- On-demand is useful for short term ad-hoc requirements for which the job cannot afford to be interrupted and are typically more expensive than Spot instances
- There's no such thing as flexible instances

References:

https://digitalcloud.training/certification-training/aws-solutions-architect-associate/compute/amazon-ec2/

https://aws.amazon.com/ec2/pricing/reserved-instances/

## 11. Question

You have recently enabled Access Logs on your Application Load Balancer (ALB). One of your colleagues would like to process the log files using a hosted Hadoop service. What configuration changes and services can be leveraged to deliver this requirement?

1. Configure Access Logs to be delivered to S3 and use Kinesis for processing the log files
2. Configure Access Logs to be delivered to DynamoDB and use EMR for processing the log files
3. Configure Access Logs to be delivered to S3 and use EMR for processing the log files
4. Configure Access Logs to be delivered to EC2 and install Hadoop for processing the log files

Answer: 3

Explanation:

- Access Logs can be enabled on ALB and configured to store data in an S3 bucket. Amazon EMR is a web service that enables businesses, researchers, data analysts, and developers to easily and cost-effectively process vast amounts of data. EMR utilizes a hosted Hadoop framework running on Amazon EC2 and Amazon S3
- Neither Kinesis or EC2 provide a hosted Hadoop service
- You cannot configure access logs to be delivered to DynamoDB

**References:**

https://digitalcloud.training/certification-training/aws-solutions-architect-associate/analytics/amazon-emr/

https://digitalcloud.training/certification-training/aws-solutions-architect-associate/compute/elastic-load-balancing/

## 12. Question

You created a new IAM user account for a temporary employee who recently joined the company. The user does not have permissions to perform any actions, which statement is true about newly created users in IAM?

1. They are created with user privileges
2. They are created with full permissions
3. They are created with limited permissions
4. They are created with no permissions

**Answer: 4**

**Explanation:**

- Every IAM user starts with no permissions
- In other words, by default, users can do nothing, not even view their own access keys
- To give a user permission to do something, you can add the permission to the user (that is, attach a policy to the user)
- Or you can add the user to a group that has the intended permission.

**References:**

https://docs.aws.amazon.com/IAM/latest/UserGuide/access_controlling.html

https://digitalcloud.training/certification-training/aws-solutions-architect-associate/security-identity-compliance/aws-iam/

## 13. Question

In your VPC you have several EC2 instances that have been running for some time. You have logged into an instance and need to determine a few pieces of information including what IAM role is assigned, the instance ID and the names of the security groups that are assigned to the instance.

From the options below, what would be a source of this information?

1. Parameters
2. Tags
3. Metadata
4. User data

**Answer: 3**

**Explanation:**

- Instance metadata is data about your instance that you can use to configure or manage the running instance and is available at http://169.254.169.254/latest/meta-data
- Tags are used to categorize and label resources
- Parameters are used in databases
- User data is used to configure the system at launch time and specify scripts

**References:**

https://digitalcloud.training/certification-training/aws-solutions-architect-associate/compute/amazon-ec2/

https://docs.aws.amazon.com/AWSEC2/latest/UserGuide/ec2-instance-metadata.html#instancedata-data-categories

## 14. Question

The application development team in your company have developed a Java application and saved the source code in a .war file. They would like to run the application on AWS resources and are looking for a service that can handle the provisioning and management of the underlying resources it will run on.

What AWS service would allow the developers to upload the Java source code file and provide capacity provisioning and infrastructure management?

1. AWS CodeDeploy
2. AWS Elastic Beanstalk
3. AWS CloudFormation
4. AWS OpsWorks

**Answer: 2**

**Explanation:**

- AWS Elastic Beanstalk can be used to quickly deploy and manage applications in the AWS Cloud. Developers upload applications and Elastic Beanstalk handles the deployment details of capacity provisioning, load balancing, auto-scaling, and application health monitoring
- Elastic Beanstalk supports applications developed in Go, Java, .NET, Node.js, PHP, Python, and Ruby, as well as different platform configurations for each language. To use Elastic Beanstalk, you create an application, upload an application version in the form of an application source bundle (for example, a Java .war file) to Elastic Beanstalk, and then provide some information about the application
- AWS CloudFormation uses templates to deploy infrastructure as code. It is not a PaaS service like Elastic Beanstalk and is more focussed on infrastructure than applications and management of applications
- AWS CodeDeploy is a deployment service that automates application deployments to Amazon EC2 instances, on-premises instances, serverless Lambda functions, or Amazon ECS services
- AWS OpsWorks is a configuration management service that provides managed instances of Chef and Puppet

**References:**

https://digitalcloud.training/certification-training/aws-solutions-architect-associate/compute/aws-elastic-beanstalk/

https://docs.aws.amazon.com/elasticbeanstalk/latest/dg/Welcome.html

## 15. Question

You have launched an EC2 instance into a VPC. You need to ensure that instances have both a private and public DNS hostname. Assuming you did not change any settings during creation of the VPC, how will DNS hostnames be assigned by default? (choose 2)

1. In a default VPC instances will be assigned a private but not a public DNS hostname
2. In a non-default VPC instances will be assigned a public and private DNS hostname
3. In a non-default VPC instances will be assigned a private but not a public DNS hostname
4. In all VPCs instances no DNS hostnames will be assigned
5. In a default VPC instances will be assigned a public and private DNS hostname

**Answer: 3,5**

**Explanation:**

- When you launch an instance into a default VPC, we provide the instance with public and private DNS hostnames that correspond to the public IPv4 and private IPv4 addresses for the instance
- When you launch an instance into a nondefault VPC, we provide the instance with a private DNS hostname and we might provide a public DNS hostname, depending on the DNS attributes you specify for the VPC and if your instance has a public IPv4 address

**References:**

https://docs.aws.amazon.com/vpc/latest/userguide/vpc-dns.html

## 16. Question

A Solutions Architect has created a VPC and is in the process of formulating the subnet design. The VPC will be used to host a two-tier application that will include Internet facing web servers, and internal-only DB servers. Zonal redundancy is required.

How many subnets are required to support this requirement?

1. 1 subnet
2. 2 subnets
3. 6 subnets
4. 4 subnets

**Answer: 4**

**Explanation:**

- Zonal redundancy indicates that the architecture should be split across multiple Availability Zones. Subnets are mapped 1:1 to AZs
- A public subnet should be used for the Internet-facing web servers and a separate private subnet should be used for the internal-only DB servers. Therefore you need 4 subnets – 2 (for redundancy) per public/private subnet

References:

https://digitalcloud.training/certification-training/aws-solutions-architect-associate/networking-and-content-delivery/amazon-vpc/

## 17. Question

A security officer has requested that all data associated with a specific customer is encrypted. The data resides on Elastic Block Store (EBS) volumes. Which of the following statements about using EBS encryption are correct? (choose 2)

1. Not all EBS types support encryption
2. Data in transit between an instance and an encrypted volume is also encrypted
3. All attached EBS volumes must share the same encryption state
4. There is no direct way to change the encryption state of a volume
5. All instance types support encryption

**Answer: 2,4**

**Explanation:**

- All EBS types and all instance families support encryption
- Not all instance types support encryption
- There is no direct way to change the encryption state of a volume
- Data in transit between an instance and an encrypted volume is also encrypted
- You can have encrypted and non-encrypted EBS volumes on a single instance

References:

https://digitalcloud.training/certification-training/aws-solutions-architect-associate/compute/amazon-ebs/

## 18. Question

You have just created a new security group in your VPC. You have not yet created any rules. Which of the statements below are correct regarding the default state of the security group? (choose 2)

1. There are is an inbound rule that allows traffic from the Internet Gateway
2. There is an inbound rule allowing traffic from the Internet to port 22 for management
3. There is an outbound rule allowing traffic to the Internet Gateway
4. There is an outbound rule that allows all traffic to all IP addresses
5. There are no inbound rules and traffic will be implicitly denied

**Answer: 4,5**

**Explanation:**

- Custom security groups do not have inbound allow rules (all inbound traffic is denied by default)
- Default security groups do have inbound allow rules (allowing traffic from within the group)
- All outbound traffic is allowed by default in both custom and default security groups
- Security groups act like a stateful firewall at the instance level. Specifically security groups operate at the network interface level of an EC2 instance. You can only assign permit rules in a security group, you cannot assign deny rules and there is an implicit deny rule at the end of the security

group. All rules are evaluated until a permit is encountered or continues until the implicit deny. You can create ingress and egress rules

References:

https://digitalcloud.training/certification-training/aws-solutions-architect-associate/networking-and-content-delivery/amazon-vpc/

## 19. Question

You are running a database on an EC2 instance in your VPC. The load on the DB is increasing and you have noticed that the performance has been impacted. Which of the options below would help to increase storage performance? (choose 2)

1. Use EBS optimized instances
2. Use HDD, Cold (SC1) EBS volumes
3. Use Provisioned IOPS (I01) EBS volumes
4. Use a larger instance size within the instance family
5. Create a RAID 1 array from multiple EBS volumes

Answer: 1,3

Explanation:

- EBS optimized instances provide dedicated capacity for Amazon EBS I/O. EBS optimized instances are designed for use with all EBS volume types
- Provisioned IOPS EBS volumes allow you to specify the amount of IOPS you require up to 50 IOPS per GB. Within this limitation you can therefore choose to select the IOPS required to improve the performance of your volume
- RAID can be used to increase IOPS, however RAID 1 does not. For example:
  - RAID 0 = 0 striping – data is written across multiple disks and increases performance but no redundancy
  - RAID 1 = 1 mirroring – creates 2 copies of the data but does not increase performance, only redundancy
- HDD, Cold – (SC1) provides the lowest cost storage and low performance

References:

https://digitalcloud.training/certification-training/aws-solutions-architect-associate/compute/amazon-ebs/

## 20. Question

One of you clients has asked for assistance with a performance issue they are experiencing. The client has a fleet of EC2 instances behind an Elastic Load Balancer (ELB) that are a mixture of c4.2xlarge instance types and c5.large instances. The load on the CPUs on the c5.large instances has been very high, often hitting 100% utilization, whereas the c4.2xlarge instances have been performing well. The client has asked for advice on the most cost-effective way to resolve the performance problems?

1. Add more c5.large instances to spread the load more evenly
2. Change the configuration to use only c4.2xlarge instance types
3. Add all of the instances into a Placement Group
4. Enable the weighted routing policy on the ELB and

**Answer: 2**

**Explanation:**

- The 2xlarge instance type provides more CPUs. The best answer is to use this instance type for all instances
- A placement group helps provide low-latency connectivity between instances and would not help here
- The weighted routing policy is a Route 53 feature that would not assist in this situation

**References:**

https://digitalcloud.training/certification-training/aws-solutions-architect-associate/compute/amazon-ec2/

## 21. Question

A large quantity of data that is rarely accessed is being archived onto Amazon Glacier. Your CIO wants to understand the resilience of the service. Which of the statements below is correct about Amazon Glacier storage? (choose 2)

1. Data is replicated globally
2. Provides 99.999999999% durability of archives
3. Data is resilient in the event of one entire region destruction
4. Provides 99.9% availability of archives
5. Data is resilient in the event of one entire Availability Zone destruction

**Answer: 2,5**

**Explanation:**

- Glacier is designed for durability of 99.999999999% of objects across multiple Availability Zones. Data is resilient in the event of one entire Availability Zone destruction. Glacier supports SSL for data in transit and encryption of data at rest. Glacier is extremely low cost and is ideal for long-term archival
- Data is not resilient to the failure of an entire region
- Data is not replicated globally
- Glacier is "designed for" availability of 99.99%

**References:**

https://aws.amazon.com/s3/storage-classes/

## 22. Question

An EC2 instance you manage is generating very high packets-per-second and performance of the application stack is being impacted. You have been asked for a resolution to the issue that results in improved performance from the EC2 instance. What would you suggest?

1. Configure a RAID 1 array from multiple EBS volumes
2. Create a placement group and put the EC2 instance in it
3. Use enhanced networking
4. Add multiple Elastic IP addresses to the instance

**Answer: 3**

**Explanation:**

- Enhanced networking provides higher bandwidth, higher packet-per-second (PPS) performance, and consistently lower inter-instance latencies. If your packets-per-second rate appears to have reached its ceiling, you should consider moving to enhanced networking because you have likely reached the upper thresholds of the VIF driver. It is only available for certain instance types and only supported in VPC. You must also launch an HVM AMI with the appropriate drivers
- AWS currently supports enhanced networking capabilities using SR-IOV. SR-IOV provides direct access to network adapters, provides higher performance (packets-per-second) and lower latency
- You do not need to create a RAID 1 array (which is more for redundancy than performance anyway)
- A placement group is used to increase network performance between instances. In this case there is only a single instance so it won't help
- Adding multiple IP addresses is not a way to increase performance of the instance as the same amount of bandwidth is available to the Elastic Network Interface (ENI)

**References:**

https://digitalcloud.training/certification-training/aws-solutions-architect-associate/compute/amazon-ec2/

https://aws.amazon.com/premiumsupport/knowledge-center/enable-configure-enhanced-networking/

## 23. Question

One of your EC2 instances that is behind an Elastic Load Balancer (ELB) is in the process of being de-registered. Which ELB feature can be used to allow existing connections to close cleanly?

1. Sticky Sessions
2. Deletion Protection
3. Proxy Protocol
4. Connection Draining

**Answer: 4**

**Explanation:**

- Connection draining is enabled by default and provides a period of time for existing connections to close cleanly. When connection draining is in action an CLB will be in the status "InService: Instance deregistration currently in progress"
- Session stickiness uses cookies and ensures a client is bound to an individual back-end instance for the duration of the cookie lifetime
- Deletion protection is used to protect the ELB from deletion
- The Proxy Protocol header helps you identify the IP address of a client when you have a load balancer that uses TCP for back-end connections

**References:**

https://digitalcloud.training/certification-training/aws-solutions-architect-associate/compute/elastic-load-balancing/

## 24. Question

Your manager has asked you to explain some of the security features available in the AWS cloud. How can you describe the function of Amazon CloudHSM?

1. It is a firewall for use with web applications
2. It can be used to generate, use and manage encryption keys in the cloud
3. It provides server-side encryption for S3 objects
4. It is a Public Key Infrastructure (PKI)

**Answer: 2**

**Explanation:**

- AWS CloudHSM is a cloud-based hardware security module (HSM) that allows you to easily add secure key storage and high-performance crypto operations to your AWS applications. CloudHSM has no upfront costs and provides the ability to start and stop HSMs on-demand, allowing you to provision capacity when and where it is needed quickly and cost-effectively. CloudHSM is a managed service that automates time-consuming administrative tasks, such as hardware provisioning, software patching, high availability, and backups
- CloudHSM is a part of a PKI but a PKI is a broader term that does not specifically describe its function
- CloudHSM does not provide server-side encryption for S3 objects, it provides encryption keys that can be used to encrypt data
- CloudHSM is not a firewall

**References:**

https://aws.amazon.com/cloudhsm/details/


## 25. Question

One of your clients has multiple VPCs that are peered with each other. The client would like to use a single Elastic Load Balancer (ELB) to route traffic to multiple EC2 instances in peered VPCs within the same region. Is this possible?

1. This is not possible with ELB, you would need to use Route 53
2. This is possible using the Network Load Balancer (NLB) and Application Load Balancer (ALB) if using IP addresses as targets
3. This is possible using the Classic Load Balancer (CLB) if using Instance IDs
4. No, the instances that an ELB routes traffic to must be in the same VPC

**Answer: 2**

**Explanation:**

With ALB and NLB IP addresses can be used to register:

- Instances in a peered VPC
- AWS resources that are addressable by IP address and port
- On-premises resources linked to AWS through Direct Connect or a VPN connection

**References:**

## 26. Question

An application you manage runs a series of EC2 instances with a web application behind an Application Load Balancer (ALB). You are updating the configuration with a health check and need to select the protocol to use. What options are available to you? (choose 2)

1. HTTP
2. TCP
3. ICMP
4. SSL
5. HTTPS

**Answer:1,5**

**Explanation:**

- The Classic Load Balancer (CLB) supports health checks on HTTP, TCP, HTTPS and SSL
- The Application Load Balancer (ALB) only supports health checks on HTTP and HTTPS

**References:**

## 27. Question

You have just created a new Network ACL in your VPC. You have not yet created any rules. Which of the statements below are correct regarding the default state of the Network ACL? (choose 2)

1. There is a default outbound rule denying all traffic
2. There is a default outbound rule allowing traffic to the Internet Gateway
3. There is a default inbound rule allowing traffic from the VPC CIDR block
4. There is a default outbound rule allowing all traffic
5. There is a default inbound rule denying all traffic

**Answer: 1,5**

**Explanation:**

- A VPC automatically comes with a default network ACL which allows all inbound/outbound traffic
- A custom NACL denies all traffic both inbound and outbound by default
- Network ACL's function at the subnet level and you can have permit and deny rules. Network ACLs have separate inbound and outbound rules and each rule can allow or deny traffic. Network ACLs are stateless so responses are subject to the rules for the direction of traffic. NACLs only apply to traffic that is ingress or egress to the subnet not to traffic within the subnet

**References:**

## 28. Question

You are trying to SSH into an EC2 instance running Linux but cannot connect. The EC2 instance has been launched in a public subnet with an Internet Gateway. Upon investigation you have verified that the instance has a public IP address and that the route table does reference the Internet Gateway correctly. What else needs to be checked to enable connectivity?

1. Check that there is a Bastion Host in the subnet and connect to it first
2. Check that the subnet CIDR block is referenced properly in the route table
3. Check that the VPN is configured correctly
4. Check that the Security Groups and Network ACLs have the correct rules configured

Answer: 4

Explanation:

- Security Groups and Network ACLs do need to be configured to enable connectivity. Check the there relevant rules exist to allow port 22 inbound to your EC2 instance
- Bastion Hosts are used as an admin tools so you can connect to a single, secured EC2 instance and then jump from there to other instances (typically in private subnets but not always)
- The subnet CIDR block is configured automatically as part of the creation of the VPC/subnet so should not be the issue here
- You do not need a VPN connection to connect to an instance in a public subnet

References:

https://digitalcloud.training/certification-training/aws-solutions-architect-associate/compute/amazon-ec2/

https://digitalcloud.training/certification-training/aws-solutions-architect-associate/networking-and-content-delivery/amazon-vpc/

## 29. Question

You launched an EBS-backed EC2 instance into your VPC. A requirement has come up for some high-performance ephemeral storage and so you would like to add an instance-store backed volume. How can you add the new instance store volume?

1. You can specify the instance store volumes for your instance only when you launch an instance
2. You can use a block device mapping to specify additional instance store volumes when you launch your instance, or you can attach additional instance store volumes after your instance is running
3. You must use an Elastic Network Adapter (ENA) to add instance store volumes. First, attach an ENA, and then attach the instance store volume
4. You must shutdown the instance in order to be able to add the instance store volume

Answer: 1

Explanation:

- You can specify the instance store volumes for your instance only when you launch an instance. You can't attach instance store volumes to an instance after you've launched it
- You can use a block device mapping to specify additional EBS volumes when you launch your instance, or you can attach additional EBS volumes after your instance is running
- An Elastic Network Adapter has nothing to do with adding instance store volumes

**References:**

https://docs.aws.amazon.com/AWSEC2/latest/UserGuide/add-instance-store-volumes.html

## 30. Question

You are creating a CloudFormation Stack that will create EC2 instances that will record log files to an S3 bucket. When creating the template which optional section is used to return the name of the S3 bucket?

1. Resources
2. Parameters
3. Outputs
4. Mappings

**Answer: 3**

**Explanation:**

- The optional Outputs section declares output values that you can import into other stacks (to create cross-stack references), return in response (to describe stack calls), or view on the AWS CloudFormation console. For example, you can output the S3 bucket name for a stack to make the bucket easier to find
- Template elements include:

  - File format and version (mandatory)

  - List of resources and associated configuration values (mandatory)

  - Template parameters (optional)

  - Output values (optional)

  - List of data tables (optional)

**References:**

https://digitalcloud.training/certification-training/aws-solutions-architect-associate/management-tools/aws-cloudformation/

https://docs.aws.amazon.com/AWSCloudFormation/latest/UserGuide/outputs-section-structure.html

## 31. Question

Your company has started using the AWS CloudHSM for secure key storage. A recent administrative error resulted in the loss of credentials to access the CloudHSM. You need access to data that was encrypted using keys stored on the hardware security module. How can you recover the keys that are no longer accessible?

1. There is no way to recover your keys if you lose your credentials
2. Reset the CloudHSM device and create a new set of credentials

3. Log a case with AWS support and they will use MFA to recover the credentials
4. Restore a snapshot of the CloudHSM

**Answer: 1**

**Explanation:**

- Amazon does not have access to your keys or credentials and therefore has no way to recover your keys if you lose your credentials

**References:**

https://aws.amazon.com/cloudhsm/faqs/

## 32. Question

A development team needs to run up a few lab servers on a weekend for a new project. The servers will need to run uninterrupted for a few hours. Which EC2 pricing option would be most suitable?

1. Spot
2. Reserved
3. On-Demand
4. Dedicated Instances

**Answer: 3**

**Explanation:**

- Spot pricing may be the most economical option for a short duration over a weekend but you may have the instances terminated by AWS and there is a requirement that the servers run uninterrupted
- On-Demand pricing ensures that instances will not be terminated and is the most economical option
- Reserved pricing provides a reduced cost for a contracted period (1 or 3 years), and is not suitable for ad hoc requirements
- Dedicated instances run on hardware that's dedicated to a single customer and are more expensive than regular On-Demand instances

**References:**

https://aws.amazon.com/ec2/pricing/

## 33. Question

You are a Solutions Architect at Digital Cloud Training. A client has asked you for some advice about how they can capture detailed information about all HTTP requests that are processed by their Internet facing Application Load Balancer (ALB). The client requires information on the requester, IP address, and request type for analyzing traffic patterns to better understand their customer base.

What would you recommend to the client?

1. Use CloudTrail to capture all API calls made to the ALB
2. Enable Access Logs and store the data on S3
3. Configure metrics in CloudWatch for the ALB

4.  Enable EC2 detailed monitoring

**Answer: 2**

**Explanation:**

- You can enable access logs on the ALB and this will provide the information required including requester, IP, and request type. Access logs are not enabled by default. You can optionally store and retain the log files on S3
- CloudWatch is used for performance monitoring and CloudTrail is used for auditing API access
- Enabling EC2 detailed monitoring will not capture the information requested

**References:**

https://digitalcloud.training/certification-training/aws-solutions-architect-associate/compute/elastic-load-balancing/

## 34. Question

You are planning to launch a fleet of EC2 instances running Linux. As part of the launch you would like to install some application development frameworks and custom software onto the instances. The installation will be initiated using some scripts you have written. What feature allows you to specify the scripts so you can install the software during the EC2 instance launch?

1.  Run Command
2.  User Data
3.  Metadata
4.  AWS Config

**Answer: 2**

**Explanation:**

- When you launch an instance in Amazon EC2, you have the option of passing user data to the instance that can be used to perform common automated configuration tasks and even run scripts after the instance starts. You can pass two types of user data to Amazon EC2: shell scripts and cloud-init directives
- User data is data that is supplied by the user at instance launch in the form of a script and is limited to 16KB
- User data and meta data are not encrypted. Instance metadata is available at http://169.254.169.254/latest/meta-data. The Instance Metadata Query tool allows you to query the instance metadata without having to type out the full URI or category names
- The AWS Systems Manager run command is used to manage the configuration of existing instances by using remotely executed commands. User data is better for specifying scripts to run at startup

**References:**

https://docs.aws.amazon.com/AWSEC2/latest/UserGuide/user-data.html

https://digitalcloud.training/certification-training/aws-solutions-architect-associate/compute/amazon-ec2/

## 35. Question

An application you manage uses RDS in a multi-AZ configuration as the database back-end. There is a failure of the primary DB instance. Which of the following statements are correct in relation to the process RDS uses to failover to the standby DB instance? (choose 2)

1. The failover mechanism automatically moves the Elastic IP address of the instance to the standby DB instance
2. Multi-AZ uses synchronous replication; therefore, the failover is instantaneous
3. Failover times are typically 60-120 seconds
4. The failover mechanism automatically changes the DNS record of the DB instance to point to the standby DB instance

Answer: 3,4

Explanation:

- The failover mechanism automatically changes the DNS record of the DB instance to point to the standby DB instance. As a result, you need to re-establish any existing connections to your DB instance
- The time it takes for the failover to complete depends on the database activity and other conditions at the time the primary DB instance became unavailable. Failover times are typically 60-120 seconds
- Multi-AZ does use synchronous replication but failover is not instantaneous
- The DN record is updated, not the IP address

References:

https://docs.aws.amazon.com/AmazonRDS/latest/UserGuide/Concepts.MultiAZ.html

https://digitalcloud.training/certification-training/aws-solutions-architect-associate/database/amazon-rds/

## 36. Question

A Solutions Architect is designing the system monitoring and deployment layers of a serverless application. The system monitoring layer will manage system visibility through recording logs and metrics and the deployment layer will deploy the application stack and manage workload changes through a release management process.

The Architect needs to select the most appropriate AWS services for these functions. Which services and frameworks should be used for the system monitoring and deployment layers? (choose 2)

1. Use AWS SAM to package, test, and deploy the serverless application stack
2. Use AWS X-Ray to package, test, and deploy the serverless application stack
3. Use AWS Lambda to package, test, and deploy the serverless application stack
4. Use Amazon CloudWatch for consolidating system and application logs and monitoring custom metrics
5. Use Amazon CloudTrail for consolidating system and application logs and monitoring custom metrics

Answer: 1,4

Explanation:

- AWS Serverless Application Model (AWS SAM) is an extension of AWS CloudFormation that is used to package, test, and deploy serverless applications
- With Amazon CloudWatch, you can access system metrics on all the AWS services you use, consolidate system and application level logs, and create business key performance indicators (KPIs) as custom metrics for your specific needs
- AWS Lambda is used for executing your code as functions, it is not used for packaging, testing and deployment. AWS Lambda is used with AWS SAM
- AWS X-Ray lets you analyze and debug serverless applications by providing distributed tracing and service maps to easily identify performance bottlenecks by visualizing a request end-to-end

References:

https://docs.aws.amazon.com/lambda/latest/dg/serverless_app.html

https://digitalcloud.training/certification-training/aws-solutions-architect-associate/management-tools/amazon-cloudwatch/

## 37. Question

You need to upload a large (2GB) file to an S3 bucket. What is the recommended way to upload a single large file to an S3 bucket?

1. Use AWS Import/Export
2. Use Multipart Upload
3. Use a single PUT request to upload the large file
4. Use Amazon Snowball

Answer: 2

Explanation:

- In general, when your object size reaches 100 MB, you should consider using multipart uploads instead of uploading the object in a single operation. The largest object that can be uploaded in a single PUT is 5 gigabytes
- Snowball is used for migrating large quantities (TB/PB) of data into AWS, it is overkill for this requirement
- AWS Import/Export is a service in which you send in HDDs with data on to AWS and they import your data into S3. It is not used for single files

References:

https://docs.aws.amazon.com/AmazonS3/latest/dev/uploadobjusingmpu.html

https://digitalcloud.training/certification-training/aws-solutions-architect-associate/storage/amazon-s3/

## 38. Question

You are using a series of Spot instances that process messages from an SQS queue and store results in a DynamoDB table. Shortly after picking up a message from the queue AWS terminated the Spot instance. The Spot instance had not finished processing the message. What will happen to the message?

1. The results may be duplicated in DynamoDB as the message will likely be processed multiple times
2. The message will be lost as it would have been deleted from the queue when processed

3. The message will remain in the queue and be immediately picked up by another instance
4. The message will become available for processing again after the visibility timeout expires

**Answer: 4**

**Explanation:**

- The visibility timeout is the amount of time a message is invisible in the queue after a reader picks up the message. If a job is processed within the visibility timeout the message will be deleted. If a job is not processed within the visibility timeout the message will become visible again (could be delivered twice). The maximum visibility timeout for an Amazon SQS message is 12 hours
- The message will not be lost and will not be immediately picked up by another instance. As mentioned above it will be available for processing in the queue again after the timeout expires
- As the instance had not finished processing the message it should only be fully processed once. Depending on your application process however it is possible some data was written to DynamoDB

**References:**

https://digitalcloud.training/certification-training/aws-solutions-architect-associate/application-integration/amazon-sqs/


## 39. Question

A DynamoDB table you manage has a variable load, ranging from sustained heavy usage some days, to only having small spikes on others. The load is 80% read and 20% write. The provisioned throughput capacity has been configured to account for the heavy load to ensure throttling does not occur.

You have been asked to find a solution for saving cost. What would be the most efficient and cost-effective solution?

1. Create a CloudWatch alarm that notifies you of increased/decreased load, and manually adjust the provisioned throughput
2. Create a DynamoDB Auto Scaling scaling policy
3. Create a CloudWatch alarm that triggers an AWS Lambda function that adjusts the provisioned throughput
4. Use DynamoDB DAX to increase the performance of the database


**Answer: 2**

**Explanation:**

- DynamoDB auto scalinguses the AWS Application Auto Scaling service to dynamically adjust provisioned throughput capacity on your behalf, in response to actual traffic patterns. This is the most efficient and cost-effective solution
- Manually adjusting the provisioned throughput is not efficient
- Using AWS Lambda to modify the provisioned throughput is possible but it would be more cost-effective to use DynamoDB Auto Scaling as there is no cost to using it
- DynamoDB DAX is an in-memory cache that increases the performance of DynamoDB. However, it costs money and there is no requirement to increase performance

**References:**

https://docs.aws.amazon.com/amazondynamodb/latest/developerguide/AutoScaling.html

## 40. Question

A financial services company regularly runs an analysis of the day's transaction costs, execution reporting, and market performance. The company currently uses third-party commercial software for provisioning, managing, monitoring, and scaling the computing jobs which utilize a large fleet of EC2 instances.

The company is seeking to reduce costs and utilize AWS services. Which AWS service could be used in place of the third-party software?

1. Amazon Lex
2. Amazon Athena
3. AWS Systems Manager
4. AWS Batch

**Answer: 4**

**Explanation:**

- AWS Batch eliminates the need to operate third-party commercial or open source batch processing solutions. There is no batch software or servers to install or manage. AWS Batch manages all the infrastructure for you, avoiding the complexities of provisioning, managing, monitoring, and scaling your batch computing jobs
- AWS Systems Manager gives you visibility and control of your infrastructure on AWS
- Amazon Athena is an interactive query service that makes it easy to analyze data in Amazon S3 using standard SQL
- Amazon Lex is a service for building conversational interfaces into any application using voice and text

**References:**

https://aws.amazon.com/batch/

## 41. Question

One of the applications you manage receives a high traffic load between 7:30am and 9:30am daily. The application uses an Auto Scaling Group (ASG) to maintain 3 EC2 instances most of the time but during the peak period requires 6 EC2 instances. How can you configure ASG to perform a regular scale-out event at 7:30am and a scale-in event at 9:30am daily to account for the peak load?

1. Use a Simple scaling policy
2. Use a Scheduled scaling policy
3. Use a Step scaling policy
4. Use a Dynamic scaling policy

**Answer: 2**

**Explanation:**

- Simple – maintains a current number of instances, you can manually change the ASGs min/desired/max and attach/detach instances
- Scheduled – Used for predictable load changes, can be a single event or a recurring schedule
- Dynamic (event based) – scale in response to an event/alarm
- Step – configure multiple scaling steps in response to multiple alarms

References:

https://digitalcloud.training/certification-training/aws-solutions-architect-associate/compute/aws-auto-scaling/

## 42. Question

A large multi-national client has requested a design for a multi-region database. The master database will be in the EU (Frankfurt) region and databases will be located in 4 other regions to service local read traffic. The database should be a managed service including the replication.

The solution should be cost-effective and secure. Which AWS service can deliver these requirements?

1. RDS with cross-region Read Replicas
2. RDS with Multi-AZ
3. ElastiCache with Redis and clustering mode enabled
4. EC2 instances with EBS replication

**Answer: 1**

**Explanation:**

- RDS Read replicas are used for read heavy DBs and replication is asynchronous. Read replicas are for workload sharing and offloading. Read replicas can be in another region (uses asynchronous replication)
- RDS with Multi-AZ is within a region only
- ElastiCache is an in-memory key/value storedatabase (more OLAP than OLTP) and is not suitable for this scenario. Clustering mode is only available within the same region
- EC2 instances with EBS replication is not a suitable solution

References:

https://digitalcloud.training/certification-training/aws-solutions-architect-associate/database/amazon-rds/

## 43. Question

You have just created a new AWS account and selected the Asia Pacific (Sydney) region. Within the default VPC there is a default security group. What settings are configured within this security group by default? (choose 2)

1. There is an outbound rule that allows all traffic to all addresses
2. There is an outbound rule that allows traffic to the VPC router
3. There is an outbound rule that allows all traffic to the security group itself
4. There is an inbound rule that allows all traffic from any address
5. There is an inbound rule that allows all traffic from the security group itself

**Answer: 1,5**

**Explanation:**

- Default security groups have inbound allow rules (allowing traffic from within the group)
- Custom security groups do not have inbound allow rules (all inbound traffic is denied by default)
- All outbound traffic is allowed by default in custom and default security groups

**References:**

https://digitalcloud.training/certification-training/aws-solutions-architect-associate/networking-and-content-delivery/amazon-vpc/

## 44. Question

You are running an Auto Scaling Group (ASG) with an Elastic Load Balancer (ELB) and a fleet of EC2 instances. Health checks are configured on the ASG to use EC2 status checks. The ELB has determined that an EC2 instance is unhealthy and has removed it from service. However, you noticed that the instance is still running and has not been terminated by the ASG.

What would be an explanation for this behavior?

1. The ELB health check type has not been selected for the ASG and so it is unaware that the instance has been determined to be unhealthy by the ELB and has been removed from service
2. Connection draining is enabled and the ASG is waiting for in-flight requests to complete
3. The health check grace period has not yet expired
4. The ASG is waiting for the cooldown timer to expire before terminating the instance

**Answer: 1**

**Explanation:**

- If using an ELB it is best to enable ELB health checks as otherwise EC2 status checks may show an instance as being healthy that the ELB has determined is unhealthy. In this case the instance will be removed from service by the ELB but will not be terminated by Auto Scaling
- Connection draining is not the correct answer as the ELB has taken the instance out of service so there are no active connections
- The health check grace period allows a period of time for a new instance to warm up before performing a health check
- More information on ASG health checks:

    - By default uses EC2 status checks

    - Can also use ELB health checks and custom health checks

    - ELB health checks are in addition to the EC2 status checks

    - If any health check returns an unhealthy status the instance will be terminated

    - With ELB an instance is marked as unhealthy if ELB reports it as OutOfService

    - A healthy instance enters the InService state

    - If an instance is marked as unhealthy it will be scheduled for replacement

    - If connection draining is enabled, Auto Scaling waits for in-flight requests to complete or timeout before terminating instances

    - The health check grace period allows a period of time for a new instance to warm up before performing a health check (300 seconds by default)

**References:**

https://digitalcloud.training/certification-training/aws-solutions-architect-associate/compute/aws-auto-scaling/

## 45. Question

A developer is writing code for AWS Lambda and is looking to automate the release process. Which AWS services can be used to automate the release process of Lambda applications? (choose 2)

1. AWS Glue
2. AWS OpsWorks
3. AWS CodeDeploy
4. AWS Cognito
5. AWS CodePipeline

**Answer: 3,5**

**Explanation:**

- You can automate your serverless application's release process using AWS CodePipeline and AWS CodeDeploy
- The following AWS services can be used to fully automate the deployment process:
    - You use CodePipeline to model, visualize, and automate the steps required to release your serverless application
    - You use AWS CodeDeploy to gradually deploy updates to your serverless applications
    - You use CodeBuild to build, locally test, and package your serverless application
    - You use AWS CloudFormation to deploy your application

**References:**

https://digitalcloud.training/certification-training/aws-solutions-architect-associate/compute/aws-lambda/

https://docs.aws.amazon.com/lambda/latest/dg/build-pipeline.html

## 46. Question

When using the MySQL database with AWS RDS, features such as Point-In-Time restore and snapshot restore require a recoverable storage engine. Which storage engine must be used to enable these features?

1. Memory
2. MyISAM
3. InnoDB
4. Federated

**Answer: 3**

**Explanation:**

- RDS fully supports the InnoDB storage engine for MySQL DB instances. RDS features such as Point-In-Time restore and snapshot restore require a recoverable storage engine and are supported for the InnoDB storage engine only
- Automated backups and snapshots are not supported for MyISAM
- There is no storage engine called "memory" or "federated"

**References:**

https://docs.aws.amazon.com/AmazonRDS/latest/UserGuide/CHAP_MySQL.html

https://digitalcloud.training/certification-training/aws-solutions-architect-associate/database/amazon-rds/

## 47. Question

One of your clients is transitioning their web presence into the AWS cloud. As part of the migration the client will be running a web application both on-premises and in AWS for a period of time. During the period of co-existence the client would like 80% of the traffic to hit the AWS-based web servers and 20% to be directed to the on-premises web servers.

What method can you use to distribute traffic as requested?

1. Use Route 53 with a simple routing policy
2. Use Route 53 with a weighted routing policy and configure the respective weights
3. Use an Application Load Balancer to distribute traffic based on IP address
4. Use a Network Load Balancer to distribute traffic based on Instance ID

**Answer: 2**

**Explanation:**

- Route 53 weighted routing policy is similar to simple but you can specify a weight per IP address. You create records that have the same name and type and assign each record a relative weight which is a numerical value that favours one IP over another (values must total 100). To stop sending traffic to a resource you can change the weight of the record to 0
- Network Load Balancer can distribute traffic to AWS and on-premise resources using IP addresses (not Instance IDs)
- Application Load Balancer can distribute traffic to AWS and on-premise resources using IP addresses but cannot be used to distribute traffic in a weighted manner

**References:**

https://digitalcloud.training/certification-training/aws-solutions-architect-associate/compute/elastic-load-balancing/

https://digitalcloud.training/certification-training/aws-solutions-architect-associate/networking-and-content-delivery/amazon-route-53/

## 48. Question

A government agency is using CloudFront for a web application that receives personally identifiable information (PII) from citizens. What feature of CloudFront applies an extra level of encryption at CloudFront edge locations to ensure the PII data is secured end-to-end?

1. Origin access identity
2. Field-level encryption
3. Object invalidation
4. RTMP distribution

**Answer: 2**

**Explanation:**

- Field-level encryption adds an additional layer of security on top of HTTPS that lets you protect specific data so that it is only visible to specific applications
- Origin access identity applies to S3 bucket origins, not web servers
- Object invalidation is a method to remove objects from the cache
- An RTMP distribution is a method of streaming media using Adobe Flash

**References:**

https://digitalcloud.training/certification-training/aws-solutions-architect-associate/networking-and-content-delivery/amazon-cloudfront/

https://aws.amazon.com/about-aws/whats-new/2017/12/introducing-field-level-encryption-on-amazon-cloudfront/

## 49. Question

An application is generating a large amount of clickstream events data that is being stored on S3. The business needs to understand customer behaviour and want to run complex analytics queries against the data.

**Which AWS service can be used for this requirement?**

1. Amazon Kinesis Firehose
2. Amazon RDS
3. Amazon Neptune
4. Amazon RedShift

**Answer: 4**

**Explanation:**

- Amazon Redshift is a fast, fully managed data warehouse that makes it simple and cost-effective to analyze all your data using standard SQL and existing Business Intelligence (BI) tools.
- RedShift is used for running complex analytic queries against petabytes of structured data, using sophisticated query optimization, columnar storage on high-performance local disks, and massively parallel query execution.
- With RedShift you can load data from Amazon S3 and perform analytics queries. RedShift Spectrum can analyze data directly in Amazon S3, but was not presented as an option.
- RDS is a relational database that is used for transactional workloads not analytics workloads.
- Amazon Neptune is a new product that offers a fully-managed Graph database.
- Amazon Kinesis Firehose processes streaming data, not data stored on S3.

**References:**

https://digitalcloud.training/certification-training/aws-solutions-architect-associate/database/amazon-redshift/

## 50. Question

You need to setup a distribution method for some static files. The requests will be mainly GET requests and you are expecting a high volume of GETs often exceeding 2000 per second. The files are currently stored in an S3 bucket. According to AWS best practices, what can you do to optimize performance?

1. Integrate CloudFront with S3 to cache the content
2. Use cross-region replication to spread the load across regions
3. Use ElastiCache to cache the content
4. Use S3 Transfer Acceleration

**Answer: 1**

**Explanation:**

- Amazon S3 automatically scales to high request rates. For example, your application can achieve at least 3,500 PUT/POST/DELETE and 5,500 GET requests per second per prefix in a bucket. There are no limits to the number of prefixes in a bucket
- If your workload is mainly sending GET requests, in addition to the preceding guidelines, you should consider using Amazon CloudFront for performance optimization. By integrating CloudFront with Amazon S3, you can distribute content to your users with low latency and a high data transfer rate
- Transfer Acceleration is used to accelerate object uploads to S3 over long distances (latency)
- Cross-region replication creates a replica copy in another region but should not be used for spreading read requests across regions. There will be 2 S3 endpoints and CRR is not designed for 2 way sync so this would not work well
- ElastiCache is used for caching database content not S3 content

**References:**

https://docs.aws.amazon.com/AmazonS3/latest/dev/request-rate-perf-considerations.html

https://digitalcloud.training/certification-training/aws-solutions-architect-associate/storage/amazon-s3/

## 51. Question

An RDS database is experiencing heavy read traffic. You are planning on creating read replicas. When using Amazon RDS with Read Replicas, which of the deployment options below are valid? (choose 2)

1. Cross-Continent
2. Within an Availability Zone
3. Cross-subnet
4. Cross-Availability Zone
5. Cross-Facility

**Answer: 2,4**

**Explanation:**

- Read Replicas can be within an AZ, Cross-AZ and Cross-Region
- Read replicas are used for read heavy DBs and replication is asynchronous. Read replicas are for workload sharing and offloading
- Read replicas cannot be cross-continent, cross-subnet or cross-facility

**References:**

https://digitalcloud.training/certification-training/aws-solutions-architect-associate/database/amazon-rds/

## 52. Question

You are planning on using AWS Auto Scaling to ensure that you have the correct number of Amazon EC2 instances available to handle the load for your applications. Which of the following statements is correct about Auto Scaling? (choose 2)

1. Auto Scaling is a region-specific service
2. Auto Scaling can span multiple AZs within the same AWS region
3. Auto Scaling is charged by the hour when registered
4. You create collections of EC2 instances, called Launch Groups
5. Auto Scaling relies on Elastic Load Balancing

**Answer: 1,2**

**Explanation:**

- Auto Scaling is a region specific service
- Auto Scaling can span multiple AZs within the same AWS region
- You create collections of EC2 instances, called Auto Scaling groups
- There is no additional cost for Auto Scaling, you just pay for the resources (EC2 instances) provisioned
- Auto Scaling does not rely on ELB but can be used with ELB.

**References:**

https://digitalcloud.training/certification-training/aws-solutions-architect-associate/compute/aws-auto-scaling/

## 53. Question

As a Solutions Architect at Digital Cloud Training you are helping a client to design a multi-tier web application architecture. The client has requested that the architecture provide low-latency connectivity between all servers and be resilient across multiple locations. The client uses Microsoft SQL Server for existing databases. The client has a limited budget for staff costs and does not need to access the underlying operating system

What would you recommend as the most efficient solution?

1. Amazon RDS with Microsoft SQL Server
2. Amazon EC2 instances with Microsoft SQL Server and data replication within an AZ
3. Amazon RDS with Microsoft SQL Server in a Multi-AZ configuration
4. Amazon EC2 instances with Microsoft SQL Server and data replication between two different AZs

**Answer: 3**

**Explanation:**

- As the client does not need to manage the underlying operating system and they have a limited budget for staff, they should use a managed service such as RDS. Multi-AZ RDS creates a replica in another AZ and synchronously replicates to it which enables the required resilience across multiple locations
- With EC2 you have full control at the operating system layer (not required) and can install your own database. However, you would then need to manage the entire stack and therefore staff costs would increase so this is not the best solution

**References:**

https://digitalcloud.training/certification-training/aws-solutions-architect-associate/networking-and-content-delivery/amazon-vpc/

https://digitalcloud.training/certification-training/aws-solutions-architect-associate/compute/amazon-ec2/

https://digitalcloud.training/certification-training/aws-solutions-architect-associate/database/amazon-rds/

## 54. Question

A company is investigating ways to analyze and process large amounts of data in the cloud faster, without needing to load or transform the data in a data warehouse. The data resides in Amazon S3.

Which AWS services would allow the company to query the data in place? (choose 2)

1. Amazon RedShift Spectrum
2. Amazon Elasticsearch
3. Amazon Kinesis Data Streams
4. Amazon SWF
5. Amazon S3 Select

**Answer: 1,5**

**Explanation:**

- Amazon S3 Select is designed to help analyze and process data within an object in Amazon S3 buckets, faster and cheaper. It works by providing the ability to retrieve a subset of data from an object in Amazon S3 using simple SQL expressions
- Amazon Redshift Spectrum allows you to directly run SQL queries against exabytes of unstructured data in Amazon S3. No loading or transformation is required
- Amazon Kinesis Data Streams (KDS) is a massively scalable and durable real-time data streaming service. It does not allow you to perform query-in-place operations on S3
- Amazon Elasticsearch Service, is a fully managed service that makes it easy for you to deploy, secure, operate, and scale Elasticsearch to search, analyze, and visualize data in real-time
- Amazon SWF helps developers build, run, and scale background jobs that have parallel or sequential steps

**References:**

https://digitalcloud.training/certification-training/aws-solutions-architect-associate/database/amazon-redshift/

https://aws.amazon.com/blogs/aws/s3-glacier-select/

https://aws.amazon.com/about-aws/whats-new/2017/11/amazon-redshift-spectrum-is-now-available-in-four-additional-aws-regions-and-enhances-query-performance-in-all-available-aws-regions/

## 55. Question

You work as an Enterprise Architect for a global organization which employs 20,000 people. The company is growing at around 5% per annum. The company strategy is to increasingly adopt AWS cloud services. There is an existing Microsoft Active Directory (AD) service that is used as the on-premise identity and access management system. You want to enable users to authenticate using their existing identities and access AWS resources (including the AWS Management Console) using single sign-on (SSO).

**What is the simplest way to enable SSO to the AWS management console using the existing domain?**

1. Launch a large AWS Directory Service AD Connector to proxy all authentication back to your on-premise AD service for authentication
2. Use a large AWS Simple AD in AWS
3. Launch an Enterprise Edition AWS Active Directory Service for Microsoft Active Directory and setup trust relationships with your on-premise domain
4. Install a Microsoft Active Directory Domain Controller on AWS and add it into your existing on-premise domain

**Answer: 3**

**Explanation:**

- With the AWS Active Directory Service for Microsoft Active Directory you can setup trust relationships to extend authentication from on-premises Active Directories into the AWS cloud. You can also use Active Directory credentials to authenticate to the AWS management console without having to set up SAML authentication. It is a fully managed AWS service on AWS infrastructure and is the best choice if you have more than 5000 users and/or need a trust relationship set up.
- You could install a Microsoft AD DC on an EC2 instance and add it to the existing domain. However, you would then have to setup federation / SAML infrastructure for SSO. This is not therefore the simplest solution
- AWS Simple AD does not support trust relationships or synchronisation with Active Directory
- AD Connector would be a good solution for this use case however the best practice is to use AWS Active Directory Service for Microsoft Active Directory for more than 5,000 users

**References:**

https://digitalcloud.training/certification-training/aws-solutions-architect-associate/security-identity-compliance/aws-directory-service/

## 56. Question

One of the departments in your company has been generating a large amount of data on S3 and you are considering the increasing costs of hosting it. You have discussed the matter with the department head and he explained that data older than 90 days is rarely accessed but must be retained for several years. If this data does need to be accessed at least 24 hours notice will be provided.

**How can you optimize the costs associated with storage of this data whilst ensuring it is accessible if required?**

1. Use S3 lifecycle policies to move data to GLACIER after 90 days
2. Implement archival software that automatically moves the data to tape
3. Select the older data and manually migrate it to GLACIER
4. Use S3 lifecycle policies to move data to the STANDARD_IA storage class

**Answer: 1**

**Explanation:**

- To manage your objects so that they are stored cost effectively throughout their lifecycle, configure their lifecycle. A lifecycle configuration is a set of rules that define actions that Amazon S3 applies to a group of objects. Transition actions define when objects transition to another storage class
- For example, you might choose to transition objects to the STANDARD_IA storage class 30 days after you created them, or archive objects to the GLACIER storage class one year after creating them
- STANDARD_IA is good for infrequently accessed data and provides faster access times than GLACIER but is more expensive so not the best option here
- GLACIER retrieval times:
  - Standard retrieval is 3-5 hours which is well within the requirements here
  - You can use Expedited retrievals to access data in $1 - 5$ minutes
  - You can use Bulk retrievals to access up to petabytes of data in approximately $5 - 12$ hours

**References:**

https://digitalcloud.training/certification-training/aws-solutions-architect-associate/storage/amazon-s3/

https://docs.aws.amazon.com/AmazonS3/latest/dev/object-lifecycle-mgmt.html

https://aws.amazon.com/about-aws/whats-new/2016/11/access-your-amazon-glacier-data-in-minutes-with-new-retrieval-options/

## 57. Question

**You need to launch a series of EC2 instances with multiple attached volumes by modifying the block device mapping. Which block device can be specified in a block device mapping to be used with an EC2 instance? (choose 2)**

1. EFS volume
2. Snapshot
3. S3 bucket
4. Instance store volume
5. EBS volume

**Answer: 4,5**

**Explanation:**

- Each instance that you launch has an associated root device volume, either an Amazon EBS volume or an instance store volume
- You can use block device mapping to specify additional EBS volumes or instance store volumes to attach to an instance when it's launched. You can also attach additional EBS volumes to a running instance
- You cannot use a block device mapping to specify a snapshot, EFS volume or S3 bucket

**References:**

https://docs.aws.amazon.com/AWSEC2/latest/UserGuide/block-device-mapping-concepts.html

https://digitalcloud.training/certification-training/aws-solutions-architect-associate/compute/amazon-ebs/

## 58. Question

Some data has become corrupt in an RDS database you manage. You are planning to use point-in-time restore to recover the data to the last known good configuration. Which of the following statements is correct about restoring an RDS database to a specific point-in-time? (choose 2)

1. The database restore overwrites the existing database
2. The default DB security group is applied to the new DB instance
3. You can restore up to the last 1 minute
4. Custom DB security groups are applied to the new DB instance
5. You can restore up to the last 5 minutes

### Answer: 2,5

### Explanation:

- Restored DBs will always be a new RDS instance with a new DNS endpoint and you can restore up to the last 5 minutes
- You cannot restore from a DB snapshot to an existing DB – a new instance is created when you restore
- Only default DB parameters and security groups are restored – you must manually associate all other DB parameters and SGs

### References:

https://digitalcloud.training/certification-training/aws-solutions-architect-associate/database/amazon-rds/

https://docs.aws.amazon.com/AmazonRDS/latest/UserGuide/USER_PIT.html

## 59. Question

You are designing the disk configuration for an EC2 instance. The instance needs to support a MapReduce process that requires high throughput for a large dataset with large I/O sizes. You need to provision the most cost-effective storage solution option.

### What EBS volume type will you select?

1. EBS General Purpose SSD in a RAID 1 configuration
2. EBS Throughput Optimized HDD
3. EBS Provisioned IOPS SSD
4. EBS General Purpose SSD

### Answer: 2

### Explanation:

- EBS Throughput Optimized HDD is good for the following use cases (and is the most cost-effective option:
  Frequently accessed, throughput intensive workloads with large datasets and large I/O sizes, such as MapReduce, Kafka, log processing, data warehouse, and ETL workloads
- Throughput is measured in MB/s, and includes the ability to burst up to 250 MB/s per TB, with a baseline throughput of 40 MB/s per TB and a maximum throughput of 500 MB/s per volume
- The SSD options are more expensive

References:

https://digitalcloud.training/certification-training/aws-solutions-architect-associate/compute/amazon-ebs/

## 60. Question

A company is deploying a new two-tier web application that uses EC2 web servers and a DynamoDB database backend. An Internet facing ELB distributes connections between the web servers.

The Solutions Architect has created a security group for the web servers and needs to create a security group for the ELB. What rules should be added? (choose 2)

1. Add an Inbound rule that allows HTTP/HTTPS, and specify the source as 0.0.0.0/32
2. Add an Outbound rule that allows ALL TCP, and specify the destination as the Internet Gateway
3. Add an Inbound rule that allows HTTP/HTTPS, and specify the source as 0.0.0.0/0
4. Add an Outbound rule that allows HTTP/HTTPS, and specify the destination as the web server security group
5. Add an Outbound rule that allows HTTP/HTTPS, and specify the destination as VPC CIDR

Answer: 3,4

Explanation:

- An inbound rule should be created for the relevant protocols (HTTP/HTTPS) and the source should be set to any address (0.0.0.0/0)
- The address 0.0.0.0/32 is incorrect as the 32 mask means an exact match is required (0.0.0.0)
- The outbound rule should forward the relevant protocols (HTTP/HTTPS) and the destination should be set to the web server security group
- Using the VPC CIDR would not be secure and you cannot specify an Internet Gateway in a security group (not that you'd want to anyway)
- FYI on the web server security group you'd want to add an Inbound rule allowing HTTP/HTTPS from the ELB security group

References:

https://digitalcloud.training/certification-training/aws-solutions-architect-associate/compute/elastic-load-balancing/

## 61. Question

A High Performance Computing (HPC) application will be migrated to AWS. The application requires low network latency and high throughput between nodes and will be deployed in a single AZ.

How should the application be deployed for best inter-node performance?

1. Behind a Network Load Balancer (NLB)
2. In a partition placement group
3. In a cluster placement group
4. In a spread placement group

Answer: 3

Explanation:

- A cluster placement group provides low latency and high throughput for instances deployed in a single AZ. It is the best way to provide the performance required for this application.
- A partition placement group is used for grouping instances into logical segments. It provides control and visibility into instance placement but is not the best option for performance.
- A spread placement group is used to spread instances across underlying hardware. It is not the best option for performance.
- A network load balancer is used for distributing incoming connections, this does assist with inter-node performance.

**References:**

https://digitalcloud.training/certification-training/aws-solutions-architect-associate/compute/amazon-ec2/

https://docs.aws.amazon.com/AWSEC2/latest/UserGuide/placement-groups.html

## 62. Question

**A web application is deployed in multiple regions behind an ELB Application Load Balancer. You need deterministic routing to the closest region and automatic failover. Traffic should traverse the AWS global network for consistent performance.**

**How can this be achieved?**

1. Use a CloudFront distribution with multiple custom origins in each region and configure for high availability
2. Create a Route 53 Alias record for each ALB and configure a latency-based routing policy
3. Place an EC2 Proxy in front of the ALB and configure automatic failover
4. Configure AWS Global Accelerator and configure the ALBs as targets

**Answer: 4**

**Explanation:**

- AWS Global Accelerator is a service that improves the availability and performance of applications with local or global users. You can configure the ALB as a target and Global Accelerator will automatically route users to the closest point of presence. Failover is automatic and does not rely on any client side cache changes as the IP addresses for Global Accelerator are static anycast addresses. Global Accelerator also uses the AWS global network which ensures consistent performance.
- Placing an EC2 proxy in front of the ALB does not meet the requirements. This solution does not ensure deterministic routing the closest region and failover is happening within a region which does not protect against regional failure. Also, this introduces a potential bottleneck and lack of redundancy.
- A Route 53 Alias record for each ALB with latency-based routing does provide routing based on latency and failover. However, the traffic will not traverse the AWS global network.
- You can use CloudFront with multiple custom origins and configure for HA. However, the traffic will not traverse the AWS global network.

**References:**

https://digitalcloud.training/certification-training/aws-solutions-architect-associate/networking-and-content-delivery/aws-global-accelerator/

https://aws.amazon.com/global-accelerator/

## 63. Question

An application on Amazon Elastic Container Service (ECS) performs data processing in two parts. The second part takes much longer to complete. How can an Architect decouple the data processing from the backend application component?

1. Process both parts using the same ECS task. Create an Amazon Kinesis Firehose stream
2. Process each part using a separate ECS task. Create an Amazon SQS queue
3. Create an Amazon DynamoDB table and save the output of the first part to the table
4. Process each part using a separate ECS task. Create an Amazon SNS topic and send a notification when the processing completes

**Answer: 2**

**Explanation:**

- Processing each part using a separate ECS task may not be essential but means you can separate the processing of the data. An Amazon Simple Queue Service (SQS) is used for decoupling applications. It is a message queue on which you place messages for processing by application components. In this case you can process each data processing part in separate ECS tasks and have them write an Amazon SQS queue. That way the backend can pick up the messages from the queue when they're ready and there is no delay due to the second part not being complete.
- Amazon Kinesis Firehose is used for streaming data. This is not an example of streaming data. In this case SQS is better as a message can be placed on a queue to indicate that the job is complete and ready to be picked up by the backend application component.
- Amazon DynamoDB is unlikely to be a good solution for this requirement. There is a limit on the maximum amount of data that you can store in an entry in a DynamoDB table.
- Amazon Simple Notification Service (SNS) can be used for sending notifications. It is useful when you need to notify multiple AWS services. In this case an Amazon SQS queue is a better solution as there is no mention of multiple AWS services and this is an ideal use case for SQS.

**References:**

https://digitalcloud.training/certification-training/aws-solutions-architect-associate/application-integration/amazon-sqs/

## 64. Question

A new relational database is being deployed on AWS. The performance requirements are unknown. Which database service does not require you to make capacity decisions upfront?

1. Amazon RDS
2. Amazon ElastiCache
3. Amazon Aurora Serverless
4. Amazon DynamoDB

**Answer: 3**

**Explanation:**

- If you don't know the performance requirements it will be difficult to determine the correct instance type to use. Amazon Aurora Serverless does not require you to make capacity decisions upfront as you do not select an instance type. As a serverless service it will automatically scale as needed.
- Amazon DynamoDB is not a relational database, it is a NoSQL database.
- Amazon ElastiCache is more suitable for caching and also requires an instance type to be selected.
- Amazon RDS requires an instance type to be selected.

**References:**

https://digitalcloud.training/certification-training/aws-solutions-architect-associate/database/amazon-aurora/

https://aws.amazon.com/rds/aurora/serverless/

## 65. Question

**The database tier of a web application is running on a Windows server on-premises. The database is a Microsoft SQL Server database. The application owner would like to migrate the database to an Amazon RDS instance.**

**How can the migration be executed with minimal administrative effort and downtime?**

1. Use AWS DataSync to migrate the data from the database to Amazon S3. Use AWS Database Migration Service (DMS) to migrate the database to RDS
2. Use the AWS Database Migration Service (DMS) to directly migrate the database to RDS. Use the Schema Conversion Tool (SCT) to enable conversion from Microsoft SQL Server to Amazon RDS
3. Use the AWS Database Migration Service (DMS) to directly migrate the database to RDS
4. Use the AWS Server Migration Service (SMS) to migrate the server to Amazon EC2. Use AWS Database Migration Service (DMS) to migrate the database to RDS

**Answer: 3**

**Explanation:**

- You can directly migrate Microsoft SQL Server from an on-premises server into Amazon RDS using the Microsoft SQL Server database engine.
- You do not need to use the SCT as you are migrating into the same destination database engine (RDS is just the platform).
- You do not need to use the AWS SMS service to migrate the server into EC2 first. You can directly migrate the database online with minimal downtime.
- AWS DataSync is used for migrating data, not databases.

**References:**

https://docs.aws.amazon.com/dms/latest/userguide/CHAP_Source.html

https://docs.aws.amazon.com/dms/latest/userguide/CHAP_Target.html

https://aws.amazon.com/dms/schema-conversion-tool/

https://digitalcloud.training/certification-training/aws-solutions-architect-associate/migration/aws-database-migration-service/

# CONCLUSION

Congratulations on completing these exam-difficulty practice tests! We truly hope that these high-quality questions along with the supporting explanations and reference links helped to fully prepare you for the AWS Certified Solutions Architect Associate exam.

The SAA-C02 exam covers a broad set of technologies and it's vital to ensure you are armed with the knowledge to answer whatever questions come up in your certification exam, so it's best to review these practice questions until you're confident in all areas. We recommend re-taking these practice tests until you consistently score 80% or higher - that's when you're ready to sit the exam and achieve a great score!

## Reach out with any question

If anything is not 100% to your liking, please email us at feedback@digitalcloud.training. We promise to address all questions and concerns. For technical support, contact us at:

support@digitalcloud.training.

Also, remember to join our private Facebook group to ask questions and share knowledge and exam tips with the AWS community:

https://www.facebook.com/groups/awscertificationqa

## Limited Time Bonus Offer

As a special bonus, we are now offering **FREE Access to the Online Exam Simulator** on the Digital Cloud Training website. The exam simulator randomly selects 65 questions from our pool of over 500 unique questions - mimicking the real AWS exam environment. The practice exam has the same format, style, time limit, and passing score as the real AWS exam.

To gain FREE access to these 500 Practice Questions, simply send us a **screenshot of your review on Amazon** to info@digitalcloud.training with "CSAA500" in the subject line. You will then get FREE access to our Online Exam Simulator within 48 hours.

Your review helps us improve our courses and help your fellow AWS students make the right choices. We celebrate every honest review and truly appreciate it. You can leave a review at any time by visiting amazon.com/ryp.

### Best wishes for your AWS certification journey!

# OTHER BOOKS & COURSES BY NEAL DAVIS

## AWS Certified Solutions Architect Associate Video Course

AVAILABLE ON DIGITALCLOUD.TRAINING

This popular AWS Certified Solutions Architect Associate (SAA-C02) video course is delivered through guided  Hands-On Labs exercises. Here's what to expect:

- 25 hours Video Lessons
- Covers SAA-C02
- Exam Cram Lectures
- 90 Quiz Questions
- High-Quality Visuals
- Guided Hands-on Exercises
- Build Applications on AWS

You will be looking over my shoulder and building applications on Amazon Web Services. By the end of the course, you will have a strong experience-based skillset thanks to the guided AWS Practice Labs.

We will use a process of repetition and incremental learning to ensure that you retain the knowledge as repeated practice is the best way to learn and build your cloud skills. We take you from opening your first AWS Free Tier account through to creating complex multi-tier architectures, always sticking to the **SAA-C02 exam blueprint** to ensure you're learning practical skills and also preparing for your exam.

We back the 25 hours of AWS Hands-On Labs with high-quality logical diagrams so you can visualize what you're building and check your progress.

Our AWS Hands-On Labs teach you how to design and build multi-tier web architectures with services such as EC2 Auto Scaling, Elastic Load Balancing, Route 53, ECS, Lambda, API Gateway and Elastic File System.

To learn more, visit: https://digitalcloud.training/aws-training-courses/

# AWS Certified Solutions Architect Associate (online) Practice Tests

Get access to the **online Exam Simulator** from Digital Cloud Training with over 500 Questions **plus 6 sets of practice exams** with 65 Questions each. All questions are unique, 100% scenario-based and conform to the latest AWS SAA-C02 exam blueprint.

Our AWS Practice Tests are delivered in 3 different modes:

**Simulation mode:** the number of questions, time limit, and pass mark are the same as the real AWS exam. You must complete the exam before you are able to check your score and review answers and explanations.

**Training mode:** You are shown the answer and explanation for every question after clicking "check". Upon completion of the exam the score report shows your overall score and performance in each knowledge area.

**Knowledge reviews:** Collections of practice questions for a specific knowledge area. When you complete a practice exam you can use the score report to identify your strengths and weaknesses and then use the knowledge reviews to focus your efforts where they're needed most.

Each exam includes questions from the four domains of the SAA-C02 AWS exam blueprint. All questions are also available in the knowledge reviews where they are split into more than 15 categories for focused training.

Learn more on how to fast-track your AWS Certified Solutions Architect Associate Exam Success:

https://digitalcloud.training/aws-certified-solutions-architect-associate-practice-tests-2019/

# AWS Certified Solutions Architect Associate Training Notes

AVAILABLE ON <u>AMAZON</u> AND <u>DIGITAL CLOUD TRAINING</u>

Save valuable time by getting straight to the facts you need to know to pass your AWS Certified Solutions Architect Associate exam first time!

This book is based on the **2020 SAA-C02 exam blueprint** and provides a deep dive into the subject matter in a concise and easy-to-read format so you can fast-track your time to success.

AWS Solutions Architect and successful instructor, Neal Davis, has consolidated the information you need to be successful from numerous training sources and AWS FAQ pages to save you time.

In addition to the book, you are provided with access to a **65-question practice exam** on an interactive exam simulator to evaluate your progress and ensure you're prepared for the style and difficulty of the real AWS exam.

This book will help you prepare for your AWS Certified Solutions Architect – Associate exam in the following ways:

• **Deep dive into the SAA-C02 exam objectives** with over 300 pages of detailed facts, tables and diagrams.

• **Familiarize yourself with the exam question format** with the practice questions included in each section.

• **Use our online exam simulator to evaluate progress** and ensure you're ready for the real thing.

To learn more, visit: https://digitalcloud.training/product/aws-certified-solutions-architect-associate-offline-training-notes/

# AWS Certified Cloud Practitioner Video Course

AVAILABLE ON DIGITALCLOUD.TRAINING

We have fully aligned this instructor-led video training with the AWS Certified Cloud Practitioner exam blueprint (CLF-C01) and structured the course so that you can study at a pace that suits you best. We start with some basic background to get everyone up to speed on what cloud computing is, before progressing through each knowledge domain.

**Here's why this ultimate exam prep is your best chance to ace your AWS certification exam:**

**HIGHLY FLEXIBLE COURSE STRUCTURE**: We understand that not everyone has the time to go through lengthy lectures. That's why we give you options to maximize your time efficiency and accommodate different learning styles

**6 HOURS OF THEORY LECTURES**: You can move quickly through the course, focusing on the theory lectures that are 100% conform with the CLF-C01 exam blueprint - everything you need to know to pass your exam first attempt

**4 HOURS OF GUIDED HANDS-ON EXERCISES:** To gain more practical experience with AWS services, you have the option to explore the guided hands-on exercises

**1 HOUR OF EXAM-CRAM LECTURES**: Get through the key exam facts in the shortest time possible with the exam-cram lectures that you'll find at the end of each section

**HIGH-QUALITY VISUALS**: We've spared no effort to create a highly visual training course with lots of table and graphs to illustrate the concepts. All practical exercises are backed by logical diagrams so you can visualize what we're building.

To learn more, visit: https://digitalcloud.training/aws-certified-cloud-practitioner-training-course/

# AWS Certified Cloud Practitioner (online) Practice Tests

AVAILABLE ON DIGITALCLOUD.TRAINING

Get access to the online Exam Simulator from Digital Cloud Training with over **500 Practice questions plus 6 sets of practice exams** with 65 Questions each. All questions are unique and conform to the latest AWS CLF-C01 exam blueprint.

Our AWS Practice Tests are delivered in 3 different modes:

**Simulation mode**: the number of questions, time limit and pass mark are the same as the real AWS exam. You need to complete the exam before you get to check your score and review answers and explanations.

**Training mode**: You are shown the answer and explanation for every question after clicking "check". Upon completion of the exam, the score report shows your overall score and performance in each knowledge area.

**Knowledge reviews**: Collections of practice questions for a specific knowledge area. When you complete a practice exam you can use the score report to identify your strengths and weaknesses and then use the knowledge reviews to focus your efforts where they are needed most.

Learn more on how to fast-track your AWS Certified Cloud Practitioner Exam Success:

https://digitalcloud.training/aws-certified-cloud-practitioner-practice-tests-2019

# AWS Certified Cloud Practitioner (offline) Practice Tests

The Cloud Practitioner exam is a foundational level exam that nonetheless includes tricky questions that test your knowledge and experience of the AWS Cloud. Our practice tests are patterned to reflect the difficulty of the AWS exam and are the closest to the real AWS exam experience available anywhere.

There are 6 practice exams with 65 questions each covering the five domains of the AWS exam blueprint. Each set of questions is repeated once without answers and explanations, and once with answers and explanations, so you get to choose from two methods of preparation:

To simulate the exam experience and assess your exam readiness, use the "PRACTICE QUESTIONS ONLY" sets.

To use the practice questions as a learning tool, use the "PRACTICE QUESTIONS, ANSWERS & EXPLANATIONS" sets to view the answers and read the in-depth explanations as you move through the questions.

These Practice Questions will prepare you for your AWS exam in the following ways:

     • Master the latest exam pattern: All 390 practice questions are based on the latest version of the CLF-C01 exam blueprint and use the question format of the real AWS exam

     • 6 sets of exam-difficulty practice questions: Presented with and without answers so you can study or simulate an exam

     • Ideal exam prep tool that will shortcut your study time: Assess your exam readiness to maximize your chance of passing the AWS exam first time.

The exam covers a broad set of technologies and it's vital to ensure you are armed with the knowledge to answer whatever questions come up in your certification exam. We recommend reviewing these practice questions until you're confident in all areas and ready to ace your AWS exam.

To learn more, visit: https://www.amazon.com/Certified-Cloud-Practitioner-Practice-Tests-ebook/dp/B07VKN5RZ1/

# AWS Certified Cloud Practitioner Training Notes

AVAILABLE ON AMAZON AND DIGITALCLOUD.TRAINING

Save valuable time by getting straight to the facts you need to know to be successful and ensure you pass your AWS Certified Cloud Practitioner exam first time!

This book is based on the **CLF-C01 exam blueprint** and provides a deep dive into the subject matter in a concise and easy-to-read format so you can fast-track your time to success.

The Cloud Practitioner certification is a great first step into the world of Cloud Computing and requires a foundational knowledge of the AWS Cloud, its architectural principles, value proposition, billing and pricing, key services and more.

AWS Solutions Architect and successful instructor, Neal Davis, has consolidated the information you need to be successful from numerous training sources and AWS FAQ pages to save you time.

In addition to the book, you are provided with **access to a 65-question practice exam** on an interactive exam simulator to evaluate your progress and ensure you're prepared for the style and difficulty of the real AWS exam.

**Deep dive into the CLF-C01 exam objectives with over 200 pages of detailed facts, tables, and diagrams – everything you need to know!**

To learn more, visit:

https://digitalcloud.training/product/aws-certified-cloud-practitioner-offline-training-notes/

# ABOUT THE AUTHOR

**Neal Davis** is the founder of Digital Cloud Training, AWS Cloud Solutions Architect and successful IT instructor. With more than 20 years of experience in the tech industry, Neal is a true expert in virtualization and cloud computing. His passion is to help others achieve career success by offering in-depth AWS certification training resources.

Neal started **Digital Cloud Training** to provide a variety of training resources for Amazon Web Services (AWS) certifications that represent a higher standard of quality than is otherwise available in the market. Digital Cloud Training provides **AWS Certification exam preparation resources** including instructor-led Video Courses, guided Hands-on Labs, in-depth Training Notes, Exam-Cram lessons for quick revision, Quizzes to test your knowledge and exam-difficulty Practice Exams to assess your exam readiness.

With Digital Cloud Training, you get access to highly experienced staff who support you on your AWS Certification journey and help you elevate your career through achieving highly valuable certifications. Join the AWS Community of over 40,000 happy students that are currently enrolled in Digital Cloud Training courses

**Connect with Neal / Digital Cloud Training on social media**:

digitalcloud.training

facebook.com/digitalcloudtraining/

linkedin.com/company/digitalcloudtraining

Twitter @DigitalCloudT

Instagram @digitalcloudtraining

Made in the USA
San Bernardino, CA
10 March 2020

65501679R00197